ENGLISH MEDIEVAL MYSTICS

LONGMAN MEDIEVAL AND RENAISSANCE LIBRARY

General Editors:
CHARLOTTE BREWER, Hertford College, Oxford
N. H. KEEBLE, University of Stirling

Published Titles:

Piers Plowman: An Introduction to the B-Text
James Simpson

Shakespeare's Mouldy Tales: Recurrent Plot Motifs in Shakespearian Drama
Leah Scragg

The Fabliau in English
John Hines

English Medieval Mystics: Games of Faith
Marion Glasscoe

Marion Glasscoe

ENGLISH MEDIEVAL MYSTICS
Games of Faith

LONGMAN
LONDON AND NEW YORK

Longman Group UK Limited,
Longman House, Burnt Mill,
Harlow, Essex CM20 2JE, England
and Associated Companies throughout the world.

*Published in the United States of America
by Longman Publishing, New York*

First published 1993

ISBN 0 582 49516 4 CSD
ISBN 0 582 49517 2 PPR

British Library Cataloguing-in-Publication Data

A catalogue record for this book is
available from the British Library

Library of Congress Cataloging-in-Publication Data

Glasscoe, Marion.
English medieval mystics : games of faith / Marion Glasscoe.
p. cm. – (Longman medieval and Renaissance library)
Includes bibliographical references and index.
ISBN 0-582-49516-4. – ISBN 0-582-49517-2 (pbk.)
1. Mysticism – England. 2. Mysticism – History – Middle Ages, 600–1500. 3. Mysticism – Catholic Church – History. 4. Catholic Church – Doctrines – History. I. Title. II. Series.
BV5077.E54G53 1993
248.2'2'09420902 – dc20 92–32411
CIP

Set by 7PP in 10/12 pt Bembo
Produced by Longman Singapore Publishers (Pte) Ltd.
Printed in Singapore

Contents

Preface

Mysticism within the English Christian tradition manifests itself in many ways; its perceptions surface in poetry and art from the Middle Ages to the present day; it is renewed in the actively expressed vision of religious reformers like the first Franciscans and later the Quakers and Shakers, but its mainstream flows, silently for the most part, through the hidden channels of the inner lives of contemplative prayer within a demanding religious discipline. The mystics with whom this book is concerned open windows on to the claims of such a life; they have a gift for language which points to vistas of fundamental creativity beyond the powers of language to express. Mysticism always presents a challenge to the materially based criteria for success, whether in the self or in society, which tend to belong to the social establishment. There are times, too, when its self-authenticating witness to spiritual reality and visionary consciousness may be viewed with unease by innately conservative authority in the institutionalised religious establishment who fear the disintegration that may follow when religion breaks free of accepted frameworks and definitions. But it is through such tensions that living truth is renewed – and at the same time humanly contrived notions of eccentricity are exposed.

Many cultural influences converged in the flowering of mystical literature which occurred at the end of the Middle Ages. Although the writers with whom this book is concerned are certainly conditioned in their thinking and practices by the complex theological traditions and doctrinal teaching of the Church, what they know and write about is not a body of intellectually formulated doctrine but a growth in experience. In the last analysis mystics have to do with 'being' and arguably therefore an introductory analysis of their writings in these terms may make them more immediately accessible. For them knowledge was not academic but experiential. Hence although other studies on these mystics have properly attempted to locate them in appropriate theological traditions, this book will not attempt to follow them in hunting out patristic sources, pronouncing on whether or not these writers express themselves correctly within particular systems of thought and evaluating their achievements. The approach developed arose from the challenge presented by looking at the literature of medieval English mystics with students who possess varying degrees of background knowledge of, and sympathy with, the Christian tradition. I am grateful for all their responses – excited, sceptical, baffled, curious, enthusiastic and hostile (especially the hostile) – which present a constant pressure to find ways of approaching the theological format of these texts as differing forms of convention used in creative literary ways to express a very particular kind of human experience – that of God. This book will not assume familiarity with conventional terms which belong peculiarly to Christian theology; although many readers will be familiar at some level of understanding with Christian teaching, others may not. In order to cater for the second group without unduly detaining the first, particular terms used in the context of Christian teaching may be found in the Glossary.

Among all those who have knowingly and unknowingly contributed to this book and to whom I am grateful, I especially thank colleagues world-wide who have participated in the Exeter Symposia on the Medieval Mystical Tradition in England over the last twelve years, the staff of Exeter University Library especially Heather Eva, Susanna Guy and Stuart MacWilliam, Longman staff for their helpful patience in difficult circumstances, and the Sisters of Syon Abbey to whose friendship and wisdom I owe a great deal. For the kind of particular support it is quite impossible to acknowledge adequately I am in debt to Roger Ellis and Michael Swanton. Their extraordinary generosity with time and expertise and their discerning judgements were unfailing when most needed. The shortcomings of this book are, of course, my own.

Marion Glasscoe
Exeter

For that friend who assures me that keeping cheerful is probably the secret of the universe!

By reson we mowe trace how miȝty, how wise, & how good he is in his creatures, but not in himself. Bot euer whan reson defaileþ, þan list loue liue and lerne for to plei; for bi loue we may fynde him, fele him, and hit him euen in himself.

(We may search out by reason how mighty, how wise, and how good he is in his creatures, but not in himself. But always, when reason fails, then it pleases love to live and to teach how to play; for by love we may find him, feel him and reach him right in himself).

Chapter 1

The Game is Begun

There are people who know that they have experienced deep within themselves a reality which gives them simple and overwhelming certainties about the real goals of human existence and which transforms their lives. This reality is not primarily one of sense experience or of the conscious intellect, though it may suffuse and illuminate both. This book introduces the writings of five of them who lived in fourteenth- and early fifteenth-century England. Although all felt that they had found a means of living which enabled them to be open to this reality, they nevertheless say that it was experienced as a gift and a grace beyond anything that could be achieved by conscious effort. Because the nature of this experience subtly eludes the normal processes of human thought and feeling and is felt to engage with a power beyond them, it is termed 'mystical' and one who knows it a 'mystic'. The label is awkward as it is also used loosely of anything inspiring a sense of inexplicable awe and mystery, however vaguely, or anyone thus moved. However, although these five writers belonged to a minority group in their society, and although they say that their experience derives from a source greater than human reason can comprehend, they are fired with a certainty that it is intimately related to the deepest needs and purposes of human being, and has about it the simple inevitability of fulfilment. It both transcends the self-evident imperfections and problems of human existence and provides the means of so living with them that they can be transformed. They called it God, understood it in terms of Christian theology and used the terms 'meditative', and 'contemplative' rather than 'mystical' to talk about their experience.

Three of the five were men: Richard Rolle, a hermit from North Yorkshire; Walter Hilton, an Augustinian canon; and an anonymous writer, probably a religious, known best for his treatise

The Cloud of Unknowing. Two were women: one lived as a recluse at St Julian's church in Norwich and is known as Julian of Norwich; the other was an ebullient housewife from King's Lynn – Margery Kempe. The fact that all five wrote of their understanding of 'mystical' experience not in Latin but in English is a sign of their times. There was a great yearning among lay people to understand in terms of their own vernacular this inner experience of the faith, which, through the institutional influence of the Church, formally governed the structure of their lives, although their education may not have been such as to enable them to cope with the official language of the Church or highly intellectual theological exposition.

Much has been written about the theology expressed by these writers, and the theological influences which seem relevant to it. Such study is certainly important historically. But speculative source-study can reveal more about the reading of the scholar than about the actual text whose possible sources are the object of the exercise and, after all, it is only to be expected that those who share a faith will also share a way of expressing it. The study of origins and influences is no substitute for looking directly at what these texts actually say and the very particular felt understanding that they mediate. That source-study has been so common is at least partly due to the fact that the interpretation of the writings of the mystics has, from the start, been felt to be the preserve of theologians. In the medieval period these were seen as the custodians of an orthodoxy which was felt to be, if only potentially, challenged by self-authenticating mystical writings – a custodial role which seems to have lingered into the twentieth century. There must, of course, always be a proper and fruitful relationship between intellectually worked out theological doctrine and the witness of individual experience. However, in the medieval period theology was 'queen of the sciences', a discipline which subsumed all other branches of knowledge and social activity and was itself luminously informed by them. Today it tends to be a more exclusive activity in which theologians talk straight to each other and down to the faithful. As far as study of the mystics is concerned, this has meant that modern readers have felt inhibited about discussing these texts and have attributed to them an abstruse esoteric quality; this is ironic in view of the fact that the mystics themselves proclaim their experience to be of fundamental human importance – and essentially simple.[1]

This book is not designed to engage with exposition of doctrine though it will inevitably point to its importance; rather it attempts a mode of appreciation of these texts to help readers, whether or not they have prior knowledge of the subject, to respond to them as literary witnesses to a life of faith understood as a game. Such a concept does itself have roots in theological tradition. The playing of this 'game' is enabled by the transcendent reality which is then manifested through its play. The aims of this first chapter are: first, to provide pointers to the nature of the experience with which these writers were concerned and an approach through which the sympathetic but uninformed reader of our own time might be able to respond to it; second, to clarify those aspects of the medieval cultural context which particularly governed the mode of expression of these writers and, importantly, the expectations of their readers.

NAMING THE GAME: CONTEMPLATIVE EXPERIENCE

Mysticism in the precise sense of an ultimate spiritual reality experienced both within the structure of the human personality and as a transcendent power is not confined to Christianity but common to all religions,[2] and mystics from differing faiths share at least elements of a common experience. They witness to a certainty that all the diversity of living beings are a part of a transcendent unifying spiritual whole which is by definition difficult to grasp in its totality; individual dancers cannot see the pattern of the whole dance – that is perceived only from outside. Mystics are certain that for brief periods they have been enabled to experience such perception and know themselves to be part of a meaningful whole – one with the way things ultimately are. So Thomas Traherne in the seventeenth century saw 'something infinite behind everything' and expressed his joy at the feeling of unity with creation:

> You never Enjoy the World aright, till the
> sea itself floweth in your Veins, till you are Clothed
> with the Heavens, and Crowned with the Stars: . . .
> Till you can sing and Rejoyce and Delight in GOD
> as Misers do in Gold, and Kings in Scepters, you never
> Enjoy the World.[3]

Blake, over a hundred years later, similarly perceived that true vision was:

To see a World in a Grain of Sand
And a Heaven in a Wild Flower,
Hold Infinity in the palm of your hand
And Eternity in an hour.[4]

These are states that a Buddhist might recognise as 'enlightenment'. Such knowledge brings a feeling of fulfilment and liberation from the immediate pressures and problems of material existence, and values derived from them, and a sense that time is the medium through which eternal realities are distilled. From within its limits it is experienced as linear, and life is organised in accordance with this. People aim at achievements to be completed in a time process and talk about how they order their priorities accordingly. Mystics are overwhelmed by a consciousness that there is a dimension beyond that of time, experience of which brings such certainty of fulfilling joy, such transfiguring of the material order, that the only possible priorities for existence in time can be to find a way of life that will allow access to this dimension. The restlessness of the striving and alienated ego is given its proper direction in a fixed longing for this joyful reality, a longing which is the ground and means of its own fulfilment.

The deep-seated feeling that man's nature is essentially structured to survive nomadically[5] and that he needs to be on the move in some way if he is to be satisfied, is complemented by the mystics' witness that true human fulfilment is the concomitant of what is experienced as a spiritual journey to a goal beyond time that is occasionally anticipated and known in time, the element within which our curiously mixed physical and spiritual natures cohere and mature. They convey a double sense of experience: that of a linear process; but also of an eternal state of being which informs and transcends it, and which is accessed within the structure of human nature, itself programmed with a restlessness that can be assuaged by nothing less.

It may be useful to a twentieth-century reader unfamiliar with the theology of Christian mysticism to turn to a particularly luminous account of such awareness in more immediately accessible terms. For example, Peter Matthiessen's account of his astonishing journey on foot, with limited supplies in the face of overwhelming winter snows, from Nepal to the Crystal Mountain in Tibet where he goes fired with the hope of seeing the rare, almost mythical, snow leopard, expresses a pattern of experience that is at the heart of the awareness of the medieval mystics with whom this book is concerned.[6] The beauties and rigours of the literal journey, the only means of seeing the creature now threatened with extinction through the dark destructive energies of man, are inseparable from the spiritual experience given and expressed through their means. High among the bright snows of the Crystal Mountain, cut off from the immediate claims and responsibilities of life in time in the twentieth century, Matthiessen experiences a joy at the heart of the created order to which he belongs, a oneness with it. He engages with a sense of Being eternally present, not driven and limited by the demands of time. He does not see what he so much wants to, the snow leopard, though he sees the evidence of its being which is, curiously, sufficient for him, despite his disappointment. What he does see is a crippled lama living in extreme simplicity and frugality in a mountain hermitage, whose being is irradiated with a joy which has an even keener edge because his infirmities offer him no possibility of escape.

Coming down off the mountains, Matthiessen first finds that he loses the calm and joy of the transfiguration of his perception in high places and becomes a prey to irritation and a sense of desolation and purposelessness – his past experience apparently rendered hallucinatory in the face of his present sense of failure. But then, like the lama, he discovers his disabilities and the constraints of life to be the very conditions for experiencing the validity of transfiguration – the two are concomitant. The whole experience of the pains and startling joys of the hazardous journey becomes for him paradigmatic of the realities of life lived fully from moment to moment, and the teaching of the lama 'not the enlightened wisdom of one man but the splendid utterance of the divine in all mankind'.[7]

The mystics with whom this book is concerned understood this sense of an ultimate reality inherent in, yet transcending, the created world, with the power to transform its pain to joy, in Christian terms. They did not travel to Tibet to seek enlightenment in high places and in an alien culture – though one at least knew the capacity of the literal pilgrimage journey to trigger an existential experience of this power,[8] and they all believed some kind of solitude and withdrawal from the normal conditions of social life to be an enabler of such knowledge. All witness to experiencing the process during which such knowledge is given as a 'way', a 'journey', and the moments of the certainty of transfiguring joy as the attainment of high places in inner experience. For them 'the splendid utterance of the divine in all mankind' had been definitively expressed over a thousand years previously in the way of life and teaching of Jesus Christ in Palestine, in his death at the hands of violently destructive men and in his restoration in life with the source of all being, God. It is their understanding and experience of the meaning of this story of the Incarnation transmitted to them in the Bible, and in the interpretations of the Scriptures by the Church Fathers, which gives their Christian mysticism its definitive characteristics. They saw in it a narrative paradigm which offered the possibility of meaning in their individual experience to all men. In their lives they could both validate, renew and thus extend its significance, for it was understood as the Incarnation of meaning, of that Word which informs the partiality of all words.

The writings of these authors have a very particular literary function. Whereas the meeting-point between reader and author in imaginative creative literature is the recognition of particular aspects of experience shaped and clarified, these authors are trying to share their understanding of the means by which all experience can be understood. Their writings are designed as spring-boards for that action which enables the understanding which is felt experience. They are not designed as artistic structures from which to stand back but as vital nourishment for the journey to which they point. They perform the function of a rite of passage whereby the reader is enabled not only to glimpse imaginatively the possibility of a reality which transcends the limitations of sense and intellect but also to validate it.

For all these writers the key which gives access to this experience is understanding the essentially dynamic implications of the Incarnation. To all of them the story pattern of Mary's assent to God's will at the Annunciation, enabling the birth of his Son who was involved with suffering, death, but also with resurrection and ascension in time, discloses a means of re-ordering (literally transforming) their own experience. They witness to a process of realisation of the confusion, frustration, failure and partiality at the heart of even the best of human experience, let alone the worst, which makes them essentially accessible to all; but they also witness to an awakening understanding of the fact that these are the very means of the experience of transformation. They feel that they can engage with a dynamic power which orders the confusion into meaning and enables them to become participants in creating a pattern that redeems the losses and chances in the contingencies of life in time – to play a game that extends the significance of the Incarnation. The awareness of the working of this dynamic power, and awareness of the need for a disciplined way of life essential to its operation, is characteristic of the mystics.

All five of these writers engage in various ways with, and with differing emphasis on, the component parts of this story. Some concentrate on their experience of the significance of the birth, death and resurrection of Christ as a fully revealed paradigm of human potential, others witness more immediately to an experience of the ultimate and ineffable reality which informs the story. Margery Kempe finds the actual humanity of Christ's life and death a pattern of living which transfigures the ordinary demands of daily life with a sense of the holy – an emotional engagement with the humanity of Christ which she shares with the 'affective piety' of her age.[9] In his English writings Richard Rolle, too, sees Christ's suffering as the pragmatic key to a form of living both as regards external circumstances and internal consciousness, which will free followers to engage with the ineffable reality of the love mediated at the Incarnation. Walter Hilton is concerned in a much more abstract and organised way with the whole story of the Incarnation as a paradigm for understanding the self and realising its fullest potential. For Julian of Norwich, meditation on Christ's Passion is the means to her visionary experience of the ultimately redemptive reality of love in the suffering and alienation of time. For her there is no way to 'endles knowyng' of God but by 'time of passion'.[10] The *Cloud*-author would not dispute this but, whereas Julian and the others communicate their experience of the being of the transcendent God in the inner self by means of focus on the combination of literal and figurative truths revealed in the story of the Incarnation and Passion, he is so concerned with the reality of a God who cannot be 'known' by intellect or sense, that he plays down these 'means'.

Some commentators see the affective piety of Margery Kempe as radically distinguished from that of the *Cloud*-author, and indeed in danger of missing the essential spirituality of God.[11] It is helpful to approach the spiritual continuum which in fact unites them by way of the teaching of the thirteenth-century Franciscan Bonaventura's description of the light of God as the sun of his divinity and the moon of his humanity.[12] Whereas the moon can be looked at directly, although its luminosity derives from the sun, the sun itself, if gazed at, blinds man with excess of light. It is this kind of darkness which is at the heart of the *Cloud*-author's work and constitutes the cloud of unknowing. Both these lights are operative in the writings of the mystics as means by which man sees his own true nature and in doing so also a reflection of God; it is a state in which they feel themselves to be most fully alive.

One thing all the writers share is an agreement that the progress to the special knowledge in the game of faith involves a reordering and an integration of the personality which gives birth to an essential lightness of spirit within man. This answers to a wider theological concept that the whole universe itself of which man is part is an expression of the play of God bringing creative order out of chaos. The concept of play as an activity entered into with delight for its own sake is important for both the theology and the psychology of religion. The Christian belief in God's being as a Trinity of Father, Son and Holy Spirit was traditionally interpreted by the Church Fathers who formulated theology, as an interplay of power, wisdom and love. The creative power of the Father is expressed in the Son as his wisdom and, in the Holy Spirit, as the creative love which binds them. Thomas Aquinas understood the relationship between Father and Son as that of the joy of divine wisdom playing before the face of God and contemplative life as sharing in such play.[13]

The mystics understood the story of the Incarnation as the game of love in time, and the life of faith as engaging with, and extending it. All agree that it involves a process of discipline and self-knowledge as a means to liberate the spirit, much as the grace and apparently effortless expressiveness of dance is, paradoxically, the fruit of rigorous physical discipline. The whole process enacts redemption. Living by faith in the story of the Incarnation turns out to be for these writers a totally absorbing game, the playing of which is a self-validating exercise that releases human creative energies to the full and extends the play of divine wisdom before the face of God. In the human situation it can be played only by means of failure and suffering: these are the elements by which the triumph of joy and love seen in Christ is constantly rediscovered.

The following chapters will look at how each of these mystics understood the nature and rules of the game. For all of them the story of the Incarnation interprets and orders all possibilities of human experience. In their time there was a general recognition of an ultimately important spiritual dimension to life that is lacking in our own – a sense of the universe given meaning by God so that man's words interpenetrate with the Word, that whole transcendent meaning so fragmented and distorted by the Fall. This fundamental relevance of a religious view of the universe to all aspects of experience is encapsulated in the figurative mode of reading Biblical history as the revelation of a divine purpose whereby the events of the Old Testament prefigure those of the New, and both together reveal the pattern of salvation whereby all future history may be interpreted. This pattern was traditionally expounded as involving four kinds of reality: literal historical truth; allegorical significance in the way in which events in the Old Testament are fulfilled by those in the New and in the life of the Church; moral teaching (labelled troplogical interpretation); and fourthly, anagogical understanding relating to ultimate spiritual realities – this is particularly important for mystical works. These four ways of understanding Scripture permeated medieval habits of reading and writing.[14] The sense of joy and spiritual opportunity at the heart of this interpretation of human history and the life of faith is vibrantly embodied in a fifteenth-century carol:

Nowel, nowel, nowel,
Nowel, nowel, nowel!

Owt of your slepe aryse and wake,
For God mankynd nowe hath ytake
Al of a maide without any make;
Of al women she bereth the belle.
Nowel!

And thorwe a maide faire and wys
Now man is made of ful gret pris;
Now angelys knelen to mannys servys,
And at this tyme al this byfel.
Nowel!

Now man is brighter than the sonne;
Now man in heven an hye shal wone;
Blessyd be God this game is begonne,

And his moder emperesse of helle.
Nowel!

That ever was thralle, now ys he fre;
That ever was smalle, now grete is she;
Now shal God deme bothe the and me
Unto his blysse yf we do wel.
Nowel!

Now man may to heven wende;
Now heven and erthe to hym they bende;
He that was foo now is oure frende;
This is no nay that y yow telle.
Nowel!

Now blessyd brother, graunte us grace
A domesday to se thy face
And in thy courte to have a place,
That we mow there synge nowel.
Nowel![15]

make: mate; *bereth the belle*: takes the prize; *pris*: value; *wone*: dwell; *wende*: go.

It has been suggested that this carol is guilty of reducing the mystery of God to human terms and redemption itself to 'little more than a lark'.[16] But such a response to the literal meaning of this carol completely misses the spiritual dimension inherent in the form of the carol and signalled by its context of affective piety.[17] The swinging rhythm and rather pleasantly exhibitionist rhyme-scheme, together with the reconciled paradoxical terms of the maiden-mother, angels kneeling to men, prisoners freed, small become great and foe become friend, enact rhetorically a delight that redemption is indeed a game, the playing of which reverses all the normal expectations of mortality. The final quieter, prayerful stanza contrasts with the single line declamations of the previous verses and witnesses to the recognition that this game is not always played with ease, that the very measure of the exultation felt arises from realisation of the ultimate issues at stake.

The mystic's understanding of this joy at the heart of experience is called visionary; it is to ordinary human perception as waking is to sleeping; and this carol, in its excited evocation of the significance of redemption in words and images, answers to this understanding. It also points to a fundamental truth that the mystics perceived in the story of the Incarnation – that the 'purpose of the Word become flesh was indeed to make mystics of us all'.[18]

INHERITED APPROACHES TO THE GAME

Mystical experience as a peculiarly human goal has a long cultural history which bears on the way these writers express themselves. The tradition to which they belong evolved an accommodation of Christian doctrine to a body of teaching inherited from Greek philosophy about a kind of knowledge – *noesis* – which is neither intellectual nor sensual, but in essence experiential and manifested in the human soul. It involves the completion of all partiality, the overcoming of all senses of alienation and it brings a fulfilment of desire for the good and the beautiful beyond the capacity of human understanding. There is an unresolved tension between the fact that the perceptions of mystics are seen as fundamentally important to the human condition and the fact that they are given to so few.[19] But it is particularly ironic that this body of teaching on to which Christian mysticism was grafted was élitist in its view of those to whom such knowledge was possible.

Philosophers like Plato and Plotinus believed that the longing for this knowledge is innate in the human soul which had itself emanated, albeit to the furthest possible extent, from the source of all being to which it longs to return. The Christian accommodation of such inherent longing for fulfilment had, however, to take account of the teaching of Nicene Orthodoxy[20] concerning the Biblical account of creation. It held that God is the Creator *ex nihilo* thus implying a divide rather than a continuum of being between man's soul and God.

In both Classical and Christian thinking mysticism represents a way back to the source of being, but in Christian thinking from the fourth century on, the gulf between Creator and created was seen as mysteriously bridged by the love of God incarnate in Jesus Christ, God's Word, the expression of himself manifest in time, which, in turn, enables human knowledge and love which are the way back. It is this essentially dynamic experience – energy releasing energy, which gives medieval Christian mysticism its special characteristics, many of which were directly derived from the teaching of St Augustine (fifth century), the most seminal figure in the West for orthodox mystical theology. He formulated in haunting terms the longing expressed by Platonists for the source of all beauty: 'late have I loved Thee, O Beauty so ancient and so new', but he recognised this longing as itself the working of God's gift of love in man – in theological terms, the grace of the Holy Spirit. For Augustine, God in giving man life quite literally inspired in him a longing for its source:

> Thou didst breathe fragrance upon me, and I draw in my breath and do now pant for Thee . . . Thou didst touch me, and I have burned for thy peace[21]

and growth in mystical knowledge concerned a process of recognition of the nature of God's involvement with his creatures in time. Unlike the Platonists he saw no ontological continuity between the soul and God, but a relationship of likeness based on the Biblical account of man's creation in Genesis (1:26–7) where his peculiar property was to be made in the image of God. Augustine conceived the structure of man's inner being, his mind, to be activated by the interaction of memory and understanding through will. This trinity of faculties constituted the image of God and enabled in him a wisdom based on the knowledge of the reality of the love of God revealed at the Incarnation. It is in this felt understanding that the image of God in man, obscured by the disintegration of sin, is regenerated. For Augustine, mystical experience operated in the gap between the Creator and creature, enabling man to recognise his own true nature and so come to a knowledge of God – a process possible only because of the Incarnation, the love poured out from the being of God to his creatures which revealed how He could be known.

However, just as the fourteenth-century English mystics present a variety of responses to a core of dogmatically formulated belief, the tradition they inherited developed a variety of particular views on the nature of mystical experience in relation to Christian orthodoxy.[22] And if Augustine's understanding of how God can indeed be known incarnationally influenced the thinking of later mystics like Walter Hilton, Richard Rolle and Julian of Norwich, another tradition, which stressed not the links between Creator and created, but the darkness of the divide, was undoubtedly formative in the experience of the *Cloud*-author. He inherited a tradition of teaching which stressed the essential unknowability of God by human faculties. A key figure in this 'negative' approach is Denys, or Dionysius, the Areopagite, probably a sixth-century Syrian monk, whose theology acquired a quasi-apostolic authority in the Middle

Ages because he was confused with the Areopagite converted by St Paul (Acts 17:19–34). He is sometimes referred to as pseudo-Dionysius or pseudo-Denys. He does not dwell on the significance of the Incarnation, but rather on the process by which the individual can, despite partial knowledge and creatureliness, enter into a darkness where nothing is known, yet God is existentially encountered in love. He finds an icon for his teaching in the Old Testament account (Exodus 19) of Moses' ascent of Sinai where he is separated from the people and priests by a cloud in the darkness of which he encounters God. This image he inherited from the fourth-century teaching of Gregory of Nyssa,[23] the most influential among those who earlier developed this negative approach to Christian mystical theology.

Whether the emphasis in mystical theology is on the interaction of those God-given human faculties which are understood as an image of his being and the means by which man may realise the love and truth manifested in the Incarnation, or on the essential unknowability of the transcendent source from whence that love and truth emanated in time, there is common ground between the two approaches in the sense of a dynamic with which man may engage. For Augustine mystical knowledge of God is the essence of Christianity involving a lifelong process of growth in the recognition of the reality of the Incarnation, enabled through the grace of God working in man's powers of will, memory and understanding. Although Dionysius stresses the utter inadequacy of any created being to know the nature of the one God who created everything from nothing, he also asserts that He is immanent in His creation and that man can encounter the reality of the energy of divine love at the heart of his being. This is the truth manifest in the Incarnation, and Dionysius says that at such a moment the mystic is like St Paul who said: 'I live and yet not I, but Christ lives in me'.[24] Both theologians find man's highest development to be his participation in the living energy of the love of a transcendent God who, both would agree, cannot be fully known in time. At the heart of both of them is a witness to the vital relationship between the historical reality of the Incarnation and a way of living by which man may engage with the spiritual reality it manifested and thus extend it in time.

Concomitant with the mystical theology inherited by the medieval English mystics, and also governing their thought and expression was a dialectic about the mode of living which enabled mystical experience and a vocabulary to express it. Broadly speaking, as far as these writers are concerned, psychological understanding of the self was Augustinian in its emphasis on memory as the power of the mind which brings to consciousness that which is the object of the will – itself the indicator of the affections and disposition of the mind and intellect. These inner faculties provide both the ability to reasonably organise one's daily survival in time and also the means by which God is known. There was, however, considerably detailed discussion as to the nature of the interaction of those inner powers in mystical knowledge. It was generally agreed that there was a difference between human science and the knowledge of God, in that while human knowledge was concerned with that which reason could analyse, theology was concerned with the way in which the transcendent love of God is known. Writers from the twelfth century onwards like Bernard of Clairvaux, Thomas Gallus and Bishop Grosseteste stressed the role of the will, the affective faculty, in this knowledge which was the desired wisdom of felt understanding. Others, like Albert the Great or Richard of St Victor emphasised more strongly the role of the intellect in that which is known.[25] This dialectic concerning the balance of human cognitive powers in theological understanding certainly influenced the way in which the medieval mystics expressed themselves, and it is necessary to be aware of the context of argument within which they wrote. Nevertheless their aim was the expression of the experience of a knowledge which integrates human faculties, not a scholastic dissection of its separate parts, important though this is to the history of thought. It is this knowledge prompted by, and answering to, divinely inspired longing that William Langland gestures towards in *Piers Plowman*. Will and intellect are united in the significantly named 'Will' who is also a searcher after Truth. The allegorical figure of Holy Church sets him on an inner journey as she teaches him that the object of his being is to discover a natural inward knowledge of a love for God that is greater than any other preoccupation.

'It is a kynde knowynge that kenneth in thyn herte
For to loven thi Lord levere than thiselve'.[26]

kenneth: gives teaching; *levere*: more dearly.

The poem, of epic proportions, illuminates the way in which Will arrives at such 'kynde knowynge' which embraces both knowledge of himself and of the love of God.

TRAINING TO PLAY: INNER DISCIPLINE

Whatever discussion there was about the faculties operative in mystical knowledge, there was a consensus of agreement that it was enabled by a process of inward self-discipline with recognisable stages of progress. The groundwork was concerned with the acquirement of self-control facilitated by the recognition of the emotional drives and mental preoccupations that would sidetrack the seeker after the love of God and impede his progress. One vivid account of the means by which this may be achieved is set out in *Ancrene Wisse*, an early Middle English text written originally for particular sisters in the late twelfth century who wanted to live as recluses dedicated to God but later adopted more widely in other such communities.[27] It illuminates the medieval understanding of the interior life subject to impulses whose gratification may satisfy the immediate demands of the self for ease, anger, pleasure, esteem, but which also impede the freedom of the spirit to seek that ultimate good which in reality is the only means of satisfying man's inherent need for fulfilment. The key to the repressive discipline advocated in this manual of behaviour is that it is to be the means by which man is liberated from all that thwarts his true nature, just as the dancer can only use his body expressively if he trains his muscles: 'those move easiest who have learnt to dance'.[28]

The sisters are taught to think of those impulses that impede the spirit as sins with the strength of predatory beasts ravening in the wilderness of the interior landscape of the fallen world. The process of achievement of a state where the self is receptive to the love of God is that of a balancing act. The author embodies his sense of this in the cumulative use of the verb *leap* to point towards the poise achieved above the abyss of self-destruction. So he calls the heart a wild beast liable to impulsive leaps out of control,[29] a situation archetypally illustrated in the story of the Fall when Eve's eyes leapt to the apple and her heart followed and so she leapt from Paradise to the pains of mortality and took all men with her.[30] This inner life is projected as a theatre for the right direction of energy: the soul in temptation is ready to leap into pride,[31] indeed the devil himself is seen as a leaper constantly alert to seize his chance to get hold of the direction of man's life.[32]

But if man is vulnerable to impulses which send him spiralling down into darkness, that very vulnerability is the means by which he can existentially know the strength whereby it can be healed and stabilised. The precarious nature of the human effort to balance is steadied by the strength of the love of God which itself leapt down into time to show it could be done. So that which makes man vulnerable to the force of the leaping devil, also opens him to the effortless strength of the leaping God which is known through the experience of inadequacy. The author sees the spiritual strength released in the sisters through their disciplined aspiration to the love of God as part of the work of that love in them; they share in the pattern of Incarnation.[33]

If the process of learning to conquer the impulses to self-gratification seems too painful to be borne, the author reminds the sisters that ultimately a complaint will seem as misguided as that of a prisoner thrown a bag of money to buy his release who moans that the bag hit and bruised him. The pain is the price of freedom: not just freedom in a spiritual kingdom after death, but realised in an inner freedom to love. The process of the recognition of the self's capacity to sin but also to engage with the strength of the leaping God which enables it to make good its losses, is ritually enacted in the sacrament of penance.[34] The process of confession, contrition and restitution was originally instituted as a public act through which individual members of society were reconciled to each other in that social harmony signified by the kiss of peace at the Mass which was the condition for the reception of Christ at the eucharist.[35] For the individual seeking an inner personal relationship with that God whose Incarnation enabled the socially redemptive love celebrated at the Mass, it was an interior process mediated by the priest and one formally encouraged by the Church after the Lateran Council of 1215. This penance was the ground for growth in the interior realisation of the love of God.

Those who wished to foster it further were encouraged in a process of meditation and prayer. Individual writers may differ in their exposition of how these two mental activities interact[36] but a classic exposition of the dynamics of the whole spiritual exercise involved in the contemplative process is found in the twelfth-century *Scala Claustralium (The Ladder of Monks)* by a

Carthusian, Guigo II.[37] He understands meditation and prayer as two sides of growth in the knowledge of God: meditation on the truth of what is read in Scripture informs the focus of the mind and the will in prayer. Meditation is that process of mental digestion that gives rise to understanding which integrates the energies of mind and will in a desire for God which is prayer.

It is in this prayerful meditation that mystics say that they receive an illumination of the reality of God over and above anything they can reach by their own efforts. Clearly the whole game has a dimension of linear extension which enables a continual process of growth in recognition. The effort involved in the activity of penance may become less rigorous as the self achieves a habit of self-control born out of self-knowledge, although, clearly, the kind of self-awareness which is the necessary ingredient for penance must constantly be maintained. But the growth in knowledge enabled by the activities of reading, meditation and contemplative prayer grows in time; it engages with the inexhaustible wisdom of God.

For teaching purposes, writers in the contemplative tradition followed Richard of St Victor in allegorising the process by which the soul comes to know God through the Old Testament story (Genesis 29) of Jacob's marriage to Leah and Rachel.[38] Jacob loved Rachel for whom he was set to work for seven years, but was then tricked into marrying the older sister, Leah, first, and working a further seven years for the greatly desired Rachel. Leah bore him children, but Rachel was barren for a long period during which Jacob had children by her maidservant before she eventually gave birth to Joseph and then Benjamin. Richard of St Victor used the story to schematise his understanding of how God (Jacob) works in the human will and affections (Leah) and the reason (Rachel) so that they become fruitful with the knowledge of himself. The story provided a flow-chart to clarify the dynamic sense of man's inner drives and faculties integrated in an ordered recognition of the reality of God. The awakened will gives rise to fear of God, sorrow for sin, hope for forgiveness and love of God (Leah's first four children). They are understood by the ability of the imagination (Rachel's servant, Bilhah) to relate these emotions to anticipation of the joys of heaven and pains of hell, and helped by the practice of self-discipline, abstinence and patience in the desires of sensuality (Zilpah, Leah's servant). This growth in, and ordering of, the impulses of the will brings an inner peace and joy (the fifth child of

Leah) which is accompanied by hatred of, and shame for, sin (the sixth and seventh children). Such a state of ordered affection enables man to recognise the achievement of inner balance and reconciliation of powers in the longing for God, the necessary condition for knowledge of Him. This recognition is the first child of Rachel and a function of reason, known by the mystics as the state of *discretion*. It represents an instinctive knowledge (a 'kynde knowynge') acquired by trial and error of how to maintain an inner balance, and reason's active initiative ends here, giving way to a new kind of knowledge of God experienced as a gift that *discretion* enables man to receive. This knowledge is contemplative, and contemplation is Rachel's last child (Benjamin) before she dies.

PLAYING-FIELDS: ACTIVE AND COMTEMPLATIVE LIFE AND THE LITURGY

These two states of the inner activity of integration giving way to the gift of contemplation are related to a complex of ideas inherited by the mystics about two modes of living known as 'active' and 'contemplative'. The story of Jacob's marriage to Leah and Rachel had also been used since the time of Augustine to symbolise these two ways of Christian living; the fundamental activities necessary to the well-being of society being represented by Leah, contemplative knowledge of the love that is the ground for these activities by Rachel.[39]

Even if it is arguable for the purposes of theological discussion that the mode of being in which contemplative knowledge of God becomes a reality is superior to the demands of the active life, Augustine recognised that in the fallen world the two were indissolubly linked and complementary:

> for no one ought to be so leisured as to take no thought in that leisure for the interest of his neighbour, nor so active as to feel no need for the contemplation of God.[40]

Gregory the Great made a similar point.[41] Active life is a condition of existence in time, translating the love of God into actions that will repair the fallen inner world of the psyche and the external world of society. It will cease with time, whereas contemplative life may be begun in time, but it will be perfected beyond it.[42] In the fourteenth century the *Cloud*-author makes the same point quite explicitly:

> þe condicion of actyue liif is soche, þat it is boþe bygonne & eended in þis liif. Bot not so of contemplatiue liif; for it is bigonne in þis liif, & schal last wiþouten eende . . . .[43]

The *Cloud*-author also provides an acute analysis of the way these terms interact in a continuum of activity both external and internal which leads finally to the possibility of the gift of contemplation. Thus he explains that the lower part of active life consists in the works of mercy and charity in society, the higher in the activities involved in penance and meditation which are also the lower part and the groundwork for contemplative knowledge of God who is beyond the ability of man's active faculties to comprehend. Yet although God is dark to man's understanding, the reality of his being may be reached out to through love.[44]

This ideal of an essential continuity between active and contemplative life is often worked out in practice in terms of their opposition. The *Cloud*-author points out that they cannot be pursued simultaneously. As in a modern context it is immediately clear that students find it hard to combine study with a full-time job; so, addressing a would-be contemplative, the *Cloud*-author explains his view that it is impossible for man to pursue the discipline of meditation and study unless he first ceases external activity, and impossible to come to mystical knowledge of God if the mind is engaged in discursive thought.[45] In practice active and contemplative life get in each other's way.

This kind of emphasis on the opposition between, rather than the complementary nature of, the active and contemplative lives was reflected in the patristic interpretation of the story of Martha and Mary (Luke 10:38–42) in which Christ excuses Mary's lack of active help in Martha's household chores because she was listening to him, on the grounds that she was concentrating on that which was most essential.[46] An opposition between active and contemplative life is fostered by the fact that not all people feel able to pursue the discipline of contemplative life – some are notably more suited to the necessary functions of active life. Thus the two terms came to be used not just of modes of being with which individuals engaged but the outward life-styles they embraced.

Contemplatives often lived solitary and reclusive lives whether or not they were in religious orders.

In thinking about the terms 'active' and 'contemplative' in medieval devotional writing, however, it is important not to confuse their use to designate outward life-styles with their designation of modes of being which enable argument about the purposes of man's existence. While it could be, and was, argued that the contemplative knowledge of God should inform the goals of active life for all men, it was acknowledged that in practice very few individuals could combine both states in balance.[47] Evidence of the difficulties experienced in trying to combine the demands of active life with those of inner quietness can be found in the request for help answered by Walter Hilton in his *Mixed Life*[48] and by the courageous attempt of Margery Kempe to live out her faith. The relationship between the two ways of being was, however, always a live issue. If few could attain the peculiar sanctity of St Francis who united contemplative consciousness of God's love with a life of exemplary action, such integrity was seen as a *desideratum*.

But what might be impossible for individuals was possible within the larger body of society. The essentially complementary nature of contemplative and active life fully expressed in the Incarnation but experienced often as a tension for individuals could be reflected more freely in the whole society of Christians understood as the body of Christ. In this context each individual can emphasise that aspect of the two modes of being for which he has the greatest gift and both may further the understanding of the work of love.[49] The opposition inherent in the terms active and contemplative is a useful way of delineating issues fundamental to the structure of the human personality and therefore of Christian society. Theologically this opposition is perceived as an accident of the Fall; essentially there is no gap between action and contemplation in the being of God. That is part of the meaning revealed through the Incarnation and it is this spontaneous integrity of being that mystics glimpse and in so doing serve and inspire the Christian society, of which they are a part, struggling to repair the ravages of sin.

This transcending of the differences of individual gifts in a corporate wholeness in which the love of God could be manifest and known[50] was constantly enacted in the ritual of the Mass at the centre of parish worship. There the emphasis in late medieval times was on the transcendental unity of the whole body of Christ embracing both the living and the dead, a unity constantly in creation through the energy of love. The breaking of the Host, the round wafer of bread signifying the body of Christ at the end of the canon of the Mass after the consecration, pointed to the continual enactment of the Passion linking Christ's body broken by the actions of sin at the Crucifixion with the divided community; but simultaneously revealing the means by which the divisions are healed since, precisely because of its breaking, the Host is the shared bread of life.[51] The sacrament embodies the reality of the power of love, known through suffering and division, as a healing power. This was emphasised by the peace – a ritual kiss of reconciliation with which the congregation were occupied while the priest made his communion. The peace of society was thus assimilated to the sacrament; it was enacted as both the condition and the effect of the reality of Christ's presence.

This sacramental process by which the body of Christ was healed was further stressed by the execution of the statutory obligation on parishioners to receive communion at least once a year. This generally took place at Easter preceded by confession, often in public, in which the social duty of making restitution for sin was stressed; it might be succeeded by a parish party which played out at its own level the eternal being of love celebrated in the Mass.[52] Indeed the power of the Church rituals in society to provide icons through which the reality they were designed to express could be felt, should not be underestimated as Margery Kempe's reaction, however extreme, bears witness.[53]

One in particular strongly reinforced this strong sense of the essential unity of the whole body of believers, despite the accidents of time – the celebration of the feast of *Corpus Christi*. It has been well argued that the great procession, headed by the Host and including the orders of the Church and social guilds, interrupted by the plays performed by the guild members reminding followers of the archetypal story of God's plan of salvation from the Creation to the Last Judgement,[54] provided opportunity for participating in that sense of unity beyond division which is the heart of Christian belief,[55] and which underpins the social value put on the more isolated lives of contemplatives.

Such emphasis on corporate wholeness can also be seen in the prayers recommended for the use of lay people during the Latin Mass. After the Sanctus and before the elevation of the Host, the reader is bidden to remember Christ's Passion and his own sin, and also to pray for all estates in the land from Pope and King to the 'poure and smale',[56] for good harvests to sustain them and for entry into God's joy at death. This prayerful reminder of Christ as the sustainer of men in society is concluded as the Host is elevated. Then follow prayers for the dead by both priest, and people who have their own version, that the Mass may be 'mede & medecyne' to them.[57] After the peace and while the priest receives the sacrament, the layman reflects on that love which is the reflection of God in society and constitutes the peace; love of God, proper love of self demonstrated in the harnessing of both spiritual and physical energies to serve God,[58] and love of society – 'alle manere of men'.[59]

At the end of the Mass there is a touching prayer as men go out into the world linking the sacrament of the one bread which binds all men in God with the bread and ale of human meeting:

> God, that his brede brake
> at his mawnde whanne he sate
> Amonge his postyllis twelue,
> He bles oure brede & oure ayl
> þat we haw & haw schal,
> And be with vs him-selwe.[60]
>
> *haw*: have; *mawnde:* the last supper – Maundy.

In the bidding prayers where the priest directs the people to pray and tells them what to pray for, probably after the offering and the anthem, again attention is directed to all estates of society, living and dead, including religious, both monastic and secular.[61] Pilgrims also are remembered, that 'god of his goodnes graunt them parte of our good prayers and us parte of theyr good pylgrimages'.[62] And certainly those treatises which deal with the spiritual and physical advantages of hearing the Mass (which ranged from not ageing during the period of the Mass to its efficacy in promoting work or journeys) stress the belief in the power of the sacrament to affect all aspects of life.[63]

This stress on *communitas* [the bond of community] is one in which the potential divisions between active and contemplative life are healed, and provides the structure within which the prayer of contemplatives is a channel for the release of the love of God, not just within the self, but within society. Those devoted to contemplation might have lived enclosed lives, but they were open to society as advisers and counsellors. And if the Mass enacted the social reality of the body of Christ, it also enacted the recognised pattern of personal contemplative experience, moving as it did from confession, the recognition of the condition of sin and fallen man, through the articulation of faith as revealed in Scripture and Creed, to the offering to God of the God-given fruits of human labour through which the gift of his presence is made known.[64]

The contemplative who had a cell adjoining the church would have a window through which the altar could be seen. Thus at the canon of the Mass he or she would be able to identify the realities of personal experience and the sacred participation in *communitas* with the presence of Christ. Small wonder that the eucharist was the centre of mystical devotion for some notable female mystics like Catherine of Siena.[65] It is significant that one of the few occasions when the author of *Ancrene Wisse* hints at the contemplative experience occurs in his account of the behaviour appropriate at the Mass:

> Efter þe measse cos hwen þe preost sacreð þer for ȝeoteð
> al þe world. þer beoð al ut of bodi þer i sperclinde
> luue bicluppeð ower leofman þe in to ower breostes
> bur is iliht of heouene. & haldeð him heteueste aþet
> he habbe iȝettet ow al þat ȝe eauer easki. (21. 18–23)

> (After the kiss of peace in the Mass, when the priest
> communicates, forget the world, be completely out of the
> body, and with burning love embrace your Beloved who has
> come down from heaven to your heart's bower, and hold Him
> fast until He has granted you all that you ask.)[66]

Liturgy provides both a public focus of the structure of the contemplative life and a ritual in which the individual's experience of the reality of God's presence within the self is one with his sense of *communitas* in the body of Christ. It also offers a continual rite of passage to mystical understanding and experience for those less advanced in that particular understanding of the reality of the faith. The whole complex structure of the liturgy throughout the year orders and enacts believers' common sense of how an ultimate reality engages with the processes of time: the Mass through the celebration of a corporate sense of all life as a divine gift sustained by processes of death and resurrection; the office by a daily pattern of worship varying throughout the year to commemorate the significance of the events of the Incarnation and link the activities of the Church in time present with the saints. The complex pattern of prayers, hymns, readings, versicles and responses performed daily throughout the year enables a private faith to be projected in a shared experience and assume a ritualised existential quality. The liturgy offers all Christians the opportunity to balance the discipline of habit and formal order with spontaneous renewal of that experience which the order of the liturgy is designed to clarify. Margery Kempe witnesses to the way in which the visual icons of the Easter ceremonies activated her inner sense of the reality of the Incarnation. Thus when she saw the priests kneel in darkness lit only by burning torches, to place the crucifix and Host in the Easter sepulchre to symbolise the darkness of the physical death and burial of Christ prior to the joy of resurrection, this ritual precipitated her inner sense of the significance of the Passion and a corresponding outpouring of love and compassion in tears as she spread her arms like her crucified Lord.[67] Margery's reactions may have been physically extreme, but her account highlights the peculiar potential in the liturgy to trigger existential experiences of the faith.

This sense of Christian unity in the faith enacted in liturgical structures which catered for the needs of lay individuals seeking to understand their faith was lost after the Reformation, when increasing stress was put on individual communion and a personal relationship with God.[68] In the late medieval period, although the sense of unity in the Church was stretched to near breaking point as the upsurge of spiritual enthusiasm from the grass roots which had been fostered by the Church's own mission for reform since the thirteenth century became viewed as a potential threat by the establishment, there was nevertheless a fruitful tension between individual and corporate senses of identity. It fostered the personal exploration of spirituality within the framework of the Church's teaching that characterises late medieval English texts.

DEFINING THE RULES: RELIGIOUS INSTRUCTION TO THE LAITY

The social dynamics which foregrounded a consciousness of individual identity have been clearly analysed: primo-genitive inheritance forcing younger sons to seek a role outside the family;

the growth of a socially fluid urban society and of cathedral schools and the resultant rise of an administrative class; the climate of learning and debate about the purposes of life, ideals to be followed and choice of life-style – whether to pursue an active life of involvement with the world of affairs or the inner contemplative ideals of a personal relationship with God within the renunciation and shelter of a cloister; the stress on personal relationships between friends and lovers; all these factors contributed to raise the profile of the individual within society rather than submerge it in low relief within a predetermined authoritarian hierarchy.[69] Culture flourished on the tension between a perception of the unique reality of individual beings and the corporate structures to which they belonged. Chaucer's art of ambiguity in presenting his Canterbury pilgrims balances the levels at which they are bonded by the literal and figurative goals of their journey and stereotyped by their social functions, with an awareness of an individual reality which cannot be adequately contained by either. So the Wife of Bath and the Prioress together challenge the social norms of women's roles; the shifting surfaces of the Pardoner's blatant hypocrisy tease the reader into an uncomfortable awareness of the unfathomable nature of human motivation for the onlooker; the Nun's priest's juxtaposition of intellectual solemnity with quick-witted pragmatism and his stress on the saving grace of social charity cuts self-importance down to size. In *Piers Plowman*, Will's discovery of the reality of his salvation is inextricably bound up with his exasperation at the gap between the ideals of the faith and their realisation within the social fabric of Church and State. His journey is one of growth in patient awareness that the truth of the Gospel cannot be enforced by social legislation but only fostered in the consciousness of individuals from whose hearts alone the reality of social salvation can spring. Langland's imaginative perception of Will's growth from experiencing this tension as destructive to a state where he sees it as the opportunity for love parallels the written witness of the mystics.

In the visual arts the more immediate appeal of the physical and emotional realities of Gothic replaced the more remote, albeit intensely moving, complexities of Romanesque and Celtic styles. The archetypal stiff-leaf decorating the movement from summit of pillar to springing of arch, burgeons into recognisable foliage: oak, hawthorn, buttercup. The specifically indeterminate forms that inhabit the underside of misericords – birds with human heads, dragons with foliage tails – give way to bats, cats, men – on horseback or performing somersaults under the ledge to balance it on various parts of their anatomy. The geometrical patterning and grotesques in the margins of holy books disappear in favour of conventional realism, birds, hunting scenes, agricultural activities.[70]

The English mystical texts in the fourteenth century are symptomatic of this whole ethos. They were produced at a time when lay people were being targeted for instruction in ways which further fostered their consciousness as individuals with self-defining choices to be made by the programme for revitalising the mission of the Church instituted by the fourth Lateran Council in 1215. This called for confession as a yearly obligation for all Christians and officially sanctioned the growing practice of private, as opposed to public, penance, although the social dimension of the sacrament as a healer of social division remained.[71] The actual implementation of reform and teaching in the Church was left to the initiative of individual bishops through the organisation of provincial synods. The English bishops were conscientious in the provision of manuals of instruction on how to hear confession and on how to teach the laity the rudiments of the faith.[72]

The most influential model of such instruction to be produced was that of John Pecham, Archbishop of Canterbury (1279–92). His Lambeth Constitutions of 1281 laid down that the priest should instruct the people in the basics of the faith and preach at least four time a year in English. Since not all of the clergy were capable of this, model sermons were produced to help them. One collection of such[73] gives insight into the literal way spiritual truths were inculcated. The sermons illuminate not only the sometimes seemingly awkward literal mode of the piety of Margery Kempe, but also the *Cloud*-author's nervousness that his readers should not confuse physical and spiritual realities.[74] One sermon to urge the duty of penance and confession tells of a woman who had committed a sin which she could not bring herself to confess for shame. 'Crist see well þat she shuld haue be dampned for þat synne'[75] so he appeared to her in her sleep, wounded as in his Passion, and told her to put her hand into his side and even to feel his internal organs and heart, commenting that if he is thus open with her, why is she so ashamed to reveal to him the secrets of her heart? When she woke she found her hand covered with blood which she could not wash off until she went to church to confess to the priest. There she wept for her sins and her tears washed away the blood;

> so be þis ensaumppull ȝe may well see þat Crist will not haue no man ne womman loste and þei will aske mercy and be shryven of here synnes.[76]

The form in which this sermon harnesses the pressure of fear as well as the promise of comfort, provides a recognisable cultural context for the form of Margery Kempe's initial vision of salvation and witnesses to the high esteem in which tears as a sign of spiritual grace were held in the fifteenth century.[77]

The instructions that John Thorseby, Archbishop of York, issued for the clergy in 1357 and which were on his instructions expounded by the Benedictine monk, John Gaytrick, in a vernacular version known as the *Lay Folks' Catechism*,[78] give insight into the framework of thought within which life was assimilated to, and ordered by, Christian belief – the groundwork of assumptions that mystical writers in the vernacular could take for granted. The *Lay Folks' Catechism* sets out the fundamentals of the faith under six headings: fourteen points of truth; the ten commandments and the two Gospel commandments; the seven sacraments; the works of mercy; the seven virtues; the seven sins. The very order implies understanding of the process of redemption whereby the Incarnation and Passion transform the *lex talionis* (the law of retaliation) of the Old Testament with the grace and love which are the means of recycling the waste products of sin. The 'fourteen points of truth', which are the foundation for all that follows, concern teaching on both the Godhead and the manhood of Christ. The seven points relevant to the Godhead are that he is true; that he is everlasting truth – 'stedefast & sothefast';[79] that Jesus is God's Son and equal with his Father; that the Holy Ghost came from both of them and is equal with them so that in God there are three aspects or powers; that this Trinity is the source of all creativity:

> Fadir and sone and haligast, thre persons and a god,
> Is maker of heuen and of erthe and of all thinges;[80]

that all believers share in the sacraments and are the Church within which lies salvation; that at judgement day all will rise up, body and soul together, and go either to hell or heaven depending on whether they have done evil or good.

The seven which are relevant to Christ's manhood are: belief in the Incarnation and Virgin birth; that in Jesus God and man are united, begotten by God, born of Mary; belief in 'Cristes passion'

> That he tholed bodily for synfulman kynd,
> Howe he was traised with his disciple, and taken with Iues,
> Beten with skourges that no skyn held,
> Nailed and (*on*) the rode, and corouned with thornes,
> And many othir hard paynes, and died atte last;[81]
>
> *tholed*: suffered; *traised*: betrayed.

that after Christ was taken down from the cross dead (the deposition), he liberated those believers subject to death before he was born, a process known as the Harrowing of Hell; that though he suffered mortality, he rose from the dead through the strength of God, and made this possible for all men; that he ascended into heaven and was crowned higher than the angels; that he will come at the end of time to judge the world and this will be the end of the era of redemption:

> For als his rightwisenesse is now menged with mercy,
> So sal it than be withouten merci.[82]
>
> *menged*: combined.

These two sets of seven points about the Godhead and Christ delineate beliefs about the nature of life subject to a process of sickness and death but also filled with the potential for healing realised definitively in the life of Christ. Both series share a common conclusion in the belief in the inevitability of the Last Judgement for which the creativity of the Trinity works through the sacraments of the Church to ensure that man can rise with Christ to 'that blis that euermore lastes'.[83] But that process is only possible at all because of the Incarnation, Passion, Resurrection and Ascension of Christ who lives the love of God triumphant in and beyond the sins of time. Thus the rest of the catechism sets out the teaching in diagrammatic form of the way in which this pattern of love can be imitated in time. At the heart of the prohibitions and directives of the ten commandments is a definition of the ways in which man inhibits love both in himself and his society:

Of the whilk ten, the thre that er first
Augh us haly to hald onentes our god,
and the seuen that er aftir, onentes our euen cristen[84]

whilk: which; *er:* are; *augh*: ought; *haly*: wholly;
hald: keep; *onentes*: concerning; *euen cristen*: fellow christian.

inhibitions which are released in the gospel commandment of love that we

love god ouer al thinges,
. . . our euen-cristen als we do
oure selven
For god augh us to love halye with hert.[85]

halye: completely.

The seven sacraments, traditionally linked to the wounds of Christ[86] because it is his suffering love which gives them efficacy, are baptism, confirmation, penance, the eucharist, extreme unction, marriage and ordination. They provide the framework by which man enters into, and sustains to the end, his spiritual life in Christian belief both personally and socially. The sacraments of marriage and ordination refer particularly to two social roles in which Christ is known, though much medieval literature betrays a piquant questioning of the gap between sacramental ideal and social reality.

The works of mercy and the virtues together show that combination of active life and inner condition that can counteract the subversive activities of the seven sins: pride, envy, wrath, gluttony, covetousness, sloth and lechery. The works of mercy are practically: to feed the hungry, to give drink to the thirsty, to clothe the naked, to shelter the homeless, to visit the sick, to help those in prison and to bury the dead; and spiritually: to give counsel, to reprove wickedness, to comfort the sorrowful, to pray for sinners, to be patient in misjudgement and to forgive wrong-doing. The seven virtues put together the three theological virtues which arise from man's relationship to God as his creator, and are the condition of all Christian action – faith, hope and charity – with the four classical virtues which relate to man as a social being: justice towards others, prudence in distinguishing good from evil in the world, fortitude in all circumstances, 'whethir so betides'[87] and temperance to achieve a balanced life-style to 'lyff skillwisely [with discretion] als the lawe techis'.[88]

This dogmatic teaching about how the faith should affect

experience is fundamental to the insight of the mystics into the living reality of the being of God and thus to the substance of the game of faith which participates in this being. Indeed the end of the *Lay Folks' Catechism* says no more or less, essentially, than they do:

For if ye kunnandly knaw this ilk sex thinges
Thurgh thaim sal ye kun knawe god almighten,
Wham als saint Iohn saies in his godspel,
Conandly for to knawe swilk als he is,
It is endeles life *and* lastand blisse . . .[89]

kunnandly, conandly: expertly.

DEMONSTRATIONS OF PLAY: PRIMERS AND LYRICS

Just as the catechism sets out the substance of the faith for the lay people, so Primers, specifically designed prayer books to enable lay people to share in the liturgical offices of the Church, incorporated it into a series of devotions that daily and poignantly remind man of the cycle of salvation. These too enter deeply into the 'play' of the mystics' faith.

The organisation of the Latin office of the Church at the Canonical Hours evolved from a complex tradition of teaching which found justification for these hours of prayer in both Old and New Testaments of the Bible; and a general pattern emerged in which they were connected with the Passion narrative.[90] Thus Matins at daybreak remembers the betrayal of Christ in the garden of Gethsemane; Prime is connected with the trial before Pilate and false accusation; Tierce with the crowning with thorns and condemnation to death; Sext (midday) with the Crucifixion; None (3 p.m.) with Christ's death; Evensong with the deposition; and Compline with the entombment. In this way the worship of each day was tied fundamentally to a constant re-enactment of the memory of Christ's death. By the fourteenth century there had developed simplified service books called Primers which were translated into English by the second half of the period.[91] The order of service in the Primers had developed from monastic devotions, added to the main office from the eighth century onwards, to remember the dead (the office of the dead), and to celebrate understanding of the role of the Virgin Mary in the working of the faith – the Hours of the Virgin. These offices were used by secular clergy and were particularly appropriate for lay use since they remained constant throughout the liturgical year and were not subject to the complex variations of the main office.[92]

Throughout the day the Hours of the Virgin celebrate Mary as the instrument of the Incarnation and intercessor for man with God but they also incorporate into this a daily memorial of Christ's Passion in the appropriate verses of the hymn *Patris Sapientia* at each Canonical Hour. Thus at Lauds at the end of Matins the verses remember how:

The wisdom of þe fadir
þe treuþe of þe hiȝ king,
God and man was takun
In þe morenyng.[93]

But the daily reminder of the shocking betrayal of truth in time is counterpointed against prayers and psalms which emphasise that this very process is the means by which redemption is accomplished and the ultimate strength of love proved. At each Hour a verse from the hymn is followed by a prayer which acknowledges this and sees the Incarnation as the means by which all men, both living and dead, can be united:

Lord ihesu crist, goddis sone of heuene, sette þi passioun, þi cros & þi deeþ, bitwixe þi iugement & oure soulis, now & in our of oure deeþ; & vouche-saaf to ȝyue to lyuynge men merci & grace in þis liyf here; and to hem þat ben deed, forȝyuenesse & reste; to þe chirche & to þe rewme, pees & accord; & to us synful men, liyf & glorie wiþ-outen ende; þou þat lyuest and regnest god bi alle worldis of worldis. amen! þe glorious passioun of oure lord ihesu crist, brynge vs to þe ioie of paradis. Amen.

our: hour; *deed:* dead; *rewme*: realm.

The office thus daily rehearsed the historical story of the Passion of Christ and its significance in such a way that it is constantly renewed in human awareness through both the linear and cyclical experience of the passing of time. This ritual process enacts a pattern which can be translated into inner experience in the contemplative discipline. There, recognition of those elements in human nature which are death to the working of the creative love of God in man, provides the grounds for its quickening into new life and knowledge of God. This liturgical pattern was also repeated in the vernacular literature produced by the Franciscans and aimed at stimulating lay piety.

John Pecham, who gave such authoritative impetus to the Church's mission to teach the laity, was a Franciscan[94] and his Constitutions and their effect owed much to the dynamic nature of Franciscan spirituality with its stress on the freedoms of love and poverty and the importance of knowledge of the Scriptures. St Francis's own mystical experience centred on his understanding of, and identification with, Christ the crucified redeemer (he received the stigmata in a visionary experience at the end of his life),[95] and at the heart of the theology of his followers was a stress on penance as a sacrament through which man can bring his nature into conformity with Christ. The idea that a contritional experience is an ongoing activity in which every man fights and conquers those elements of his fallen nature as Christ fought evil on the Cross[96] and that this is part of the continuing process of redemption – indeed its very condition[97] – was at the heart of their preaching and teaching which developed the monastic piety of an earlier period for a lay audience. The zeal for the development of spiritual life, which had flowered in Europe from the tenth to the twelfth centuries, had resulted in the reform of the Benedictine monasticism of the West and the emergence of Orders – Cluniac, Cistercian and Carthusian – committed to living apart in various communal ways which stressed above all the individual inner spiritual growth of their members. A new emphasis on the fruit of learning being inward experience of the truth of Christ was given particularly cogent expression by such men as the Carthusian Guigo II and the Cistercian Bernard of Clairvaux. In the thirteenth and fourteenth centuries this reforming enthusiasm was channelled into the foundation of Orders more oriented towards service of the whole community – the mendicant Dominicans and Franciscans were travelling preachers and the Augustinian Canons (known as Austin Friars) were committed to lives of pastoral service. Through these channels the contemplative ideals developed in monastic communities found a wider audience. The Franciscans had a specially charismatic gift for transmitting their understanding of the inward nature of redemption. It shaped the aesthetic of the lyrics and meditations concerned with the life of Christ which they wrote to convey their understanding imaginatively. In the retelling and interpretation of the events of the Incarnation to stimulate an emotional response, and to deepen understanding of its implications, they translated the affective piety of earlier reformed monasticism into a religious sensibility which dominated English popular piety.[98]

The lyrics which are found in preaching manuals like the *Fasisculus Morum*[99] and *Speculum Christiani*[100] or are specifically written or collected by Franciscans like James Ryman, William Herebert and John Grimestone[101] both encapsulate essentials of the Franciscan teaching in a way calculated to catch the imagination and stir the emotions, and incorporate standard interpretations of the meaning of Scripture. A lyric like Grimestone's little fragment draws on a verse from Lamentations (1:12) which in the office for Easter was quoted as words of Christ as a reproach to sinful man.[102] It thus provides a vernacular equivalent for the uneducated; and, by poetically fusing the Scriptural texts with the way in which they were interpreted and with emotional understanding of such meaning, it enables a response to the significance of the Incarnation. Its words in their own way incarnate the Word in the tradition of Augustinian and Franciscan epistemology. Very simply it presents, through its visual image of the Crucifixion and its present-tense appeal to passers-by to think of the uniqueness of the love it manifests, a sense of the issues of the Passion as a continual process:

Ye that pasen be the weyye,
  Abidet a litel stounde
Beholdet, al mi felawes,
  Yef ani me lik is founde.
To the tre with nailes thre
  Wol fast I hange bounde;
With a spere al thoru mi side
  To min herte is made a wounde.[103]

pasen: pass; *stounde*: time; *wol fast:* very firmly.

The final two lines complete the physical image but metaphorically signify that reality at the heart of Christianity, that through the experience of suffering the strength of love is made known. Another lyric makes even more explicit this identification of life in time with the Crucifixion as the only means by which its true value may be realised:

Gold and al this werdis wyn
 Is nouht but Cristis rode;
I wolde ben clad in Cristis skyn,
 That ran so longe on blode,
And gon t'is herte and taken myn in –
 Ther is a fulsum fode.
Than yef I litel of kith or kyn,
 For ther is alle gode.[104]

wyn: pleasure; *t'is*: to his; *fulsum fode*: abundant nourishment; *yef*: give, care.

Such lyrics embody an understanding of the process of transfiguration at the heart of the Christian faith which is realised by the mystics in experience and gestured towards in their texts. Lyrics operate in that area between intellectual reception of dogmatic teaching and mystical intuition of the reality to which this teaching points. They signal this for those who are not contemplatives and reflect it for those who are. Like the liturgy, they provide a meeting point for the two and enter deeply into the means by which a visionary like Julian of Norwich conveys to others her apprehension of God alive and working in the being of man.

Consider for example the little lyric based on Augustine's *Confessions* VIII, 5.

Louerd, thou clepedest me,
An ich nagt ne ansuarede the
Bute wordes scloe and sclepie:
'Thole yet! Thole a litel!'
But 'yiet' and 'yiet' was endelis,
And 'thole a litel' a long wey is.[105]

Louerd: Lord; *clepedest*: called; *nagt ne ansuarede*: did not answer anything; *scloe*: slow; *sclepie*: sleepy; *thole*: wait/suffer; *yiet*: yet; *endelis*: endless.

This skilfully manipulates alliteration and rhyme in a humorously wry acknowledgement of the archetypally human facility for putting off that effort of intellectual and emotional energy involved in recognising and acting on the truth. It might well have been in the mind of the *Cloud*-author when he appealed to his disciple as a weary wretch, sleeping in sloth, and deaf to the calling of the disturbingly dynamic love of God.[106]

Lyrics like these enabled the possibility of grass-roots familiarity and emotional engagement with the Incarnation. They could operate as a focus or trigger for meditative understanding. This was also directly addressed in one of the most popular books of the Middle Ages, the thirteenth-century Franciscan *Meditationes Vitae Christi.*[107] The first complete English translation was by the Carthusian Nicholas Love and licensed for reading by the Archbishop of Canterbury, Thomas Arundel, in 1410,[108] but portions were translated earlier than this. For example, the fragment by Robert Mannyng dealing with the story of the Passion known as *Meditations of the Supper of Our Lord.*[109]

Although the aim of the Meditations was to stimulate an emotional response to the humanity of Christ in an act of affective piety, this was closely tied to a theological understanding that only through a loving penitential identification with His suffering could man also experience the transfiguring reality of the power of His Resurrection and life. At the beginning of his translation, Mannyng appeals to the reader:

Opone þyn herte and hyde þy face;
For þou shalt chaunge þy chere a none,
Or elles þyn herte ys harder þan stone.[110]

chere: feeling/expression; *a none*: forthwith.

His vivid description of the Crucifixion both stresses Christ's willingness – he climbs the ladder to mount the cross, then turns at the top, laying himself vulnerable and open as he stretches out his arms and back against it – and rams home the shock of pain as the nails are driven in. Mannyng invites an emotional identification with the event to give rise to a spiritual act:

Thenk now, man, how hyt ys down
Yn þe oure of syxte of none.
Beholde þe peynes of þy sauyour,
And crucyfye þyn herte with grete dolour.[111]

down: dark; *syxte*: sext.

In the full translation by Nicholas Love, the whole story of the Incarnation integrated with comment from Patristic sources (and especially from Bernard of Clairvaux) was schematised into sections for meditation through the week. Monday's stories included that of the Annunciation, recalling both Adam's fall and Christ's redemption in such a way that sin and redemption appear as simultaneous action constantly re-enacted:

And so this day ouȝte euere to be had in mynde of man and womman: for this day was man made to the liknes and the ymage of god/and sette in that ioyful place of paradise/and forto haue liued euere with outen deth. And this day the firste man/Adam/ by the fruyte of the tre forbeden deformed in hym that ymage of god/ and loste that ioyful place of paradyse/and was dampned to deth with outen endynge. But this day the secounde Adam/crist god and man/reformed this ymage in his Incarnacioun/and after/ by vertue of the blessed fruyt of his body hangynge on the tree of the crosse/restored man to blisse and lyf euerlastynge. Also this day the first womman/Eue/thoruȝ pride assentynge to the serpent/ the deuel of helle/ was cause of mannis dampnacioun. And this day the blessed mayden Marye/thoruȝ mekenesse trowyng to the aungel Gabriel/was cause of mannis saluacioun. And so this day hath man mater of grete ioye and of grete sorwe: firste of grete ioye for the souereyne godenesse/worshippe/and grace of gode done to hym: and also of grete sorwe for his grete synne and vnkyndnesse done to god aȝeynward. And thus myȝt thou haue thy contemplacioun of this day and of this blessid feste of cristes Incarnacioun/ and oure ladyes annunciacioun.[112]

Such meditation is closely connected with Julian's visionary experience of the lord and the servant[113] in which Adam and Christ become one figure, Adam falling and Christ instantly subjected to death as sin precipitates the Incarnation in the work of mercy and love. Friday is devoted to the Passion story organised in terms of the Canonical Hours with the detail of Christ's human suffering imaginatively elaborated in order to encourage the reader to identify with the moment. The pattern is completed by the account of the Ascension and Pentecost as proper to Sunday. The historical period of time between the two events is seen in terms of the internal experience of the individual Christian seeking assurance of God. Such a one is bidden to 'preye' 'seke' 'aske' and 'knokke at the dore' in the certainty that 'he schal come . . . and coumforte thy desolate soule' as the Holy Ghost came to the apostles:

and so preyeng in his blessynges of goostly swetnesse /. . . thou schalt haue so grete likynge in his mynde and in thoo goostly drynkes that he schal make the drunken ofte in soule / that thou schalt be ioyful and glad that euere thou forsoke the false coumfortes of the worlde.[114]

goostly: ghostly.

The book ends with a meditation on the sacrament as the focus for the experience of the transforming energy of God released in time at the Incarnation. The power of the sacrament is attested to not just by stories of miracles in which the devout see Christ himself present in the Host, but in terms of inward experience 'wherof we haue knowynge onely by beleue with ynneforthe'[115] [*ynneforthe*: inwardly] and the meditation ends with a prayer for the experience of the healing presence of Christ:

> O thou swettest manna / aungels mete! O thou most likynge goostly drink / brynge in to my inward mowth that hony swete taste of thyne heleful presence. Kyndele in me the feruour of thyn charite: . . . fro thi hye heuene nowe come downe to me / that I / knytte and ioynede to the / be made oon spirit with the.[116]

Such cultivation of an inner experience of the reality of Christ's being by means of affective meditation on his life is a discipline taken for granted in the writings of all the mystics to be discussed, despite their differences in emphasis. It can be taken for granted precisely because of the kind of literature with which lay people were already familiar and the liturgical practices which stimulated their desire for further instruction and participation in the practice of the faith.

CONTEXT OF PLAY: THE CULTURAL MOMENT

This lay demand for teaching about contemplative spirituality together with the particular emphases of individual mystics who met and also stimulated it in fourteenth-century England, both represents, and engages with, a complex web of theological and socio-historical developments. Modern scholarship is beginning to bring to attention traditions of piety, particularly that of women, in Europe from the twelfth century onwards, which are significant for the understanding of medieval English mysticism. The *zeitgeist* expressed itself in a lively concern for the Christian faith and its implications for a *modus vivendi*. Among all levels of society – university teachers, those living in religious communities, women with time on their hands from the new bourgeoisie – there was a deep engagement with religious truth.

The world of learning, fired by the tension between the intellectual arguments of scholasticism and the more experiential piety of the monastic orders given a powerful voice by such men as Bernard of Clairvaux and Hugo and Richard of St Victor, was preoccupied with the relationship between the operations of reason and faith and a growing tendency to see them as distinct rather than complementary experiences, a climate of thought favourable to mystical theology.[117]

Moreover, the thrust of missionary zeal to preach the faith and to live out its realities (the *vita apostolica* [apostolic way of life]) which gave rise to the preaching and mendicant orders was of enormous importance to the development of lay piety in Europe.[118] Both the Augustinians and Dominicans sought to combine the qualities of actives and contemplatives in their way of life and teaching; they stressed the need for penance and man's dependence on God's grace for that illumination of understanding through faith and love that they believed was knowledge of God. Bonaventura articulated the theology of the Franciscans, inspired by the imitation of Christ in the life of poverty and love of their founder. The Dominicans and Franciscans had houses in England and scholars at the universities there in the thirteenth century, the Augustinians in the fourteenth century.[119] In Europe their mission found a receptive audience in the groups of holy women, *mulieres sanctae*, who came together in various ways to pursue life-styles which they thought best furthered their ideal of a Scriptural *vita apostolica*. The devotional lives of women gained increasing official recognition in all sorts of ways from the eleventh to the fifteenth century. The percentage who were considered saints for their complete rejection of worldly influence and a piety which often combined active charity with mystical prayer, increased dramatically.[120] Such dedication manifested itself not only among professional religious like the Dominican nuns in the Rhineland known for their mystical experience,[121] or Franciscan tertiaries like Angela of Foligno, who was converted after her marriage and, once a widow, devoted her life to God,[122] but among lay women in the Low Countries and Germany known as Beguines. These chose to live a life of poverty and charity supported by their own manual labours and loosely affiliated to local religious houses, from whom they might receive spiritual guidance, and to whom they gave the proceeds of their work. During the thirteenth century they associated together in communities submitting to an organised communal life of prayer,[123] including the Canonical Hours, and active charity as well as their work, though they were still dependent on the guidance of priests and religious houses. Augustinians, Dominicans, Franciscans and Cistercians all contributed to the care of such communities which were finally organised into independent parishes. This partial regularisation of the Beguine life-style in enclosed groups with restricted movement and in association with orthodox religious communities, was the condition of their recognition by the Church, and important as a safeguard from the suspicion that their free and irregular communities and enthusiastic piety were breeding grounds for heresy. The women who joined such communities were sometimes married and their aim was to live out the ideals of an apostolic life within the restrictions of their local community. They dressed with distinctive plainness[124] and aspired to a simple integrity expressed in behavioural terms defined with the authority of Scripture. It is easy to see from the list of qualities appropriate to the good Beguine listed in one thirteenth-century manuscript how their piety engaged with contemplative spirituality. They are bidden to:

> look down; to have lofty thoughts; to pray often; to travel little; to speak in the heart; to walk in the spirit; to be watchful in sleep; to be rich in poverty, wise in foolishness and strong in weakness; to cry for joy; to have a burning love, pure thoughts and an ordered way of life.[125]

The lives of some of these *mulieres sanctae* were certainly known in England. One fourteenth-century manuscript contains information about four:[126] those of Catherine of Siena, the fourteenth-century Italian girl who became a Dominican tertiary and whose teaching based on mystical certainty of the reality of her union with Christ, with whom she experienced a spiritual visionary marriage, was given official Dominican patronage; and three thirteenth-century Belgian mystics: Christina called *Mirabilis* from St Truden; Elizabeth of Spalbeck, a Belgian recluse patronised by the Cistercians; and the prototypical Beguine, Mary of Oignies, championed by Jacques de Vitry, the Bishop of Acres and later a Cardinal Legate at the court of Gregory IX who protected her and wrote her biography. Mary's exceptional piety as a child, extending to the scorning of pretty clothes, caused her parents to wonder 'what-maner womman schalle oure doghter be?' In fact she became a woman devoted to prayer 'soo þat, while she wroȝt with hir handes and spanne, she hadde a sauter set byfore hir and swetly seyde salmes þere to oure lorde' [*spanne*: spun; *sauter*: psalter; *salmes*: psalms], and practised severe self-mortification. The severity of her discipline

– she lived three years on bread and water, sometimes went barefoot to church in winter and prostrated herself on the bare floor of the church during weather so cold that the wine froze in the chalice during Mass – is typical of these women.[127]

Elizabeth of Spalbeck imitated the Passion of Christ at the Canonical Hours: at Matins, beating herself as she remembered Christ being taken with swords and staves; at Prime, walking with arms twisted behind her back like a bound thief to commemorate Christ being led from Caiaphas to Pilate and then Herod; at Sext, None and Evensong, stretching herself in a cruciform posture. The narrator comments:

> In woundes and peynes she affermiþ þe feith of þe passyone, in ioye and myrþe after peyne gladnes of þe resurrexyone, in rauishynge þe ascencyone, in rodynes of hir reuelacyouns and spritual lyfe she figurith þe sendynge of þe holy goost, and of þe sacramente of þe auter and of confessyon, and þen of desyres of alle mennes saluacyone, and of sorowe of vnkydenes and dampnacyone of mankynde.[128]
>
> *rauishynge*: ecstasy; *rodynes*: the presence.

The accounts of the torments to which Christina subjected herself convey a feeling of a disturbed personality although she apparently miraculously survived them. She cast herself into heated ovens or boiling cauldrons, was immersed in the freezing waters of a mill-race in winter and hunted by a pack of dogs through thorny thickets. Like Margery Kempe later, she had prophetic gifts.[129] The devotion of these women centred on the eucharist. Catherine sometimes lived off it alone,[130] Christine had strange out-of-body experiences during Mass[131] while Jacques de Vitry tells how Mary of Oignies had visionary experiences at the elevation of the Host and found rest and relief for her spirit in the presence of the sacrament.[132]

Mary was married but with her husband's cooperation dedicated her life to God. The same was true of the enormously influential Bridget of Sweden who, despite an early marriage and eight children, lived an increasingly ascetic and religious life to which she devoted herself completely at her husband's death. She founded a still extant Bridgettine order for whom she provided a Rule. An English Bridgettine house was founded at Sion House in Twickenham in 1415.

The aims of St Bridget in founding her order concentrate the cultural significance of this increasingly high-profile female piety in the Middle Ages. Her concern that the sisters living a life of contemplative discipline should in one respect be totally unrestricted – in their access to, and possession of, books – and the fact that, evidently, the brothers of the order both encouraged and instructed them in the knowledge of theological traditions,[133] illuminates, and is symptomatic of, the problems faced by women who wished to live out their faith and give an articulate account of their experience. Such women suffered from a lack of formally structured education[134] and from inhibitions about taking the authoritative initiative involved in composing written texts. The social engineering which placed them in positions of powerlessness ensured that the only female voice readily heard was that of the shrill tones of the satirised scold – a literary stereotype. It is no accident that in secular lyrics of the period women, apparently the cause of so much self-regarding male rhetoric, (albeit rescued by humorous and witty posturing), are conspicuous by their silence – absent from the lover's self-dramatisation and the satirist's easy jibes. The inescapable subservience of the female is ratified even when she is not manoeuvred as an object of adoration or spite:

I am as lyght as any roe
To preyse wemen wher that I goo.

To onpreyse wemen, yt were a shame,
For a woman was thy dame;
Our Blessyd Lady beryth the name
Of all women wher that they goo.

A woman ys a worthy thyng:
They do the washe and do the wrynge;
'Lullay, lullay', she dothe the syng,
And yet she hath but care and woo.

A woman ys a worthy wyght;
She seruyth a man both daye and nyght;
Therto she puttyth all her myght,
And yet she hathe bot care and woo.[135]

roe: deer; *onpreyse*: slander; *wyght*: creature.

But the effect of this fifteenth-century carol in providing a reminder that the Incarnation was realised through a woman, is to put a warning shot across the bows of those who exploit the daughters of Eve.

That Mary herself could be cultivated as an ideal of womanhood, as Virgin and Mother, without the complications of sexual politics, suited the male temper of the age.[136] It is interesting that it is in the work of a woman, Julian of Norwich, that Mary's female willingness to be open to receive embodies that attitude which lies at the heart of contemplative experience.[137] Religious experience offered a release through which women could testify to an authoritative experience in which gender was transcended. It must surely be significant that in an age when the evidence for women as writers is so sparse,[138] two out of the five writers here discussed are women and that both present their spirituality nourished by physical debility, coloured by gender-specific terms, and very evidently rooted in the affective piety stimulated by the visual iconography of the Incarnation;[139] although both found these to be factors which precipitated their experience of transcendent being and for Julian, in particular, they triggered her sense of that which is ineffable. It is true that both Julian and Margery Kempe, like their European counterparts, had to negotiate the significance of their experience through the authority of the Church; and like Catherine of Siena and Bridget of Sweden, Margery, certainly, depended on the offices of a scribe to actually write her account. Nevertheless all found an authority in their relationship to God which enabled them to find a means of articulating it.

The cultural phenomena through which we glimpse female spirituality in the Middle Ages are undoubtedly important for feminist studies.[140] But as mystics these medieval women, though 'taking the route [they] would be likely to take',[141] join with their male counterparts to point to the same inner journey into the truth of the Incarnation – a wisdom which transcends human distinctions and where 'there is neither male nor female. For you are all one in Christ Jesus' (Galatians 3:28).

It is against such a background of fervent articulate piety in Europe, always presenting the Church with the challenge of potential heresy, and occasionally erupting into mass movements like the hysterically fervent white-robed flagellants[142] who lashed themselves in hysterical penitential preparation for the Second Coming, that the English situation in the fourteenth century has to be seen.

Although there is evidence for a great growth in lay piety in England there was no equivalent to the free association of *mulieres sanctae* on the Continent. It is clear, however, that there were manifestations of ways of life shaped by an understanding of the faith that leavened society with spiritual awareness. The evidence of wills and bishops' registers points to the prevalence of recluses in society from the twelfth century onwards:[143] men and women who led solitary contemplative lives of prayer, often in cells attached to churches and chapels but who were also available to counsel those who sought help. Some were in religious orders and acted as confessors, others were lay people. All were required to get official sanction for their enclosure and to provide evidence of the means by which they were to be physically provided for. It is clear from the evidence of wills from all social classes up to the sovereign himself that society valued the spiritual input of those whose dying to worldly values (at their enclosure the burial service was read over them) was not regarded with jokey discomfort as disturbingly eccentric, but valued as contributing a unique gift to a total social welfare.

Besides anchorites who were physically enclosed, there were also those who led eremitical lives of greater physical mobility, preaching and teaching, sometimes performing labouring tasks like road-mending or keeping care of bridges,[144] sometimes living more haphazardly off the charity of others. Such a figure was the perfect model for the everyman figure seeking the meaning of salvation for both individual and society that Langland depicted in the weary, wet-shod Will, so vibrantly aware of the gap between the final metaphysical realities of heaven and hell and the immediate beguiling preoccupations of the field full of folk, for whom hot pies seemed more sustaining than the bread of life.[145]

Other outlets for lay piety which may have channelled that desire for corporate activity embodied in the European Beguinages were the lay fraternities of contemplative communities and the city guilds[146] which provided both temporary contemplative retreats for those in active life, and active expressions of social concern which embodied the love of God.

All this would have fostered among lay people awareness of a spiritual dimension to life. The strong sense of community between living and dead expressed in the frequent injunction in wills to pray for the soul of the deceased and to endow a priest for this specific purpose[147] witnesses to a feeling for a purpose in existence beyond that of material well-being. This feeling was also released in the cult of the saints – both those long dead and those whose lives of special piety inspired a demand for their canonisation. Thus John, Prior of the Augustinian House at Bridlington, was known as a holy man and canonised in 1401. The saintly Vicar of Keyingham, Philip of Beverley, who did much for local clergy, was venerated as a saint. Miracles were reported at his tomb as they were at the burial place of Richard Scrope, Archbishop of York, who was beheaded in 1405 and whose popularity as a saintly defender of Church freedoms against the usurpation of secular authority rivalled that of Thomas of Canterbury. An office was written to celebrate his memory, as also for the engaging north-country hermit, Richard Rolle, although neither was ever officially canonised.[148]

Such emotionally fervent piety was also provided with a catalyst in the devotional use of images. At best, this focused that subtle blend of doctrine and awareness of its living reality defended by Walter Hilton and Reginald Pecock,[149] at worst it encouraged the superstitious substitute for the work of faith which was labelled idolatry by the Lollards, those enthusiasts for the study of Scripture who tended to confuse its letter with its spirit. They were themselves a witness to the success of the ecclesiastical promotion of lay education in the faith although, in their case, it stimulated a sectarianism which exploded in the first quarter of the fifteenth century as a threat to both the doctrinal and social establishment of authority. The potential for subversiveness in the realisation of the equality of all men in the sight of God, and the possibility of each man reading the word of God directly for himself, sadly, proved too explosive a threat to be ignored and the Lollards were subject to persecution. Nevertheless their Bible was widely circulated not only among the middle classes but among the nobility.[150]

There is evidence of a religious enthusiasm more acceptable to the establishment among the nobility, some of whom appear to have either anticipated or eagerly embraced the official establishment of new liturgical feasts in devotional offices in their private chapels. A rite for the Mass of the Holy Name, confirmed officially in 1489 is found in a fourteenth-century missal belonging to William Beauchamp, Lord Bergavenny.[151] And there is evidence for the prompt celebration of the Feasts of the Transfiguration and the Visitation, officially instituted in 1457 and 1475 respectively, in an unusual series of screen paintings in a small Devon church connected with the Chudleigh family.[152]

This upsurge in lay piety in the fourteenth and fifteenth centuries also fostered particular reading habits. Again, the evidence of wills indicates increased lay interest in the literature of the contemplative life. Henry Lord Scrope of Masham had texts of Richard Rolle and a copy of St Bridget's *Revelations* in his library.[153] The widow of Sir Brian Stapleton left a collection of books which included Rolle's psalter. An inventory of the books of a Bridlington widow, Elizabeth Sewerby, included the *Meditations of the Passion* ascribed to Bonaventura, Rolle's meditations on the Passion, the *Revelations* of St Bridget of Sweden and an English copy of the life of St Catherine of Siena.[154]

At a time when the middle class, having acquired literacy for reasons of commercial pragmatism during the twelfth and thirteenth centuries, started to develop a more imaginative personal taste in reading, they also showed signs of being involved with vernacular piety. In the fourteenth and fifteenth centuries, wills show that books such as primers, saints' lives (*Legenda Aurea*), Boethius' *Consolation of Philosophy* and psalters belonged to such people as tailors, grocers, vintners and mercers.[155]

This desire to accommodate the life of the spirit in everyday activities is finely illustrated by the Latin instructions in a fifteenth-century manuscript as to how a devout layman should regulate his daily life, from his rising with all swiftness and signing himself with the cross, to his final return to bed when he must go to sleep in the uncertainty, salutary from a penitential, if not somnific, point of view, as to whether he will survive until the morrow.[156] As well as his ordinary business, the person addressed is expected to say Matins of the office of the Virgin and intersperse the day with prayers. Light is cast on the customs of contemporary devotion by the instruction not 'climb up to the cross' to kiss Christ's feet in tears of penitence but to do it in his heart. This presumably refers to devotional access to the rood-loft (by newel stair or ladder).[157] He is also instructed to look at the books provided in the church for such as him when he hears Mass. His whole household is permeated by a religious rule. The children must have found the silence or edifying talk at table somewhat tedious, as also the prohibitions on all dancing, dicing and wrestling. The injunction to make a small cross on the table from five breadcrumbs as a sign of devotion links him with a custom known to have been practised in monastic life, linking the daily bread of physical survival with the bread of life broken at the Passion.

This sensibility for integrating aspects of contemplative with active life is also manifest in the *Livre de Seyntz Medecines* written by Henry Duke of Lancaster; in it he writes about his own sense of that mortal sin for which Christ the healer supplies remedies, having beaten death in that tournament where he 'turned our sorrow into joy and overcame death with death'.[158] It is clear, then, that there was among laymen and women an interest in leading what Walter Hilton calls a 'mixed life', combining prayer and meditation with active duties. To cater for this audience manuscript compilations of devotional works were produced as working anthologies with a practical purpose.[159] Certainly the early printers saw the commercial viability of producing texts for this market although the writings of the English mystics were not well represented. Wynkyn de Worde printed Hilton's *Scale* at the command of Lady Margaret Beaufort and carefully arranged selections from the *Book of Margery Kempe* known as *A shorte treatyse of contemplacyon.*[160] He also printed the Middle English adaptation of the dialogue of St Catherine of Siena made for the Bridgettine sisters at Syon Abbey and known as *The Orcherd of Syon*.

The cultural context of the mystics who wrote in English in the fourteenth and fifteenth centuries witnesses to an appetite for spiritual literature which they both formed and addressed. Their writings engage with a spectrum of the cultural and theological traditions of medieval Europe. More abstractly the particularities of circumstance which attended both Julian's and Margery's report of their experiences illuminate the position of women and the roles open to them within the heirarchy of spiritual authority in the late medieval period. Clearly the subtle substructure of theological argument in the negative tradition which underlies the experiential theology of the *Cloud*-author distinguishes him from Julian of Norwich whose vibrant sense of the reality of the being of God at work in human nature was born out of her visionary meditative experience focused on Christ's Passion. Her religious sensibility is much nearer to that of the affective Franciscan devotion just as his is to the Dominican tradition of speculative thought. The enthusiasm of both Margery Kempe and Richard Rolle for adopting a life-style which would itself openly express a response to God's love as revealed in the Incarnation and their desire to teach others of this, betrays a deeply felt response to Franciscan teaching; while Walter Hilton's beautifully structured account of the progress to essential human fulfilment as inward discovery of the reality of Christ incarnate dying to sin but rising in love, one in heart and mind with God, places Walter Hilton squarely in the tradition of the theology of the Augustinian friars.

Interesting though it is to be aware of the way in which these various theological traditions bear fruit in the mystics' accounts of their experience, it is important to remember that they cannot fully account for this experience. They provide the writers with a language by which they can recognise and communicate their sense of an ineffable being with the dynamic power to transform their lives, and the purpose of their writing is to release that dynamic in the lives of others. The knowledge they seek is experiential, and they lived in the expectation of a final reality which must inevitably be in itself a judgement on the existential awareness of it at a human level.

All depend in varying degrees on the analytical activities of conscious thought, but all would say with Thomas à Kempis:

> I had sooner feel compunction than know its definition. At the last judgement we shall not be asked how many books we have read but how we have lived.[161]

It is to this existential challenge that the writers here discussed addressed themselves, all in their own ways meeting it by demonstrating how to go on the game of faith!

NOTES

1. It is true that the *Cloud*-author does deliberately address himself to a restricted audience of those who are naturally drawn to a life of prayer, but this does not alter the fact that he believes his teaching to be essentially simple. Indeed he is wary of intellectualising. See below, pp. 168–9.

2. See further: Tart (1975); Merton (1969); Johnston (1974). Smart (1965); Katz (1983); Moore (1987); Collins (1991).

3. *Centuries of Meditation* (1958, Cent.i, 29 p.15).

4. *Auguries of Innocence*, ed. Keynes (1966, p.431).

5. For a popular introduction to such a view see Chatwin (1987).

6. *The Snow Leopard* (1980).

7. Matthiessen (1980, p. 274).

8. See below pp. 279–81, 292–8, 308–12.

9. See below pp. 30–7, 277–9, 288–9, 295–6.

10. *A Revelation of Love* (1976, c.21. p.23). Unless otherwise stated all quotations from Julian of Norwich are from this text.

11. E.g. Tugwell (1984, pp. 164–5).

12. See *Sermones de Tempore*, etc. (1901, *Sermones de Sanctis in Festo Omnium Sanctorum, Sermo II*, p.601, where, commenting on Revelation (Apocalypsis) 21:23: 'And the city had no need of the sun, neither of the moon, to shine in it: for the glory of God did lighten it, and the Lamb is the light therof', he says:

    Sicut enim videmus in ista machina mundiali, quod lumine ***solis*** *per diem et lumine lunae et* ***stellarum*** *per noctem illuminatur et ornatur; sic civitas illa lumine Agni decoratur et illustratur, quia Divinitas eius est ibi loco* ***solis,*** *humanitas eius loco* ***lunae,*** *Beati* ***loco stellarum***. (For just as we see in this earthly [city] that it is lit and adorned by the light of the sun by day and the light of the moon and stars by night; so that city is decorated and lit by the light of the Lamb, since his Divinity is there in place of the sun, his humanity in place of the moon and the Blessed in place of the stars.)

13. *Expositio Super Boethium 'De Hebdomadibus'*, ed. Mandonnet (1927, p.165f). Cf. translation of the Prologue in Gilby (1951, pp.1–2): 'Notice how aptly contemplating is compared with playing, and because of two characteristics. First play is delightful, and the contemplation of wisdom brings the greatest joy; . . . Divine wisdom compares its joy with play; *I was delighted every day, playing before him at all times* [Proverbs 8:30]'. For a discussion of this concept in the early fathers and medieval theology, see Hugo Rahner (1965). See also Neale (1969).

14. See further Macqueen (1970, c.4).

15. Ed. Gray (1992, no.9. p.7).

16. Tugwell (1984, p.165).

17. See below pp.30–7.

18. Pepler (1959, 78–9).

19. Cf. the traditions of Jewish mysticism; Scholem (1955) Lectures 1–4, esp. second lecture, pp.40f. But see also below pp.20–1 on the solution provided by the concept of the corporate body of Christ.

20. Council of Nicea 325.

21. *Confessions*, ed. Sheed (1944 X, 27, pp.188–9).

22. See Louth (1981) *passim.*

23. *Life of Moses*, trans. Ferguson (1979).

24. *Divine Names*, IV, 13. Migne, *PG* 3, 712A. (Cf. Galatians 2:20.)

25. See further Chenu (1969); Minnis (1983, 1984).

26. Ed. Schmidt (1978, Passus 1, 143–4). See also Davlin (1981).

27. See Dobson (1966, 1976).

28. Pope, *An Essay on Criticism*, ed. Butt (1963, p. 155, l.363).

29. See *Ancrene Wisse*, ed. Tolkien (1962) 'þe heorte is a ful wilde beast. and makeð moni liht lupe . . .' (p. 29.9–10). [The heart is a very wild animal and often leaps lightly out . . . (Salu, 1989, p.21)].

30. 'Eue þi moder leop efter hire ehnen. from þe ehe to þe eappel. from þe eappel iparais dun to þer eorðe. from þe eorðe to helle. þer ha lei i prisun fowr þusent ȝer and mare. heo and hire were ba. and demde al hire ofsprung to leapen al after hire to deað wið uten ende' (p. 32.5–10). [Your mother Eve leaped after her eyes had leapt; from the eye to the apple, from the apple in paradise down to the earth, and from earth to hell where she remained, in prison, four thousand years and more, together with her husband, and she condemned all her children to leap after her, to endless death. (Salu, 1989, p.23)] Cf. Kaske (1960).

31. 'Ah godd nalde nawt þat ha lupe i prude' (p. 73.25–6). [But God did not want it to leap into pride. (Salu, 1989, p.62)]

32. 'lo þe sweoke hu he walde makien hire aleast to leapen in to prude' (p. 121.24–5); 'Lo þe treitre hu he seið . . .' 'Buh þe let me leapen up nule ich þe nawt longe riden. . . . Sum . . . lefde him and beah him and he leop up and rad hire baðe dei and niht twenti ȝer fulle' (p. 137.4–6, 12–14). [Notice how the deceiver wanted to make her leap, finally into pride. (Salu, 1989, p.104). Hear how he says, traitor that he is: . . . Bow yourself down, let me leap up; I do not want to ride you long . . . Someone . . . once believed him, and bowed down for him and he mounted and rode her day and night for twenty whole years. (Salu, 1989, p.118)]

33. The author projects his understanding by means of the quotation from Canticles 2:8 *venit dilectus meus saliens in montibus. transiliens colles*; [My beloved cometh leaping upon the mountains, skipping over the hills] and his gloss: 'Mi leof kimeð leapinde ha seið o þe dunes. þat is. totret ham tofuleð ham. þoleð þat me totreode ham. tuki ham al to wundre. schaweð in ham his ahne troden. þat me trudde him in ham. ifinden hu he wes totreden as his trode schaweð' (p. 193–4. 6–11). [My love comes leaping, she says, upon the mountains, that is, he treads them underfoot, making them vile, allows them, to be trodden on,

to be outrageously chastised, and shows on them his footmarks. (Salu, 1989, p.168)] The mountains represent those who try to live contemplative lives in which they identify with Christ in his suffering and thus know his love.

34. Indeed it is in chapter six on Penance that the passage allegorising Canticles 2:8 occurs. See note 33.

35. See Bossy (1975, 1983).

36. For example see below pp.85f., 135.

37. Trans. Colledge and Walsh (1978); see further Tugwell (1984, pp.93–124).

38. Richard of St Victor was a twelfth-century prior of the abbey of St Victor founded in Paris to combine the intellectual vitality of university theology with the ideals of monastic life. For his classic exposition of the process of contemplative life based on Genesis 29 see *The Twelve Patriarchs*, trans. Zinn (1979); for a detailed discussion of the relationship between Richard of St Victor's text and the *Benjamin Minor*, a free translation and adaptation of *Twelve Patriarchs*, attributed to the *Cloud*-author; see also Ellis (1992).

39. See Butler (1967, pp.157–88).

40. *City of God*, 19, 19. trans. Bettenson (1972, p.880).

41. *Moralia in Job*, ed. Adriaen (1979, *Liber*, XIX, xxv, 45, pp.991–2). See further Evans (1988, pp.105f).

42. See Gregory the Great, *Homiliarum in Ezechielem Prophetam*, Homily 2, 8, PL, 76, 953. For further reading see Butler (1967, pp.171–223).

43. *The Cloud of Unknowing*, ed. Hodgson (1982), c.8. p.17.18–21. All quotations cited from the *Cloud*-author are from this edition.

44. *Ibid*, c.8. p.17.5–40. For medieval teaching on the good works of the active life see below p. 29.

45. *Ibid*, c.8. p.18.1–14.

46. Cf. *The Cloud of Unknowing*, chapters 16–22.

47. It was traditionally held that the office of Bishop united both active and contemplative lives: see Gregory the Great *Liber Regulae Pastoralis*, where he explores the tensions in the combinations of these two ways of being for Bishops. See especially II.V:'Here the Truth itself, manifested to us through susception of our humanity, continues in prayer on the mountain, but works miracles in the cities (Luke vi:12), thus laying down the way to be followed by good rulers [bishops]; that, though already in contemplation aspiring to highest things, they should mingle in sympathy with the necessities of the infirm, since charity then rises wonderfully to high things when it is compassionately drawn to the low things of neighbours; and the more kindly it descends to the weak

things of this world, the more vigorously it recurs to the things on high' (*The Book of Pastoral Rule, and Selected Epistles of Gregory the Great*, eds Schaff and Wace (1964, p.13). Richard Rolle comments in his autobiographical account of his interior life *Incendium Amoris*, trans. Wolters (1972) *The Fire of Love*, c.21, that no one except Christ can fully integrate action and contemplation – that is perform actions while being fully absorbed in contemplative knowledge of God.

48. See below pp.119–28.

49. Cf. Augustine, *City of God* (19.19): 'we see then that it is love of truth that looks for sanctified leisure, while it is the compulsion of love that undertakes righteous engagement in affairs'; Bettenson (1972, p.880).

50. Cf. *The Orcherd of Syon*, eds Hodgson and Liegey (1966): 'a clerk & a religyous man neden seculeris, & seculeris religious. For þat oon wiþout þat oþir can noþing do; & þus of alle oþire'. (6. c.4. p.362).

51. Cf. the prayer during which the Host is broken, *Sarum Missal in English* (1868, p.314): 'Deliver us, O Lord, we beseech Thee, from all evils past, present, and to come; and at the intercession of the blessed and glorious ever-Virgin Mary, Mother of God, and of Thy blessed Apostles Peter & Paul, and Andrew, with all Saints, (Here let the Deacon give the paten to the Priest, kissing his hand; and let the Priest kiss the paten: then let him place it first before his left, then his right eye; after which let him make the sign of the cross over his head, and then let him replace it, saying,) graciously give peace in our time, that aided by the help of Thy loving kindness, we may both be ever set free from sin and secure from all disquietude. (Here let him uncover the Chalice and take the Body, with an inclination, placing It over the bowl of the chalice, holding It between the thumb and forefingers, and let him break It into three parts, the first fraction while he says) Through the same Thy Son Jesus Christ our Lord, (The second fraction) Who with Thee liveth and reigneth in the unity of the Holy Ghost, God, (Here let hin hold the two broken pieces in his left hand, and the third over the top of the chalice in his right hand, saying aloud) world without end.' See further Bossy (1983; 1985, c.4).

52. See Bossy (1985, pp.70–1) and see further (1983).

53. See below pp.24, 276f.

54. See above p.9.

55. See James (1983).

56. The prayers were translated into Middle English in the late thirteenth century from a twelfth-century French original. See *The Lay Folks Mass Book*, ed. Simmons (1879, p.35.169).

57. *Ibid*, p.45.240.

58. *Ibid*, p.51.283–92.

59. *Ibid*, p.53.299.

60. *Ibid*, p.60.59–64.

61. *Ibid*, pp.62–80.

62. *Ibid*, p.78.30–2.

63. See 'A Treatise of the Manner and Mede of the Mass' *Lay Folks Mass Book*, (1879, pp.128–47, especially 131–5 and notes, pp.366–74).

64. In the Sarum use the prayer is: 'Wherefore also, O Lord, we Thy servants together with Thy holy people, calling to mind the most blessed Passion of the same Christ Thy Son our Lord God, together with His Resurrection from the dead, and His glorious Ascension into Heaven, offer to Thy excellent Majesty of Thy gifts and bounties . . . a pure, holy, a spotless Sacrifice, the holy Bread of eternal life, and the Cup of everlasting Salvation'; *Missal* (1868, p.311). The York use is still more explicit: 'Wherefore also we thy servants, O Lord . . . do offer unto thy excellent majesty, of thine own gifts, albeit given unto us, a pure, a holy, an undefiled sacrifice, the holy bread of eternal life, and the cup of everlasting salvation' *Lay Folks Mass Book* (1879, p.109).

65. See below p.39.

66. (p.21.18–23). Trans. Salu (1990, p.14).

67. See *The Book of Margery Kempe*, eds Meech and Allen (1940, p.140.11–15).

68. See Bossy (1975).

69. See Morris (1972).

70. For example see: the carvings on the capitals of the Chapter House at Southwell Minster and the nave capitals in Exeter Cathedral; misericord carvings in Gloucester and Hereford cathedrals; examples of manuscript illumination in Bodley MS Douce 366 (the Ormesby Psalter), British Library MSS Royal 2 B.vii (the Queen Mary Psalter) and Additional 42130 (the Luttrell Psalter).

71. See Bossy (1975).

72. See Shaw (1985).

73. It is preserved in B.L.MS Royal 18 B xxiii; ed. Ross (1940).

74. See below pp.176–80.

75. Ross (1940, c.38. p.216.32–3).

76. (p.217.26–8).

77. See further below p.278.

78. Eds Simmons and Nolloth (1901).

79. *Ibid*, p.24.87.

80. *Ibid*, p.24.97–8.

81. *Ibid*, p.28.132–6.

82. *Ibid*, p.30.166–7.

83. *Ibid*, p.26.116.

84. *Ibid*, p.30.170–3.

85. *Ibid*, p.60.260–2.

86. See Rushforth (1929, pp.99–100).

87. The *Lay Folks' Catechism* (1901, p.86.433).

88. *Ibid*, p.86.446.

89. *Ibid*, p.98.571–5.

90. See Mary Philomena (1964).

91. See *The Prymer or Lay Folks' Prayer Book*, ed. Littlehales, 2 vols (1895–7).

92. See Edmund Bishop, 'On the Origin of the Prymer', in Littlehales (1895–7, 2, xi–xxxviii).

93. *The Prymer* (1895, p.15). For a fuller analysis see Glasscoe (1990).

94. See above p.26.

95. See *The Life of St Francis* (1950, c.13. pp.383–9).

96. For the teaching on the efficacy of contrition in the sacrament of penance by the thirteenth-century Franciscan teacher Alexander of Hales, see *Glossa in Quattuor Libros*, 15 (1957, *Liber*, IV: *Distinctio* IV, 17.pp.86–7; *Distinctio* XVI, 1.pp.252–4; *Distinctio* XXII, 2.pp.382–84 – see especially p.384: *In contritione enim annihilat se homo; in remissione peccati Deus annihilat culpam* (For in contrition man annihilates himself; in the forgiveness of sin God annihilates blame . . .). Also *Quaestiones Disputatae*, XX, (1960, *Quaestio XLVIII, De Sacramentis in Genere, Membrum 2, 17.pp.850–1: Christus enim, pugnans pro nobis fortiter contra diabolum, in ara crucis consecratus sacerdotus pro nobis satisfaciens, sponsus Ecclesiae*

resurrexit oleo gratiae plenae delibutus. In quantum homo suscipit Baptismum conformatur ad similitudinem Christi passi, quia ex virtute passionis Christi deletur originale quoad culpam et poenam, 6 ad Rom., 4: **Consepulti sumus** *etc. Per Confirmationem reformatur ad similitudinem Christi pugnantis contra inimicos; per Eucharistiam vero ad similitudinem Christi qui est sacrificium; per ordinem sacerdoti.* ('For Christ fighting for us stoutly against the devil, consecrated as a priest on the altar of the cross, making amends on our behalf, rose again as the spouse of the Church annointed with the full oil of grace. Inasmuch as a man receives Baptism, he is assimilated to the likeness of the suffering Christ since by virtue of the passion of Christ the original [sin] is done away with as far as blame and punishment is concerned. Romans 6:4 we are buried, etc. Through Confirmation he is reformed to the likeness of Christ who is the sacrifice through the order or priesthood'.) See also Jeffrey (1975, c.2).

97. See, for example, Bonaventure (*Sermones de Tempore, etc.,* 1901, *Domenica Quarta in Quadragesima, Sermo I,* p.232: preaching on 'And a great multitude followed him, because they saw his miracles which he did on them that were diseased' (John 6:2) he comments: *Ecce, quod Christus, Rex regum, statuit decretum quod nullus possit eum videre, nisi secum crucifixus. Et hoc decretum est tantae generalitatis, ut nullus excipiatur; tantae autem necessitatis, ut cum nullo dispensetur;* ('Behold Christ the King of kings declared that no one could see him unless he was crucified with him. And this declaration is of such general import that there is no dispensation for anyone;') and continues, referring to the words of Christ: *sed* ***qui perdit animam suam propter me inveniet eam****, id est, qui* ***carnem suam crucifigit cum vitiis et concupiscentiis,*** *assumendo vexillum victoriae, expectet suae coronationis praemium*' (but whoever loses his own life because of me will find it, that is, whoever crucifies his own flesh with vices and lusts, taking up the standard of victory, let him look out for the reward of his own coronation).

98. See further Bynum (1982); Cousins (1983); Dickinson (1950); Jeffrey (1975) Knowles (1948 and 1961); Leclercq (1961); Louth (1976); Southern (1970).

99. See Little (1917, p.139f.).

100. Ed. Hohnstedt (1937).

101. See Zipitza (1892); Carleton Brown (1970, nos 12–25, pp.55–76). For a general discussion of Franciscan influence on English lyrics see Jeffrey (1975, esp.c.6).

102. See *Brevarium Ad Usum Insignis Ecclesiae Sarum*, eds Procter and Wordsworth (1882, Vol.1, dcclxxxvii).

103. Ed. Gray (1992, 26.p.25).

104. Ed. Gray (1992, 50.p.51).

105. Ed. Gray (1992, 79b.pp.81–2).

106. *The Cloud of Unknowing*, (c.2. p.8.21–2).

107. See further Salter (1974, pp.41–6). Wallace (1984, p.177f.)

108. See Nicholas Love, *The Mirrour of the Blessed Lyf of Jesu Christ*, ed. Powell (1908).

109. Ed. J. Meadows Cowper (1875).

110. *Ibid* p.1.10–12.

111. *Ibid* p.19.605–8.

112. Love 1908, p.33.

113. See below pp.246–55.

114. Love 1908, p.299.

115. *Ibid* p.306.

116. *Ibid* pp.323–4.

117. See further Bynum (1982, c.1–3); Louth (1976); Leff (1958).

118. See above pp.32–3.

119. See further Jeffrey (1975, c.5).

120. See Weinstein and Bell (1982).

121. See Bynum (1982, c.5).

122. See *The Book of Divine Consolation of the Blessed Angela of Foligno*, trans. Steegman (1909, pp.5–6 and *passim*).

123. See McDonnell (1969, especially Part 1, chapter V and Part 2 chapters I and VII); Devlin (1984).

124. See McDonnell (1969, pp.128–9).

125. MS Bibliothèque Nationale Latin 15972. For the scriptural basis of these injunctions see: Proverbs 6:16; Lamentations 3:4; 1 Thessalonians 5:17; Lamentations 3:28; 1 Kings i:13 (Vulgate, in Authorised Version 1 Samuel); Galations 5:25; Canticles (Song of Solomon) 5:2; 2 Corinthians 6:10; 1 Corinthians 3:18; 2 Corinthians 12:10; Tobias 11:11 (Vulgate, now Apocrypha, Tobit and cf.11:14); Luke 12:49; Philippians 4:8; 1 Corinthians 14:40. See Hilka (1927, pp.156–8); Cf. McDonnell (1969, p.417).

126. Douce MS 114, ed. Horstman (*Prosalegenden,* 1885).

127. See Horstman (1885, p.135.37–8; p.141.41–2; pp.139–40.34–12; p.140.37; p.142.23; p.146.30.

128. *Ibid* p.118.32–8.

129. *Ibid* pp.122.14–38; 123.4–16; 127.10f.

130. *Ibid* p.191.14–15.

131. *Ibid* p.120.15f.

132. *Ibid Lib.* I, c.x, p.146.22–5; *Lib.*II, c.iv, p.165.1–5; c. viii, p.174.25–8, p.175.5–17. For further reading see McDonnell (1969, pp.305f.); Bolton (1978); Bynum (1982, pp.170–262).

133. See *Rewyll of Seynt Sauioure* (1978, 2, p.50); Ellis (1984, pp.115–23); Erler (1985); Hutchison (1986, pp.215–23 and references cited); Denley (1990, esp. p.221).

134. See Orme (1973, pp.52–5); Barratt (1992, pp.2–4).

135. *Early English Carols,* ed. Greene (1977, 396, p.234).

136. See Warner (1990, esp. Parts One and Four).

137. See below p.221.

138. See Barratt (1992, p.1).

139. See below, chapters 5 & 6 esp. pp.215, 254, 276–9, 288–9, 295–6.

140. See further Delany (1975, 1983, 1990); Baker (1978); Bynum (1982, 1987); Nicholas and Shuck (1984); Berman, Connell and Rothschild (1985); Aers (1988); Bennett and Clark etc. (1989); Barrett (1992).

141. T.S. Eliot, *Four Quartets*: 'Little Gidding'.

142. See further McDonnell (1969, pp.7 and 370–2); also Windeatt (*The Book of Margery Kempe*, 1985, pp.318–9, chapter 46, note 6).

143. See Warren (1985).

144. See Clay (1914, c.V).

145. *Piers Plowman*, ed.Schmidt (1978, Passus 1).

146. See Hughes (1988, p.12f.); Barron (1984, 13–37); Westlake (1919).

147. See further Hughes (1988, c.1, pp.35–57)

148. See further Hughes (1988, c.6, pp.298–346 and refs cited).

149. See the treatise 'conclusiones de ymaginibus' ascribed to Hilton in B.L. MS Royal 11 Bx, fol.178, Russell-Smith (1954) and Clark (1985); Pecock *The Repressor of Over Much Blaming of the Clergy*, ed. Babington, (1960), and Aston (1984, c.5).

150. See further Aston (1984, esp. c.5); Hudson (1985); (1988, esp. c.4 and c.5). It is interesting that the proverb used by John Ball in his sermon on Blackheath during the 1381 rebellion 'whan Adam dalf, and Eve spane, /Wo was thanne a gentilman' [*dalf*: dug, *spane*: spun; *wo*: who.] (see Walsingham, *Historia Anglicana*, ed. Riley [1864, ii, p.32] was adapted from current use and is also found in a late fourteenth-century devotional lyric attributed to Richard Rolle ((almost certainly mistakenly), see Horstman (1895, i, p.73)).

151. See Catto (1981, p.49); Pfaff (1970, pp.65–6).

152. See Glasscoe (1987); Pfaff (1970, pp.29 and 47).

153. See Allen (1966, p.29); Dillon and Hope (1897); Kingsford (1920, pp.90–8).

154. See Hughes (1988, p.293 and refs cited).

155. See Parkes (1973).

156. *Instructions for a Devout and Literate Layman*, ed. Pantin (1976, see esp.398–400).

157. *Ibid* (p.399). The rood, a large crucifix usually flanked by the figures of the Virgin and St John the Divine, was erected in medieval churches on the top of a large screen dividing nave and chancel. Access to the top of the screen (loft) was arranged for devotional purposes. See also below pp.70–1, 98.

158. Ed. Arnould (1940).

159. See further Gillespie (1989).

160. See further Holbrook (1987); Keiser (1987).

161. *The Imitation of Christ*, Book 1, chapter 3.

Chapter 2

Richard Rolle: The Form of Living

It is no accident that we know more about the lives of Richard Rolle and Margery Kempe than about the other three writers with whom this book is concerned. Biographical details are not relevant to what the *Cloud*-author and Walter Hilton have to say, and about Julian we know only those circumstances which immediately impinge on her visionary experience. The thrust of their work points away from the particularities of individuality to engage in different ways with the significance of the Incarnation which for them provides the ultimate pattern of meaning for all men. It may also be important that the two most impersonal writers of these three, Walter Hilton and the *Cloud*-author, were both almost certainly professional religious and thus already established in a tradition of self-effacement. The details of Julian's life are not known, but it is highly unlikely that she was professed at the time of her visionary experience – if at all. It is interesting that although she does begin her account with biographical experience, her concern is with its theological import for all.[1] Richard Rolle and Margery Kempe found their own routes, not without difficulty, to mystical understanding. Neither of them was in religious orders and, whether or not either of them aspired to sainthood,[2] both clearly felt that sharing their 'confessions' was an important social act.[3] For Margery they are the substance of her book – for Rolle they enter into some of his writing and illuminate his teaching. With both Rolle and Margery Kempe more is known precisely because both were articulate about adopting a life-style which answered to their spiritual needs. Margery followed her own adaptation of the tradition of the *mulieres sanctae* and Rolle was a hermit; each exhibited extraordinary qualities within his or her role.

Such was Rolle's charisma during his life that his grave at Hampole Priory in South Yorkshire just west of Doncaster,[4] became a centre of pilgrimage where miracles were recorded. The deaf, dumb, insane and dead were all said to be restored at his tomb. Sometimes it appears that the mere act of measuring them in order to manufacture a candle of corresponding dimensions to burn at the tomb was sufficient to effect the cure. For instance, it is recorded that one woman, Joan of Sprotborough, fell into a millpool and in spite of not being rescued for an hour was then revived by prayer and by being 'measured for a candle'.[5]

Towards the end of the fourteenth century an Office for St Richard Hermit was written for the Priory in the hope of his canonisation. It recorded the main events of his life, and modern scholarship has in the main verified it from independent documentary sources as well as from Rolle's own writings.[6] The picture that emerges is of a man both maddening and engaging in his inner spiritual drive, and in his search for a way of living appropriate to its demands. He had the freedom of spirit to cut through convention and authority if he felt it to be an impediment to his calling. Such courageous integrity can look like arrogance since it apparently rejected the means to an understanding of the faith acquired by the tested traditions of academic and spiritual disciplines or social *mores.* Yet his writings witness to an inner toughness and honesty which complement his sensitivity and spiritual receptiveness, and balance his obvious volatility. They compel respect for his 'venture' life-style risked to win the realities of his faith and also, on occasions, make vividly accessible the mental furniture of his faith. He is more poet than academic, or professional religious, and it is precisely because of his wilful integrity and gift for language that he is able to share a sense of the actual process – frequently frustrating – of the practice of spiritual discipline which for all the mystics is the weapon in the battle against the forces of darkness that self-evidently threaten to destroy human fulfilment. The discipline is the only means by which these forces are consumed and thus destroyed.

In a consumer society, where wealth is synonymous with money and thus both the currency and final *desideratum* in a process of endless consumption, people are in danger of knowing the 'price of everything and the value of nothing'.[7] The mystics, however, joyfully recognise a congruity between price and value. The discipline which all of them write about with varying levels of emphasis and directness is the only means in every sphere of human activity by which the *desideratum* of love is liberated and all pain finally destroyed. In his Latin work *Incendium Amoris (The Fire of Love)* Rolle talks of it as kindling for the 'fire which consumes everything which is dark' (Prologue.4),[8] an element which he recognises as the final reality. There is, however, a touching gap between the grandeur of the issues he recognises and the comical or exasperating hit and miss practical manner in which he engaged with them.

The *Office* tells us that he was born at Thornton Dale near Pickering in North Yorkshire. Such external evidence as there is points to his being the son of a fairly poor rural family who were tenants on the estate of the manor of Thornton Dale which, in 1335, was described as having:

> a chief messuage worth in garden produce and herbage 13s 4d, arable lands and meadows, a watermill, a fulling mill, a common oven.[9]
>
> *messuage*: estate.

They managed to send Richard to school and at some time he attracted the notice of the lawyer-priest Thomas de Nevill, later Archdeacon of Durham, who gave him a grant to study at Oxford when he was about thirteen or fourteen years old. The first three years of his Oxford course of studies would have included grammar, logic and rhetoric (the *trivium*), after which the student had to attend formal sessions of dispute and argument before becoming a Bachelor of Arts and going on to the second part of the course, music, astronomy, geometry and arithmetic. There is no evidence that Rolle received his Bachelor's degree, and his frequent scathing remarks on the uselessness of scholarly argument as a means to the knowledge of God indicate that the intellectual training offered at Oxford would have been uncongenial to him. In *The Fire of Love* he writes:

> Nowadays too many are consumed with a desire for knowledge rather than for love, so that they scarcely know what love is or what is its delight. Yet all their study should have been directed to this end, so that they might be consumed with the love of God as well. Shame on them! An old woman can be more expert in the love of God – and less worldly too – than your theologian with his useless studying. He does it for vanity, to get a reputation, to obtain stipends and official positions. Such a fellow ought to be entitled not 'Doctor' but 'Fool'.
>
> (5. 61)

Certainly he did not stay the full course which was seven years for the qualification of a Master's degree, the necessary precondition for further study of law, theology and medicine. He left when he was eighteen, presumably with the cry so often heard from those who look for instant wisdom in courses designed primarily to foster skills by which such discrimination may be attained: 'the course cannot give me what I am looking for'. The *Office* remarks that 'he desired rather to be imbued more fully and deeply with the theological doctrines of Holy Scripture than with the study of physical and secular science' which looks as if he left after the *trivium*. It continues:

> in his nineteenth year . . . considering the uncertain term of human life, and the fearful end especially before the fleshly and the worldly, he took thought, by the inspiration of God, providently concerning himself (remembering his end), lest he should be taken in the snares of sin.[10]

The *Office*, of course, was in the business of sanctification, but this account of Rolle's early passionate concern for a life-style which reflected his urgent sense of priorities is heard again later in his *Fire of Love*:

> As adolescence dawned in my unhappy youth, present too was the grace of my Maker. It was he who curbed my youthful lust and transformed it into a longing for spiritual embrace. He lifted and transferred my soul from the depths up to the heights, so that I ardently longed for the pleasures of heaven more than I had ever delighted in physical embrace or worldly corruption. . . . Yet I was still living amongst those who flourished in the world, and it was their food I used to eat. And I used to listen to that kind of flattery which all too often can drag the most doughty warriors from their heights down to hell itself. But when I rejected everything of this sort to set myself to one purpose, my soul was absorbed with love for my Maker. I longed for the sweet delights of eternity, and I gave my soul over to love Christ with every ounce of my power. . . . From then on I continually sought quiet, and that although I went from one place to another.
>
> (15.91–2)

By the age of nineteen he was back at home, which was probably, by this time, in Yafforth about twenty-five miles from Thornton Dale,[11] the way of development through the competitive channels of establishment institutions behind him, and his face turned towards the alternative life-style of the recluse which he embarked on with a comically home-spun rite of passage.

Since it is clear that the vocation of hermit was officially recognised in the fourteenth century,[12] the account of Richard's pursuit of his calling points to parental opposition and possibly a reluctance on Richard's part to commit himself to any officially supervised licensing. Certainly the *Office* states that he became a hermit 'without his father's knowledge and against his will . . . because he loved God more than his father in the flesh'.[13] It looks as if he decided on a do-it-yourself habit modelled on those of Augustinian hermits who wore a basic white garment and scapulary which for outside wear were covered with a black cowl and hood tied round with a black leather thong.[14] The *Office* tells us that he arranged for his sister to meet him in a nearby wood and to bring with her two of her over-dresses, one white and one grey, and his father's rainhood. As soon as he got his hands on them he cut the sleeves off the grey dress and adapted those of the white one, then stripped off, and donned first the white dress and then the grey one as a sort of sleeveless cowl of a suitably penitential colour and finally the hood and 'thus, as far as was then possible to him, he contrived a confused likeness to a hermit'.[15] As the implications of the purposes of this scarecrow figure dawned on her, his sister screamed out that he was crazy, and perhaps even threw herself at him to prevent his plan. The legend says that he 'drove her away from him menacingly'[16] and took to his heels in flight from any possible prevention of his purposes by friends and family.

The next episode reported in the *Office* has the same eccentric opportunist quality. Whether by design or accident, Richard went to 'a certain church . . . where the wife of a certain worthy esquire . . . named John de Dalton, was accustomed to pray'.[17] John Dalton was the younger son of a Lancashire family who feathered his nest by dubious means while carrying out the office of agent for the Earl of Lancaster as constable of Pickering Castle, a position he lost in 1322 as a result of the unsuccessful rebellion of the earl who was subsequently executed. Dalton was, however, granted his own estates again which included land at Pickering and further east near Snainton, first at Foulbridge and then at Kirkby Misperton. There is no certainty as to which church and manor house the account in the *Office* refers to, but it is highly probable that they were at Pickering. If this is correct Rolle was putting some distance between himself and his father but returning to territory known in childhood.[18] In the church Richard fell to prayer with such absorption that Lady Dalton forbore to disturb him when she entered, but her son recognised him as a former Oxford student. The interest he attracted was greatly increased when, with the consent of the priest-in-charge, Richard preached at Mass with such charism that the congregation were moved to tears. He was subsequently invited home to dinner by the Daltons. His behaviour at the visit seems to suggest that he was a disturbing presence, since he did not turn up in the Great Hall as expected, but disappeared into a derelict and disused part of the house from whence he had to be fetched. At dinner he was utterly silent and tried to leave as soon as he had eaten sufficient but before the table was cleared. John Dalton eventually elicited the truth of his identity from him and offered him sanctuary as a hermit in his own home (perhaps Richard had been reconnoitring in his disappearance before dinner) and at his own expense.[19] John Dalton's action seems to have been very near in time to the crisis in his own life when he was temporarily imprisoned for his support of the Earl of Lancaster. The acceptance of Dalton as his patron by the uncompromisingly idealistic Richard seems odd, though he may not have realised the character of the man at this stage. Certainly both the account in the *Office* of his later career and the remarks he let drop in his own writings point to a friction in his situation which ultimately led him to leave the Daltons to seek a quiet place elsewhere. In *The Fire of Love* he lashes out at those who have spent 'their youthful energy in getting hold of others' property by hook or by crook' for their own worldly security and who use their authority aggressively (30.139–40). His own situation as a tame hermit to be shown off to guests by the lady of the house can hardly have suited him. The account in the *Office* of one such episode makes pious capital from the situation:

> and a remarkable incident is recounted. We are told that the hermit was once sitting alone in his cell after dinner when there came to him the lady of the house . . . and many persons with her, and found him writing rapidly. They begged him to desist, in order to give them some words of edification, and for two consecutive hours he proceeded to give them excellent exhortations, while at the same time never ceasing his writing – and all the while what he was writing was not the same as what he was speaking.[20]

One wonders whether Richard's failure to look up from his work (perhaps copying a manuscript) betokened exasperation at the interruption.

He may have left the Daltons at the time of their troubles. The reconstruction of the possible sequence of events in his life which can be inferred from the *Office* and personal remarks in his writings, is at best a complicated matter of academic conjecture which is of no direct help to the reader in engaging with his English works. The *Office* hints defensively at a period of nomadic existence which was censured by critics as unstable. Certainly there are references in his works to his 'wandering like Cain' and also to disagreements with monks whom he criticises for their worldliness and describes as jealous of his own popularity and envious of his mystical experience.[21] It has even been mistakenly argued that at some point during the 1320s he fled to Paris and studied for a while at the Sorbonne.[22] What is certain is that Rolle's own inner drive was to be a solitary contemplative and to use his experience in the service of others.[23] The *Office* tells us that he eventually settled in the area known as the county of Richmond.[24]

It also gives the information that Rolle was 'accustomed to show himself very familiar to recluses, and to those who needed spiritual consolation'[25] and it must have been during this period of his life that he met his disciple Margaret de Kirkeby. She was a nun at Hampole Priory before adopting the life of a recluse at East Layton near Richmond in 1348 when Rolle wrote for her a treatise known as *The Form of Living* which was designed as both programme for, and illumination of, the solitary life-style that she had adopted. Indeed it may even be argued that many more of Rolle's English texts were written specifically for her.[26] There was clearly a close friendship between them, and the *Office* gives a moving account of his efficacy in curing her of some kind of fit:

> He came and found her mute, but when he had seated himself at her window and they had eaten together, it chanced that at the end of the dinner the recluse wished to sleep, and oppressed by slumber her head drooped towards the window where God's saint, Richard, was reclining, and as she was leaning a litle on that same Richard, suddenly, with a vehement onslaught, such a grave vexation took her in her sleep that she seemed to wish to break the window of her house, and in that strong vexation she awoke, her speech was restored, and with great

devotion she broke out into the words 'Gloria tibi Domine', and the blessed Richard completed the verse which she had begun.[27]

There are difficulties about the dating of this episode. The *Office* continues with a description of a relapse of Margaret's illness from which she was cured when Rolle promised her that she should never again suffer from it as long as he was alive. After several years, therefore, when the illness recurred, Margaret sent after Richard only to learn that he had died at the hour she was afflicted. Although the *Office* describes her as a recluse at the time of her cure, there is a discrepancy here between the date at which she was enclosed (1348) and the fact that several years elapsed between the cure and the relapse of her illness when Rolle died, since many manuscripts attest to Rolle's death in 1348.[28] Perhaps her cure took place while she was still at Hampole and the *Office* refers to her as a recluse because that is what she later became, or perhaps she had become an anchoress while still at Hampole.

Rolle died at the height of the plague, but his reputation as a loved spiritual counsellor survived him – probably furthered by his disciple William Stopes who seems to have been a young religious and acted as Rolle's literary executor after his death.[29] There is doubt as to whether he is that 'William' for whom Rolle wrote, at the end of his life, the Latin treatise, *Emendatio Vitae*,[30] translated into English in the sixteenth century.

Whatever the uncertainties of the precise dates, events and social connections in Rolle's life it is clear from external and internal evidence that he felt increasingly compelled towards a solitary life because it facilitated contemplative inner life which was for him the reality to be cultivated above all other. To those who urged the perennial claims of the virtues of community living and quoted Ecclesiastes 4:10 'Woe to him who is alone when he falls; for he has not another to help him up', Rolle answered:

> they do not define 'alone' as being 'without God' but understand it to mean 'without company'.
>
> (*Fire of Love*, 13.82)

While he condemned as pride the solitary life-style which arises from self-reliance rather than faith in God (14.87) he countered his opponents with another Scriptural quotation from Osee (Hosea) 2:14 interpreted as referring to the relationship between God and the soul: 'I will lead her into solitude, and I will speak to her heart' (13.83). His whole life was a search for quietness in which the voice of God could be heard (see 15.92). While he recognised that the essence of this quietness is an inner condition, saying of those who know it:

> many of their number, although they live physically among people, are mentally remote from them; they never falter in their heavenly longing, because in spirit they are far removed from a sinful way of life,
>
> (13.83)

yet for him such remoteness had to be physical as well as spiritual. Perhaps his own impatient temperament made this especially essential in his case:

> I myself fled to the wilderness when it proved no longer possible to live harmoniously with men, who, admittedly, were a frequent obstacle to my inner joy. Because I did not do the kind of things they did, they attributed waywardness and bad temper to me.
>
> (27.128)

Certainly he believed that his inner feeling of being most alive, most engaged with real issues, in his contemplative experience, was a gift from God and that his whole integrity depended on his furthering a life-style which he believed enabled him to receive the gift, however strong the opposition he encountered:

> Above all else I have always longed to sit and concentrate on Christ, and him alone. . . . But those who argued with me did not share this opinion, and tried to make me conform to their pattern. But I could not possibly desert the grace of Christ and accept the views of foolish men who were completely ignorant of all that was going on within me. I put up with all their talk, and I did what I had to do according to the state in which the Lord had placed me.

What he had to do was to 'live apart from men, as far as the needs of the body allow . . . continually upheld by him whom I love' (31.142).

CONTEMPLATIVE EXPERIENCE

In *The Fire of Love* Rolle gives a vivid account of his spiritual life as a progress from intellectual knowledge of the faith to 'kynde knowynge'[31] – a progress to which all the mystics witness. Rolle can only talk about it in figurative terms. First comes the inner experience of a spiritual reality described as a door opening to reveal not only the face of the Beloved but a way of love by which he can be reached (15.92). Then Rolle describes two further stages in which his experience is illuminated as the truths of God on which he meditates are felt inwardly. First he feels what he calls heat which seems to be associated with creativity: 'an unusually pleasant heat. . . . from none of his creatures but from the Creator himself'. This leads to a sense of eternal harmony 'and I knew the infusion and understanding of heavenly spiritual sounds, sounds which pertain to the song of eternal praise and to the sweetness of unheard melody' (15.93).

In his account of the final stage, it is as if the unheard melody of which he had some intimation suddenly becomes audible and transposes all his experience into its terms:

> In my prayer I was reaching out to heaven with heartfelt longing when I became aware, in a way I cannot explain, of a symphony of song, and in myself I sensed a corresponding harmony at once wholly delectable and heavenly, which persisted in my mind. Then and there my thinking itself turned into melodious song, and my meditation became a poem, and my very prayers and psalms took up the same sound. The effect of this inner sweetness was that I began to sing what previously I had spoken; only I sang inwardly, and that for my Creator.
>
> (15.93)

The extent to which the senses actually play a role in Rolle's spiritual experience has been argued.[32] Certainly later writers warn against mistaking unusual sense phenomena for genuine spiritual enlightenment.[33] What does seem to be the case is that Rolle had an experience of what he understood as divine reality which transfigured his ordinary perception and that he could only express this in terms of the way men respond to the arts of music and literature. His meditation became a poem, his thinking became a song. Poems order experience and share it; understanding them and writing them involves an act of creativity, and in both activities there is a kind of joy involved when the order of words, or insight into the effect of that order, corresponds with the way things are. Bonaventura saw human craftsmanship (which included poetry) as an image of the creativity of God revealed in the Incarnation – 'for the Son of God is the "art of the Father" ' – and known in the contemplative union of the soul with God. The work of the craftsman is to realise an inner idea in a way that is beautiful, useful and enduring, and as his work is the object of his satisfaction and delight ('if it were in his power to produce an effect which would know and love him, this he would assuredly do'), so man is created for God who alone satisfies his nature. The idea points to a kind of dynamic joy of understanding between creator and creation; that it is not constantly felt is due to sin.[34] Rolle seems to witness to an experience where the barrier to the direct experience of that joy is lifted; the Word that informs all words, the harmony behind all music, becomes real to him; 'my meditation became a poem . . . I began to sing what previously I had spoken' (15.93).

It is small wonder that he sought quiet and freedom from external pressure to follow his inner vision. His search for a style of living which would enable him to cultivate his contemplative gifts led him to equate, perhaps sometimes confuse, an interior state with the external mode of achieving it.[35] Certainly he seems to define active life in terms of outward works and to see it as inferior to the inward experience of contemplation:

> Some people are doubtful as to which life is the more meritorious and excellent, the contemplative or the active. To many of them the active life seems more deserving because of the amount of good works and preaching it performs. But this is the mistake of ignorance, because they do not know what the contemplative life stands for. True there are many actives who are better than some contemplatives. But the best contemplatives are superior to the best actives. So we say therefore that the contemplative life, taken in itself, is sweeter, nobler, worthier, and more meritorious in respect of its fundamental principle, which is delight in *uncreated good;* in other words it is because this is the life which loves God more ardently. Therefore, the contemplative life, if it is properly lived, issues in a greater love of God, and demands more grace, than the active life. . . . Actives to be sure, serve God with their toil and outward activity, but they spend little time in inner quiet. And the result is that they can only rarely and briefly know spiritual delight. On the other hand contemplatives are almost always enjoying the embrace of their Beloved.
>
> (21.109–10)

For Rolle, because God looks on the heart and not the outward appearance, and judges the will not the deed, it seems self-evident that the contemplative life, seeking to be one with God's love, must be preferred, because actives are too distracted by what they do.

But if he sometimes tends to distinguish active from contemplative life in terms of life-style, he is also aware of the strenuousness of contemplative life[36] and stresses that solitude alone will not yield the fruits of contemplative life. In *The Fire of Love* he pinpoints the experience witnessed to by all mystics of a strenuous inner effort which although it is the precondition of contemplative experience cannot actually produce it. As the *Cloud*-author might say, contemplative understanding comes from nowhere and is experienced as a gift:

> We must not be surprised if a man does not attain the heights of contemplation or experience its sweetness at the beginning of his Christian life. It is quite simple: to acquire contemplation means much time and hard work, and it is not given to anyone any time anyhow, even though its possession brings unspeakable joy. It is not within man's power to achieve it, and however great his efforts they will be inadequate. But God is generous, and it is granted to those who truly love him, and who have sought Christ beyond what men consider possible.
>
> (31.142–3)

THE FORM OF LIVING

The events of Rolle's life as given in *The Fire of Love* and the *Office* illustrate his growing discoveries in his game of faith. Rolle was a prolific writer in Latin about his mystical theology.[37] His English texts which almost certainly belong to the last ten years of his life relate to his role as a spiritual counsellor, and they are consistent with what we know of him – their strength lying not in systematic exposition but in his skill with language to illuminate the goals of spiritual life and so awake his readers to their reality. It is as if they might be responses to requests to 'write up' exchanged conversation and counsel – some are lyrics and short prose poems on the nature of contemplative life.[38] This chapter will introduce Rolle's qualities as an English writer about mystical experience by concentrating chiefly on two kinds of text. The first, *The Form of Living*, is a treatise which Rolle wrote for Margaret de Kirkeby to explain the shape of contemplative life to which it is an excellently manageable introduction. It is characteristic of Rolle's mystical theology, and it is the most extended and systematic of the English treatises, combining imaginative use of language and a relatively well-controlled intellectual structure to effect a psychological understanding of the desire for, and experiences of, the life of faith, and a taste of its nature. The second kind of text – meditation on the Passion – is illuminated by the wider perspective of *The Form of Living*. Rolle's *Meditations* embody at a literary level his appreciation of the shaping energies of the form of the inner life. Through a high level of devotional art they enact stages of the contemplative game – indeed provide means of play.

Rolle uses the phrase 'form of lyvyng' twice in the text of that name. He signs off: 'Loo, Margarete, I have schortly sayde þe þe forme of lyvyng, and how þou may come til perfeccion' (12.119.76–7),[39] using the phrase to denote a pattern of life. Earlier he ends chapter three with a hint of humour saying that many people are not what they seem despite the appearances and begs her to try her utmost not to be worse than she appears, concluding :

> and if þou will do als I lere þe in þis schort forme of lyvyng, I hope, thorou þe grace of God, þat if men halde þe gude, þou sall be wele better.
>
> (3.94.41–3)
>
> *als*: as, *lere*: teach; *halde*: hold/esteem; *sall*: shall.

Here the word 'form' is ambiguous referring to his writing as well as to a life-style. The literary work is to define the mould which is to be instrumental in shaping the life's work. The use of 'form' meaning an instrument for shaping in crafts, like a template or a cobbler's last, was normal in the 1340s, the more modern usage of the word as 'prescribed course', 'formative principle', not being found until later.[40] The register of 'form' as 'template' seems to catch exactly the potentially creative status of the text whose full form will only be realised when it is enacted. Moreover, it follows in its own terms a design which is fundamental to medieval Christian culture, underlying the liturgy of the Mass and informing the architecture of church buildings. The Mass offers the sacrifice of the Passion through which man becomes part of the kingdom of God and the redeeming action of Christ.[41] The church interior was dominated by the rood-screen and rood with the visual images of the dying Christ flanked by the sorrowing and faithful Mary and

John. Passing beneath it from the lay part of the church, the nave, to the chancel, where the priest celebrated, figuratively marked the rite of passage from earth to heaven. In an age when lay people did not participate in the celebration of the Latin Mass the mystics writing in the vernacular interpreted their own experience of the reality expressed in both ritual and architecture, that it is only by means of suffering that redemptive love is proved and inherits the kingdom.

The Form of Living illuminates the stages of the way of life which Rolle believed would enable these beliefs enacted in building and ritual to become psychological realities. It seems clearly to be divided into two parts.[42] Each concentrates on the means and ends, preparation for, and fulfilment of, spiritual life, the first part dealing with the self-regulation necessary to release the desire for God from all impediment; the second dealing more directly with contemplative experience. But while it is true that such a division is discernible, it is also true that the goal is in sight from the start. In the first chapter Rolle juxtaposes the issues of life and death in terms of everlasting and perishable goods, and says strikingly:

> he þat hase noght Jhesu Criste, he tynes all þat he has, and all þat he es, and all þat he myght gete
>
> (85.19–21)

tynes: loses.

thus identifying the Incarnation with the fulfilment of human identity. In one of the meditations on the Passion to be examined in the last part of the chapter Rolle vividly explores the nature of such a loss. This treatise, however, is designed to clarify the process by which man turns from death to life and finds 'all þat he has', Jesus. Rolle has to try to meet the linguistic challenge which faces any mystical writer: to define and point towards the nature of an experience which is in essence ineffable. Characteristically he uses the imagery of song to point to the highest kind of contemplative experience of God:

> a wonderful joy of Goddes luf, þe whilk joy es lovyng of God, þat may noght be talde; . . . . (12.118.46–7). I say þe þat no man wate, bot he or scho þat feles it, þat has it, and þat loves God, syngand þarwyth.
>
> (8.106.72–4)

wate: knows; *syngand þarwyth*: singing with it.

The *Form* unfolds a process of definition which comes full circle back to its beginning so that that can be understood in a new way:

> the end of all our exploring
> will be to arrive where we started
> And know the place for the first time.[43]

The value of the writing is that it provides points of reference for the voyager within.

Chapters 1–6: lighting the fire of love

The first three chapters of *The Form* address themselves chiefly to the solitary religious, pointing the contrast between the reality of inward holiness and the outward appearances – 'habett of halyness' (3.94.39) – a term which seems to cover not just the clothing but the outward practices of piety, fasting and abstinence. Rolle stresses the need to acquire *discretion* in these observances so that they do not become ends in themselves and counter-productive to their true purpose – to release the practitioner to a freedom to love.[44] Rolle stresses at the beginning the joy which is the obverse of the discipline:

> Men wenes þat we er in pyne and in penance grete, bot we have mare joy and mare verray delyte in a day, þan þai have in þe worlde all þar lyve.
>
> (2.89.12–15)

wenes: think; *pyne*: torment; *mare*: more; *verray*: true; *þar*: their.

But although it is characteristic of Rolle's writing to stress the joy of the contemplative, it would be a mistake to suppose that he ever suggests that the passage to it is easy:

> Na man till swylk revelacion and grace on þe first day may kom, bot thurgh lang travell and bysines to loue Jhesu Criste, als þou sall here afterward.
>
> (2.90.36–8)

At the very start he warns against the specific danger attendant on solitary life – hallucination; a point to remember when considering the arguments of those who tend to be distrustful of Rolle's theology.[45] There is a delightful passage where he addresses himself to the role of dreams and faces out the difficulty inherent in medieval lore which others like Chaucer resolve through ambiguity: namely, that in a situation where some dreams were held to reveal truth and others to be the products of a disordered digestive system, it is difficult to distinguish true from false. Rolle warns against taking any of it seriously:

> Bot sa mykell we sall latlyer gyf fayth till any dreme, þat we may not sone wyt whilk es soth, whilk es fals, whilk es of oure enmy, whilk es of þe Hali Gaste.
>
> (2.93.134–7)

sa mykell: so much; *latlyer*: less readily; *wyt*: know; *es*: is.

He ends the address to the solitary with his playful warning on the necessity of distinguishing between inner holiness and outward habit having previously established that:

> þai er anly hali, what state or degre þai be in, þe whilk despises all erthly thyng, þat es at say, lufs it noght, and byrnes in þe luf of Jhesu Criste . . . and feles a swetnes in þaire hert of þe lufe withouten ende.
>
> (3.93.9–14)

er anly: are only; *þe whilk*: the which; *at say*: to say; *þaire*: their.

The phrase, characteristic of Rolle, 'byrnes in þe luf of Jhesu Criste' combines man's love for God with God's for man in a fire which sets man alight. This is the 'fire which consumes everything that is dark'(*Fire of Love*, prologue, p.47); at this stage of the treatise it is a metaphor whose full implications have not been developed, but it is the goal of this form of living.

The kindling that ignites the desire for knowledge of God into leaping flames rising 'ay upwarde, als fire, sekand þe heghest place in heven'(4.95.1) is inner discipline. Rolle suggests that this is begun in thought of the four last things: death, for 'we lyve bot in a poynt' in 'uncertente of owre endyng'; judgement, when we account for our use of time 'and ilk tyme þat we thynk not on God, we may cownt it als þe þyng þat we have tynt' (4.95.19–22, 38–9); heaven, the joy which is 'mare þan any may tell'; and hell, where also is burning in fire (4.96.46–7, 54). The perspectives Rolle brings into focus stress the urgency of the situation. He presses it home, 'I wyll þat þou be ay clymbande tyll Jhesu-warde' (5.96.1).

The end of the first half of *The Form* is concerned with clarifying the ordering of inner life – laying the fire – through an analysis of the human capacity for sin.[46] Its positive side is that it implies man's ability to recognise his aptitude for self-pollution, and thus trigger the dynamic power which first clears the mess through the sacrament of penance (repentance, confession, satisfaction) and then works through self-discipline to keep the channels running clear in thought, word and deed. This involves working mentally and physically to keep distractions at bay, guarding the tongue to speak little and to the point, taking especial care not to misrepresent others, living as if death might come tomorrow and balancing the needs of the body with the longings of the spirit in *discretion*.[47] Rolle is emphatic that 'ryghtwysnes' is not in the discipline itself, but it is the fruit of it, a state of inner freedom untouched by the constraints of outward circumstances:

> bot þou ert ryghtwys, if all ilyke be to þe, despyte and lovyng, povert and rytches, hunger and nede, als delytes and dayntes.
>
> (6.101–2.176–1)

bot: but; *ert*: are.

He recognises that the will to effect such inner effort has to be awakened – drawn –[48] that it is the response to goodness in men and in Christ, and to the joy of heaven, which starts to work man's salvation. So far Rolle has been concerned to delineate strategies to prevent man losing all his creative potential, a stage roughly corresponding to that which other mystics label the purgative stage; now he tries to bring into focus what is saved. This involves finding a language for the goal of contemplative life – 'I vate wele þat þou desyres to here some special poynt of þe luf of Jhesu Criste, and of contemplatyf lyfe' [*vate wele:* know well; *here*: hear] (6.102–3.214–2) – to bridge the gap between doctrine and reality. In the first part of *The Form*, language is used to denote action and inner states that are immediately recognisable so that, for instance, cleanness of mouth is defined as not talking for the sake of it and telling no lies (c.5). Now words become means to mediate a visionary experience of love and enlarge understanding. They point beyond themselves to the possibility of an all-encompassing reality to which they are a vital witness because they are constituent parts, words signifying the Word. The prose in this section starts to function like poetry, ordering images and rhythmical cadences to convey an intimation of the way that Rolle believed that things are. In its own terms it is sacramental.

Chapter 7: the song of love

Chapter seven, the hinge by which *The Form* opens to this level of significance, directly addresses itself to the essence of the contemplative life – certainty of being, through which all experience is transfigured to joy. Rolle expresses it metaphorically as speech becomes song. In *Emendatio Vitae* he acknowledges the variety of modes of expressing this kind of insight:

> Sum says, contemplatyfe lyf is not ellis bot knawlegis of þingis to cum & hyde, or to be voyde fro all wardly occupacion, or study of godis lettyrs. Odyr says þat contemplacion is free sight in þe spectakyls of wisdom, with a full he meruayll. Odyr says þat contemplacion is a boke, & wys behaldynge of þe saule, spred all abowt to behald his myghtis. Odyr says, & wel, þat contemplacion is Ioy of heuenly þingis. Odyr says, & best, þat contemplacion is deed of fleschly desires be Ioye of þe mynde raisyd. To me it semys þat contemplacion is Ioyfull songe of godis lufe takyn in mynde, with swetnes of augell louynge.
>
> (12.127.16–28)

knawlegis: knowledge; *hyde*: hid; *wardly*: worldly; *full he meruayll*: very great wonder; *deed*: death; *raisyd*: elevated.

He continues with a memorable expression of the joy in the play of faith 'þis is þe myrth in mynde had gostely for þe lufar euerlastynge, with grete voys oowt brekand' (12.127.16–28).

In chapter seven of *The Form*, leading his disciple on from the initial perspective of striving to order her inner life as if she should die tomorrow – a challenge which sets the adrenalin running and wonderfully sharpens awareness – he potently reminds her in terms of his own cultural coinage that the world is indeed 'charged with the grandeur of God'[49] by instructing her to see all her physical experience in terms of the sacrifice also offered at the Mass:

> And when þou ert at þi mete, love ay God in þi thoght at ilk a morsel, and say þus in þi hert:
>
> Loved be þou, keyng,
> and thanked be þou, keyng,
> and blyssed be þou, keyng,
> Jhesu, all my joyng,

Of all þi giftes gude,
þat for me spylt þi blude
and died on þe rode;
þou gyf me grace to syng
þe sang of þi lovyng.

(7.103–4.28–38)

keyng: king.

By means of keeping in remembrance this little incantatory prayer at meals and indeed at all times not otherwise taken up with prayer or speech ('and thynk it noght anely whils þou etes, bot bath before and after, ay bot when þou prayes or spekes', 7.104.39–40) the disciple will maintain a constant perception of all aspects of sustaining life as a divine gift mysteriously available in time only through the processes of death and resurrection. It is no accident that it was recommended for use in the fifteenth-century *Lay Folks Mass Book* at the elevation of the Host.[50] All the devotions recommended for the laity during the Mass reinforce a sense of this pattern. The prayers recommended before the consecration are for the spiritual welfare of all estates and conditions of men in terms of a literal and spiritual harvest which not only ensures their survival in this world but also in the next.

þis world þat turnes mony wayes
Make gode til vs in alle oure dayes;
þo weders gret and vnstable,
lord make gode & sesonable;
þo froytes of þo erthe make plenteuus,
Als þou sees best, ordayn for vs,
Swilk grace til vs þou sende,
þat in oure last day, at oure ende,
when þis worlde & we sal seuer
Bring vs til ioy þat lastis euer.[51]

froytes: fruits; *seuer*: sever.

Such prayers are then easily assimilated to the offering of the Mass, a ritual which keeps alive the paradigmatic reality of the Incarnation. So the priest addresses God

> Wherefore also we thy servants, O Lord, and also thy holy people, in memory as well of the blessed passion of the same Christ, thy Son, our Lord, as of his resurrection from the dead, and also of his glorious ascension into the heavens do offer unto thy excellent majesty, of thine own gifts albeit given unto us, a pure, a holy, an undefiled sacrifice, the holy bread of eternal life, and the cup of everlasting salvation.[52]

As he continues with the prayer that those who receive the sacrament may 'be fulfilled with all hevenly benediction and grace through Jesus Christ', so Rolle in *The Form of Living* now turns to a description of the interior awareness of this fulfilment.

Chapter 8: the three degrees of love

Like all mystics Rolle understands the essence of contemplative life to be a progress and he borrows terminology from Richard of St Victor[53] when he describes this progress as three degrees of love 'insuperable' 'inseparable' and 'singular'.

For Rolle the first stage, 'insuperable' involves a love of God which nothing can shake:

> On þis maneer sal þi luf be insuperabel, þat na thyng may downe bryng, bot spryngand on heght.
>
> (8.105.13–14)

He uses the same degrees translated as 'vnouercomyn' 'indepartyd' and 'singuler' (11.123–4.26,32,5) in *Emendatio Vitae* and it illuminates his thinking in *The Form*. He says of the first degree that it happens when no other desire can divert love from God and 'all labyr is lyght to a lufar', signalling a vivid apprehension of the joy at the heart of the work of redemption. The second stage 'inseparabel' represents a state of being constantly centred on a consciousness of Jesus. The heart 'cryes with his lufe to be haldyn' [*haldyn*: held fast]. The third degree involves a sense of complete comfort in Jesus 'all multyn in fyre of lufe' (11. 123.30,35; 125.34–5). In *The Form* he comments that in the first two degrees it is possible to say 'I languysch for lufe' or 'Me langes in lufe' (106.53–4) but in the third degree all is comfort and joy. Speech becomes song: 'þan þe sange of lovyng and of lufe es commen'(105.45), longing is satisfied and the lover becomes part of the fire of love. In *The Form* the prose style shows Rolle at his best embodying his sense of 'the expanding of love beyond desire':[54]

> Bot þat fire, if it be hate, es swa delitabell and wondyrful þat I kan noght tell it. þan þi sawle es Jhesu lufand, Jhesu thynkand, Jhesu desirand, anly in þe covayties of hym anedande, til hym syngand, of hym byrnand, in hym restand. þan þe sange of lovyng and of lufe es commen, þan þi thoght turnes intil sang and intil melody, þan þe behoves syng þe psalmes þat þou before sayde, þan þou mon be lang

> abowte few psalmes, þan þe wil thynk þe deed swettar þan hony, for þan þou ert ful syker to se hym þat þou lufes: þan may þou hardely say: 'I languysch for lufe'; þan may þou say: 'I slepe, and my hert wakes'.
>
> (105–6.40–52)
>
> *hate*: hot; *lufand*: loving; *anedande*: breathing; *mon*: will; *deed:* death; *syker*: sure; *hardely*: boldly.

The first sentence uses the inexpressibility *topos* – the rhetorical trick for gesturing towards the ineffable. It is followed by a sentence of seven verbal phrases dependent on one main verb 'is' which builds up a sense of being actively extended 'lufand – thynkand – desirand – anedande – syngand – byrnand' yet also paradoxically 'restand'. The incantatory run of present participles with their weak-syllable endings gives way to the strong definitive statement which has gathered resonance of meaning both within the text and from other of Rolle's writings: 'þan þe sange of lovynge and of lufe es cummen'. Its rhythm is hauntingly evocative of the Canticle of Canticles (Song of Songs) (2:11): 'For winter is now past, the rain is over and gone. The flowers have appeared in our land, the time of pruning is come'. It is then developed in seven statements to a climactic definition of the nature of the fire of love; they are brought to a triumphant conclusion by juxtaposing a negative statement with its positive form to indicate ways in which the third degree of singular love fulfils and transcends the longing of the earlier stages:

> þan may þou hardely say: 'I languysch for lufe'; þan may þou say 'I slepe, and my hert wakes'.

The phrase from The Song of Songs (5:2) which heralds the arrival of the beloved, here conveys a sense of a transformed newly awakened consciousness where longing and the unquiet ego are quenched.

It has been suggested that because Rolle does not make use of Richard of St Victor's fourth stage, *insatiabilis* the love that can never be satisfied because of the inexhaustible nature of God, he did not in fact enter so profound a mystical experience as others.[55] This argument, however, is countered by drawing attention to the passage in *Emendatio Vitae* (c.11) describing singular love:

> and þe more þus in hym it lifis, þe more in lufe it is kyndyld & to hym it is lykkar
>
> (11.124.26–7)
>
> *lykkar*: more like.

which shows that he conceived of an unlimited and thus, literally, unfulfilled desire for God.[56] This sense is not contradicted by anything in *The Form*.

Rolle also refers to three degrees of love in two earlier treatises known as *Ego Dormio* and *The Commandment* both written for a nun in the early stages of religious life (possibly Margaret Kirkeby).[57] *The Commandment* anticipates *The Form* but is less comprehensive in its analysis, whereas in *Ego Dormio* although he does not borrow Victorine terminology for his analysis, he nevertheless outlines a growth in religious experience similar to that in *The Form* but starting at an earlier stage in religious life. The first degree of love in *Ego Dormio* shown by an unshakeable adherence to the teaching of the Church and necessary to every man 'þat will be safe' (63.91) seems to be taken for granted by the time of the later text. But the second degree expressed outwardly in giving up the world with a heart wholly centred on Christ, seems to correspond in some ways to both the insuperable and inseparable stages of *The Form* and like them gives way to a third stage when the contemplative sees into heaven and is filled with the joy Rolle expresses as song: 'þi prayers turnes intil joyful sange, and þi thoghtes to melody' (69.284–5). Rolle says that the first two stages defined in *Ego Dormio* are possible for actives as well as contemplatives, though he does comment that during the second stage his pupil will want to be alone 'to thynk on Criste, and to be in mykel praying' (65–66.158–9). At the end of chapter eight of *The Form* Rolle comments that in the 'fyrst degre er many, in þe toþer degree er ful faa, bot in þe thyrde degre unnethes er any' [*faa:* few; *unnethes:* scarcely] (107.83–5) confirming this view. It is one that is echoed by the *Cloud*-author.[58]

Chapters 8–10: poetic teaching

In *The Form* the first two degrees of love seem to correspond to the stages in the contemplative's life that Rolle has addressed in chapters one to six. In chapter four the 'turnyng til Jhesu' from all worldly things (94.2) is like the 'insuperabel' love, while the second degree, 'inseperabel' relates to the injunction to remember that all time is lost which is not God-centred and to contemplate the joy of those who are stable in this love until death (95.38f.). The element of active effort in the discipline of the inner life in the first part of *The Form* seems linked to the sense of the first two degrees. The third degree is not felt to be acquired by effort but given by grace, 'God gyfes it til wham he wil, bot noght withouten grete grace comand before'(8.106.75–6). Nevertheless Rolle concludes this chapter with a song which acts as a kind of rite of passage – an enabler for the reception of this gift. Its rhetorical structures enact a felt understanding of an interior spiritual state which illuminates the reader's imagination.

When will þow com to comforth me, and bryng me owt of care,
And gyf me þe, þat I may se, havand evermare?
þi lufe es ay swettest of al þat ever war.
My hert, when sal it brest for lufe? þan languyst I na mare.
For lufe my thoght has fest, and I am fayne to fare.
I stand in still mowrnyng. Of all lufelyst of lare
Es lufe langyng, it drawes me til my day,
þe band of swete byrnyng, for it haldes me ay
Fra place and fra plaiyng til þat I get may
þe syght of my swetyng, þat wendes never away.
In welth bees oure wakyng wythowten noy or nyght.
My lufe es in lastyng, and langes to þat syght.

languyst: would languish; *fest*: securely; *fayne to fare*: eager to go on; *lare:* teaching; *haldes*: keeps; *fra*: from; *noy*: hurt.

In this *cantus amoris* Rolle creates a literary experience of the longing to have Jesus illuminated by the intellectual understanding of what this means. To achieve this he creates a sense of the gap between the speaker and God by contrasting verbs of action which embody a sense of the dynamic power of the love of God to the speaker's trapped stillness, and then resolves these apparent opposites as he perceives his stillness to be the very condition of the inner movement he desires. He is both 'still and still moving'.[59] In the first six lines he asks when that love which is incarnated in Jesus will 'com to comforth me' 'bryng me owt of care' 'gyf me þe', and sets these verbs of power potentially activated on his behalf with his own sense of motionless deprivation: 'I stand in still mowrnyng'. The quickening presence of the love he longs for seems conspicuous by its absence, a feeling emphasised by the strong-stressed, medially-stopped half-line. But the second half of the lyric moves on from this: the completion of the line looks back to what has gone before in its rhyme, but syntactically and alliteratively it moves forward to convey the perception of that very still mourning symptomatic of the inner spiritual movement of Christ's coming.

With perhaps a pun on mourning he continues: 'of all lufelyst of lare/Es lufe langyng, it drawes me til my day'. Thus he expresses the realisation that in the still mourning is a moving power and the lyric ends with another juxtaposition, this time of two positive certainties, of the reality of the vision longed for, and of the recognition that the power to realise it is love which on man's part essentially expresses its dynamic nature by means of patience, 'the faith and the love and the hope are all in the waiting'.[60] The lyric unites feeling and understanding in that wisdom which is the goal of affective piety.[61]

Anyone who comes to Rolle's lyrics looking for the subtle music of variety of stress within a regular syllabic pattern will be brought up short by an unpredictability of both syllabic and stress systems which lurch uneasily from one banal sing-song pattern to another. But Rolle's great strength as a lyric writer is in his ability to approximate the rhythms and emphases of the speaking voice to incantation. It is positively helpful if his poems are written out as prose (as they actually often are in the case of those lyrics embedded in prose treatises as opposed to independent lyrics)[62] because they are then naturally read for the speaking voice and not with any expectation of the regularity roused by the sight of poetic form. The result is a lyrical prose particularly effective when it serves to embody a singing climax at strategic points – a not unsurprising tactical manoeuvre on the part of a writer trying to intimate the reality of a mystical experience which he expresses as transposing everyday speech to song.

This poetic teaching which enacts a surrogate experience of the operation of grace is extended in Rolle's recommendation of a form of prayer which, though obviously popular in the Middle Ages, he yet made peculiarly his own, devotion to the name of Jesus. It was a form of devotion found not only among the learned[63] but in prayers designed for the laity, as for instance, in another prayer recommended for lay folk at the elevation of the Host:

O Jesu lorde wellcum thou be
In forme of brede as y the se;
O Jesu, for thy holy name;
Schelde me thys day from syn and schame

or in the prayer, a fragment of which was carved on a church bench in Oxfordshire:

Jesu for thy holy name
And for thy bitter passion,
Save us fro synne and shame
And endles dampnacion.[64]

In chapter nine Rolle writes a prose-poem about the efficacy of a prayer in which the Holy Name is a focus for all that he understands about the process of redemption. The name of 'Jhesu' concentrates an understanding of the energy of love which continually works to this end and used in prayer becomes a kind of brief mnemonic for this whole area of understanding and longing. It concentrates the will to God who transcends all particularity and it acts like the kind of short prayer that the *Cloud*-author recommends: 'take þee bot a litil worde of o silable; for so it is betir þen of two, for euer þe schorter it is, the betir it acordeþ wiþ þe werk of þe spirite . . . þis worde schal be þi scheeld & þi spere, wheþer þou ridest on pees or on werre'.[65] In chapter nine of *The Form* Rolle uses this Jesus prayer to recapitulate the whole progress in love he has so far described – it becomes as it were the tool which shapes and conveys his understanding of redemption:

> If þou thynk Jhesu contynuly, and halde it stabely, it purges þi syn, and kyndels þi hert; it clarifies þi sawle, it removes anger, and dose away slawnes; it woundes in lufe, and fulfilles of charite; it chaces þe devel, and puttes oute drede: it opens heven, and makes a contemplatif man.
>
> (9.108.8–13)
>
> *dose away slawnes*: does away with sloth.

The prose is orchestrated to a climax. The series of short paratactical main clauses with two (occasionally three) strong stresses answers the opening conditional clause, 'if þou thynk Jhesu contynuly'. They first describe the work of love as a double edged activity with positive and negative effect – purging sin and kindling the heart, clearing the soul and removing anger and sloth, wounding in love and fulfilling with charity, chasing off the devil and extinguishing fear – and then level out to the strongly stressed affirmation which defines the positive potential of the negative statement in chapter one 'he þat hase noght Jhesu Criste, he tynes all þat he has, and all þat he es, and all þat he myght gete'(85.19–21) for he that has 'Jhesu' grows through prayer to the fulfilment of human potential: heaven is open to him and he is made a 'contemplatif man'. The chapter ends with a succinct statement about the divine energy which works through discipline to the freedom to love and is manifested in the relationship between the Old and New Covenants: 'for fulnes of þe law es charite; in þat hynges all'. This leads naturally to the splendid definitions of love in chapter ten as Rolle anticipates the disciple bringing him down to earth with a question: 'You talk a great deal about love but what is it? Where is it? How do I best practise it and know that I am loving God?' The systematic answers reveal that love is essentially in the inner heart of man not in works, which are merely a sign of love, though it is true that 'luf wil noght be ydel: it es wirkand som gude evermare' (111.96–7). By re-examining the three degrees in ways which are closer to those of *Emendatio Vitae* Rolle now expands understanding of the implications of his earlier definitions in chapter eight of *The Form*. He answers that first God should be loved with the humility and strength which makes all labour light[66] so that no shame or anguish can destabilise the delight (111–12.99–137). Secondly, he should be loved wisely and that involves complete detachment from earthly values (112–13.138–70).[67] Thirdly he should be loved devoutly (113.171f.) and sweetly and that is when the soul feels overcome with joy, burning in the heat of the Holy Ghost – a Noah's ark of security in the love of God that nothing can destroy:

> And þan þou comes intil swilk rest and pees in sawle, and quiete withowten thoghtes of vanitese or of vices, als þou war in sylence and slepe and sette in Noe schyppe, þat na thyng may lette þe of devocion and byrnying of swete lufe.[68]
>
> (113.180–5)

war: were.

On the question of how the lover can recognise whether he is loving, Rolle warns that apart from the overwhelming assurance which accompanies the gift of the experience of singular love, man cannot live by certainty, but faith, since that is the nature of the game; but he does suggest a do-it-yourself questionnaire which is really designed to reveal to the user where his heart is fixed. So he is doing well if he genuinely feels no lusting after earthly things but such a burning love of God that it is the only thing he wants to talk about, the only activity he wishes to pursue; and if anything which furthers it, however apparently difficult, is easily done, and any hardship suffered gladly with genuinely indestructible inner joy. Answering the question as to the state in which this love can best be practised, Rolle points to an inner quietness which seems for him to be achievable only in literal solitude and constrained stability: 'þai er Goddes trone, þat dwelles still in a stede, and er noght abowte rennand' [*trone*: throne; *a stede:* one place] (10.116.258–9). For himself, he finds that the sitting posture most effectively releases his contemplative energy. But the high point of the chapter is the definition of love which precedes these questions of where and how it may be pursued. It is another example of Rolle's singing prose as he moves through a series of figures which accumulate a delighted perception of love as the Word which informs all meaning. The initial image of fire and light clarifying the sight/understanding and consuming the whole being is left behind in a series of more abstract metaphors which relate to its dynamic quality drawing men to its source. The style is emotive but the intellectual understanding informing it has an astringent clarity which is very moving. It points to truth which has become wisdom born of experience:

> Trowth may be withowten lufe, bot it may noght helpe withouten it. Lufe es perfeccion of letters, vertu of prophecy, frute of trowth, help of sacramentes, stablyng of witt and conyng, rytches of pure men, lyfe of dyand men.
>
> (10.109.29–33)

stablyng of witt and conyng: the firm foundation of wisdom and knowledge.

This is Rolle's version of 1 Corinthians 13:2:

> And if I should have prophecy and should know all mysteries, and all knowledge, and if I should have all faith, so that I could remove mountains, and have not charity, I am nothing.

But he is more immediate in his evocation of the reality of a power that activates the potential efficacy in all areas of human endeavour and experience and runs counter to death. He creates a sense of a primal energy suffusing man as the sun does the air and fire a coal (10.110.56–72) and in his writing he tries to bridge the gap between intellectual acknowledgement of such a truth and experience of its reality.

Chapter 11: the gift virtues and the form of living

In only one manuscript[69] is the form of living related to the wider but familiar theological framework of the gift virtues. These were developed from qualities defined by Isaiah (c.11) in his prophecy traditionally associated with the Incarnation, and interpreted by the Church Fathers as gifts of the Holy Spirit.[70] The inclusion of them at this point in the text, defines the whole process of the experience of love, 'insuperable' 'inseparable' and 'singular' as the activity of the Holy Spirit in man. The section exists elsewhere in separate form[71] but it has a propriety at this point, stressing that the dynamic shaping inherent in the process Rolle describes is a property of God and a divine gift; and it leads into the final summarising chapter focused on active and contemplative life. In traditional manner Rolle treats the gifts of the Holy Spirit listed as Wisdom, Understanding, Counsel, Might, Knowledge Piety and Fear of the Lord in Isaiah 11 in the inverted hierarchical order Counsel, Understanding, Wisdom to relate them to the process of withdrawal from the world and achievement of that inner *discretion* which is the ground of contemplation;[72] he then deals with strength, piety, knowledge and the fear of the Lord itemised as forces which stimulate man to self-knowledge and help the soul to endure against sin, all aspects of a more active spirituality.

Chapter 12: reading, meditation and prayer

In the final chapter Rolle looks at active and contemplative life both as inner states and outward practices. Active life, keeping the commandments and loving one's neighbour as oneself[73], is compatible with, indeed may express, the first degree of love, while contemplative life grows from this to the more inward experience of all three degrees of love. Here Rolle recognises the two stages in mystical experience, one actively willed the other a transcendent gift, to which all those engaged with spiritual life witness. These stages relate to the spiritual exercises which embrace reading of scripture (*lectio*), meditation (*meditatio*), prayer and contemplation although those who use this terminology do not always do so in a precisely similar denotative way. Thus, for instance, in the twelfth century the Carthusian Guigo II said that 'reading seeks for the sweetness of a blessed life, meditation perceives it, prayer asks for it, contemplation tastes it. Reading, as it were, puts food whole into the mouth, meditation chews it and breaks it up, prayer extracts its flavor, contemplation is the sweetness itself which gladdens and refreshes.'[74] Here meditation is closely connected to what is read in terms of its retention in the memory as the grounds for prayer. However, with the growth in emphasis on the importance of what is called 'affective devotion' – that is, experienced, rather than intellectual, knowledge of the faith – meditation came to refer to an exercise not necessarily based directly on Scripture but designed to stir the will by an intense appeal to the emotions through meditations on the manhood of Christ.[75] As the definition of meditation developed in scope, so prayer came to denote not just intellectually formulated structures but a desire for God which sometimes rises to a direct consciousness of his presence. This has been described as 'the affection of a man that clingeth to God, a homely and pious speaking, a standing of the enlightened soul unto enjoying for so long as may be'.[76] Thus prayer became seen not as formulated exercise, which may or may not concentrate the mind, but as a state of consciousness.

This development is particularly important in the study of those who wrote in the vernacular for laymen who were cut off from the richness of recollected prayer in the practice of the liturgy and in search of modes by which they could realise the substance of their faith. In chapter twelve of *The Form* Rolle says that the 'lower part' of contemplative life, or first stage, is concerned with meditation, prayer and hymns. This seems to coincide with the experience of love he calls 'inseparabel' when:

> þi thoght and þi myght es swa haly, swa enterely, and swa perfytely festend, sett, and stabeld in Jhesu Cryste, þat þi thoght comes never of hym, never departyd fra hym
>
> *festend*: fastened; *sett*: settled; *stabeld*: established; *of*: off.

and the solitary is urged to prayer as a focus for the love:

> and als sone als þou wackens, þi hert es on hym, sayand *Ave Maria* or *Gloria tibi Domine* or *Pater noster* or *Miserere mei Deus* if þou have bene temped in þi slepe, or thynkand on his lufe and his lovyng, als þou dyd wakand'.
>
> (105.19–26)
>
> *wackens*: wake up; *Ave Maria*: Hail Mary; *Pater noster*: our Father; *Miserere mei Deus*: have mercy on me O God; *temped*: tempted.

The second stage he labels contemplation which is 'a wonderful joy of Goddes luf, þe whilk joy es lovyng of God, þat may noght be talde' (118.46–7). And he describes the moment when the second stage is entered as seeing (with all its connotations of understanding) into heaven 'for contemplacion es a syght, and þai se intil heven with þar gastly egh' (119.68–9). This signals clearly that the dynamic of singular love is operative when everyday reality is transfigured from speech to song and the contemplative feels the ordinary demands of the self stilled as he awakes to the wider reality: 'þan may þou say: "I slepe and my hert wakes" ' (8.106.51–2).

For Rolle it seems that this 'sight' can arise from both meditation and prayer, two conditions which look alike in his writing. In *The Form* he says that the lower part of the contemplative life is:

> meditacion of haly wrytyng, þat es Goddes wordes, and in other gude thoghtes and swete, þat men hase of þe grace of God abowt þe lufe of Jhesu Criste, and also in lovyng of God in psalmes and ympnes, or in prayers.
>
> (118.36–40)

haly: holy; *ympnes*: hymns.

This is consistent with his account of his own quickened consciousness in *The Fire of Love* when he says that prior to his feeling of *calor* he was sitting in a chapel 'delighting in the sweetness of prayer and meditation' and in his experience of *canor* 'my thinking itself turned into melodious song, and my meditation became a poem, and my very prayers and psalms took up the same sound' (15.93).

In *Emendatio Vitae* he deals with prayer, meditation and reading in that order, but in the actual chapter on contemplation he spells out a sequence which agrees with what he tells us of his own experience and which does not contradict his account in *The Form*.

> Meditacion in god & godly þingis, aftyr prayer and redynge is to be takyn, qwher is þe halsynge of rachell. To redynge, longis reson & inquisicion of treuyth, þat is a gudely lightte markyd apon vs. To prayer, longis louynge sange, passynge in behaldynge and meruayll: and so in prayer standis contemplatyfe lyfe or contemplacion. To meditacione, longis inspiracion of godd, vndirstandynge, wysdome and syghynge.
>
> (12.127.8–15)

halsynge: embracing; *rachell*: Rachel; *longis*: belongs; *sange*: song; *meruayll*: wonder; *syghynge*: sighing.

It is clear from this that for Rolle prayer was the most important exercise by which the reality of faith is realised, which is why he deals with it first after the section on the necessity for patience in adversity:

> Iff þou in temptacion or tribulacion be sett, to prayer o-none ryn.
>
> (7.118.4)
>
> *o-none*: forthwith.

Prayer is the means by which the transforming dynamic of the love of God is accessed in the innermost marrow ('inhirliest mergh') of our hearts (7.118.28) and labour becomes light (11.123.30). It is fundamental to all stages of spiritual life. But he does acknowledge, even while giving prayer priority, that 'meditacion helpis' (7.119.5).[77]

His sense of the delicate interrelation between reading, meditation and prayer is set out at the beginning of the chapter on contemplation:

> Contemplatyfe lyfe or contemplacion has thre partys: Redyng, Prayer, & Meditacion. In redynge, god spekis to vs; In prayer, we speke to god; In meditacion, awngels to vs cum down & techis vs, þat we erre nott. In prayer þa go vp and offyrs owr prayers to god, ioyand of owr profett, þat ar messyngers be-twix god and vs.[78]
>
> (12.127.1–7)
>
> *þa*: they; *profett*: profit.

Here meditation has a mediating function: a process in which insight is received like a gift, much as the process of analysing a poem mysteriously yields a new integrated perception of its whole meaning which transcends the conscious process of study. For Rolle this kind of understanding is assimilated to the consciousness of God in prayer. The angels that descended in meditation ascend in prayer, and so meditation is the very 'halsynge of rachell' (12.127.10), that is contemplative experience,[79] which Rolle points towards in affective anagogical terms as the 'ioyfull songe of godis lufe' (12.127.25). But for him, as for all the mystics, such joy is not realised without suffering. The pattern revealed in the story of the Incarnation of constraint, death and resurrection is fundamental to the Christian mystical perception of being human. Salvation lies only in working with the system of redemptive choices. In chapter six of *Emendatio Vitae* he says that man must either be burnt in this life with the fire of God's love and of tribulation (the last being a means to proving the strength of the first) or, after this life, bitterly in hell[80] – a perception that Eliot transposes into a modern idiom in *Little Gidding*:

> We only live, only suspire
> Consumed by either fire or fire.

For Rolle meditation was clearly a means of activating the inner work of love and freeing the self. In *Ego Dormio* he explains to the Sister that as she grows in her love of Christ, she will find nothing matters to her but this love and the sin of man which disfigures it, and that all this is focused by thinking on the Passion of Christ:

> And I will þat þou have it mykel in mynde for it will kyndel þi hert to sett at noght all þe gudes of þis worlde and þe joy þarof, and to desyre byrnandly þe lyght of heven.
>
> (65.152–5)

Although in *The Form* he makes it clear to Margaret that it is difficult to be too prescriptive about meditation, since God will put the kind of thoughts into her heart that are right for her,[81] he does say in *Emendatio Vitae* that beginners in spiritual life may find the words of others helpful (8.120.31–2) and on occasions he himself wrote meditations on the Passion which embody his understanding of the catalysis they are designed to help.

The rest of this chapter is concerned with Rolle's ability to find literary means of engaging in various ways with the Passion story so that he can point to the transforming experience of truth, 'kynde knowynge', which is the aim of the meditative exercise. His deliberately composed meditations exemplify his particularly characteristic gifts as a mystical writer in English – to project the elusive processes of the inner experiences of the human condition as live issues. Study of these meditations therefore also illuminates aspects of the inner journey which all the medieval mystics take for granted. For all of them the Passion focuses the terrifyingly destructive forces in human nature and signals the one way by which they are to be rendered ultimately ineffective – a way not isolated in history, but constantly repeated by means of the game of faith. It is a hard game to engage with but meditations on the Passion are designed to enable play. In *Emendatio Vitae* Rolle explains:

> þerfore truly is schewyd þe manhede of Ihesu criste, in þe qwhilk emong man suld be glad, in qwhilk he has mater of Ioy and also mournyng. Ioy for sikyrnes of owr gaynbiyng, heuynes for filth of owr synning, for þe qwhilk it is to heuy þat so worþi a offirynge is offyrd. For þe boystus fleschly sawle into behaldyng of þe godhede is not rauischyd bot if it be gostely, all fleschly lettyngis vastyd.
>
> (8.119.18–24)

> *qwhilk*: which; *sikyrnes*: assurance; *gaynbiyng*: redemption; *heuynes*: distress; *heuy*: grevious; *worþi*: distinguished/excellent; *boystus*: coarse; *rauischyd*: transported; *lettyngis*: obstacles; *vastyd*: destroyed.

His own meditations focus on the paradoxical response of 'Ioy and mournyng' in various ways appropriate to differing stages of inner development. The lyrical meditation proper to the second degree of love that he includes in *Ego Dormio* projects a lightness of spirit as it embodies rhetorically a sense of the joyful reality behind the story which is the goal of the contemplative. The two most powerful prose meditations attributed to Rolle, on the other hand, enact a painful penitential sense of the gap between the sour sterility which is a concomitant of what St Paul calls 'the body of this death' (Romans 7:24) and the joy and creativity of God, though comparison between them reveals different levels of engagement with the same theme.

THE PROSE MEDITATIONS ON THE PASSION

The question of authorship

The shorter and most effective from a literary standpoint survives in only one manuscript where it is attributed to Rolle.[82] It is closely related to a longer version extant in four manuscripts three of which assign it to him.[83] There is, however, a third prose meditation attributed to Rolle. It exists in incomplete form in a manuscript at Longleat House[84] which contains an anthology of Rolle's English writings all, there, recorded as dedicated to Margaret de Kirkeby, and it also exists in an extended form where it is entitled *De passione secundum Ricardum*.[85] It is far less powerful than the other two. In them the meditator projects a dramatisation of his own reaction to the Passion as a present reality. In this, an authoritarian voice addresses the would-be meditator in a series of injunctions to remember the various events in the Passion story and to pray for mercy. The moving immediacy of the situation is diluted and exchanged for a homiletic tone. If it is by Rolle, it would seem to be more of a series of prompts for meditation on the Passion than a fully worked out structure.

Despite the agreement on the attributions to Rolle in the manuscripts, his authorship has been questioned, partly because of the lack of certainty about the authority of scribal attributions, partly because of the absence in the texts of that sense of joy springing from an inner knowledge of the reality of redemption which generally characterises his work.[86] Yet the very specially acute sense of deprivation found in the shorter of the two versions to be examined here argues the recognition of the possibility of the presence of just such joy; 'absence is not non-existence, and we are therefore entitled to repeat, "come, come, come, come:" '[87] and both Rolle's meditations on the Passion are such powerful works precisely because he enacts a sense of the gap between the body of sin and the joy of God and a longing to close it through penitence and love. It is true that knowledge of the probable origins of the meditations in a series of Anglo-Norman prayers points to the possibility that they have been freely adapted by various compilers who may or may not have included Rolle.[88] But it is also true that Rolle was in the habit of reworking old material with variations in different works[89] and that the manuscript ascriptions to him suggest that there was no discomfort in seeing the *Meditations* as part of the Rolle canon in the late medieval period. Certainly they are powerful examples of how meditations on the Passion were designed to work in inner experience and they illuminate aspects of the 'form' of contemplative living in ways characteristic of Rolle.

Liturgical context

It is important to remember the liturgical context of these meditations for it supplies other expressed structures of meaning only latent within them but crucial to their full impact. The meditations project an experience of alienation and deadness from which the meditator longs to be released; he knows at one level that Christ's death is the key to such release:

> whe, lord, a drope of þi blood to droppe on my soule in mynde of þi passyoun may hele al my sore, souple and softe in þi grace þat is so harde, and so dyen whan þi wylle is.
>
> (90.cf.102)

whe: ah!; *mynde*: remembrance; *hele*: heal; *dyen*: dying.

But in this work such knowledge is not projected as that of experience, though it depends on recognition of the possibility of such experience for its validity. Such a recognition was, of course, a commonplace of the faith. It was formulated dogmatically in the catechism and daily celebrated in the memorial of the Passion inherent in the Canonical Hours.[90] It was also embodied in the Hours of the Virgin that daily reminded the devout laity as well as religious, of an archetypal pattern of suffering through which the nature of redemption was manifested and which established the means by which it would be experienced. The pattern of these Hours entered deeply in various ways into the structure of deliberately composed meditations on the Passion and enabled them to imply a greater meaning than they explicitly formulate. The series of vernacular meditations based on the Franciscan *Meditationes Vitae Christi* are quite specifically organised in terms of the Canonical Hours[91] as is the series in the thirteenth-century *Mirror* of St Edmund of Abingdon which was translated from the Latin in the fourteenth century and almost certainly known to Rolle.[92] It throws light on the role of meditation in the 'form' of contemplative living.

The *Mirror*, a work of Victorine piety, is designed to reveal both the state of fallen human nature and what could be if all its potential was fulfilled. The text opens with the words of St Paul to the Ephesians (4:1) *videte vocacionem vestram*; the copy in the manuscript belonging to the Yorkshire man, Robert Thornton, renders this vividly as 'seese ȝowre callynge' [*seese:* take possession of].[93] The calling is to holiness which inheres in knowing the truth and loving goodness ('knowynge of soþnesse, and Loue of godnesse')[94] and comes only with self-knowledge and contemplation of God. The text sets out guidelines for coming to a true sense of priorities in the self, not unlike those in Rolle's *Form*, and then examines three ways in which man can contemplate God: in nature (which shows us our place in creation), in Scripture (which teaches the faith) and on 'God self'. This 'may beo in two Maners: Wiþ-outen, in his Monhede, and wiþ-Innen in his heiȝe Godhede'.[95] The contemplation of the manhood is organised as a series of meditations on the Passion attached to the Canonical Hours in the same order of events as in the Primer but in a more extended form. Juxtaposed to each detail from the Passion sequence is another about the life of Christ which sets the Passion in the context of the scheme of salvation. For example, the betrayal remembered at Matins is juxtaposed with the Nativity; the Crucifixion at Sext with the Annunciation; the death of 'þe makere of lyf, for þi loue' and the withdrawal of sunlight at Nones with the Ascencion.[96] The contemplation on the Godhead is an explanation of the Trinity as God, the original creative power, who enjoys the goodness of company in the Son whose wisdom is bound to himself by the love which is the Holy Ghost. And, says the writer, 'þe selue may eueri man sen in himself' for he has within him the image of the Trinity: a creative power which enables him to know, and to love what he knows. The passage concludes: 'in þis manere þou schalt knowen þi god. Such manere of knowyng is foundement of Contemplacion' [*foundement:* foundation].[97] He then describes the inner movements of contemplative experience in which man is raised above the limits of his nature to a sense of the ultimate reality of God. In the progress of the *Mirror* the meditations (which this text also calls contemplation) on the Passion are one part of the process by which man sees God in himself since it activates the trinitarian structure of the soul and is the means by which the Incarnation is realised and man becomes holy. The process of recollecting the events of the Passion is the catalyst for two kinds of knowledge: knowledge of sin which awakens sorrow, and knowledge of love which awakens joy. This is the knowledge which redeems man and is the basis for the contemplative experience of God as the final transforming reality in which joy and sorrow are perceived as harmony not discord.[98] It is in the context of such liturgical and meditative patterning of the Passion narrative that the two most powerful meditations attributed to Rolle should be studied in order to understand their full potential for helping that transformation of consciousness which is at the heart of mystical experience.

The long and the short prose meditations on the Passion

Both the long and short meditations are presented as prayers in which Rolle counterpoints awareness of the suffering caused by sin in the events of the Passion with a growth in horrified consciousness of the death blows of sin in the self, for which the only remedy is that love manifested in the death of Christ working in man: what Julian will call 'the werkyng of mercy', which lasts as long as sin pursues man, and of grace which works our 'dredful faylyng' into solace and our 'shamefull' 'falling' to resurrection.[99] Rolle's meditations enact the meaning of such grace. In them he isolates the main events of the Passion story for attention in particular ways in the sequence in which they appear in the Hours, except that he begins with the agony in the garden not included there. In this respect his practice contrasts interestingly with that of the *Mirror* of St Edmund where this is remembered at Compline along with the entombment thus suggesting a constant cycle of enactment of the Passion. As one day closes, the agony in the garden reminds man of the whole round of suffering starting again thus prompting that continual sorrow which activates the sacrament of penance, the start of the redemptive process.[100] The suffering involved in facing the enormity of man's potential for sin is the only cure for the greater suffering. The same effect is achieved in the continual cycle of meditations on the Passion in the liturgical Hours of the Cross; they remind man not just of death conquered by death once in the historical events of the Passion, but of a continual process to last until the end of time.

But if Rolle's positioning of the agony in the garden has a simpler impact than that in the *Mirror*, his meditations nevertheless achieve a similar overall effect through his prayerful response to the series of emphasised moments in the Passion narrative. But despite their close similarity there is a marked difference in emphasis and tone between the two versions. The longer one opens with a series of petitions in which the meditator prays for grace to serve God with his whole being. These culminate in the prayer that was also used at each Canonical Hour of the Cross and that brings to mind the glory, joy and life which was man's birthright, forfeited at the Fall but renewed by Incarnation. In the meditation it is given in Latin, the Middle English version from the Primer is:

> Lord ihesu crist, goddis sone of heuene, sette þi passioun, þi cros & þi deeþ, bitwixe þi iugement & oure soulis, now & in our of oure deeþ; & vouche-saaf to ȝyue to lyuynge men merci & grace in þis liyf here; and to hem þat ben deed, forȝyuenesse & reste; to þe chirche & to þe rewme, pees & acoord; & to us synful men, liyf & glorie wiþ-outen ende; þou þat lyuest and regnest god, bi alle worldis of worldis. amen!
>
> *our:* hour.

This tone of penitent confidence in the grace made available through Christ dominates the longer meditation which sustains a formal devotional element that constantly acts as a buffer between the meditator and the subject of his meditation. In the shorter version there are no preliminary prayers recorded and the formal prayer structure which introduces the opening events of the Passion story (as in the long version) is early abandoned in the account of the crucifixion itself in favour of an uninterrupted meditation on Christ's Passion with which the observer is closely identified at many levels.

The nature of this particular kind of identification and of the differences between the two versions can be illustrated even in the formally constructed prayerful episodes. Each opens with thanks addressed to Jesus for the particular incident of the Passion under consideration and closes with a prayer which first applies this incident to aspects of the meditator's own life and then modulates into a set pattern indicated by the Latin directives *Pater Noster, Et ne nos, Adoramus, Aue* [Our Father, And [lead] us not, we praise, Hail]. The seventh prayer in the long version concerns the suffering before Annas, Caiaphas, Pilate and Herod, but more especially the moment when Christ looks at Peter after he has denied him (Luke 22:55–62):

> Swete Ihesu, I þanke þee for alle þe schames, anguischis, & felonyes, þat þou suffridist biforen Annas & Caifas, Pilat & Eroud, & nameli I þanke þee, swete Ihesu, for þat merciful lokinge, þat þou turnynge aȝen biheld upon seint Petir þi disciple þat forsook þee & ȝit in myche anguische þou schewedist þi loue openli to him, so þat neiþer schame ne peine myȝt drawe þin herte fro him. Now, swete Ihesu, turne þin iȝe of merci toward us synful, so þat þoru þi merci and grace we moun repente of oure trespas & mys-dedis with seint Petir. Pater noster.
>
> (p.94)

ȝit: yet; *iȝe*: eye.

The short version, typically, focuses more sharply, concentrating only on the episode with Peter so that there is an identification made between him and the meditator and, by implication, all men who by their natures inevitably betray Christ:

> And among oþere I thanke þe, lord, of þat lokynge þat þou lokyd to þi decyple þat þe hadde forsakyn, seynt Petyr: þou lokyd to hym with syȝt of mercy when þou were in þi most angwysch and in þi most peyne; opynly þou schewyd þere þe loue and þe charyte þat þou hadde to vs, þat schame no peyne ne no thyng may drawe þin herte fro vs, . . .

> Swete lord ful of mercy and of pyte, þere we thorow þi blessyd lokyng may turne to þi grace and repent vs of owre trespas and of owre mysdede, so þat we may come with seynt Petyr to þi mercy. Adoramus; Pater. Aue.
>
> (p.83)

The Longleat version of this subject shows by comparison how much less effective than either of the others it is. The meditator is simply bidden to remember Peter although the identification with him is implicit in the way the incident is juxtaposed to the injunctions to pray:

> Thinke . . . how Iesus bihilde Petir denyande him, and Petir than ȝede forthe and wepte ful sore. . . . Than say this psalme *Miserere mei, deus, secundum magnam misericordiam tuam*, [Have mercy on me O God, according to thy great mercy] and say to the ende, and this orisoun *Absolue, quesumus domine, animas famulorum famularumque tuarum* [We pray thee Lord forgive the souls of thy maidservants and manservants].[101]

Although the formal prayer structure in the long version operates more rigidly and systematically, it is punctuated by lengthy emotive meditations. Thus the account of the scourging opens out into a series of extravagant similes to meditate on Christ's wounded body. It is likened to a heaven full of stars, yet better than such because his wounds are efficacious by day as well as by night, and not only cannot be obscured by clouds but positively drive away clouds of sin; a net full of holes in which the meditator prays to be drawn to the bank of death; a dovecote full of holes of refuge and a honeycomb full of cells of sweet honey; a book written in red ink – matter for the meditator's attention at 'matyns, pryme, houris, euesong & complin'; a meadow full of healing and delightful flowers and herbs (96–7). Here the similes seem to enact a devotional extravaganza which conveys a remarkable feeling of that very elation and joy the absence of which has been remarked upon.[102] The passage brings sharply to attention the powerful and complex ways in which elements of the Passion story may provoke a meditative response. There is a kind of confidence, typified in the prayer to Christ the source of sweet honey-cells of devotion, which is at odds with the stark mood provoked by a revulsion from sin in the whole piece and which is very different from the whole thrust of the short version:

> Now, sweet Ihesu, graunte me grace to touche þee wiþ criynge merci for my synnes, wiþ desiris to gostly contemplacioun, wiþ amendinge of my lijf & contynuaunce in goodnes, in stodie to fulfille þin heestis, & delicat abidinge in mynde of thi passioun. Pater noster. Et ne.
>
> (p.97)

heestis: commands.

The profound realisation of Jesus as a source of grace at the heart of this passage in the long version colours the meditator's longing for it in the other expanded meditations that open out of this sequence of prayers. When he remembers Christ condemned to carry his cross out of Jerusalem to the place of execution, he prays for compassion to identify with the sufferings of Mary, and when Christ is nailed to the cross the meditator's awareness of the deadly processes of sin in himself appropriately obtrudes into the meditation. The tone is distinctly altered from that in the earlier passage on the grace in Christ but it is not unaffected by it:

> I studie in þi passioun & I fynde noo taast: my synnes ben so manye and so wickid þat þei han schit out deuocioun & han stoppid al þe sauour of swetnes from my soule
>
> (p.100)

taast: taste; *schit*: shut.

and the formal Latin prayer which concludes the section is followed by one for grace to feel the love of God, addressed to 'swete Ihesu, þat quikenest þe dede'.

Hereafter, although each meditation on the process of Christ's death is ended by Latin prayers, the opening is only once a formal expression of thanks (significantly when Rolle remembers Christ's cry that he feels forsaken); the other moments are initiated by cries of prayer or remembrance.

> Swete Ihesu, þanne þe iewis heuen up þe cros; . . . Swete ladi maiden & modir, wo was þee bigoon whanne Crist hadde take his leue at þee; . . . Swete Ihesu, þanne criedist þou dolefulli on þe rode.
>
> (100–1)

iewis: Jews; *heuen*: heave; *wo . . . bigoon*: overcome with grief.

The cadences of intense sadness and horror serve to intensify the feeling of devotional longing for a love which will somehow heal this dying process yet is integrally linked with, and expressed through it:

> A, swete Ihesu, þei ȝauen þee poisoun to kele þi þrist wiþ: & þou ȝaue hem þin herte blood to quenche her synnes, & to hele her soulis.[103]
>
> (p.101)
>
> *kele*: cool/quench; *þrist*: thirst; *hele*: heal.

The very repetition of the invocation 'swete Ihesu' which does not appear in the short version gives a feeling of relief.

In this long version the final moment brought to consciousness is the death of Christ when light drains from the cosmos itself and Mary and John are left in sorrow at the foot of the Cross. So, at the point when the meditator ends in prayer that he may always keep this passion in mind, he presents to himself an image which might easily coincide with that on a rood-screen, or painted panel. This might thus serve to bridge the transition between prayer and other forms of activity and also embody a perpetual icon for that prayer and for penitence:

> graunte me, swete ladi, to haue & to holde þis passioun in mynde as hertili & as studiousli in al my lijf, as þou, ladi, & Ioon, hadde it in mynde whanne þe peple weren goon & ȝe abiden bi þe rode foot. Amen.
>
> (p.103)

The shorter version engages with the Passion story much more starkly to project a powerful realisation of the horror of being cut off from all that Christ is – in the words of *The Form of Living* 'he þat hase noght Jhesu Criste, he tynes all þat he has, and all þat he es, and all þat he myght gete' (1.85.19–21). It starts off with the prayer-framed sequence of events up to the point in the narrative when Christ is crowned with thorns and condemned to death, but in a more compressed form. At this point the short version abandons the formal prayer frames and opens out into uninterrupted prose in which meditation on the enormity of what is happening to him 'þat schop the sonne & al þat is ouȝt, of al þe gode in erþe' [*schop*: created; *ouȝt*: anything] (p.85) carries the narrative to the point where Christ leaves Jerusalem; then the meditation on the sorrow of Mary modulates into the account of the death of Christ, the major stages of which are marked by cries of remembrance but unpunctuated by any suggestions for Latin prayer.

The cadence of the prose in the short version often emphasises meaning with a more telling precision than in the long version.

When Christ, beaten and weak, is made to carry the cross, the long version presents it as one element in a series which together compose a 'ruful siȝt'

> þe cros heuy & huge & so hard trust upon þi bak, þat þou art cruyschid to hepe & schrinkist þer-vndir.
>
> (p.98)
>
> *trust*: trussed; *cruyschid*: crushed.

Whereas the short version makes a flat statement:

> þe cros is so heuy, so hye, and so stark, þat þei hangyd on þi bare bac, trossyd so harde
>
> (p.85)
>
> *trossyd*: trussed.

where the strong stresses of sense are counterpointed with the underlying metrically rhythmical dactyls, and the half rhyme on 'stark' and 'harde' brings the whole description to a brutal head. Similarly a few lines further on, in the description of the journey to Golgotha, the long version has 'þus þou goost, swete Ihesu out of Ierusalem toward þi deeþ' (p.99), where the interjection of 'swete Ihesu' interrupts the action of the scene and lends the whole description a devotional tone. The short version moves from polysyllabic words to the final monosyllabic 'deth' and creates a tone of inexorable finality:

> þus in þis gronynge & in þis mychel pyne, þou gost owt of Ierusaleȝ toward þi deth.
>
> (p.85)
>
> *Ierusaleȝ*: Jerusalem.

In both versions Christ is imagined as suffering in all his human senses through the cruel process of crucifixion 'so was þou pyned in þi fiue wyttes, to hele with oure trespas þat we þere-with han wrouȝt' [*pyned*: tormented; *fiue wyttes*: five senses] (87.cf.100) but, unlike the long version, the short version pins this down precisely in a process of blow-by-blow equivalents between sin and sufferings. For example:

> Agayn þe synne of felyng & of euele gatys, were þi handys and þi feet with harde nayles thyrlyd, and fro þe hed to þe feet, with coronynge and scourgynge, with bofetynge and betynge, with spornynge and

puttynge, with harde cordys knyttynge, and on þe cros streynynge, þou wolde, gloryous lord, for me harde be pyned.[104]

(p.88)

gatys: ways; *thyrlyd*: pierced; *spornynge*: scorning; *puttynge*: rejection; *harde be pyned:* sorely be tormented.

The understood realities of redemptive love and a feeling of separation from them break into the narrative sequence of both versions. In the short text the account of the Crucifixion and the meditator's awareness of his own sin come to a climax in an outpouring of lyrical prose which has been printed as verse[105] though it seems more effective if the surge of the rhymes and the alliterative cadences rise within the very structure of the prose like great waves to break in the bitter realisation that it is the meditator's sin which both nails Christ to the cross and blocks the free expression of love in himself:

A, lord kyng of myȝt, þat leuyn woldust þi myȝt & os vnmyȝty become my wrongys to ryȝte: what is it þat I speke & bete þe wynd? I speke of þe felyng of þe & fynde I no taste, I blondre in my wyrkyng os man þat is blynd, I studye in my thouȝtes and þei wyrken al wast: it is tokenyng of my deth, and fylthe of my synne, þat slayn hath my sowle & stoke is þere-Inne, and stoppyth al þe sauoure, þat I may nouȝt the fele, þat so schamely haue ben þi tretoure vntrewe; it myȝt be a prison, gloryouse lord, to þi godhed; þe stynke of my schame, þe sorwe of my soule, þe fylthe of my mouthe, ȝyf I lykke þere-onne it fylyth þi name: so may I no manere þe swetnesse of the taste, þat I haue lost thorow synne to han lykyng of swyche comfort – for I blondre gladly in lustys of many dyuerse blamys.

(p.87)

os: as; *blondre*: blunder; *wyrken al wast*: come to nothing; *stoke*: fastened; *tretoure*: traitor; *lykke*: lick; *fylyth*: defiles.

All the internal rhyme, play on words (myȝty/vnmyȝty, wrongys to ryȝte) and alliteration, which intensify the sense of the meditator's awareness of both the creative power of God 'king of myȝt' and the impotence of all his own functions, are lost in the long version which omits much of the intense self-disgust present in the short:

A, lord swete Ihesu, þat woldist vnmyȝti bicome to make me myȝti & mende my synne, I speke, lord, of þi passioun and of hiȝ deuocioun & I fynde no swetnes, but speke as a iay & noot what I meene; I studie in þi passioun & I fynde noo taast: my synnes ben so manye and so wickid þat þei han schit out deuocioun & han stoppid al þe sauour of swetnes from my soule, & þerfore I speke & blundere forþ as a blinde creature, & speke wiþouten wisdom or kunnynge of so deuoute mater.

(p.100)

iay: jay; *noot*: do not know; *schit*: shut.

The emphasis on Christ as the source of life and creativity is similarly highlighted in the short version in the skilful use made of rhyme, cadence and monosyllabic, strong-stressed ends of sentences to graphically convey the moment when he dies and the created cosmos fails:

. . . þou saydest at þe laste: *Consummatum est*, þat is: 'Al is endyd.' þanne fel doun þine hed, and þe gost went owt. þe erþe þanne tremblede, þe sonne lost hys lyȝt: þat al merk was þe wedur os it hadde ben nyȝt.

(p.91)

merk: dark.

These effects are lost in the prosaic longer version:

Swete Ihesu, þanne seidist þou last 'Al is endid': þan fel þin heed doun, þi goost passide from þe, þe erþe tremblide, þe sunne lost his liȝt, dede men risen out of her graues, þe temple to-cleef, – stones al to-bursten; – þo weren witnessis of þi godhede.

(p.103)

to-cleef: split.

In both versions the meditator contemplates the appalling inversion of the created order with its lord suffering greater deprivation than the foxes and birds as he hangs 'in þe eyre' (88.cf.101) with nowhere to lay his head – a reference to Matthew 8:20 traditionally used to emphasise the poverty of God embraced at the Incarnation.[106] Both bring into play the Easter office and order for the Mass on Good Friday where Christ is given words of reproach based on texts from Lamentations, Jeremias and Micheas (Micah) to stress the contrast between God's goodness to his people under the old covenant and their crucifixion of his Son. But whereas the long version refers only to the words in Lamentations 1:12 (O all ye that pass by the way, attend, and see if there be any sorrow like unto my sorrow), the short version incorporates all the references to focus more sharply on the organic relationship between man and Christ whose natural growth is blasted by sin:

> Ihesu, why were it nouȝt my deth þe dool and þe sorewe, whan I thenk in my thouȝt whou reufully þou spake whan þou sayde: 'Alle ȝe þat passyth by þe way, abydeth and byholdyth ȝyf euere ony peyne þat euere soffred any man, or ony wordely woo, be lyk þe sorwe þat I soffre for synful mannys sake,' Nay, lord, nay, þere was neuere non so hard, for it was makeles; of alle peynys þat euere were, so hard was neuur fowndyn. And ȝyt seydys þou, lord, so swetely and so mekely: *Vinea mea electa, ego te plantaui*: þat is: 'My dere vynȝerde', seydust þou, þat is, my dere chosen, 'haue I nouȝt my-self þe plauntyd? why art þou so bytter?' *Popule meus, quid feci tibi* : þat is 'My swete, what haue I þe don? haue I þe wratthyd, þat þou dost me þis woo? haue I not ȝeuyn þe al my self, and al þat euere þou hast, and lyf with-owten ende ȝef þou it wyl take, my body to þi foode, and to deth on rode, and hyȝt þe al my-selue in heuene to þi mede? haue I with my gode dede hyrtyd þe so sore, or with my swete dawntynge greuyd þin herte? [107]
>
> (p.88)

dool: grief; *whou*: how; *wordely*: worldly; *makeles*: without equal; *mede*: reward; *dawntynge*: overcoming.

And only in the short version does the meditator acknowledge this by identifying himself with the penitent thief pleading for pardon to be extended to him, and confessing his failure to acknowledge Christ as the true source of his integrity:

> Lord, for þi mercy, þat welle art of mercy, say to me þat am þi thef þat þou to hym sayde – for I haue stole þi gode dedys, and vsyd mys þi grace, þe wyttus and þe vertues þat þou to me hast lent.
>
> (p.88)

mys: wrongly; *wyttus*: senses.

In both versions the meditator admits that the very ability to recognise the life-giving power in Christ is a sign that he in fact has the love of God even if he does not feel it:

> But wel I wot þis þat I haue rad, þat who-so ȝernyth and sekyth a-ryȝte: þou he fele þe nouȝt, he hath þat he wot nouȝt, þi loue of godhede . . .
>
> (p.87.cf.p.100)

rad: read; *ȝernyth*: desires; *wot*: know.

And in both, as the meditator sees his betrayal and sense of deprivation borne by Christ in His words: 'My god, my dere god, why hastow al forsakyn me . . . (89.cf.102) he imagines himself lying down among the bones of dead men on mount Calvary, taking the foot of the Cross in his arms, the stench of death in his nostrils. It is a powerful icon: Christ and man identified in accepting the consequences of sin, but differentiated by the sign of the unfailing creativity of the love of God – life-blood. Both versions thus make play with the paradox of life and health through suffering and death, but the short version makes a much more pointed and concentrated use of the theme. Right at the very beginning, in the prayer which arises from the memory of Christ's anguish in the garden of Gethsemane when the narrator remembers 'þou swattest blod for angwysche', the shorter version identifies this sweat with that which marks the healing and turning point of human fever conflating it with the sweat of human anguish struggling against evil. In this way Christ's suffering from sin at the Passion, and man's penance, are seen as part of one sacramental healing process:

> I preye þe, lord, and byseche þe for þi swete mercy, þat þou be myn help in al myn angwysch and my fondynges, and send me, lord, þe aungel of red and of confort in alle my nedys: þat I myȝte turne thorow þat swet owt of al sekenesse of soule in to lyf of hele of body.
>
> (p.83)

fondynges: trials; *red*: counsel; *confort*: comfort.

Such perception is foregrounded again at the point when the meditator devotionally embraces the cross. Like Eliot's sharply witty version of this paradox:

> The wounded surgeon plies the steel
> That questions the distempered part;
> Beneath the bleeding hands we feel
> The sharp compassion of the healer's art
> Resolving the enigma of the fever chart,[108]

the meditator in the short text exclaims:

> Come þanne at þi wylle, heuenelyche leche, and lyȝten me sone os þou my nede knowyst; a sparkle of þi passyoun, of loue and of reuthe, kyndele in myn herte to quycnen it with: so þat al brennyng in loue ouur al thynge, al þe world I may forgete, and baþe me in þi blood.
>
> (p.90)

leche: physician; *brennyng*: burning; *ouur*: over.

But the force of this metaphor of healing is lost, together with the lyrical cadences of alliteration, in the long version:

Come þanne, swete Ihesu, at þi wille, & liȝte in to my soule as þou for best knowist a sparcle of loue.

(p.103)

liȝte: light.

This existentially known contrast between the body of death through which is encountered the possibility of life is at the heart of Christian mysticism itself experienced in playing the game of faith which renews the truth of the Incarnation. A few years later than the time Rolle was writing, Langland made verbal play with the paradox to point to the transcending truth that Will perceives. The figure of Mercy points to the nature of the redemptive process:

'Thorugh experience' quod heo, ' I hope thei shul be saved.
For venym fordooth venym – and that I preve by reson.
For of alle venymes foulest is the scorpion;
May no medicyne amende the place ther he styngeth,
Til he be deed and do therto – the yvel he destruyeth,
The firste venymouste, thorough vertu of hymselve.
So shal this deeth fordo – I dar my lif legge
Al deeth dide first thorugh the develes entisyng;
And right as thorugh [gilours] gile [bigiled was man],
So shal grace that al bigan make a goode ende
[And bigile the gilour – and that is good] sleighte:
Ars ut artem falleret.[109]

heo: she; *preve*: prove; *and do therto*: placed upon it; *venymouste*: poison; *vertu*: power; *fordo*: destroy; *legge*: wager; *entisyng*: tempting; *gilours gile*: deceiver's guile; *sleighte*: stratagem; *Ars ut artem falleret*: strategy to foil strategy.

Later still, Julian of Norwich, whose mystical experience arose out of meditation on the Passion, defined her sense of a dynamic power of divine love working to process the effects of sin as the work of Christ: 'and there is in him bleding and praying for us to the Father – and is and shall be as long as it nedith'.[110]

The purpose of both versions of Rolle's Meditations on the Passion is the same: to stimulate that penance and love which can bridge the gap between man and God – a gap that Julian was to express in her realisation that in her longing for God 'nothyng letted me but synne, and so I beheld generally in us al'.[111] But whereas the long version sustains a note of quiet confidence in the efficacy of penitential meditation on the Passion to enable this, the short version uses literary resources to embody a horrifying sense of what it means to be trapped in the body of this death (sin) contrasted to the life in love to be embraced in Christ where death has no actual dominion. The contrast in emphasis in meditative engagement with the same theme between the two pieces is taken further in their endings. The long version leaves the sinner in sustained penitential mood with Mary at the foot of the Cross – ('still mowrning').[112] But the short version points to a promise of progress in experience beyond the stage of penitent sorrow. It moves to the description of the deposition at 'os it were tyme of euynsonge'(p.91) and entombment, ending quietly with the event recorded in Matthew's Gospel (27:66) 'þenne was þere warde set of armede kny3tes, to kepe þe monument tyl þe thrydde day'.(p.91) This final sentence is evocative of all that is not stated about the sequel to the Passion. The sorrow and guarded watchfulness in the darkness of the external events of the story is counterpart for the inner penitential awareness of the meditator, but at the heart of the darkness there is certainty of light in the Resurrection of the 'thrydde day'. This is the faith which underlies the bleakest expressions of the meditator's sense of evil. The most negative moment of withdrawal contains all the potential for new growth. The Primer expresses it:

Fro cros, crist was takun doun
  At euesong tyme, we fynde;
Power of resurreccioun
  Was hid in goddis mynde[113]

and in contemplative understanding the historical resurrection of love is experienced as an inner reality more powerful than the block of sin (guarded tomb) that separates man from Christ. It is to such renewed life and joy that the meditation on the Passion in *Ego Dormio* points.

MEDITATION ON THE PASSION IN *EGO DORMIO*

It has been said that the *Meditations on the Passion* are proper to beginners in spiritual life.[114] It is certainly true that they enact an awareness of the efficacy of penance which is at the very foundation of Christian spirituality; but it also true that part of their potency depends on an understanding of the joy of 'brennyng in loue ouur al thynge' when:

'schal I blesse þe tyme þat I fele me so styred to þe of þi grace þat al wordely wele & fleschely lykyng ageyn þe thouȝt of þi deth lykyth me nouȝt.

(p.90)

ageyn: against, in comparison with.

The meditation on the Passion in *Ego Dormio*, on the other hand, engages directly with the experience of receiving such a gift. Its chanting quality sounds a note of buoyancy and music in the evocation of the enormity of the Crucifixion. This runs freely at the end of the lyric composition as finally the speaker explicitly asserts his capacity to sing for love.

My keyng, þat water grette and blode swette;
Sythen ful sare bette, so þat hys blode hym wette,
When þair scowrges mette.
Ful fast þai gan hym dyng and at þe pyler swyng,
And his fayre face defowlyng with spittyng.

þe thorne crownes þe keyng; ful sare es þat prickyng.
Alas! my joy and my swetyng es demed to hyng,
Nayled was his handes, nayled was hys fete,
And thyrled was hys syde, so semely and so swete.

Naked es his whit breste, and rede es his blody syde;
Wan was his fayre hew, his wowndes depe and wyde.
In fyve stedes of his flesch þe blode gan downe glyde
Als stremes of þe strande; hys pyne es noght to hyde.

þis to see es grete pyte, how he es demed to þe dede
And nayled on þe rode tre, þe bryght aungels brede.
Dryven he was to dole, þat es owre gastly gude,
And alsso in þe blys of heven es al þe aungels fude.

A wonder it es to se, wha sa understude,
How God of mageste was dyand on þe rude.
Bot suth þan es it sayde þat lufe ledes þe ryng;
þat hym sa law hase layde bot lufe it was na thyng.

Jhesu, receyve my hert, and to þi lufe me bryng;
Al my desyre þou ert, I covete þi comyng.
þow make me clene of synne, and lat us never twyn.
Kyndel me fire within, þat I þi lufe may wyn,
And se þi face, Jhesu, in joy þat never sal blyn.

Jhesu, my saule þou mend; þi lufe into me send,
þat I may with þe lend in joy withowten end.

In lufe þow wownde my thoght, and lyft my hert to þe.
My sawle þou dere hase boght; þi lufer make it to be.
þe I covete, þis worlde noght, and for it I fle.
þou ert þat I have soght, þi face when may I see?
þow make my sawle clere, for lufe chawnges my chere.
How lang sal I be here?
When mai I negh þe nere, þi melody to here,
Oft to here sang,
þat es lastand so lang?
þou be my lufyng,
þat I lufe may syng.

keyng: king; *grette*: wept; *sythen ful sare bette*: afterwards very severely beaten; *dyng*: beat; *swyng*: scourge; *demed*: condemned; *hyng*: hang; *thyrled*: pierced; *hew*: complexion; *brede*: bread; *owre:* our; *lufe ledes þe ryng*: love leads the ring; *law*: low; *twyn*: part; *blyn*: cease; *lend*: dwell; *lufer:* lover; *for:* from; *chere*: expression; *negh*: approach.

Athough the text is sometimes represented in stanzas,[115] it does not appear as verse in all the manuscripts.[116] In fact it makes its point more powerfully if it is seen as prose but heard or read as poetry since the meditation then enacts for the reader that speech-become-song meditation-become-poem that Rolle talks of in *The Fire of Love*. It thus points to the way in which meditation is the very 'halsynge of Rachel'. Furthermore, the stanzas obscure the fact that the use of rhyme shapes significant units of sense, since the rhyme scheme then cuts across the stanza forms. This becomes clearer by looking at the first two stanzas.

Here the rhyming unit begun by *grette* brings to mind both interior and exterior pain: Christ's solitary agony in the garden and the pain of scourging. It nevertheless addresses the sufferer as *king*, thus defining the relationship between meditator and Christ and establishing the twin poles of thought – sovereignty and suffering. The second rhyme on *dying* emphasises the deforming physical violence which precedes the final judgement to death, and provides the stark reminder that this action kills joy: 'alas! my joy and my swetyng es demed to hyng'. The third rhyme on *fete* isolates the image of the five wounds and modulates into an extended description of this on a new rhyme. This fourth unit, edited as the third stanza, is, in fact, borrowed from a current Middle English verse paraphrase of lines in a Latin meditation[117] and provides some justification for printing out the whole piece in stanza form. The description of the five wounds prepares for the fifth unit, which fuses memory of the outrage of the historical Passion story with its sacramental meaning, as the bread of heaven is, in effect, rubbished on the Cross. The sixth unit rams home the enormity of such an act, but the sacramental references have already introduced the joy latent in the horror. Then, just at the moment when the full sacrilege of what happened is described, there is a change of tone as Rolle initiates the seventh rhyme scheme chiming with *ryng*, and refocuses the actions of hideous brutality as the means by which the voluntary ring-dance of love is patterned. The leader has shown the way and the dancers respond:

> Bot suth þan es it sayde þat lufe ledes þe ryng;
> þat hym sa law hase layde bot lufe it was na thyng.
>
> Ihesu, receyve my hert, and to þi lufe me bryng;
> Al my desyre þou ert, I covete þi comyng.

This 'comyng', works at several levels: that of the reality of the sacraments, the promise of the Second Coming, and the anticipation of a longed-for coming in mystical experience. All three are part of one pattern, defined by Christ, but experienced within the penitential life of the meditator: no resurrection without death, no joy without sorrow, no feeling of the presence of love without sometimes consciousness of its absence, and all three comings relate to an overcoming of sin.

So the rest of the meditation turns on overcoming of separation from God through the fire of love. The tenth rhyming unit on *thoght* and *þe* brings together the Passion that started the meditation and the inner desire of the speaker, through the image of the wound of love which will impel the soul to God. Stressed monosyllables enforce the recognition of Jesus as the goal of longing: þou ert þat I have soght'. The last seven lines on three rhymes break the pattern of units of sense on single rhymes as the meditator signals by means of the present tense: 'lufe chawnges my chere', the possibility of transformation to a state where he can hear the melody to which love dances, and he ends with a statement of faith, 'þou be my lufyng, þat I lufe may syng'. This meditation works by recalling the isolated moments of the Passion story familiar in other meditations and in the liturgy – the agony in the garden, the scourging, the crowning with thorns, the Crucifixion itself – but using the resources of rhetoric to embody a sense of the joyful reality behind the story which such meditation is designed to enable. It enacts in its form a faith that the experience of broken suffering in time is in reality the choreography and notation for the dance and music of love and Rolle advises his disciple that meditation on this reality will draw up her heart 'so þat þe egh of þi hert mai loke intil heven' (69.261–2).

Rolle's gifts as a writer enable him to convey the flavour of a variety of levels of religious awareness and all his English writings are worth exploring with this in mind. In *The Form of Living* he charts the sacramental understanding at the heart of the Mass, as a whole way of life and perceived growth in consciousness; his *Meditations on the Passion* engage with different stages of such growth and, indeed, are designed to act as catalysts for its progress. All are devotional art work to signify the nature of the contemplative journey for those starting out.

NOTES

1. See below pp.215–6, 218.
2. See Collis (1964); Watson (1991). References to this study of Rolle's work which appeared after this book was completed are included where possible.
3. Cf. in our own day Merton (1949); Harvey (1991).
4. The priory is now in ruins but originally lay across what is now a street, on land sloping down to a stream. See further, Allen (1966), pp.524–5.
5. See Comper (1969),p.314. See further *Officium De S Ricardo De Hampole* in *The York Breviary*, (1882) vol.2, Appendix v.
6. Rolle's canonisation was never finally effected. For translation of the material relating to his life in the *Office* prepared for him see Allen (1966), pp.51–61; Comper (1969), pp.301–14. All page references given below to translations from the *Office* refer to Allen (1966).
7. Oscar Wilde: *Lady Windermere's Fan*, Act 3.
8. Trans. Wolters (1972). All references are to chapter and page numbers in this edition.
9. See *The Honor and Forest of Pickering* (1895, 2, p.273).
10. pp.55–6. Cf. the tone of the *Instructions to a Devout and Literate Layman*, p.45 above.
11. See Allen (1966), p.436.

12. See above p.43.

13. p.57.

14. See Dugdale *Monasticon* vi.pt iii.p.1590. (Cf. Comper, 1969.p.56.)

15. p.56. See further Watson (1991, p.42).

16. p.56.

17. p.56.

18. See further Allen (1966), pp.458–9.

19. See *Office*, p.57.

20. *Ibid*, p.58.

21. See Allen (1966), pp.77, 121, 487 and references cited.

22. See Allen (1966), pp.490–500; Sargent (1988); Watson (1991, p.37).

23. See further Watson (1991, esp. Introd. and Chapters 6 and 7).

24. *Ibid*, p.59. Richmondshire covered the western parts of Yorkshire and Lancashire and part of what is now Cumbria. See McCall (1910, xxiii).

25. *Office*, p.59.

26. See Ogilvie-Thomson (1988), xv and lxvii. She points out that the contents of MS Longleat 29, Rolle's English texts, *The Form of Living, Ego Dormio, The Commandment, Desire and Delight, Ghostly Gladness*, five lyrics and a fragment of a prose meditation on the Passion are all dedicated to *Margaretam reclusam de Kyrkby*. She develops Allen's argument (1963, p. 60) that *Ego Dormio* (see below pp.79 and 105f). which, in one manuscript (Cambridge University Library Dd v 64) is dedicated to a nun of Yedingham, is in fact written for a secular before entering religious life, and conjectures that it may have been written for Margaret in 1343 when she entered on her religious vocation.

27. Allen (1966), p.60.

28. Allen (1966), p.430.

29. See Allen (1966, pp.518–20) but cf Watson (1991, p.325n.8).

30. *The Mending of Life*, ed. Harvey (1896).

31. See above p.14–15.

32. See Knowles (1927, pp.78–80); (1961, p.54); Wakelin (1979, esp. p.198); R. Allen (1984, p.32); Clark (1983, p.116); Watson (1991, pp.260f.).

33. See Hilton, *Scale 1*, c.10; *Scale 2*, c.30; (see below pp.152–3); *The Cloud of Unknowing*, chapters 52–3.

34. *De Reductione Artium ad Theologiam* (1955. pp.30–7, 11–20).

35. See above pp.18–20, 65–6.

36. For background to this aspect of contemplative life see for example Augustine *De Consensu Evangelistarum* I. Chapter V. 8. *PL* 34. 1045–6; *De Trinitate* Book XII; Gregory the Great, *Moralia in Job*, ed. M. Adriaen (1979, *Liber*, V, xxxi, 55. pp.256–8. See also *The Cloud of Unknowing*, where the author sees the inner activity involved in penance and meditation as an area of overlap between the active and contemplative lives: 'þe hiȝer party of actyue liif & þe lower party of contemplatiue' (8.17.35).

37. For an account of his Latin works see Allen (1966), chapters 4, 5, 6, 7, 10. See also Watson (1991).

38. His English works consist of an *English Psalter*, several lyrics, three treatises: *Ego Dormio, The Commandment, The Form of Living*, some short prose pieces which approximate to poetry, *The Bee and the Stork, Desire and Delight, Ghostly Gladness* and the *Meditations on the Passion.*

39. All references for the *Form, Ego Dormio* and *The Commandment* are to Allen (1963) in the order chapter, page, line.

40. See *MED, sub* 'forme', esp 3.

41. See above p.21 See further Dix (1945, chapter IX).

42. See Allen (1963), pp.83f.; Rygiel (1978).

43. T.S. Eliot, *Four Quartets*: 'Little Gidding'.

44. Cf. *Ancrene Wisse*, p.15 above.

45. See above p.67, notes 32 and 33.

46. Rolle borrowed this schematic analysis from *Compendium Theologicae Veritatis*, by Hugo Argentinensis. See references given in Ogilvie-Thomson (1988), p.196.

47. See above p.18.

48. Cf. *The Cloud of Unknowing*, 2.8.19–22.

49. Gerard Manley Hopkins, *God's Grandeur.*

50. See Robbins (1942). Cf *Lay Folks Mass Book* (1879, p.40).

51. *Lay Folks Mass Book* (1879), p.36. See also above pp.21–2.

52. *Ibid*, p.108. *Unde et memores, Domine, nos tui servi, sed et plebs tua sancta ejusdem Christi Filii tui Domini Dei nostri tam beatae passionis,necnon et ab inferis resurrectionis, sed et in caelos gloriosae ascensionis, offerimus praeclarae maiestati tuae de tuis donis ac datis. Hostiam puram, hostiam sanctam, hostiam immaculatam, panem sanctum vitae eternae, et calicem salutis perpetuae.*

53. *De Quattuor Gradibus Violentae Charitatis, PL* 196, 1213.

54. T.S. Eliot, *Four Quartets:* 'Little Gidding'.

55. See Jennings (1975, pp.198–9).

56. See further Clark (1983. p.125).

57. See above note 26.

58. Cf. *The Cloud of Unknowing*, 8. and pp.18–19 above.

59. T.S. Eliot, *Four Quartets:* 'East Coker'.

60. *Ibid.*

61. See further Gillespie (1982).

62. See for instance *The Form* in Oxford Bodleian Library, MS Rawlinson A. 389; Vernon Sum. Cat, 3938; Cambridge University Library MS Dd V 64. London British Library, MS Add 22283; Add 37790.

63. See Comper (1969) pp. 141f. and references cited. See also Gray (1992), lyrics no. 47, 48, 49, 51, 53b and d.

64. See Gray (1967).

65. *The Cloud of Unknowing*, 7.15.31–3, 38.

66. Cf. *Mending*, 11.123.30.

67. Cf. *Mending*, 11.123–4, 38–1.

68. Cf. *Mending*, 11.124.14–15.

69. CUL MS Dd V 64.

70. See Isaiah 11.1–3 *Et egredietur virga de radice Iesse, et flos de radice eius ascendet. Et requiescat super eum spiritus Domini: spiritus sapientiae, et intellectus, spiritus consilii, et fortitudinis, spiritus scientiae, et pietatis. Et replebit eum spiritus timoris Domini:* (Vulgate). [And there shall come forth a rod out of the root of Jesse, and a flower shall rise up out of his root. And the spirit of the Lord shall rest upon him: the spirit of wisdom, and of understanding, the spirit of counsel, and of fortitude, the spirit of knowledge, and of godliness. And he shall be filled with the spirit of the fear of the Lord.] These seven qualities were early interpreted as virtues given by the Holy Spirit and linked with other series of sevens, the petitions of the Lord's prayer, the beatitudes and the seven deadly sins. For a medieval exposition see *The Book of Vices and Virtues*, ed. Francis (1942, pp. 116f.).

71. In MS Thornton, Lincoln Cathedral 91, and BL Arundel 507.

72. See above p.18.

73. See above p.29.

74. See Guigo II translated by Colledge and Walsh (1978, III, pp.82–3). For further discussion see Tugwell (1984) chapters 9–11.

75. See *Aelred of Rievaulx's De Institutione Inclusarum,* Ayto and Barrett (1984, chapter 14, pp.17 and 39).

76. See William of St Thierry, *Golden Epistle*, trans. Shewring (1930, c14, 44, p.79). For a further account of the development of prayer see William of St Thierry, *Exposition on the Song of Songs,* trans. Hart (1970, Preface, 12–25, pp.10–19).

77. See further Clark (1983).

78. Cf. St Augustine, *Enarratio in Psalmum LXXXV, PL* 37, 1086.

79. See above p.18.

80. 'Gladly þerfore tribulaciions ar to be suffyrd in aduersite . . . for be þis & slike oþer owr synnes ar clensyd & medis encryssyd. Truly awder behoues vs in þis lyfe with fyre of purgatory or hell bitterliest be crucifyd & ponyschid. Cheis þerfore, þe tone we sall not scape' [*slike oþer:* other similar; *medis*: rewards]. *Mending*, 6.116.15–20.

81. cf. Hilton, *Scale* 1.34. where he talks of meditation as the free gift of God bestowed in ways peculiarly appropriate to the make-up of particular individuals.

82. CUL MS Ll I 8. The colophon reads: *Explicit quedam meditacio Ricardi heremite de hampole de passione domini* . . . [Here is set out a certain meditation of Richard, hermit of Hampole, about the passion of the Lord.]

83. CUL Addit. MS 3042: 'Here bigynneþ deuoute meditaciouns of þe passioun of Crist whiche weren compilid of Richard Rolle hermyte of Hampol, . . . ; Bodley e Museo 232: Here begynnethe a deuout meditacion vp þe passioun of crist Imade by Richard Rolle heremyt of hampoll'; Uppsala Univ C 494.

84. MS Longleat 29.

85. BL Cotton Titus cxix. See further Ogilvie-Thomson (1988), xcii.

86. For an account of the manuscripts see Allen (1966), pp.278–87; see also Morgan (1953), p.101. For further reading on Rolle and the theme of the Passion see Madigan (1978).

87. E. M. Forster, *Passage to India*, c.19.

88. See Morgan (1953).

89. See for instance the similarities between the *Commandment* and *The Form*. See also Allen (1966, p. 281); note 46 above; Watson (1991, e.g. Introd.).

90. See above pp.30–31.

91. Eg. *The Privity of the Passion: Bonaventura de mysteriis passionis Iesu Christi,* (Thornton MS) ed. Horstman (1895), I, pp.198–218; *Medytacyuns of þe Soper of oure lorde Ihesu,* ed. Cowper (1885), 1–24; Nicholas Love, *The Mirrour of the Blessyd Lyf of Jesu Christ,* ed. Powell (1908).

92. Ed. Horstman (1895, I. pp.219–61). See further Sister Mary Philomena (1964); Forshaw (1971, 1972).

93. Horstman, I. p.219.

94. Horstman, I. III. p.241. All further references to this text are from this volume of Horstman.

95. *Ibid*, p.254.

96. *Ibid*, pp.254–7.

97. *Ibid*, p.259.

98. See also Pollard (1985).

99. See *A Revelation of Love* (1976), c.35, p.36; c. 48. p.51.

100. In the Longleat version of Rolle's meditation the speaker spells it out rather ponderously: 'I say, thou wrecched caitife, sithen, thou schalt ʒiue a rekenyng of the leste thouʒte, vmbithinke the how thou hast spended this day, whiche is ordened to the to spende to the loouynge of thi lord and helthe of thi soule. Bethinke the, and begynne at morne, and so from houre to houre and fro tyme to tyme til thou comme at euene, and than of that thou hast trespassed aske mercy. And also soon as thou mayist, comme to thi confessioun, and rise oute þereof and than say "Lord, I haue this day and al my life falsly and wickedly despended aʒeyns thi louynge and the helthe of my soule".' Ogilvie-Thomson (1988), p.67.147–155).

101. Ogilvie-Thomson (1988), pp.65–6, 75–84.

102. See Morgan (1953).

103. See Schmidt (1983), p.174f.

104. Cf. the long version: 'in felinge, swete Ihesu, þou were þeined in þi bindinge and hariynge, buffetinge, blindfelling, scourginge, crowninge, in beringe of þe cros' (p.101).

105. See Allen (1963), pp.24–5, 183–192.

106. See Schmidt (1983) pp.188–92 and references cited.

107. The following references to the liturgy are taken from *Brevarium Ad Usum Insignis Ecclesiae Sarum*, eds Procter and Wordworth (1882); *The Sarum Missal*, ed. Legge (1916); *The York Breviary* (1879, 1882); *The York Missal* (1872).
The relationship of the passage from Rolle to the liturgy is as follows:

(a) 'Alle ȝe þat passyth . . . mannys sake' based on Lamentations 1:12 used in Sarum Office for Good Friday, Matins, in primo Nocturno, lectio i: *O vos omnes qui transitis per viam, attendite et videte si est dolor sicut dolor meus*. [O all ye that pass by the way, attend, and see if there be any sorrow like to my sorrow.] (I.dcclxxxvii). Cf. *York Breviary*, 71, 401, Sabbato Pasche, Lauds, Antiphon.

(b) *Vinea mea electa* . . . so bytter' based on Jeremias 2:21 used in Sarum Office for Good Friday, Matins, in secundo Nocturno, after Lectio iii: Response 4. *Vinea mea electa ego te plantavi. Quomodo conversa es in amaritudinem: ut me crucifigeres et Barabam dimitteres*. [My chosen vineyard I planted thee. How are you turned into bitterness that you Crucify me and release Barabas.] Versicle. *Ego quidem plantavi te vinea mea electa omne semen verum. Quomodo conversa es*. [Yet I planted thee a chosen vineyard, all true seed. How then art thou turned . . .] (I.dcclxxxix). Cf. *York Breviary*, 71, 390, Good Friday, Matins, in Primo nocturno, Response and Versicle after Lectio iii.

(c) *Popule meus* . . . þe don?' based on Micheas (Micah) 6:3 used in Sarum Mass on Good Friday in the Reproaches which occur after the Epistle, Gospel and subsequent prayers: *Populus meus, quid feci tibi aut in quo contristavi te?* [O my people, what have I done to thee, or in what have I molested thee?] (*Sarum Missal*, p.112). Cf. *York Missal*, 105. This is also an Antiphon at Lauds on Passion Sunday in the Sarum Office (I,dccxxviii).

108. *Four Quartets*: 'East Coker'.

109. *Piers Plowman* (1978), Passus XVIII, pp.224–5, 151–62.

110. *A Revelation of Love*, c.12. p.15.

111. *Ibid*, c.27. p.28.

112. See above p.98 and p.80.

113. The *Prymer* (1895), p.30.

114. See Allen (1963), p.18. See above p.35.

115. Allen (1963), pp.67–9.

116. See Oxford Bodleian Library, MS Rawlinson A 389 ff. 77–81; Vernon Sum. Cat. 3938, ff.369–70; CUL, MS Dd V 64, ff.22b–9. BL, MS Add. 22283f. 150b-1b; Add. 37790f. 132.–5b.

117. See Carleton Brown (1952), p.1. It appears to derive ultimately from lines in *Liber Meditationem* attributed to Augustine, see *PL* XI.906.

Chapter 3

Walter Hilton: The Heritage of Health

Richard Rolle's at times flamboyant attempt to arrive at a form of living which would express his compulsive and impulsive drive towards personal realisation of the love of God, brought the circumstances of his life into prominence. In contrast we know little of the life of Walter Hilton. Manuscript sources state that he was an Augustinian canon at Thurgarton in Nottinghamshire[1] and some also state that he died there on 23 or 24 March, 1395–96.[2] His major work, however, which became known as *The Scale of Perfection* was extremely popular in his own time. A large number of manuscript copies survive, some owned by lay people like John Kilham, a London merchant[3], and it was printed in 1494 at the command of Lady Margaret Tudor the mother of Henry Vll. Whereas Rolle's poetic understanding of spiritual life embodied in his English works makes them like flares sent up to illuminate dark ground, each a light but each separate, Hilton's *Scale* brings into the daylight a carefully worked out map of spiritual life with each of the major stages interconnected.

There is some evidence that he received formal academic training at Cambridge.[4] He is called *Magister* in the manuscripts, a title reserved for doctors of theology.[5] In addition to this, one manuscript describes him as 'comensour of decrees and Chanoun of Thurgurtoun', another as *decretorum inceptoris* and it has been argued that this implies a training in Canon Law.[6] Certainly the careful structuring and methodical scrupulosity of his vernacular works on the development of spiritual life betoken an academic training.

His involvement with the practicalities of such development seems to have been at the level of experience as well as theory. Harley MS 2397 calls him 'maister Watir hiltone hermyte'.[7] Sometime about 1382 he wrote an epistle (*De Imagine Peccati*) to his friend Adam Horsley, a priest, who was an official of the

Exchequer, encouraging him in his intention to become an enclosed religious. In this epistle he indicates that he himself, at the time of writing, is a solitary attracted by the disciplined life of service in a religious order, but does not feel any burning conviction that that is his calling:

> I confess, alas, that I do not feel that burning spiritual desire for entry into religion, inspired by that divine grace, as it ought to be felt by those who from zealous devotion and pure desire of the mind plan to enter religion. . . . Indeed I own myself unworthy and I long to be the servant of even the least religious in the Church of God and I hope by God's grace to be made a sharer with them. . . . If, on the other hand, God should have ordained for me thus, miserable and wretched as I am, and should have called me by His grace to sit solitary and serve him in that manner, as he deigns to grant to me, shall I not persevere in that calling?[8]

There is no means of knowing how near to the regularised life of Thurgarton he was at this date. There is no certainty either as to where he wrote his main English works: the treatise known as *Mixed Life*, giving advice to the upmarket man of affairs who also wished to create opportunities to cultivate his inner spiritual life (one manuscript describes it as 'a luitel Boc þat was writen to a worldli lord to teche him hou he schulde haue him in his state in ordeynd loue to god and to his euencristene'),[9] and the two books of *The Scale of Perfection*. It is generally supposed that it was at Thurgarton. Certainly both books are attributed to Walter Hilton *Canonicus de* Thurgarton, though the mood he expresses in *Scale 1*, which is addressed to a female recluse, seems similar to that he expressed while he was still a solitary and suffering the kind of feelings of purposelessness he expresses in the *De Imagine Peccati*. In *Scale 1* he protests that he speaks of more than he has directly experienced:

> Lo, I haue told þe a litel as me thynke first of contemplatif life, what it is, and siþen of þe weyes whilk by grace leden þe þerto; noȝt for I haue in felyng and in wirkyng as I haue in seying; neuerþeles I wold by þise wordes, wilk as þer arn, first stire myn own negligence forto do betere þen I haue don and also my purpose is forto stire þe or any oþere man or woman þat has taken þe state of life contemplatif forto trauaile more bisily and more mekely . . .[10]
>
> (92.361a. –160).

In the second book which complements the material in the first, there is an often remarked upon change of tone: the reservation and distancing of *Scale 1* is absent from the imagistic structures which embody his thought and insight in *Scale 2*.

Certainly the ethos of an Augustinian priory with its stress on the expression of an inner religious faith in the active life of the community would have been sympathetic to the characteristic concern Hilton displays in his writing not just for professional religious but for all those, whether in active or enclosed life, who feel that their religious faith holds the secret of a dimension of fulfilment to which they desire access. He recognises that there are many levels at which people engage with religion. For many it will involve no more than a ritualised acknowledgement, mediated by the Church, of a realm of ultimate value which, if it does in fact inform their existence, they know only through blind obedience to the Church's teaching:

> . . . þese simple soules þat trowen stidefastly as holy kirke trowes, and putten hem fully in þe mercy of God and meken hem vndire þe sacramente and þe laghes of holikirk mad sauf þorw praier and trowþ of her gostly moder whilk is holikirk.
>
> (*Scale* 2,10.71v. –207)

laghes: laws; *sauf*: safe.

They have:

> bot a childes knowyng of God and ful litel felyng of hym bot arne broȝt forþ in þe bosum of holy kirke and norisched wiþ þe sacramentes as children are fed wiþ milk.
>
> (10.71r. –206–7)

Those for whom Hilton is writing, however, are those who are driven either intellectually (*Scale 1*, c.4) or emotionally (*Scale 1*, c.5) towards integrating an inner life of moral values and spiritual sensitivity with Christian teaching.

Hilton's mystical theology is not conveyed with the passionate poetry that characterises Rolle's writing, it is not attended by the rigours of the *Cloud*-author's sense of that transcendent God who cannot be known in any recognisable sense of the word, the visionary experience of Julian of Norwich, or the endearingly unbalanced enthusiasm of Margery Kempe. His work is, however, central to an understanding of Christian mysticism and the spiritual sensibility which informed the surge of lay devotion in the late medieval period. His great literary achievement is to have found images and structures to convey theologically understood experience and to articulate with luminous clarity an understanding of how the Incarnation reveals a pattern in which all modes of human fulfilment are subsumed. Hilton sees this as a 'form' (in Rolle's sense of the word) which provides the means of integrating and ordering human experience. In all his work he addresses not just those who are enclosed as religious solitaries with special time for attention to their inner development – though he admits that this life-style is most conducive to it[11] – but all those who are predisposed to pursue an inner life.

MIXED LIFE: KINDLING FOR LOVE

It is not clear whether the date of composition of *The Epistle of Mixed Life* precedes or follows *Scale 1* with which it has close affinities.[12] Certainly its thinking is complemented by a knowledge of the longer text which may be the reason for its appearing after both books of the *Scale* in the early printed editions. It does, however, provide a useful introductory focus on Hilton's breadth of appeal, and also on his understanding of the terms 'active' and 'contemplative' as they appear in the more sophisticated books of *The Scale*. It is also a cultural document of prime importance for understanding the sensibilities of the lay audience for whom the mystical writers in the vernacular were providing texts. Obviously popular, it survives complete (or nearly so) in sixteen manuscripts many of which divide the text into chapters although they do not all agree as to how. Six of these manuscripts include passages absent from the other ten at the beginning and the end of the text.[13] They relate to what is coming and what has gone respectively.

Whatever disagreement there is about the internal divisions of the texts in the manuscripts, the whole treatise has a shape. It first sets in a social and theological context the desire of the unknown nobleman to devote himself to God without the distractions that arise from involvement with secular responsibilities. It then argues that this very desire for God is God immanent in man's being and shows how it may, in his particular case, come to inform all sides of his life which are reconciled as they are turned into fuel to feed the fire of love – itself lit in his desire for God. The implication at the beginning of the text is that the lord feels his worldly duty and his love for God to be pulling against each other and unbalancing him:

> Y knowe weel þe desire of þyn herte, þat þou ȝernest gretli to serue oure lord bi goostli occupacioun al holli wiþoute lettynge or trobolynge of wordeli bisynesse.
>
> (7.73–5)
>
> *ȝernest*: long, desire; *lettynge*: hindrance.

The state to which Hilton hopes to point him is one of *discretion* in which self-knowledge and the love of God are the means of integrating what seem like opposites in equilibrium. The text from the Canticle of Canticles 2:4 *ordinavit in me caritatem* (he set in order charity in me) distils imaginatively Hilton's understanding that love can only be properly expressed through a disciplined orientation of the particular gifts and powers of the self to God.[14] This involves responsible self-knowledge; not a striving after a spirituality which may not be appropriate to one's particular capacity, but a creative inner process. In *The Scale* Hilton will talk about it in terms of remaking – reforming – those elements of the self which he calls the 'miȝtes' [powers] of the soul (*Scale 2*, 31.106v–258) – mind, reason and will – in such a way that they reflect the likeness of God in whose image they were created. *Scale 2* is structured to manifest the nature of this likeness; *Mixed Life* is less ambitious, but the moderate clarity of its argument is based on, and goes some way towards revealing, an understanding of the structure of personality as the means by which God is conceived in time.

Hilton addressed himself to the practical situation of his friend who felt himself torn by the demands of the active life impinging on his desire to pursue contemplation, and helps by showing that these two terms, so often used as opposites to refer to a manner of living, either as a professed religious or as a man of affairs, take their fundamental meaning from different inner conditions. He is much clearer analytically and more comprehensive than Rolle in his discussion of this matter and realises that the terms distinguish essentially complementary modes of living. Active life in the sense of engagement with the physical necessities and well-being of society belongs properly and sensibly to people who feel no inner compulsion towards, or understanding of, spiritual issues – as he much more trenchantly put it, they have 'no sauour' of 'goostli occupacioun' (12.123–4). Contemplative life belongs to those who not only have a keen awareness that life in the world hangs by a thread, but a sense that their own identity and reality does not inhere fundamentally in physical things. Hilton says they turn away from involvement in the world, and, in words which more immediately evoke the liberation and peace which are the goals of the rigours of contemplative life, he says that they:

> maken hem self pore & naked to þe bare nede of þe bodili kynde, and fleen fro souereynte of alle oþere men to þe seruice of God.
>
> (13.135–7)

That is, they rid themselves from involvement with any possessions not strictly needed for physical survival and escape from the demands and goals of social success to a different kind of service. But immediately Hilton makes it clear that such a life-style involves an active life of its own if the peace that is sought is to be found, for it may not be had:

> wiþoute grete exercise of bodi, and contynuel traueile of spirit in deuoute praieres, feruent desires, and goostli meditacions.
>
> (13–14.141–3)

This has been defined earlier as:

> good werkes þat þi soule dooth by þe wittes and þe membres of þi bodi vnto þi silf, as in fastynge, wakynge, & in refreynyng of þi fleschli lustis bi oþir penaunce doynge, or to þyn euen-Cristen bi fulfillinge of þe dedes of merci bodili or goosteli, or vnto God bi suffrynge of all maner [bodili] myscheues for þe loue of ryȝtwisenesse.
>
> (4.34–9)

Such an active component of spiritual endeavour is a concomitant of man's temporal nature. He may be naturally drawn towards a discovery of a state which does not depend on time and space for its reality, but the medium of the imperfect world into which he is born means that:

> we haue neiþir þe gostli knowynge of God bi liȝt of vndirstondynge, ne goostli felynge of hym bi clene desire of louynge.
>
> (3.21–4)

Such knowing and feeling, the mystics say, is given in response to a process – an ordering of the drives in human nature so that they can be expressed as love. The development is one of recovery of health from sickness; Hilton sees that man's dual nature has a double inheritance: the sickness of the self that we are born to (3.19–20) and the transcendent 'heritage of helþe' (*Scale* 2. 46.139r. –301) that we can work towards:

> þerefore we mosten abide & worche bi proces of tyme.
>
> (*Mixed Life*, 4.28)

In *The Scale* Hilton developed at greater length the nature of the active and passive elements that belong to the contemplative life through which those who pursue it discover in the structure of their own experience the very being of Christ. Here, in *Mixed Life*, he relates that individual experience of Christ in every man to the Christ who transcends individual limitations and is expressed by the whole body of those in whom he is born in time through their knowing and doing:

> þou schalt vndirstonde þat oure lord Ihesu Crist, as man, is heed of þe goosteli bodi whiche is holy chirche. þe membres of þis bodi aren alle Cristene men. Summe aren armes, and summe feet, and summe aren oþere membres aftir sundri wirchynges þat þei vsen in heere lyuynge.
>
> (25.273–7)
>
> *heere*: their.

It is precisely because of these 'sundri wirchynges' in the lives of individuals dictated by their particular talents and circumstances that discussion of active and contemplative life tends to polarise life-styles which are then also subject to evaluation in which contemplation is more highly esteemed simply because it relates to a greater state of spiritual awareness.[15] In recommending what Hilton calls 'medeled liyf' to his noble lord, he calls on the earlier tradition of awareness of a fundamental harmony between these two conditions – both crucial to temporal life as exemplified in the Incarnation.

> oure lord, for to stire summe to vse þis medeled liyf, . . . ȝaue hem ensample bi his owen worchynge þat þei schulden vsen þis medeled liyf as he dide. O tyme he comouned wiþ men, and medeled wiþ men, schewynge to hem his deedes of merci, for he tauȝte þe vncouþ and vnkunynge bi his prechynge, he vesited þe sike & heeled hem of here

> sooris, he fedde þe hongry, and he comforted þe sori. And anoþer tyme he lefte þe conuersacioun of al wordeli men and of his disciples [also], and wente in to dissert upon þe hillis, and contynued alle þe nyȝt in praieres aloone, as þe gospel seiþ.[16]
>
> (17–18.177–88)

vnkunynge: ignorant.

So he persuades his man with a natural talent for the proper administration of worldly affairs that to neglect this because of a preoccupation with spiritual meditation could be unwise. Indeed in view of the tradition of seeing Christ as combining both active and contemplative lives it is perhaps surprising that mixed life was not more specifically advocated as an ideal. It is true that Franciscan spirituality put new stress on the necessity for integrating action and contemplation. But perhaps the obvious disparity between individual talents and dispositions which clearly fit some for action more than others, the obvious tension involved between the pressures of active involvement in affairs and the inner detachment necessary for thought and contemplation, and the history of the development of Western institutional Christianity with its strong tradition of groups separated from the world in convents and monasteries, or priests distinguished from the laity by their religious calling, make it after all not so surprising that the discussions of active and contemplative life tended to stress their separation from each other rather than draw attention to a more fruitful affinity.

It is a mark of Hilton's clarity of thought and practical spirituality that he should pick up the episcopal ideal of a composite life-style and set it up as the *modus vivendi* for a spiritually-minded temporal lord.[17] In the graphic image taken from contemporary devotion of the lord who aspires to kiss Christ's mouth in spiritual devotions and in doing so neglects acts of charity and so treads on his feet, Hilton skilfully combines all the strands of thought on the roles of action and contemplation in the Christian life as the means by which the individual works out his full spiritual potential (25–6.273–88).

He immediately commands attention by grasping the nettle of the difficulty that the lord feels in combining the apparently opposing demands on his natural gifts. It is just here, Hilton points out, that his particular opportunity to show love arises. The point of his advice is not just to authorise 'medeled liyf' which the lord is anyhow pursuing:

> but I wolde þat þou schuldest doo þus gladli, and not þenke looþ for to leve sumtyme goostli occupacion and entirmete þee wiþ wordli bisynesse, . . . but þat þou schuldest doo boþe werkes in diuers tymes, and wiþ as good wille þat oon as þat oþir, ȝif þou myȝt.
>
> (28.312–9)

He can cut from one kind of state to the other with joy; this is for him precisely how love is to be ordained.

To emphasise the very essential connection between the two modes of being, Hilton introduces the metaphorical interpretation of the Old Testament story of Jacob's marriage to Leah and Rachel.[18] Although this has the weight of patristic authority behind it, Hilton very simply outlines the bare essentials of the story and its interpretation giving it particular emphasis to highlight implications peculiarly relevant to the noble lord. Thus instead of following the traditional linear progression of the allegory – a development towards contemplation based on Jacob's union with Rachel after his marriage to Leah – Hilton is more interested in emphasising the coexistence of the two wives:

> so schalt þou doo aftir þe ensample of Jacob: take þise two lyues, actif and contemplatif, siþen God haþ sent þe boþe, and vse hem boþe, þat toon wiþ þat toþir.
>
> (32.362–4)

In his reference to another facet of the story, that concerning Jacob's change of name to Israel, allegorised as a man seeing God,[19] Hilton does suggest a progression in contemplation for his pupil saying that he will become Israel, that is, fully contemplative, in the next world, certainly, and possibly even in this if his circumstances change so that he is relieved of worldly responsibility altogether. But Hilton is chiefly concerned with exploring how it is possible for contemplation and action to be states which are mutually creative and fulfilling for the lord. He suggests that, rightly managed with a light heart, the demands of the active service of love will positively stimulate desire for contemplative perception – a rest in the recognition of the ground of all love. The key to healing the divisions in man's nature which produce the tension between active and contemplative life is love, only realised in playing the game of faith that this is true. When you are interrupted in contemplative devotion, says Hilton, don't be angry and depressed but leue of liȝteli þi deuocioun, wheþir it be in praiere or in meditacioun, and goo doo þi dette and þi seruice to þyne euene-Cristene as redili as oure lord him silf badde þee doo so, and suffre mekeli for his loue, wiþouten grucching if þou may.

(34–5.388–92)

This is the mode by which man following a mixed life realises in himself the creative love of God – the fire of love that Rolle talked of as consuming all that is dark. The disciplines of active life in the sense of worldly help to others, or the necessity for study,[20] are to be like 'stikkes' laid on the burning coal that represents man's innate desire for God and needs to be nourished if it is to provide full light and heat (35–9.397–449).

Indeed this is the heart of Hilton's argument for the validity of mixed life for the aspiring contemplative, for he says that this very desire, the burning coal which has to be thus nourished by a positive attitude to the demands of both active and contemplative life, is in fact God himself at the very ground of our being. In *Scale 2* Hilton talks of his understanding of the dynamic nature of God's love working in man:

If þu wilt witen þen what þis desire is, soþly it is Iesu. For he makiþ þis desire in þe and he gifiþ it þe and he it is þat desiriþ in þe and he it is þat is desired. He is al and he doþ al if þu miȝte seen him.

(24.89r. –234)

The goal of contemplative life is to *see* this, a seeing which is a felt understanding of love, and Hilton accounts for the curious process by which a person grows towards this state as the interaction between the being of God – unformed love in which all men participate – and the response enabled by God to this dynamic potential at the heart of their being – love formed.[21] Finally the contemplative grows to recognise that in his life of love for God the being of God is extended in time: 'he is boþ þe gifer and þe gifte and makiþ vs þan bi þat gifte for to knowen and lufen him' (*Scale 2*, 34.111r.–264). And time, the medium in which Jesus is discovered as 'tresour hidd in þi soule' (*Scale 1*, 49.322b.–122), is the dimension of the Incarnation, necessitated by the Fall.

Here in *Mixed Life*, a text that must be seen in relation to *Scale 1* and *Scale 2*, Hilton adumbrates the same progress in chapter fourteen:

> . . . oure lord haþ sent in to þyn herte a litil sparcle of þis blissid fier, þat is him silf as hooli writ seiþ: *Deus noster ignis consumens est*; oure lord God is fier wastynge – for as bodili fier wasteþ alle bodili þynges þat mai be wasted, riȝt so goosteli fier, þat is God, wastiþ al maner of synne where-so hit falleþ, and forþi oure lord is likened to a fier wastynge – I praie þee norische þis fier. þis fier is not ellis but loue and charite.
>
> (39–40.450–7)
>
> *goosteli*: spiritual.

Following Augustinian theology, he locates the very essence of Christian life in the continual sustained desire for God – the only way in this life to perceive the nature of the love which joins God and man's soul. This desire should govern every aspect of living as desire for health dominates a sick man – it is the very mainspring of action, 'rote of al þi wirkynge'(47.558). The lord has to learn how best to pace himself spiritually to allow this desire to integrate all his potential. The kind of awareness this induces is *discretion*.[22]

> þan is it good þat al oure bisynesse be for to stire þis desire and vse it bi discrecioun, now in oo deede, now in an oþir, aftir we aren disposyd & haue grace þerto.
>
> (47.555–8)

The last eleven chapters of the treatise address themselves to the nature of the discretion appropriate to mixed life. Hilton is aware that ultimately the lord will be best judge of what helps him most, but he suggests that every day should start with an effort to discipline his whole attention to God. It may be that thinking of his own fragile balance between goodness and a propensity to go wrong, or thinking of the sins of others with compassion, will be salutary. Such thoughts lead naturally to the manhood of Christ, the sharp reminder that the Incarnation provides of both the destructive nature of sin and the means by which this destruction is turned back on itself – laid waste. Hilton stresses that a quickened sense of the inner meaning of the Incarnation cannot be forced; it is essentially experienced as a gift and those eager to know God should always try to work with the grain of their own particular natures rather than force any prescribed activity: 'take esili þat wolen come'(53.637). Nevertheless he does signal some, as Julian would call them, 'means' that might help. A careful consideration of the nature of virtues, or of the lives of the saints and apostles may help, as will meditation on the Passion and Mary, whose virtues enabled Christ to be born and make manifest the wisdom and goodness of God. Prayer and meditation may be alternated to foster a recollected attention, but no activity, however fruitful, should be pursued to the point of extremes:

> it is spedefulle for to haue discrecioun in ȝoure wirchynge, not fully falle þerto for to folwe it as moche as wole come.
>
> (65.787–9)

Hilton thus encourages a constant awareness of an inner life to be fostered. The area of conscious energy he is seeking to nourish is one which can engage with the means by which sorrow, lethargy, darkness and ill health are transfigured to joy, energy, light, strength and peace. It is this sharp awareness of an inner process which will release men from the constraints of time, that makes those who make enormous emotional investment in material enterprises look incredibly foolish:

> þei aren like to children þat rennen aftir botirflies, and, for þei loke not to her feet, þei falle sumtyme doun and breken heer legges.
>
> (60.715–17)

Heaven is the only true object of human desire and it must be particularly and discreetly nourished in a continual process of growth.

> no man sodeynli is maad souereyne in grace, but fro litil he bigynneþ, and bi processe wexeþ, vntil he come to þe moste.
>
> (69.838–9)

This awareness of a process is the governing concept of *The Scale of Perfection*.

Despite the fact that Hilton says in chapter ten of *Mixed Life* that the nobleman who is like Jacob married to Rachel and Leah will only become Israel 'þat is verri contemplatif' (33.374–5),[23] if he is released from worldly responsibilites there is no ground for suggesting that he meant to rule out the possibility of the most profound kind of contemplative experience for the man in mixed life. It is true that his definition of Rachel as 'reste [and] goosteli swettenesse in deuocioun and contemplacion', and 'grace of deuocioun and reste in conscience' (31–2. 351–2,360–1) seems to correspond with his thinking about the stage of spiritual development which he describes in *Scale 1* chapter seven as preceding an experience where man's awareness in love of the life within him as Christ, is expressed as a 'mariage made bitwix god and þe soule'(8.283a. –82). But it is also true that he describes this final state as one illumined so as 'forto se by vnderstondyng soþfastnes whilk is god, and also gostly thynges with a soft swete brennand loue in hym' (8.282b. –82); and in *Mixed Life* Rachel is also defined as 'siȝt of bigynnynge þat is God, and bitokeneþ liyf contemplatif' (30–1.342–3). Moreover in *Scale 2* he moves away from using the language of progressively numbered stages to formulate his thinking about the nature of contemplative experience. Instead he explores a number of aspects that all inhere in a state of contemplative awareness of a reality beyond time. Here inward stillness and peace of conscience (aspects of Rachel in *Mixed Life*) are incorporated into the experience of union.[24]

In *Scale 1* chapter nine Hilton says that the fullness of contemplative experience can be given to those in active life, though he adds the rider that they will not be able to make such full use of it as those living more sheltered lives as solitaries or in a contemplative order. It is this reference to contemplative life as a state that Hilton refers to as 'verrei contemplatif' in *Mixed Life*.

In line with his unprescriptive manner of teaching about how to develop contemplative life which is governed by his awareness of the intensely individual nature of discretionary achievement, Hilton is deliberately leaving his terms open, or using those likely to be directly applicable to actives, so that the recipient should not be constrained by definitions as he develops in his contemplative life. The scale and tone of the little treatise on mixed life does not allow for the complex work and breadth of thinking such definitions would entail. It is in the two books of *The Scale of Perfection* that Hilton develops structures to convey his understanding of the nature of contemplative life; these two books form the most sustained analysis and illumination of the subject in the writings of the five authors here studied.

SCALE 1 AND 2: FROM SICKNESS TO HEALTH

Hilton's powers of analysis have attracted studies in a historical theological context and comparisons of his account of the stages of contemplative life with those formulated by other writers, especially St John of the Cross.[25] Such work is of obvious value to the understanding of Hilton's ideas and to the overall academic perspective on the documentation of contemplative experience. The original recipients of Hilton's text, however, as is clear from the very fact that he wrote for them in the vernacular,[26] were not interested in comparative academic study, but in particular guidance which would enable them to fully integrate their religious faith in their lives. The approach of the historian of theological ideas may obscure the literary integrity of such a text as Hilton's *Scale*. Ironically, it may, indeed, frighten the lay reader away altogether. Yet Hilton's text is remarkable in its power to bring alive conceptually the nature and ultimate implications of the life of faith in its own terms. As has already been observed by the Dominican, Conrad Pepler:

> we need not to labour the fact that Hilton is writing the same things as St John of the Cross, . . . What is remarkable is that the same basic truths can be experienced and expressed in such outwardly differing modes. If any proof were needed to insist that confessors and directors should avoid pressing their penitents into any clearly established scheme but instead should simply wait upon the Lord and watch and assist his working in the individual soul, this diversity among the great masters of the spiritual life should be sufficient. The way is one in Christ who is the way, it is the way of love – the love of Christ, but Christ is lived in each person according to the construction of that personality and the love works through the individual's free will.
>
> Hilton's *Scale* gains, perhaps, over some other later descriptions of the way in being very wide and very general so that the individual can find his own way therein without being embarrassed by a bundle of inapplicable particularities.[27]

The 'particularities' of scholarly comparison can also embarrass the lay reader of *The Scale* where Hilton, particularly in *Scale* 2, illuminates something about the inner relevance of what is meant by 'Christ lived in each person according to the construction of that personality'.

Manuscript copies of *The Scale* survive in large numbers. Sometimes they include both books, sometimes 1 or 2 by themselves. Some of those which contain Book 1 only, for example the fourteenth-century Vernon and Simeon manuscripts, include it as part of a large collection of medieval texts. Those manuscripts with both books or only Book 2 belong to the fifteenth century.[28] Although in both books Hilton never loses sight of the spirituality possible for actives each book is addressed to a different audience: *Scale 1* to an enclosed and apparently illiterate anchoress 'redyng of holy writt may þou noȝt wel vse' (15.288a. –88); while *Scale 2* seems more generally addressed to a wider and not necessarily wholly contemplative audience.[29] It looks as if the two books were not conceived as a single entity although they interrelate in the way that Hilton picks up and elaborates aspects of the subject of *Scale 1* in *Scale 2*. Clearly contemporary readers who knew both books considered them connected. For instance, one of the manuscripts containing a copy of only Book 1, describes it as the first part of the book called 'The Mirror of Contemplation by Canon Walter Hilton'(Lansdowne MS 362: *Prima pars libri qui dicitur Speculum contemplacionis – Walterus hiltoun canonicus*[30]) while one of the few manuscripts to contain Book 2 alone refers to it as 'the secunde part of the reformyng of mannys soule drawyn of maister Watir hiltone hermyte'.[31] Only where the two books appear together is it called *Scala Perfeccionis, The Scale of Perfection*. Although this title is not very appropriate, since Hilton never explicitly develops the metaphor, it nevertheless presents a view of the two books treating an overall development of an inner spiritual life.

Furthermore, not only does Hilton imply that he is implementing his treatment of the subject in *Scale 1* at the beginning of *Scale 2*,[32] there are also points in *Scale 1* where he anticipates a development of his subject beyond that relevant for his immediate recipient. On occasions when he is developing thought about contemplative prayer as an experience where man feels his faculties of reason and will to be at rest, informed by a loving knowledge of God, or about this experience both restoring what man lost at the Fall and anticipating the life to come, he acknowledges that he has outstripped the immediate needs of his particular audience: 'þou has noȝt ȝit fully seen what it is, for þi gostly eȝe is noȝt ȝit opened' (46.319a.–119).[33]

In *The Scale* as a whole Hilton brings into focus a double image of human nature. One, relating to its ability to get things wrong, is sick and frustrated: 'now euere ilk man þat lyueȝ in þis wrecched lyfe is gostly seke' (*Scale 1,* 44.316a. –116); Hilton's view of this state is like that of Rolle's view of the body of this death in his *Meditations on the Passion.* The other image is of man cured of his sickness, delighting in the freedom of a state where knowledge and desire are fully answered in an experience of love. The experienced reality of this image is the recognition of the nature of God in man that will grow beyond time: 'for in þat siȝt and in þat knowynge of Iesu is fully þe blis of a resonable soule and endles lif' (2.33.110v. –263). For Hilton, the key to the means of curing the sickness which obscures and thwarts the brightness and power of the image of God lies in the Incarnation. The intellectual and emotional clarity of his understanding, his sensitivity to language, and the potential of traditional figurative modes of writing, come together in a work of literature which conveys a sense of the Incarnation as a live issue. *The Scale of Perfection* is a key text for its own period and beyond it.

Scale 1 concentrates more on the image of sickness, its diagnosis and treatment, but all the time it is informed by a vibrant sense of the health aspired to; whereas *Scale 2* is concerned with the nature of the experience by which the image of sin is transfigured to a likeness of the being of God. It is at the point in *Scale 2*, where Hilton starts to emphasise this, that he uses the image of the ladder to look back at what has gone before, and to point the way ahead:

> bot fro þe lowest to þe heiȝest may not a soule sodeynly stirte nomore þan a man þat wil clymbe vp on an hiȝe laddre and settiþ his fot vp on þo lowest stele may at þe neȝst flien vp to þe heiȝst, bot hym behouiþ gon by processe on aftir a noþer til he may come to þe ouerest. Riȝt so it is gostly; no man is made sodenly souerayn in grace bot þurw longe exercise and sleiȝ wirkyng a soule may come þerto namely whan he helpiþ and techiþ a wrecched soule in whom alle grace liþ. For wiþouten special helpe and inwardly techyng of him may no soule come þerto.
>
> (*Scale 2*, 17.79v. –220)

stele: rung; *neȝst*: next; *behouip*: needs; *sleiȝ*: skilful.

The rest of the book illuminates the subtle inner movements of the personality in which man engages with the power of God to come to a knowledge of his being, the 'sleiȝ wirkyng in a soul' when

> he helpiþ and techiþ a wrecched soule in whom all grace liþ. For wiþouten special helpe and inwardly techyng of him may no soule come þer to.
>
> (*Scale 2*, 17.79v. –220)

Scale 2 is more engaging as a work which marshals literary resources to illuminate Christian mystical theology. But Hilton himself starts the book with a statement of its purpose to describe 'more of an ymage þe whilk I haue bifore tymes in pertie discried to þe' (1.63r.–193) and the image here taken for granted is the subject of *Scale 1* to which some reference must be made.

SCALE 1

The text

Establishing the text for *Scale 1* is a less straightforward matter than that for *Scale 2* where all the manuscripts agree on the basic substance of the book. In *Scale 1* three main issues divide the manuscript versions. The first is the passage on the cult of the Holy Name of Jesus which, where it is included, completes chapter 44 and begins 'bot now seiȝ þou: "If þis be soth" '(316a.–115). The second is the presence in some manuscripts of short expansions of the text which tend to tie in very explicitly what is being said to the Incarnation of Christ. For example, the following passage dealing with a remedy against temptation contains in some manuscripts an expansion which is here taken from B.L. Harley MS 6579 and marked by italics:

> first þat þei wilen *putten al her trist in our lord Iesu Crist and brynge to mende often his passioun and þe peynes þat he suffred for vs, and þat þei þanne* trowen stedfastli þat al þis sorwe and trauaile þat þei suffren . . . is . . . assaynge for here betture.
>
> (38.23r.)

Or further, in chapter forty-six, where Hilton is talking about the word 'Iesu' as a means of focusing all the inheritance of life that the recluse desires, he says:

> bute I mene Iesu *Crist þ*at *blissed persone God and man, sone of Virgyn Marie whom þis name bitokneth, þ*at *is* al goodnesse, endles wisdom, luf, . . . and þi saluacioun.[34]
>
> (46.31r.)

These insertions do not add anything new, they simply expand in a particular way what has been said and they are not absolutely consistent in all the manuscripts in which they appear. The third element, the presence or absence of which cuts across the manuscript relationships, is a short passage influenced by the teaching of St Augustine on charity which occurs in some, but not all of the manuscripts in *Scale 1*, chapter seventy.

Some manuscripts of *Scale 1* contain neither the passage on the Holy Name nor the insertions; some have the Holy Name passage but not the shorter additions; some have both; still others have the insertions but not the passage on the Holy Name. The conclusion of scholars is that the passage on the Holy Name and the addition to chapter seventy is original to Hilton whereas the shorter passages were probably originated and incorporated by transcribers as glosses on the text.[35] The text here quoted for *Scale 1* is from Cambridge University Library Add. MS 6686 which includes the passage on the Holy Name and that in chapter seventy but not the shorter additions. Certainly both elements bring into high relief the incarnational element in Hilton's thinking which is, in fact, central to both books.

Chapters 1–41: 'work as you may'

The opening fourteen chapters of *Scale 1* provide a context of definitions for Hilton's particular address to a recluse asking advice on the contemplative life which, in the first chapter, he acknowledges to be a demanding process:

> I sey noȝt þat þou so liȝtly on þe first day may be turned to hym in þi soule by fulhed of vertus, as þou may with þi bodie be spered in a hous.
>
> (278b. –77)

fulhed: completeness; *spered*: enclosed.

Although in defining active and contemplative life Hilton makes it clear that contemplative life belongs especially

> to hem þe whilk forsaken for þe loue of God all worldly ryches, worschipes and outward bisynes and holly ȝyuen hem bodie and soule up her myȝt and her conyng to þe seruice of god by gostly occupacioun
>
> (3.279b. –78)

myȝt: strength; *conyng*: ability.

he, characteristically, makes it clear that it is not ruled out for actives. Hilton sees three divisions in contemplative life which, broadly speaking, cover the range of modes of inner knowledge of God. The first is that acquired solely by study and reading which is only a pale imitation of the real thing since it is not accompanied by an experience of love which answers to the intellectual knowledge (c.4). The second concerns a love for God which is a gift and has nothing to do with learning (c.5–7); this itself has two aspects covering that which is experienced sporadically by both actives and contemplatives, and a stabler devotion given after a long process of discipline in which the contemplative feels a 'grete rest of bodie and of soule' (7.282a. –81). The third refers to a state of love in which man realises the love of God in his being and is one with Him. This state is the goal of the contemplative life, if not here, then certainly after death. Hilton says that the concomitant of this state is to be reformed to the image of Jesus, that is to the wisdom of God, the traditional title of the Son, and such reformation will combine both knowledge and love 'cognicioun and affeccioun' (8.282b. –82). Theologically trained readers of his time would recognise a background of scholarly debate on whether it is primarily through man's intellect or capacity to love, that the soul engages with God[36], and they would be able to acknowledge Hilton's synthesis of understanding and desire.

Hilton's uneducated disciple, however, is learning at this stage that the goal of the contemplative life is a remaking of the self to be like God through a loving practice, and thus knowledge, of goodness:

> ay seke þat þou myȝtest come to þe gostly felyng of God: and þat is þat þow myȝtest knowe and fele þe wisdom of Gode, þe endeles myȝt of hym and þe grete godenes of hym in hymself and in his creatures.
>
> (12.286b–7a. –86)

Such contemplation is experienced as a gift which lifts the conscious effort to know and love God into an activity of delight which expresses the whole man:

> when by grace of Iesu and by gostly and bodily exercise þe resoun is turned in to liȝt and will in to loue.
>
> (14.288a. –87)

Although this goal is thus acknowledged from the start, the rest of the book is devoted to the means by which the contemplative can work towards it. Since she is illiterate, reading of the Bible is ruled out, but, in whatever activity she finds herself, she can pursue prayer and meditation in meekness, and faith in the teachings of the Church, and the same 'continuel desire to God' that he advocated in *Mixed Life* (41.472) here stressed as an inner dynamic, where she is never idle 'bot alwey liftand up þi hert by desire to God and to þe blisse of heuen' (22.296a. –96).[37]

Like Rolle, Hilton sees prayer as the primary activity, recognising it as a state of consciousness which enables man to receive the gift of God; and while it does not cause it to be given, nevertheless prayer is a way in which such grace comes (c.24) He sharpens a constant awareness of two modes of activity in the inner life: that of conscious effort, and that of an effortless creative power of love and understanding which is sometimes experienced and believed by the mystics to be the work of God in man. *Scale 2* enlarges on this release of creative being in the self. Here Hilton is more concerned with advising formal patterns of prayer which may help the recluse towards the ability to meditate, though all the time his description of the exercise of spoken prayer is informed by an excited awareness of a form that needs no words in its joyful and peaceful awareness of God. This is the object of his pupil's desire, though at present she is like the man who

> can noȝt renne liȝtly by gostly preyere for his fete of knowyng and louyng arn seke for synne,
>
> *renne*: run; *fete*: feet; *seke*: sick.

and for this reason

> hym nedeȝ forto haue a siker staff forto hold hym by.
>
> (27.299b. –99)
>
> *siker:* firm.

Such a staff is spoken prayer.

The technique in *Scale 1* is to fuel the recluse's imaginative understanding of a condition where she can freely maximise her spiritual potential and, at the same time, promote the discipline which allows her to do so. This discipline is the way through which the full meaning of the Incarnation is experienced and the creative love of God expressed through the constraints of human nature. Thus is Christ known. Hilton here formulates the same perceptions that govern Rolle's understanding of the role of meditations on the Passion when he says:

> for a man schal noȝt come comunly to gostly delite in contemplacioun of þe Godhed bot if he come first in ymaginacion by bitternes and compassioun of his manhed.[38]
>
> (35.306b. –106)

In fact Hilton gives no very precise rules about meditation itself because he is aware that it relates intimately to each individual's unique personality and gifts. But he is in one sense or another occupied with it for the rest of the book as he directs the recluse in understanding her experience in terms of a pattern established by the Incarnation, and anchors his teaching to Scripture. His understanding of the illuminative potential of meditation as a gift from God is indicated by his comparison of the meditative state to that of the disciples between the Ascension and Pentecost. As they longed for a spiritual assurance of Christ's presence and received it in the Holy Spirit which literally inspired in them knowledge and love of God so the meditator may grow in inner spiritual knowledge (c.33, 36). But he does not shirk the reality that the exercise is often accompanied by distracting temptation arising out of a sense of futility, doubt and weakness.[39] When this happens, meditation on the Passion of Christ is an obvious source of strength together with the constantly held realisation that it provides an opportunity to play the game of faith by which its reality is proved.[40]

> When þou art broȝt so lowe by trauaile in temptacioun þat þe thynkeȝ no help ne no comforth bot as þou were a fordon man ȝit preye to God and sothly þou schalt sodenly spryng up as þe day sterne in gladnes of hert and haue verrei treist in god as Job seiȝ.
>
> (38.309b. –109)

It can also thus be the entrée into a further development:

> bot þou schalt if þou wilt biginne a new gamen and a new trauaile and þat is forto entre in to þin oun soule by meditacioun forto knowe what it is: and by knowyng þereof forto come to þe gostly knowyng of God.
>
> (40.311a.–111)

Hilton stresses that this may not be part of the natural development of his particular correspondent. He rather hauntingly characterises the life of the contemplative as a God-hunt and compares those hounds who see the hare and never weary of the chase until they have their quarry with those who run simply because others in the pack do so. Just as a hound who is not on the scent will not get his quarry, so the contemplative cannot violate the integrity of her own feeling and understanding and force her development. This must come by the delicate interaction of her own willed effort and the creative understanding which Hilton calls grace. All she can do is to desire God, 'bot wirk as þou may and crie God mercie for þat þat þou may noȝt' (41.312a. –112). Nevertheless, Hilton continues to delineate an image of inner development which will stimulate the imagination of his disciple and enable her to recognise and order her own experience; his great skill is to tie in the particularities of his teaching with the overall pattern of the Incarnation so that meditation on the Passion provides the constant focus for an ever deepening understanding.

Chapters 42–92: the image of sin

His starting point is with the inward consciousness, common to human nature, of the duality every person experiences – the awareness of the possibility of an inner poise and fulfilment apparent by its absence from an opposing experience of disorder and discontent. He interprets this in terms of the story of the Fall saying that by 'inward biholdyng' man can see in his nature:

> þe worschipe and þe dignite whilk it schuld haue bi kynde of þe first makyng: and þou schalt se also þe wrecchednes and myschef whilk þou art fallen inne for synne.
>
> (42.312b. –112)

kynde: nature.

and fastens on the dynamic nature of the longing to recover what appears to be lost as the material to be worked with. It is what, in *Mixed Life* he would call the 'sparcle of þis blissid fier, þat is him silf' (39.450–1). But the longing will draw its follower into hard places, so Hilton quotes Matthew 16:24: *Si quis vult post me venire, abneget semetipsum, et tollat crucem suam, et sequatur me* [If any man will come after me, let him deny himself, and take up his cross, and follow me] and relates it explicitly to the anchoress's mode of religious life:

> Whoso wil come aftere me, forsake hymself and hate his oune soule, þat is forto sey, forsake all fleschly loue and hate all his oun fleschly lif and his bodily felyng for all his wittes for loue of me and take þe cros, þat is to sey suffre þe peyn of þis a while and þen folue: þat is to sey in to contemplacioun of me.
>
> (42.313b. –113)
>
> *wittes*: senses; *folue*: follow.

This is the way she shares the work of redemption which is Christ's.

In order to bring into clear focus what it is that has been lost but can be regained through meditative discipline, Hilton advances an orthodox Augustinian analysis of the structure of personality as essentially tripartite and, thus, trinitarian.[41] Mind or memory is that total creative capacity for consciousness, which also contains that which is below the level of immediate recognition – man's full potential for knowledge, which is like God himself

> in als mykel as þe mynde was made myȝtie and stedfast by þe fadere almyȝtied forto hold hym withouten forȝetyng, distractyng or lettyng of any creature.
>
> (43.314a. –113)
>
> *mykel*: much.

It is the theatre of human integrity which involves the other two faculties, 'resoun' and 'will'. 'Reason', Hilton defines as the faculty by which things are understood – the process by which they are brought to conscious recognition and so can be, metaphorically, 'seen', like the wisdom of God the Father, – Christ. 'Will' is driven by love and desire and so is like the Holy Ghost. Hilton describes the story of man before the Fall as a time when reason was clear and bright, love directed only towards the goodness of God and man's potential fulfilled as his soul 'whilk may be called a made trinite was fulfilled in mynde siȝt and loue of þe vnmade blissed trinite whilk is oure lord' (43a.314. –114).

It is this spontaneous participation in the being of God in whom is 'full rest' (43.314b. –114) that was lost at the Fall. In place of the original image of the power of God in which man was created, came a distorted travesty of it 'a foule merk wrecched trinite' (43b.314. –114) in which God is not recognised and things which of their very nature cannot fully satisfy desire become its object. This is the human nature (the heritage of sickness) with which every man is familiar, and which is nevertheless still capable of conceiving what is lost, just as health is desired by the sick. Although the image of the Trinity is distorted, its powers are not destroyed and this is the activity of God in the soul – the ability to understand what could be, and to desire it:

> if þou hadest lost alle þe resoun of þi soule bi þe first synne, þi soule schuld neuere haue founden hym aȝeyn; bot he left to þe resoun and so he is in þi soule and neuere schal be lost out of it.
>
> (49.322a. –122)

But it is a question of 'so near and yet so far' as Hilton adds that man is not near Christ or in him until he has actually found him. The key to the whole process of 'finding' is Christ's Incarnation. It is the ground for the faith and effective action of all men, in whatever state of life, who desire the spiritual health that they know they lack. This desire, Hilton says, is the 'love of Iesu'[42] which is the ground of salvation whether or not man experiences the joy and love in the kind of illuminated understanding which is the special gift of the contemplative:

> And þoȝ we myȝt neuere gete it here fully, ȝit we schul desire þat we myȝt recouere here lyuand a figure and a liknes of þat dignite, þat oure soule myȝt be reformed as it were in a schadue by grace to þe ymage of þe Trinite whilk we haden by kynde and aftere schulun haue fully in blisse. For þat is þe life whilk is verreile contemplatif vnto bigynne here, in þat felyng of loue and gostly knowyng of God, by openyng of þe gostly eȝe whilk schal neuere be lost ne be taken awey, bot þe same schal be filled oþere wise in þe blisse of heuen.
>
> (45.318a. –118)
>
> *schadue*: shadow; *schulun*: shall.

Hilton spends some time at this stage of the book finding imaginative ways of pointing to the goal of contemplative discipline – the finding of Jesus who is lost in man's soul as a treasure buried in a field (c.49) but who also is a joy beyond all that desiring can encompass (c.46).[43] These pointers serve to motivate the inner discipline – the subject which occupies the rest of the book. Hilton stimulates a conception of the contemplative vocation as essentially dynamic – an interaction between the creative powers of God and man. In so far as the anchoress is seeking Christ lost in the soul, she is like the disciples in the boat on the sea of Galilee lost in the storm (Matthew 13:44) who woke the sleeping Jesus to save them from destruction:

> stire hym by prayere and waken hym with crying of desire and he schal sone ryse and helpe þe.
>
> (49.322b.–323a. –122)

But underlying the cry of the anchoress is the constant calling of God which alone enables her cry: 'oure lord calleȝ þe and all oþere whilk wilen herken to hym (50.323a. –122). Here Hilton comes to the heart of his treatment of the inner life in *Scale 1*. He asks: 'what letteȝ þe þen þat þou may neiþere se hym ne here hym?' [*letteȝ*: hinders] (*ibid*) The new 'gamen' and 'trauaile' of which he spoke in chapter forty is to find out.

It is small wonder that Hilton wrote a sequel to *Scale 1*. Its centre lies in the recognition of what impedes the sight of love, whereas *Scale 2* is occupied with facilitating recognition of the nature of God's being – love – in man. In *Scale 1* Hilton defines the obstruction to the sight and sound of Jesus as the body of sin and death from which Paul cried to be delivered (Romans 7:24–5) and which the anchoress encounters in the progress of her meditative life. The more she tries to fix her heart on God who is beyond all man can think and desire, the more she encounters an inner darkness which has 'neiþire liȝt of knowyng ne felyng of loue ne likyng' (52.324b. –124). As Rolle uses his *Meditations on the Passion* as a means to recognise what is meant by the death of Christ, in terms of the life within ('it is tokenyng of my deth, and fylthe of my synne, þat slayn hath my sowle . . . þat I may nouȝt the fele' (p.87)) Hilton spends thirty chapters (55–84) in defining that within man which hides his integrity and its source from him. If you wish to stop pollution, then you must be able to identify it. But Hilton is always careful to stress that the cleansing process to eradicate sin involves patient inner effort (the expression of the anchoress's fixed intention to God) not violent physical punishment (chapters 72–5). It is a case of going with the grain of one's nature – the heart of which is the wisdom of God. The analysis of sin[44] that occupies much of the second half of the book and which, perhaps fittingly from a literary point of view, distorts the balanced analytic framework of the role and nature of contemplative life in the first half, is frozen in a definitive icon in which the body of death is horriby manifested with a head of pride, back of covetousness (worldly things that the anchoress turns away from), a heart of envy, arms of anger, a belly of greed, genitals of lechery and feet of despairing sloth which find it difficult to stir themselves to good works (prayer and meditation for the anchoress) (85.355a–6a. –154–5). This image is of that mortality which perverts the realisation of the image of God and travesties it. If man is to be delivered from this, he must, like Christ, suffer a form of crucifixion. As Hilton puts it we are born into this image of sin which 'if þu wilt be like to Crist' must be crucified (86.356b. –156). The very desire to break the image will meet with the response of love which enables it to happen. Hilton sees this destruction as a continual process, but he also recognises in it a major stage that other mystics call the 'dark night of the senses' a particularly sharp period of suffering during which the will is firmly dislodged from false values and reoriented towards God.[45] Thereafter, he says, if the stirrings of the old image are felt they may disturb the peace but will not radically contaminate the knowledge and love of God, the image of Jesus, conceived now in contemplation as a shadow of ultimate reality.

And if the whole life of the contemplative is an extension of the Incarnation, it is at this point that Christ is quickened. Hilton sums up the whole process as he has defined it in Book One through the two images of sin and Christ with a quotation from Galatians 4:19:

> of þis schapyng to þe liknes of Crist spekeȝ seinte paule þus: *Filioli quos iterum parturio donec Christus formetur in uobis*; mi dere childre whilk y bere as a woman bereȝ a barn vntil Crist be aȝeyn schapen in ȝow. þou has conceyued Crist in trouth and he has life in þe in als mykel as þou has a gode will and a desire forto serue hym and plese hym; bot he is noȝt ȝit full schapen in þe ne þou in hym by fulhed of charite.
>
> (91.360b. –160).

whilk: which; *bere*: carry; *barn*: child; *fulhed*: fullness.

Scale 1, then, maps the whole area of the contemplative life and shows it may be accessed through inner participation in the truth revealed at the Incarnation:

> noman may come to þe contemplacioun of þe Godhed bot he be first reformed by fulhed of mekenes and charite to þe liknes of Iesu in his manhede.
>
> (91.361a. –160).

Most of the book, however, is occupied with the effort to clarify the process by which the reformation to the likeness of Jesus in his manhood may be begun, the experience of this likeness in the reformed 'myȝtes' of the soul and how it leads to contemplation of the Godhead is not explored in any fullness although it is present as a stated goal. It is to this image of the reformed soul and the nature of its experience that Hilton turns at greater length in *Scale 2*.

SCALE 2:

Chapters 1–17: wholeness and health

The first seventeen chapters of *Scale 2* provide a context for this discussion which looks back to *Scale 1*. Chapters one to six recapitulate in a more explicitly dogmatic form the implications of his treatment of the image of sin in *Scale 1*. The means of all reformation is the Incarnation and Passion of Christ through which love is known both by divine revelation and experience. Hilton says that the possibility of reformation thus open to man's free choice has two aspects: first, reformation in faith which is based on the process of recognition and destruction of the image of sin which has occupied the greater part of *Scale 1*; and second, reformation in feeling which involves a development possible for some who can progress further to an inner freedom and joy which such discipline enables. At the heart of Hilton's conception of reformation in faith is a belief in the efficacy of the sacraments and the authority of the Church; at the heart of his conception of reformation in feeling is his understanding of the nature of human cognition of God.

In the first sixteen chapters he looks at reformation in faith which is open to all through the sacraments of baptism – the means of restoration from the consequences of original sin – and penance, the means of recovery from individual sin. The crucial element for Hilton is the reorientation of the will. In baptism this occurs through the faith of Holy Church.[46] In penance Hilton stresses contrition because it, rather than confession itself, signifies the reorientation of the will, although it is clear that the act of confession can also aid contrition. This stress on will – 'loke what þi wil is for þar in standeþ al' (70r. –205) – is an aspect of the concern he expresses in *Mixed Life* for the importance of a 'continuel desire to God' and in *Scale 1* (22.295b. –95) for a 'hole and a stable entencoun' to please God which must underly all that the anchoress does.[47]

The reformation in faith is of fundamental importance to all who wish to lay hold on their inheritance of health. And in language which extends the representation in *Scale 1* of man's struggles against sin in terms of the Passion, Hilton says that it is the reformation in faith which enables man to carry the image of sin rather than be carried away by it:

> þis soule is not borun in þis ymage of syn as a seke man þauȝ he fele it; bot he beriþ it.
>
> (12.74v. –212)
>
> *borun*: borne.

For some this reformation in faith is sufficient in itself. The contemplatives, however, with whom *Scale 2* is chiefly concerned, go further into reformation in feeling. Their natural capacity to achieve self-knowledge (hence the stress on recognising the image of sin in *Scale 1*) enables them to receive what feels like a gift of freedom from the pressures of the destructive impulses in the self, and a personal inner experience of the God.[48] For Hilton, as for those in the Augustinian tradition, faith is the condition of understanding, *nisi credideritis non intelligetis*.[49]

At the beginning of *Scale 2*, Hilton puts its subject in a conceptual framework which picks up and indirectly rehearses his teaching in *Scale 1*. But he stresses that the progress in contemplative experience, reformation in feeling developing from reformation in faith, is part of an organic process of growth to a peace and fulfilment the longing for which is innate in man who may mistakenly and unnaturally think it resides in material circumstances:

> vnkyndely he doþ and vnresonablely he wirkiþ þat lefiþ þe souerayn gode and aylastande lif þat is God vnsoȝt . . . and chesiþ his reste and his blis in a passand delit of an erþly þinge.[50]
>
> (14.76r. –214)
>
> *vnkyndely*: unreasonably; *aylastande*: everlasting; *vnsoȝt*: unsought.

Scale 2 is pervaded by a sense of the reality of a dimension to human experience beyond the confines of time and sin, though it is only accessed through them. Hilton uses words like 'shape' and 'image' ('oure lord God schope man in soule to his owne ymage and liknes') (1.63r. –193) which depend on spatial dimension for their meaning; but as he defines them they point to an integration of human sentient powers in a consciousness of transcendent love and knowledge. There is a potency in his warning at the end of chapter fourteen that the world is dependent on time which will end, and man's most urgent and natural work, therefore, should be to find the means by which he can pass beyond it. People should love God and 'bisily seken and travailen how þei miȝten be reformed to his liknes or þei passed hennus' (14.77r. –216). Reformation in feeling is the state in which man experiences something of an ultimate reality of which he will only be fully aware after death. It is to the processes of this second reformation that Hilton now turns in chapter seventeen onwards, likening them to the gradual progress in recovery of full health after the medicine that effects the basic cure of the disease (spiritually speaking, penance). It is in this context that Hilton uses the image which was later used as the title of the work. Reforming in faith is the fundamental starting-point for those concerned with the heritage of health; reforming in feeling is the highest state in this life that a soul may come to, but the climb towards it is gradual. The image of the ascent of the ladder is relevant not only to the process of spiritual development he is about to describe, but also to the careful sequential structuring of his teaching where images and arguments accumulate to point towards a greater synthetic understanding.

Hilton's use of language in *Scale 2* is more creative than in *Scale 1*. He finds a means of using the language of both physical experience and Scripture in an anagogical sense whereby mystical experience may be both recognised and shared by those to whom it is known, and to some extent desired, because imagined, by others less involved. Imagination played an important, if intermediate, role in Hilton's theology. All through *The Scale* Hilton hangs his thinking on the pegs of Scriptural texts interpreted as revealing figuratively the nature of spiritual reality.[51] We know from his other writings that he defended the use of images in understanding the faith.[52] He aligned himself with the traditional view that the Scriptures describe unseen things by the form of visible things[53] so as to stimulate reason in cognitive understanding, itself a spiritual reality which is an image of full contemplative knowledge.[54] In the seventeenth century Herbert saw this kind of understanding as a form of prayer which he describes not only as 'God's breath in man returning to his birth' but as an illumination in terms which Rolle and Hilton would have recognised:

> Church bels beyond the starres heard, the soul's bloud,
> The land of spices; something understood.[55]

Hilton describes imagination as serving understanding when the need arises and although he is clear that the imaginative faculty is dependent on physical experience in a way in which mystical experience of God is not, he none the less saw it as able to precipitate a more spiritual understanding.[56] Thus in chapter thirty he restates the threefold division of the spiritual life which he starts in *Scale 1*: the basic faith without any inner experience of God, a felt love of Christ and finally an experience of the spiritual reality of God.[57] Imagination 'stirrid bi grace' is the faculty he names as active in the second stage: 'for whi, þe gostly eiȝe is opened in beholdynge of oure lordes manhede' (30.103r. –253). It would seem that imagination rightly directed enables the extension of meaning which is involved in the Incarnation; but as the Incarnation points beyond itself in the risen and ascended Christ, so imaginative knowledge of God is transcended by a more purely spiritual experience. Thus Hilton says:

> the þridde luf þat þe soule feliþ þurgh gostly siȝt of þe Godhed in þe manhede as it may be seen here, þat is best and most worþi and þat is perfit luf.
>
> (30.103r. –253)

But he is aware of the extremely close if not absolutely inseparable connection between the two modes of knowing, for:

> oure lord Iesu in his Godhed is a spirit, þat may not be seen of vs lifande in flesche as he is in his blissid liȝt þerfore we schal lifen vnder þe schadwe of his manhede as longe as we are here.
>
> (30.104v. –255)

This shadow is cast by the body of Christ through the light of God. The world of shadow is the condition of human knowledge, and imagination deals in the meanings inherent in it but points to the light beyond where it will no longer be of use:

> þawȝ þis be soþ þat þis luf in ymaginacioun be gode, nerþeles a soule schuld desiren for to hafe gostly luf in vndirstandynge of þe Godhede: for þat is þe ende and þe ful blis of þe soule and alle oþer bodyly biholdynges are bot menes ledend a soule to it.[58]
>
> (30.104v. –255).

Chapters 18–30: inward journeys

Such a conception of the imagination as mediator controls Hilton's use of language in chapters eighteen to thirty as he tries to convey understanding of reformation in feeling: a state which combines both a sense of continual movement with an awareness of a state of being in which such movement is no longer necessary. The movement is the condition of being in time:

> for a soule may not stonde stille alwey in on stat while þat it is in þe flesche for it is eiþer profitend in grace or peirynde in synne
>
> (18.80v. –221).
>
> *stat*: condition; *profitend*: improving; *peirynde*: deteriorating.

and the most sustained metaphor for this process of profiting in grace, that of the journey to Jerusalem,[59] is one with immediate connotations for the medieval reader. In the medieval maps of the known world (Europe, Africa and Asia) Jerusalem was depicted at its centre. In the Hereford world map it is drawn as a walled city surmounted by the hill of the Crucifixion – a visual reminder of the central significance of temporal life subject to change and death. The gold letters M O R S encircle the globe, and ultimate judgement is depicted in the heavens above where angels blow the last trumpet and Christ reigns in glory. The dual image of Christ in eternal glory and Christ crucified in time are an icon of Christian understanding of the human situation. Devotion in the Middle Ages was often expressed by means of penitential journeys to famous shrines. The Hereford world map marks the main stages of one such – the famous pilgrimage to the shrine of St James of Compostella.[60] But the most famous and prestigious pilgrimage of all was that to Jerusalem itself which could be conceived at a literal level as a journey to the centre of the earth.[61] Hilton urges those who would know God to think of themselves as pilgrims to 'Ierusalem-ward' set out on a journey to the centre of their own inner world:

> gostly to oure purpos, Ierusalem is as mikel for to seyen as siȝt of pes and bitokeneþ contemplacioun in perfit luf of God. For contemplacioun is not ellis bot a siȝt of Iesu whilk is verrey pes.
>
> (21.85r. –227)
>
> *bitokenep*: signifies.

He thus brings into play resonances from the traditional Augustinian image of the City of God the desire for which activates the Christian life[62] and from allegorical exegesis where Jerusalem signifies, morally, the soul of the faithful Christian striving for the vision of peace and, anagogically, the life of those in heaven who see God face to face.[63] For Hilton, as for the *Cloud*-author, the road to this Jerusalem is 'ronne by desires & not by pases of feet'.[64]

The journey represents the great escape from destruction; it is begun in time and ended beyond it. For those who are going to progress from reformation in faith to reformation in feeling Hilton brings into focus a vivid sense of the existential insecurity of the soul in the world. He describes the reformation in faith, secured at baptism and by penance, leaving the soul as if on the very brink of a pit from which it has been rescued but into which it is in imminent danger of falling back. Wisdom consists in putting some distance between the soul and such destruction. This is the distance travelled to the greater security of reformation in feeling.

Just as the pilgrim who travels to the earthly Jerusalem leaves behind him all his possessions to enable his journey, so Hilton teaches that that which propels the inner journey is a balancing of the will and the mind in the simultaneous awareness that nothing is possible without God who must therefore be desired above all else. He gives the disciple a mantra to concentrate his faculties: 'I am noȝt, I hafe noȝt, I coueite noȝt bot onely þe luf of Iesu' (22.87r. –231).[65] Hilton recognises that while it is apparently unreasonable for man governed by reason utterly to devalue himself and attribute any good things which he does to Christ[66] it is nevertheless the route to true identity, away from the temporal accidents which attract the self, to its essential which is discovered in Christ himself. Such a recognition liberates the potential of the self from the restrictive claims of the conscious ego; it also liberates thought about Christ. The peculiar nature of this journey, that the willed progress is experienced as a divine gift, is a consequence of this theology:

> for he is free and gifiþ him self where he wille and when he wil neiþer for þis werk ne for þat, ne in þis tyme ne after þat tyme. For þawȝ a soule wirke al þat he kan and may al his lif tyme, perfit luf of Iesu schal he neuer haue til oure lord Iesu wil frely gife it. Nerþeles on þe toþer side I say also þat I hope he ȝifiþ it not bot if a man wirke and trauaile al þat he kan and may, ȝe til him þinkiþ he may no more or elles be in ful wil þer to ȝif he miȝte.
>
> (20.83r. –225)

In chapter twenty-four Hilton uses the repetitions and cadences of rhetoric to convey this recognition of the activities of a God whose powers are conceived in Trinitarian terms of creating giving and responding in love at the heart of the self:

> If þu wilt witen þen what þis desire is soþly it is Iesu. For he makiþ þis desire in þe an he gifiþ it þe and he it is þat desiriþ in þe and he it is þat is desired. He is al and he doþ al if þou miȝte seen him. Þou dost noȝt bot suffrest him wirke in þi soule and assentes to hym with grete gladnes of herte þat he fouchiþ saufe for to do so in þe. þu art not elles bot a resonable instrument wher in þat he wirkiþ.
>
> (24.89r. –234)
>
> *fouchiþ saufe*: vouchsafes.

At this point Hilton widens the scope of the metaphor of the journey to Jerusalem – the knowledge of Christ in the soul – by warning that the way from the light of the world to the light of heaven leads through darkness which he describes as ' a tymeful space bitwix two daies' (24.89v. –234). A sense of being in darkness is common in mystical accounts of spiritual life though it may not indicate precisely the same experiences in each writer.[67] In Hilton it represents stages in the journey to God when the soul is no longer engaged with worldly things and as it were asleep to sin (24.90r. –235) but is not yet fully illuminated by the knowledge of Christ:

> he is in þe soule as travailand in desire and longynde to liȝt; bot he is not ȝit as restend in luf, and shewend his liȝt. And þerfor hit is callid niȝt and mirknes, in als mikel as þe soule is hid fro the fals liȝt of þe werld and haþ not ȝit fully felyng of trewe liȝt . . . .
>
> (24.91v. –237)

The experience of the dark can be either painful or restful: painful in so far as the soul is still troubled by the pressures of the worldly attractions from which it is hiding; or restful in so far as the soul is waiting untroubled in its longing for Christ.

Hilton embodies his understanding of this journey in images of light and darkness based on an anagogical reading of two texts from Isaiah 26:9 : 'mi soule haþ desired þe in þe niȝt' and 9:2: *Habitantibus in regione umbrae mortis, lux orta est eis* which he translates 'to the wonend in þe contre of shadwe of dede, liȝt was spronge' [*wonend:* dwellers] (25.92r. –238). Memorably he describes the soul's glimpses of its distant goal, as 'smale sodeyn liȝtynges þat glideren out þurgh smale caues fro þat citee' [*caues:* crannies] (25.92v. –238). And just as the dimensions of a city seen from afar belie their true nature, so the soul seeking contemplation 'if he may come within þe citee of contemplacioun þan seeþ he mikel more þan he sawȝ first' (25.93r. –239).

This anagogical use of language points to a realm of experience beyond that of its immediate field of reference, and draws on the alternative life-style of the contemplative. For Hilton openness to the reality of the dark shadows of the inner world carries a promise of life more exciting than the glare of everyday physical reality 'þat semiþ so shynende and so confortable to hem þat are blynde in knowynge of gostly liȝt' (25.92r. –238). For him it becomes so self-evident where true fulfilment lies that those who are content to rest in the basic reformation in faith appear ludicrous. Hilton comments:

> Whan I see a werdly man þawȝ he haue of werdly gode mikel more þan hym nediþ ȝit he wil neuer saien 'hoo! I haue inow, I wil [no] more of þis. Bot he wil ai coueiten more and more, ... Mikel more þan schude a chosen soule coueiten goostly goode þat is ay lastand and makeþ a soule blissed.[68]
>
> (18.81r. –222)
>
> *mikel:* much.

All through *Scale 2* Hilton implies that the pursuit of this inner calling is open to all:

> þer mown be mony sundry weies and sere werkes ledend sundry soules to contemplacioun. For after sundry disposynges of men and after sundry states, as are religious and seculers þat þei are in, are diuers exercices in wirkynge.
>
> (27.96v. –245)
>
> *sere:* several; *diuers*: diverse.

He is careful not to be over-precise in formulating rules of practice which might not be helpful to all temperaments and all needs. But one thing is common to all who follow the process of reforming in feeling: that is experience of the life of desire for God, freed from any earthly considerations, as an entry from the light of the world into a darkness in which things normally hidden from sight can gradually be discerned, and in which ultimately there grows a vision of a greater light. Hilton also assimilates this imagery to his understanding of the Christian life as an extension of the Incarnation. Referring to Christ's teaching in John 10 that he is the good shepherd and the door to the sheepfold through which alone salvation lies so that anyone 'that entereth not by the door into the sheepfold, but climbeth up another way, the same is a thief and a robber', Hilton remarks that anyone who thinks they can bypass the way of darkness is such a 'þefe and a breker of þe wal' (27.97r. –245). And in this darkness the process of crucifying the image of sin in the practice of penance is completed for the contemplative is dead to the world. Hilton stresses that without this death there is no entry into the City of God, the contemplative state – 'þer is no gate bot on' (27.96v. –245).

He also interprets St Paul's teaching to the Colossians (3:3) in these terms:

> *Mortui enim estis, et vita vestra abscondita est cum Christo in Deo.* ȝe are dede, þat is ȝe þat for þe luf of God forsaken alle þe luf of þe werld are ded to þe werld bot ȝoure life is hid fro werdly men. As Crist lifiþ and is hid in his Godhed fro þe luf and þe siȝt of fleschly lufers.
>
> (27.97r. –245)

Mortui . . . in Deo: For you are dead; and your life is hid with Christ in God.

His evocation of a silent darkness at the heart of which the soul is alive only in faith and expectant longing, combines the same sense of both end and beginning that Rolle creates at the end of his shorter Passion meditation when the process of penance linked with the stages of the Crucifixion concludes in the darkness of the entombment – a darkness which in the pattern of Incarnation is the prelude to dawn and Resurrection. The darkness of which Hilton speaks, and the darkness of the penitential understanding in the Passion meditations, may belong to different stages of development in the knowledge of God, but they are part of a continuous pattern of experience of death and resurrection which underlies them all.

This is exemplified in Hilton's summary of the four stages in reformation in feeling (Chapter twenty-eight). First is the excitement of the sense of calling; second, the passionate and painful struggles in overcoming sin which bring him into a darkness which initially is without savour or delight; third, the experience of light and comfort in the darkness which he describes as the work of Christ illuminating the soul 'with schynynges' (27.98r. –345); and fourth, the full light and bliss of heaven which this light in the darkness anticipates.

In chapter thirty Hilton's analysis of the process of reformation of feeling comes to a climax as he brings together the implications of his analysis and imagery in a synthesis embodying his full sense of the process of contemplative life as lived discovery of the meaning of the Incarnation.The experience of the darkness reveals to the soul its essence which is that its being does not inhere in the dimensions of time: 'for þi soule is no body bot a lif vnseable' (30.102r. –252) and has its own mode of knowing that is not entirely dependent on bodily senses or imagination. Hilton defines this using the traditional mirror image:[69] 'for þi soule is bot a mirrour, in þe whilk þu schalt see God gostly' (30.102v. –253). The mirror reflects the being which in fact sustains and underlies physical existence, validates the perceptions of faith and imagination, and is revealed in the Incarnation – the pattern of existence which constrains the Word. Hilton is aware that the Incarnation must always be the starting-point for reforming in feeling, and only through the processes of faith and penance for the sins which deform the body of Christ can the soul come to see the reality of the being of God in man – Christ:

> I sey not þat we sul departe God fro man but we schul loue Iesu boþe God and man. God in man and man in God, gostly not fleschly.
> (30.104v. –255).

It is this ghostly love that the soul glimpses in the darkness, and in doing so experiences the reality of the resurrected and ascended Christ who comes to man in the Holy Spirit and completes the story of the Incarnation.

In chapter twenty-four, when he identifies the desire for God which fuels the contemplative's journey with Jesus, he uses language which echoes Matthew's account of the Resurrection and comments:

Biholde him wel, for he goþ beforn þe not in bodily liknes, bot vnseablely by priue presence of his mi ȝte. Þerfore see him gostly if þu maiȝt, or elles trowe hym and folwe him wheder so he goþ; for he schal lede þe in þe riȝt wey to Ierusalem þat is þe siȝt of pees in contemplacioun.[70]

(24.89r. –234)

vnseablely: invisibly; *priue*: inward and private; *maiȝt*: can.

In the reformation of feeling the contemplative is moving beyond the love understood and expressed by means of the suffering involved in penance, to the fruit of the risen lord. Hilton embodies his sense of how the contemplative grows in love for Christ as God, in the image of Mary Magdalene reaching out to touch the risen Jesus who says:

Noli me tangere, nondum enim ascendi ad Patrem meum. Touche me not, I am not ȝit stied vp to my fader.

(30.104v. –255)

stied vp: ascended.

Hilton enlarges:

sette not þe reste ne þe luf of þine hert in þat forme of man þat þu seest with þi fleschly eiȝe only for to reste þer in; for in þat forme I am not stied vp to my fader. Þat is I am not euen to þe fader; for in forme of man I am lesse þan he. Touche me not so, bot sett þi þoȝt and þi luf in to þat forme in whilk I am euen to þe fader, þat is þe forme of þe Godhed, and lufe me, knowe me and worschip me as God and man godly, not as a man manly.

(30.105r. –255–6)

euen: equal.

It is this love, knowledge and worship which is experienced in the darkness; the 'lif vnseable'(30.102r.–252) of the soul' as the gift of the Holy Ghost at Pentecost who:

was vnseably felt in þe miȝtes of her soules, . . . so . . . þat þei haden sodeynly þe gostly knowynge of soþfastnes and þe perfeccioun of luf as oure lorde behiȝt hem, seiande þus: *Spiritus sanctus docebit vos omnem veritatem*. Þat is: þe Holy Gost schal teche ȝow al soþfastnes.

(30.105v. –256)

soþfastnes: truth

This is the core of contemplative knowledge, not the quasi-sensual experience of heat and sweetness and light which may accompany it. These, Hilton says, putting the over-enthusiastic followers of Rolle's spirituality into perspective, are at best outward tokens of an inner grace.

Chapters 31–46: 'this gift of love'

In the last part of *Scale 2* Hilton turns away from his powerful evocation of the inner journey that he calls 'forþgoynge', away from the reforming of faith 'to hiȝere reformynge þat is in felynge' (31.106r. –257) to look more closely at what that state is, 'and how it is made, and whilke are gostly felynges þat a soule resceifiþ. (31.106r. –257).

It is well known that Hilton's mystical theology involves a synthesis between feeling and intellectual knowledge based on an Augustinian tradition of theological exposition of a sequential relationship between faith and understanding where 'understanding' springs from a lived experience of the intellectually formulated truths of a prior faith, though it may also involve an attempt to present a rational analysis of the understanding of such experience.[71]

This synthesis is present in Hilton's constant use of light imagery in his account of the inner journey to indicate the 'gostly þinges' that are 'seen and knowen by vndirstandynge of þe soule, not bi ymaginacioun' (30.102v. –253) since imagery of light and seeing resonates with meaning at the levels of both intellect and feeling.

In order to teach how those journeying through the darkness may distinguish the light that slides out through crannies from the city of Jerusalem (25.92v. –238) from false lights, he differentiates between the light of self-righteousness, which shines out between the clouds of presumption and putting down of other Christians, and the experience of the 'sunne of riȝtwisnes þat is oure lord Iesu' that shines on meek souls.

> Vnto þise soules þe trewe sunne shal spryngen and illumine here resoun in knowynge of soþfastnes and kyndelen here affeccioun in brennnyng of luf: and þan shal þei boþ brennen and schynen. þei schul þurgh vertue of þis heuenly sunne bren in perfit luf, and shynen in knowyng of God and gostly þinges. For þan be þei reformed in felynge.
>
> (26.94v. –242)

bren: burn.

It is this light of knowing in love that informs his memorable translation of Isaiah 58:11: *Et . . . Dominus Deus . . . implebit animam tuam splendoribus* [and the Lord will fill thy soul with brightness] as 'þan schal oure lord Iesu fulfil þi soule with schynynges' (27.98r. –247).

In chapter thirty-one Hilton quite firmly establishes knowing and wisdom as reforming in feeling as he translates St Paul's prayer in Colossians 1:9 'þat ȝe may be fulfilled in knowynge of Goddis wille in alle vndirstandynge and in al maner gostly wisdom' (31.106v. –258) and comments 'this is reformyng in felinge'. But he distinguishes two modes in which the soul understands or feels: through the senses (imaginatively) and simply through its own powers of mind reason and will. These are involved in reforming in feeling when, through grace, they are 'fulfillid in al vndirstondyng of þe wille of God and gostly wisdam, þan haþ þe soule new graciouse felynges (31.106v. –258). And although he points to reason as 'properli þe image of God' it is only so when it is reformed in feeling (*ibid*). Moreover Hilton is careful to point out that this knowledge of God to which man has access is not distinguished by its intellectual content. He cannot as a creature in time fully know what God is beyond time, but he can know that he has being and that he is 'an vnchaungeable beynge, a souereyn miȝt, souereyn soþfastnes, souereyn goodnes, a blissid lif, an endeles blis' (32.107r. –259). And Hilton enjoins a further caveat: that this knowledge is not one of academic possibility known 'vnsauourly, as doþ a clerke þat seeþ him by his clergi only þurgh miȝt of his naked resoun' (32.107r&v. –259); it is a knowledge inseparable from experienced love:

> he seeþ him in vndirstandynge þat he is, counfortid and liȝtned bi þe gifte of þe Holy Gost with a wondirful reuerence and a priuy brennande lufe and with gostly sauour and heuenly delite, more clerly and more fully þen it may be wryten or seide.
>
> (32.107v. –259)

This knowledge, Hilton says, is 'þe blis of a resonable soule and endles lif' (33.110v. –263) but the role of grace, which is the gift of the Holy Ghost, is crucial to it and in chapter thirty-four he addresses himself to the way in which man gains this knowledge which is the point of his creation.

In the context of medieval theological debate as to whether theology primarily appeals to *intellectus*, the 'rational part of the mind' or *affectus*, the will or 'disposition of the mind',[72] it has been felt that for Hilton, intellect plays the leading role and affection follows since he says 'lufe comiþ oute of knowynge and not knowynge oute of luf' (34.110v. –263).[73] Such a reading is certainly sustained by the text even given the qualification with which Hilton hedges his statement that the knowing itself is a gift of God's love:

> þe luf þat oure lorde haþ to a synful soule þat kan riȝt not lufen hym is cause whi þis soule comiþ to þis knowynge.
>
> (34.110v. –264)

It is, however, possible that such a reading arises out of the dimensional confines in which language works. Hilton is constrained by a means of communication that is by definition inadequate to the job of describing an experience of a totality of meaning which transcends all partial insight:

> for we are so fleschly þat we kun not speken of God ne vndirstonden of him bot if bi swilke wordes first ben entrid in. Nerþeles, whan þe inner eiȝe is opned þurȝ grace for to hafe a litel siȝt of Iesu, þan schal þe soule turne liȝtly ynowȝ alle swilke wordes of bodily þinges in to gostly vndirstondynge.
>
> (33.110r. –263)
>
> *bot if bi swilke wordes first ben entrid in*: unless [we] are first introduced through such words.

He uses language to point the way out of the distinctions of awareness in time:

> þis gostly opynynge of þe inner iȝe in to knowynge of þe Godhed I calle reformynge in feiþ and in felynge. For þan þe soule sumewhat feliþ in vndirstandynge of þat þinge þat it had bifore in nakid trowynge.
>
> (33.110r. –263)
>
> *trowynge*: believing.

Just as in *Piers Plowman* Will travels a long route to 'kynde knowynge' of the truth which Holy Church instructs him as a matter of faith is innate in his created being:

> It is a kynde knowynge that kenneth in thyn herte
> For to loven thi Lord levere than thiselve,
> No dedly synne to do, deye theigh thou sholdest –

> This I trowe be truthe; . . .

so Hilton's reformation in feeling is a journey to the centre of the self 'to know the place for the first time' where God is immanent. And this knowledge of God in the self closes the gap between will and intellect which is too often the condition of fallen man. Hilton implies such a synthesis at every stage of his writing about contemplative experience.[74]

The context in which he talks about the primary role of the intellect since 'lufe comiþ oute of knowywnge and not knowynge oute of luf' (34.110v. –263) is his justification for suggesting that the means of accomplishing the journey to reformation in feeling is to covet only the love, not the knowledge of God,[75] an act of will, because it is the primary uncreated love of God – the Holy Ghost – which enables the soul to that knowledge and experience of God from which love grows. Love is 'boþ þe gifer and þe gifte, and makiþ vs þan bi þat gifte for to knowen and lufen him' (34.111r. –264).

The whole nature of the soul mirrors the Trinity.[76] In its existence it witnesses to the creative power of the Father; the nature of its being in will and wisdom is the medium in which Christ redeems man, and the love which activates both the reformation in faith and the reformation in feeling in which the nature of Christ as God is known and loved is the Holy Ghost. Hilton therefore identifies the dynamic power of God in the soul as the prime mover of the will to the knowledge and love of God. Elsewhere in the text Hilton identifies this willed desire as Jesus:

> he makiþ þis desire in þe and he gifiþ it þe, and he it is þat desiriþ in þe and he it is þat is desired.
>
> (24.89r. –234)

Indeed he acknowledges that he moves between the persons of the Trinity as one in creative love:

> Bot per chaunce þu bigynnist to wundre whi I sey o tyme þat grace wirkiþ al þis, and anoþer tyme I sey þat loue wirkiþ, or Iesu wirkiþ, or God wirkiþ. Vnto þis I sey þus, þat whan I sey þat grace wirkiþ I mene lufe, Iesu and God: for al is on and not bot on.
>
> (42.132v. –292)

Academically, it may help analysis of contemplative knowledge to argue about the operation of those powers designated intellect and will, but there is a practical danger that such analysis, by its very dissective nature, may distort the reality of the cognition that is its subject. It can seem like scholastic quibble to consider intellect leading in this creative process – longing for a knowledge which itself gives rise to human love. For Hilton, integration of intellect and will enabled by the dynamic power of God is the reformation of feeling in which the operations of the Trinity are mirrored in the self.

He stresses the primary duty of the soul to covet nothing but love:

> Ask þou þen of God no þinge bot þis gifte of lufe, þat is þe Holy Gost . . . for þer is no gifte of God þat is boþ þe gifer and þe gifte, bot þis gift of luf. . . . it schal opnen and liȝtnen þe resoun of þi soule for to sene soþfastnes, þat is God and gostly þinges. And it shal stire þi affeccion holli and fulli for to loue him.
>
> (36.115r. –269)

As Julian finds that the life of prayer activated by a God-given longing for fulfilment involves a growth in consciousness of the potential for love at the heart of the self in which she is united to God,[77] so Hilton describes the whole process of the reformation in feeling in contemplatives as the work of love freeing them from all the impediments of their disordered natures and impelling them to the darkness where the 'ghostly eyes' are opened to consciousness of Jesus who is both the ground of being and transcendent God, which consciousness is inseparable from love. In his attempt to point to the nature of this consciousness he uses language which traditionally refers to both knowing and loving:

> þis openynge of þe gostly eiȝe . . . may be callid: *purte of spirit and gostly reste, inward stilnes and pees of conscience, heiȝenes of þoȝt and onlynes of soule, a lifly felynge of grace and pryuete of herte, þe waker slep of þe spouse and tastynge of heuenly sauor, brynninge in lufe and schynynge in liȝt, entre of contemplacioun and reformynge in felynge.*
>
> (40.123r&v. –280–1)
>
> *purte*: purity; *onlynes*: singleness; *pryuete*: inward revelation; *waker slep*: waking sleep.

And he stresses that despite the distinctions in meaning they are one in truth, 'for a soule þat þurȝ visitynge of grace haþ on, haþ al'

(40.123v.–281). There is no division between knowledge and love in the truth of God.

This visiting of grace Hilton understands as a kind of special consciousness of the grace present in the whole process of reformation in faith and feeling[78] and he recognises that such periods of awareness are not sustained, though when they come they not only bring experience of the realities accepted in faith as the basis of Christian life but they can also transfigure the experience of formulated prayer from that of willed discipline to that of something deeply understood and loved. In words which are remarkably similar to Rolle's account of his experience where speech was transformed to singing, Hilton writes:

> þan is þe body not elles, bot as an instrument and a trumpe of þe soule, in þe whilke þe sowle blowiþ swete notes of gostly louynges to Iesu.
>
> (42.131v. –291)

trumpe: trumpet.

He continues that this gift of quickened creative understanding is also what illuminates the levels of meaning to be found in Scripture,[79] so that it is understood as providing the pattern of salvation at all levels of experience. And just as Hilton has understood the whole growth in reformation in feeling as the extension of the pattern of death and resurrection revealed in the Incarnation, so now he provides an icon for this whole process of quickened spiritual understanding in the story of the journey to Emmaus (Luke 24:13–35) where the risen Christ joins two disciples and opens their eyes to the meaning of the Scriptures though they do not at that stage recognise him physically:

> *Aperuit illis sensum, ut intelligerent Scripturas*. He opned to hem clernes of wit þat þei miȝten vndirstondyn holy writ.
>
> (43.133v. –293)

Literature offers the possibilities of many modes of meaning derived from the experiences of the individuals and cultures which interact in the process of writing and reading. A text such as Hilton's belongs to this medium but points through it to an experience of a source of all meaning which is ineffable and beyond the confines of the dimension of time. It is a matter of Christian faith for Hilton that the way to this meaning was revealed in the

Incarnation which provides a pattern of the way to understanding – Langland's 'kynde knowyng'.

This belief in the Word made flesh informs Hilton's literary method. It frees him to appeal through imaginative understanding to realities beyond it; the pattern of the Incarnation, Passion, Resurrection and Ascension of Christ informs every stage of his exploration of the ladder of perfection enabling the contemplative to find the freedom within his physical experience to transcend it with joy. It fires for the reader a sense of the reality of the integration and fulfilment of the self in the knowledge of God of which he speaks, and it brings alive the meaning of the story of Scripture at a personal level. *The Scale* is itself a sustained meditation mediating the inner relevance of received beliefs. Although Hilton, like Rolle, is wary of being over-precise about meditation because it would inhibit the inner development which must be unique to each individual,[80] he finds images and structures general enough to point the way and enable a community of understanding. Just as Rolle stresses meditation as a unique gift but acknowledges that the beginner in contemplative life may profit from 'oþer mens wordis',[81] so Hilton says he has tried to write just a little about his understanding of 'gostly þinges' for 'wissing of þi soule'.The ultimate referent for such a work, however, is in the experience which it both points to and shares:

> For a soule þat is clene, sterid bi grace to vse of þis werkynge, may see more in an houre of swilk gostly matere, þan myȝt be writen in a grete book.
>
> (46.140r. –302)

NOTES

1. For example: inscribed on the flyleaf of BL Harley MS 6579 in a fifteenth-century hand later than that of the scribe is: *Magister Walterus Hyltoun Canonicus de Thurgarton qui fuit homo venerabilis sciencia et vite sanctitate. composuit hunc librum plenum catholica doctrina et edificacione*. [Master Walter Hilton Canon of Thurgarton who was a man revered for knowledge and holy living. He wrote this book full of Catholic doctrine and instruction.] See further Russell-Smith (1954, pp.205ff).

2. See Russell-Smith (1954, pp.199, 205, 208–11). She cites colophons of the Latin text of one or both books of *The Scale* which give the date of Hilton's death as 24 March, the vigil of the feast of the Annunciation a dating which agrees with

that of other manuscripts of the English text which are of Carthusian provenance. However, CUL MS Ee iv 30 also Carthusian, gives the date as 23 March. She explains that this discrepancy may be accounted for by the fact that Carthusians kept the anniversary of the death of a monk who died *post completorium* (that is after Compline, the last office of the day) on the day following although they recorded the true date of the death.

3. See Gardner (1936a, p.108).

4. See *Walter Hilton*, ed. Clark and Dorward (1991, pp.13–14). Hereafter cited as Clark and Dorward.

5. Gardner (1936a, p.108).

6. Magdalene College (Cambridge) MS 17 and BL Add. MS 11748. See Russell-Smith (1954, pp.184–5); Clark and Dorward (1991, pp.14–15).

7. See Gardner (1936a, pp.108).

8. *Ibid*, (pp.111–12).

9. MS Vernon. fol.353. See *Yorkshire Writers*, ed. Horstman, (1895, I, p.264). Quotations from *Mixed Life* are from Ogilvie-Thomson (1986) and numbers refer to page and line. I am grateful to James Hogg for permission to quote from this text published in his series Elizabethan and Renaissance Studies 92:15.

10. Editions of the Middle English texts of *The Scale of Perfection* are not yet available although that of *Scale 1* based on CUL Add MS 6686 is being prepared by M.Sargent, and that of *Scale 2* based on BL MS Harley 6579, by S.S. Hussey, see further Clark and Dorward (1991, pp.53–6). Quotations from Books 1 and 2 of *The Scale* are taken directly from these manuscripts (capitalisation and punctuation mine, and abbreviations silently expanded), but for ease of reference a page number is also given to the modern translation in Clark and Dorward (1991). The numbering thus refers to the chapter in the book of *The Scale*, the page number and column of CUL ADD MS 6686 for Book 1 or the folio number of BL Harley 6579 for Book 2, and the page number in Clark and Dorward. I am grateful to both Professor Hussey and Dr Sargent for allowing me to consult their work.

11. See *Scale 1*, chapters 1, 3, 9; *Mixed Life*, chapter 10.

12. See Ogilvie-Thomson (1986, ix).

13. *Ibid* (xxvii-xxxii).

14. See further *ibid*, (p.8, note 82), highlighting Hilton's originality in the tradition of exegesis of this text.

15. Cf. Rolle, *Form of Living*, c.12.

16. See further Beale (1975).

17. See above chapter 1, p.20 and note 47. Cf. Beale (1975,p.385) who points out that nowhere are such Latin terms as *vita media* or *vita mixta* encountered except in fifteenth-century manuscripts of Hilton where they translate the concept of 'medeled lyf'.

18. See above pp.17–18.

19. See Augustine, *Enarratio in Psalmum* 149, 4.PL 37, 1951.

20. Here Hilton widens the scope of the address beyond that of his immediate correspondent: 'A man þat is lettered and haþ vndirstondynge of hooli writte, ȝif he haue þis fier of deuocioun in his herte, it is good vnto him for to gete him stikkes of hooli ensamples and seiynges of oure lord bi redynge in hooli writte, and norissch þe fier wiþ hem. Anoþer man, vnlettered, mai not so redeli haue at his hand hooli writ ne dottoures seiynges, and forþi it nedeþ vnto him for to doo many goode deedes outewarde to his euene-Cristene, and kendele þe fier of loue wiþ hem. And so it is good þat eche man in his degree, after þat he is disposid, þat he gete him stikkes of o þing oþer of oþer, eiþer of preieres or of good meditaciouns or reding in hooli writte, or good bodili worchynge, for to norische þe fier of loue in his soule þat it be not quenchid' [*lettered*: educated; *redeli*: easily; *dottoures*: doctors; *euene-Cristene*: fellow-Christians] (38–9.434–46).

21. See *Scale 2*. 34.111r. –264.

22. See above p.18.

23. See above p.124 and note 19.

24. See further Clark (1979b).

25. See Sitwell (1949, 1950a, b); Clark (1978b).

26. On the evidence for lay-ownership of copies of *The Scale*, see Gardner (1936a, pp.107–8).

27. Pepler (1949, pp.509–10).

28. For detailed studies of the textual history of *The Scale* see Gardner (1936b); Hussey (1964). I am grateful to Professor Hussey for clarifying the current position regarding the manuscripts of *The Scale*.

29. 'What werk þat it be þat þu schulde don after þe degre and þe state þat þu standis in bodily or gostly, if it helpe þis gracious desire þat þu haste for to lufe Iesu and make it more hol more esy and more miȝty to alle vertues and to alle goodnes þat werke hald I beste be it prechynge be it þinkynge be it redyng be it wirkynge' [*hol*: whole] (21.86r. –229).

30. See Gardner (1936b, p.13).

31. BL Harley MS 2397, see Gardner (1936b, p.14).

32. See below p.132.
33. Cf. 'bot now seiȝ þou þat I speke ouere heȝe to þe in þis maner of preyere . . .' (1.33.303a.–103); 'And þerfor if þou thynk þat I haue here bifor spoken ouere heȝe to þe for þou nay noȝt take it ne fulfill it as I haue seid or shal sey, I will fall doun to þe als lowȝe as þou wilt . . .' (1.44.315a. –115).
34. Cf. Clark and Dorward (1991, pp.108, 119).
35. See Gardner (1936b, pp.20f.; Clark and Dorward (1991, pp.53–6).
36. See Minnis (1983, 1984a).
37. For a study of Hilton's treatment of 'intention' in a medieval theological context see Clark (1978c).
38. See above pp.89–90.
39. The same perception governs Julian's understanding when she says that there is no way to 'endles knowyng in God' but by 'time of passion'(c.21. p.23). See below pp.234–5,
40. Cf. Julian c.41. p.42.
41. See Augustine, *De Trinitate* Book 10, c.11. p.17; c.12. p.19.
42. This passage comes from that part of chapter 44 known as the passage on the Holy Name, see above p.132.
43. Cf. Julian of Norwich c.51. p.58; see below pp.248, 250–1.
44. For a comparison of Hilton's analysis of sin with the standard approach to the subject in medieval handbooks see Milosh (1966, c.5).
45. Cf. Clark (1978b).
46. Hilton's view of the efficacy of baptism leads him to the unfortunate statement that the soul of a child that is unchristened is the image of the 'fende' (6.67v. –200).
47. See further Clark (1978c).
48. 'þe second reformyng distroyes þe olde felynges of þis ymage of synne' (5.67r. –200).
49. See further Clark (1982).
50. Cf. Augustine, *Confessions* (1944, I.I.p.1) where he addresses God: 'Thou hast made us for Thyself and our hearts are restless till they rest in Thee'.
51. E.g. his account of the crucifixion of the image of sin where each part of the image is linked to a passage in Scripture, *Scale 1*, c.85.355–6b .–154–5), and the call for the crucifixion of this image is linked to Galatians 5:24, (c.86.356b. –156).

52. See Russell-Smith (1954); Minnis (1983, pp.352f).

53. E.g. Richard of St Victor, *The Twelve Patriarchs* (1979) chapter 5. See further below note 54.

54. See for example *Paraphrase De L'Abbé De Verceil Thomas Gallus Sur La Heirarchie Dans Les Cieux*, chapter 1, in *Dionysiaca: Recueil Donnant L'Ensemble Des Traductions Latines des Ouvrages Attribues Au Denys de L'Areopage*, Bruges, 1937, 2 vols, vol.2 pp. 1043–4, sections 743–7 and the illuminating comparison of understanding with contemplation there made: *et cognitivam intelligentiam sacrarum scripturarum esse imaginem comprehensivae contemplationis quae mentes satiat* . . . ('the cognitive understanding of the holy Scriptures is the image of that all embracing contemplation which fully satisfies minds . . .'). I owe this reference to Minnis (1983, p.344).

55. Prayer 1.

56. Cf. above p.139.

57. Cf. Rolle's treatment of three degrees of spiritual life in *Ego Dormio*.

58. Cf. Schmidt (1980).

59. See chapter 21 (84r.–227).

60. See Crone (1965, p.452).

61. See Zacher (1976, chapters 3 and 6).

62. See Augustine, *City of God* (1972) especially Book XIX.

63. See Lubac (1959, pp.568, 645–50 and refs cited).

64. *The Cloud of Unknowing*, c.60. p.62, 31–2.

65. Cf. chapter 21. (85r. –228) where 'meknes seiþ I am noȝt, I hafe noȝt; lufe saiþ I coueite noȝt bot on and þat is Iesu'.

66. Chapter 20 (83v. –225–6).

67. See further Clark (1977, 1978b).

68. Hilton's use of the word 'chosen' is conditioned by his sense of the reality of a dimension beyond time in which all time is eternally present, and designates those whom he believes will be one with God there: 'þese þat God knew bifore þat schuld be made schaply to þe ymage of his sone, þese he called' [*made schaply*: conformed] (28.98v.–247). Such a conception does not invalidate man's freedom to respond to the call, it is simply a description in time of a reality beyond it.

69. See Bradley (1984); Park (1992).

70. Cf. Matthew 28:7: '. . . and, behold, he will go before you into Galilee; there you shall see him . . .'

71. See Clark (1982); Minnis (1983, pp.350f.).

72. See Minnis (1983, p.325).

73. *Ibid*, p.354.

74. See above p.14 and p.153.

75. See chapter 21.

76. See chapter 34, 112r –265.

77. *A Revelation of Love*, chapters 41–3. See below pp.242ff.

78. Chapter 40, 126r–284.

79. 'it is expouned and declared letterly, morally, mistily and heuenly if þe mater suffre it' [*letterly*: literally; *mistily*: allegorically.] (c.43.133v.–294). Cf. above p.9.

80. See *Scale 1*, 34, 305a–105.

81. *The Mending of Life* (1896, c.8, p.120, 31–2).

Chapter 4

The *Cloud*-Author: 'Kepyng of Tyme'

It is a mark of the rich diversity of ways in one truth that the *Cloud*-author's manner of touching on 'gostly þinges' for the 'wissing' of the soul involves the reader in a startlingly different literary experience to that of reading *The Scale of Perfection*.[1] There is no systematically structured exposition of all the stages of development in the growth of the inner life in awareness of God, though it is clear that this is available as a subtext which is taken for granted in his thinking. Instead we have a group of works in the vernacular which address particular aspects of religious life and particular needs of those who feel themselves impelled to explore it. These writings signal an authentically individual authority able to assimilate the thought and experience of others in the expression of an austere understanding of how man discovers God to be the purpose of his being. After the poetic fireworks of Rolle and the carefully sustained intellectual and emotional appeal of the imagistic analysis of Hilton, the *Cloud*-author's writing has a cutting edge of devotional astringency and humorously shrewd observations on pious posturing; it is like a fresh wind from a far country in its witness to how the inner spirit of man reaches to the truth of God that cannot be encompassed by human faculties.

There are seven treatises connected by manuscript tradition with the author of *The Cloud of Unknowing*: *The Cloud* itself; *The Book of Privy Counselling; The Epistle of Prayer; The Epistle of Discretion of Stirrings; Hid Divinity*, a translation and partial adaptation (via intermediate Latin texts) of the work of Dionysius the Areopagate; *Benjamin Minor, the Study of Wisdom*, freely adapted from *The Twelve Patriarchs* of Richard of St Victor; and *A Treatise of Discerning of Spirits* (a creative development of passages from two of St Bernard's *Sermones de Diversis 23 & 24*.[2] The focus of this chapter will be on the work for which the *Cloud*-author is best known, the

Cloud of Unknowing, and *The Book of Privy Counselling* most frequently connected with it in manuscript compilations.[3] The major work, *The Cloud of Unknowing*, is explicitly elucidated by further thought in *The Book of Privy Counselling*, in which the author also refers to *The Epistle of Prayer* and *Hid Divinity*[4] as his. This establishes the fact that these three texts preceded *The Book of Privy Counselling*. There is, however, no other certain knowledge about the other works or the order in which they were written.[5] It is generally accepted that *The Epistle of Discretion of Stirrings* is indeed likely to be the *Cloud*-author's since it expands the teaching of *The Cloud*, particularly that in *Cloud* chapter 42. Since both the *Benjamin Minor* and the *Discerning of Spirits* certainly underpin the teaching of the *Cloud*-author in various ways and are related to the other treatises in manuscript collections, the strong possibility that they too can be safely included in the canon has been argued although recent scholarship has called into question the authorship of the *Benjamin Minor*.[6]

The anonymity of the *Cloud*-author has remained impenetrable despite the suggestion of some that his style and theological perception agree sufficiently with those of Walter Hilton to make identification possible.[7] While it is true that the vocabulary of passages from both authors taken in isolation from the whole context in which they belong can look remarkably similar, and that their theological positions on the manner in which man knows God are not so far apart as is sometimes argued, nevertheless it should give pause for thought that arguments on both sides can be constructed at all. While the debate has a certain detective fascination and can serve to sharpen understanding of the theological implications of the texts involved, it is not necessary to our understanding, nor should it be allowed to distort appreciation of the literary quality and unique inner coherence of both *The Cloud of Unknowing* and *The Scale of Perfection*. Certainly the literary experience and, therefore, the theological understanding involved in reading *The Scale* and the *Cloud*-author's works are very different. Part of the pleasure in reading Hilton lies in responding to the clarity of the intellectual structure which informs his understanding of the inner life, while with the *Cloud*-author it is the nervous energy of the style, embodying the most delicate and hesitant evocation of a mode in which man's experience is suffused by awareness of the reality of God, which challenges, moves and excites. Significantly, it remains the view of the *Cloud*-author's definitive editor, and it is one with which this writer agrees, that while the linguistic evidence of the works points to a late fourteenth-century author from the east Midlands, that author was not Walter Hilton.[8]

It is, however, possible that the *Cloud*-author knew Hilton or at least his work. In chapter forty-eight of *The Cloud* the author mentions the question of how to judge the validity of bodily feelings in devotion, but he says he does not need to go into it :

> for whi þu mayst fynde it wretyn in anoþer place of anoþer mans werk a þousandfolde betir þan I kan sey or write.
>
> (48.50–1.40–1)

and Hilton deals with precisely this matter in *Scale 1* chapters ten to twelve.[9] Indeed University College Oxford Manuscript U 14 of *The Cloud* actually identifies this other 'mans werk' as 'hylton's' albeit marginally and in a later hand.[10]

The *Cloud*-author has strong connections with the Carthusian order. Not only is his mode of thinking probably influenced by the work of the Carthusian writers Guigo II and Hugo of Balma[11] but, more incontrovertibly, the order was very important in the transmission of the text.[12] However widely the manuscripts were circulated after the Reformation, it seems that their immediate distribution was among a restricted audience.[13] Many of the manuscripts are of Carthusian provenance, and even those which are not come from professional religious backgrounds. Moreover there is evidence that *The Cloud* was not included in early publishers' lists of devotional treatises[14] and although works by Rolle and Hilton are frequently mentioned in wills, there are no such references to *The Cloud of Unknowing*.[15]

AUDIENCES

The inference from all this that *The Cloud of Unknowing* was a specialist text for a specialist audience[16] is borne out by the *Cloud*-author's own remarks in the Prologue that his text is not suitable for all readers. However, the concomitant feeling among some modern commentators that it is also a very rarefied and difficult text is not thus substantiated. At the beginning of *The Book of Privy Counselling* the *Cloud*-author remarks:

> I merueyle me somtyme whan I here sum men sey (I mene not simple lewid men & wommen, bot clerkes [& men] of grete kunnyng) þat my writyng to þee & to oþer is so harde & so heiȝ, & so curious & so queinte, þat unneþes it may be conceiuid of þe sotelist clerk or wittid man or womman in þis liif, as þei seyn.
>
> (76.19–24).
>
> *I merueyle me*: I am surprised; *lewid*: uneducated; *kunnyng*: learning; *unneþes*: scarcely.

It is hard to reconcile this with the perpetuation of the view that the text 'makes considerable intellectual demands of its readers'or that *The Cloud of Unknowing* is the most difficult of spiritual writings in the fourteenth century.[17] With the exception of the translations and adaptations from earlier works (*Hid Divinity [Benjamin Minor]*, and *Discerning of Spirits*) the *Cloud*-author's writings are directed at particular individuals in specific situations. We know that the disciple addressed in *The Cloud of Unknowing* was a young man of twenty-four[18] who had turned from active to contemplative life with all the inevitability with which the falcon flown on a creance returns to the falconer:

> For first þou wote wel þat when þou were leuyng in þe comoun degree of Cristen mens leuyng in companie of þi wordely freendes, it semeþ to me þat þe euerlasting loue of his Godheed . . . miȝt not suffre þee be so fer fro him in forme & degree of leuying, & þerfore he kyndelid þi desire ful graciously, & fastnid bi it a lyame of longing, & led þee bi it into a more special state and forme of leuyng, to be a seruant of þe special seruauntes of his; where þou miȝtest lerne to liue more specialy & more goostly in his seruise þan þou dedist, or miȝtest do, in þe comoun degree of leuyng bifore.
>
> (1.7–8.39–10)
>
> *wordely*: worldly; *lyame*: leash.

The phrase to be a 'seruant of þe special seruauntes of his' has a teasing ambiguity which would have had – indeed still has – an immediate resonance for those in religious communities. By quoting in the vernacular the familiar formula of the Papal signature *servus servorum* (servant of the servants) the *Cloud*-author is making an encouraging and gently humorous remark to the young man whose calling sets him alongside all those in religious life right up to the Pope himself.[19] If this particular young man was not only a servant in the sense which applies to all religious but also, literally, a servant as a lay-brother in the community, the phrase would have an added bite which is utterly characteristic of the *Cloud*-author's style. Writing in the vernacular he often, as will be seen, approaches potentially complex matters with a deliberate simplicity and a light touch, as would be demanded by an address to a lay brother albeit one who had an innately highly-developed sense of the religious calling prompting him towards a solitary life. He imaginatively and humorously anticipates such a young man's objections and difficulties by dramatising him in the discussion,[20] but he can also take for granted a degree of natural understanding of what is meant by, and involved in, the experience called by Rolle (drawing on the terminology of Richard of St Victor) singular love.[21]

> ȝit it semeþ þat he wolde not leue þee þus liȝtly, for loue of his herte, þe whiche he haþ euermore had vnto þee siþ þou were ouȝtes. Bot what did he? Seest þou nouȝt how lystly & how graciously he haþ pulled þee to þe þrid degre & maner of leuing, þe whiche hiȝt Synguleer? In þe whiche solitari forme and maner of leuyng þou maist lerne to lift up þe fote of þi loue, & step towardes þat state & degre of leuyng þat is parfite, & þe laste state of alle.
>
> (1.8.11–17)

ouȝtes: of any account; *lystly*: readily; *hiȝt*: is called.

It has been suggested that a lay-brother with such a calling would not be sufficiently advanced in contemplation or have an 'intellect strenuous and flexible enough to match the demands of this kind of theology'.[22] However, this view seems, at best, unnecessary in the face of the *Cloud*-author's insistence that those who label his teaching 'coriouste of witte' have got it wrong for, 'ȝif it be witterly lokyd, it schal be founden bot a symple & a liȝt lesson of a lewid man' (*P.C.*76.36–7). If the disciple was a Carthusian lay-brother there is no reason to suppose that he was not sufficiently literate in the vernacular to be the recipient of such teaching.[23] Undue speculation as to the exact identity of the recipient is not appropriate here, but all the internal evidence of the text points to a man peculiarly fitted to living a solitary life but having some connection with a religious order, who was blessed with a natural religious understanding, uncomplicated by subtle intellectuality and with an obvious gift for contemplative prayer. Such a gift may also be inferred from the fact that the *Cloud*-author can take for granted a detailed knowledge of the nature of the basic disciplines of penance and meditation,[24] and is only concerned to forward the disciple in the cultivation of what he calls 'werk' – a way of prayer in which the disciple becomes directly aware of the transforming reality of God.

His discretion and maturity may be deduced from comparison with the alarmingly shrewd *Epistle of the Discretion of Stirrings* written to, it would seem, a young man with an over-solemn zeal to adopt a religious life, and an anxiety as to the form it should take:

> þou askist me counsel of silence and of spekyng, of comoun dietyng & of singulere fastyng, of dwelling in companye & of only-wonyng by þiself. And þou seist þou arte in grete were what þou schalt do; for, as þou seist, on þe to partye þou arte greetly taried wiþ spekyng, wiþ comoun etyng as oþer folk done, and wiþ comoun wonyng in companye; and, on þe toþer party, þou dredist to be streitly stille, singulere in fasting, and only in woning, for demyng of more holines þen þou arte worþi, and for many oþer periles.
>
> (109.2–10)
>
> *comoun dietyng*: ordinary eating habits; *singulere*: special; *only-wonyng*: living alone; *were*: perplexity; *þe to*: the one; *taried*: kept back; *streitly stille*: strictly silent; *for demyng of*: for fear of being judged.

The *Cloud*-author puts his finger devastatingly on the uncomfortable possibility that the young man's problems arose from confusion in his thinking: that the manner of living would produce the religious insight rather than the insight prompt the manner of living; that he was misled by the desire to imitate the religiosity of others rather than to follow the difficult but more rewarding path of coming to terms with himself.

> And touching þees steringes, of þe whiche þou askist my conseit and my counsel: I say to þee þat I conseyue of hem suspeciously; þat is, þat þei schold be conceyuid on ape maner. Men sein comonly þat ape doþ as he oþer seeþ. Forȝeue me ȝif I erre in my suspecioun, I prey þee.
>
> (113.1–5).
>
> *conseit*: opinion; *on ape maner*: apishly

The author's surmise is strengthened by the fact that someone else in the area had confusedly fallen into the same error through trying too hard to imitate a solitary in the district with a genuine gift for contemplative life. The *Cloud*-author gently tries to build on the situation:

> And leue þe corious beholdyng & seching in þi wittes to loke wheþer is betir. Bot do þou þus: sette tone on þe to honde and þe toþer on þe

> toþer, and chese þee a þing þe whiche is hid betwix hem, þe whiche þing when it is had, ȝeueþ þee leue, in fredom of spirite, to beginne and to seese in holding any of þe oþer at þin owne ful list, wiþouten any blame.
>
> Bot now þou askest me what is þat þing. I schal telle þee what I mene þat it is. It is God for whom þou schuldest be stille, ȝif þou schuldest be stylle; and for whom þou schuldest speke, ȝif þou schuldest speke; and for whom þou schuldest fast, ȝif þou schuldest fast; and for whom þou schuldest ete, ȝif þou schuldest ete; and for whom þou schuldest be only, ȝif þou schuldest be only, and for whom þou schuldest be in companie, if þou schuldest be in companie; and so forth of alle þe remenant, whatso þei be. For silence is not God, ne speking is not God; fastyng is not God, ne etyng is not God; onlines is not God, ne companye is not God; ne ȝit any of alle þe oþir soche two contraries. He is hid betwix hem, and may not be founden by any werk of þi soule, bot al only bi loue of þin herte. He may not be knowen by reson. He may not be þouȝt, getyn, ne trasid by vnderstonding. Bot he may be loued and chosen wiþ þe trewe, louely wille of þin herte. Chese þee him; and þou arte silently spekyng & spekyngly silent, fastyngly etyng and etyngly fasting; and so forþ of alle þe remenant.
>
> (114–5.32–13)

tone: the one; *seese*: cease; *list*: desire; *trasid*: discovered.

He conveys the sense that the work of the spirit cannot be forced, but only liberated in the self through humble self-knowledge gained through discipline and advice from those who practise such discipline:

> And þerfore leue to worche after oþer mens disposicions; and worche after þin owne, if þou maist knowe what it is. And vnto þe tyme be þat þou maist wite what it is, worche after þo mens counseile, þat knowen here own disposicioun, bot not after þeire disposicioun.
>
> (118.26–30)

He also points to his belief that the way forward is not one of intellectual understanding, but of learning the techniques of spiritual love-play which opens man to God and God to man.

> By reson we mowe trace how miȝty, how wise, & how good he is in his creatures, bot not in himself. Bot euer whan reson defaileþ, þan list loue liue and lerne for to plei; for by loue we may [fynde] him, [fele] him, and hit him euen in himself.
>
> (115.29–33)

trace: search out.

The author writes *The Cloud of Unknowing* for a disciple whose discretion in pursuit of his calling he trusts. It is a text which fields the resources of language with great delicacy both to convey how this love-game can be played and to point to apprehension of its nature. There are also hints in the text when he broadens a particular point to a more general discourse that the *Cloud*-author was aware that it might be read by more than one particular man.[25] Some of the difficulties registered by readers of *The Cloud of Unknowing* may stem partly from unfamiliarity with the negative theology mediated by the pseudo-Dionysius which governs the *Cloud*-author's mode of expression. He himself acknowledges that this is difficult when he says in his translation, *Hid Divinity*, that he has used the interpretations of the Victorine, Thomas Gallus, 'to declare þe hardnes of it' (*H.D.*119.9). The difficulties also stem partly from a desire to respond in terms of theological discourse to the intellectual implications of this expression rather than to its function as figurative language to move the reader to an awareness of the existence of a reality which cannot be adequately reflected in time-bound syntactical processes of semantic fragmentation. Augustine signals such awareness in his description of the Word of God as 'not an utterance in which what has been said passes away that the next thing may be said and so finally the whole utterance be complete: but all in one act, yet abiding eternally. . . . But of Your Word nothing passes or comes into being, for it is truly immortal and eternal.'[26] The whole of *The Cloud* is based on the premise that all creation witnesses to a larger reality which can also be encountered existentially. The *Cloud*-author's warning that he distrusts the speculative learning of 'þees corious lettred . . . men' [*corious*: subtle, speculative] (Prologue, 2.5) and that the book is only proper to those who have an innate feeling of desire for God – an 'inward stering after the priue sperit of God' (*Ibid*, 2.9) potential contemplatives – is not idle, for such readers would have a natural affinity with the essentially profound simplicity of his subject matter, and would understand the way in which the teaching is easy. Nevertheless the *Cloud*-author uses the premises of Dionysian theology and language so creatively that they enable a literary experience which illuminates his subject. For those with no natural sympathy for this, the text may well present difficulties but still be far from opaque, though some understanding of the apophatic approach to God is necessary.

THE *CLOUD*-AUTHOR AND THE PSEUDO-DIONYSIUS

At the heart of the *Cloud*-author's teaching about contemplation is an apprehension that God so far transcends all definitions of human knowledge that all categories of sensual feeling, imaginative meditation and abstract intellectual thought have finally to be jettisoned as partial distractions in contemplative experience. They are so inadequate to adumbrate the reality about which the *Cloud*-author knows that he can only express this paradoxically as a 'knowyng' of God 'þe whiche is knowyn by vnknowyng'. In the use of such terminology he explicitly acknowledges that he draws on the work of the pseudo-Dionysius:

> & trewly, whoso wil loke Denis bookes, he schal fynde þat his wordes wilen cleerly aferme al þat I haue seyde or schal sey, fro þe biginnyng of þis tretis to þe ende.
>
> (70.70.6–8)

aferme: ratify.

Dionysius' writings were particularly influential in the West from the twelfth century onwards in a tradition of negative theology and teaching on the contemplative life.[27] The *Cloud*-author's work is permeated by this tradition and it is thus probable that he did not derive the image which gives *The Cloud of Unknowing* its title directly from Dionysius at all. He talks of darkness rather than a cloud of unknowing, whereas Richard of St Victor's treatise on mystical theology, *Benjamin Major*, uses the exact image of the 'cloud of unknowing' (*nubes ignorantiae*) and also describes the cloud of forgetting which, like that in the *Cloud*-author, wipes out memory of the knowledge of created things.[28]

As with Hilton's theology, the study of sources is important in setting the *Cloud*-author's work in a context of presuppositions and climate of thought. But it is important not to let this obscure the fact that the teaching of the *Cloud*-author is not in terms of intellectual discourse and argument but of sharing understanding about an experiential and phenomenological approach to God which transforms man's life.[29] Indeed, the *Cloud*-author is clearly exasperated by any over-intellectual approach to theology. Not only does he disassociate his work from those who are primarily interested in intellectual speculation,[30] but in the beginning of *The Book of Privy Counselling* he inveighs against an intellectuality which gets in the way of the apprehension of truth, thus putting his finger on a constant tension in the history of religion between the apprehension of a truth the profound and dynamic simplicity of which can be known only through the convolutions of experience, and the intellectual speculation about the nature of this truth and this experience. So he writes:

> þat now þees dayes not only a fewe folkes, bot generaly niȝhond alle (bot ȝif it be one or two in a contrey of þe specyal chosen of God) ben so bleendid in here coryous kunnyng of clergie & of kynde þat þe trewe conceite of þis liȝt werk, þorow þe whiche þe boistousest [lewyd] mans soule or wommans in þis liif is verely in louely meeknes onyd to God in parfite charite, may no more, ne ȝit so moche, be conceyuid of hem in soþfastnes of spirit, for her blyndnes & her corioustee, þen may þe kunnyng of þe grettest clerk in scole of a ȝong childe at his A.B.C.
>
> (*P.C.*76.26–34)
>
> *niȝhond*: almost; *bleendid*: blinded; *coryous kunnyng of clergie & of kynde*: abstruse knowledge from academic learning and nature; *boistousest:* uncultured; *lewyd:* uneducated; *onyd*: made one with.

He also clearly shows a wariness of external forms of piety which may, as in the case of the young man in *The Epistle of Stirrings*, be mistaken as ends in themselves. In *The Cloud* he betrays extreme distaste for such practices as he contrasts the grotesque distortions of an over-literal piety, and physical straining after a grace which is essentially spiritual, with the charismatic attraction of those alight with the simplicity of the love of God.[31]

To such a man, with an austere yet passionate sense of the ineffable reality of God, the Dionysian negative approach to mystical theology supplied a language with which he could express his sense of how that God, beyond the reach of sense and reason, may yet be accessed through love: 'by loue may he be getyn & holden; bot bi þouȝt neiþer' [*getyn*: got; *holden*: held] (*The Cloud*, 6.14.23). Yet in this stress on love he actually differs from the original text of Dionysius' *De Mystica Theologia*. Just as he did not derive the image of the 'cloud' for the state of unknowing directly from Dionysius, so in his emphasis on love he was almost certainly influenced by the work of Thomas Gallus, Abbot of Vercilli in the thirteenth century. In Gallus' adaptation of Dionysius *De Mystica Theologia* for contemplatives, he stressed that it is man's capacity to love, not the power of his intellect which, helped by God's grace, is operative in contemplative union. The *Cloud*-author stresses the importance of Gallus' understanding of Dionysius in the prologue to his translation[32] *Deonise Hid Divinity* when he admits that this is a difficult text. His claim that his own teaching is easy is based on an awareness of the ironic contrast between the complex processes of human thought and feeling and the bare simplicity of the approach to God to be learnt. Indeed, he concedes that since it involves the abandonment of all sensible modes of understanding it seems extremely unreasonable to the intellect which does not like to commit itself to courses of action without good reason and so 'wil on no wise late þee consent to þis werk er þe tyme be þat þer be maad aseeþ to þe coriouste þerof by sum feire skile' [*be maad aseeþ to*: satisfaction is given; *feire skile*: fitting argument] (*P.C.*86.40–1). But he is able to gesture towards a condition about which he cannot speak directly – basically one of 'complete simplicity costing not less than everything'[33] because his understanding of the negative theological approach derived from Dionysius gave him an approach which recognises the equivocal nature of language and points beyond it towards the possibility of a timeless silence of full understanding.

In the text translated by the *Cloud*-author as *Hid Divinity* it is argued that the language of negative theology depends for its full effect on a proper understanding of the opposite affirmative approach to God in which his nature is talked about in terms of attributes which are at least partially understood at a human level. This is an approach expounded in another work of Dionysius 'Of Goddes Names' (*Divine Names*) where he explained how God could be called 'Good, how Beyng, how Liif, how Wisdome, & how Vertewe, & what oþer þat þei be of þe vnderstondable namynges of God' (125–6.35–2). In *De Mystica Theologia* (*Hid Divinity*), however, he insisted that understanding of the one who is beyond all particularities and distinctions is actually limited, made 'streite', by an affirmative approach (III.126.18); so if language cannot of its nature positively define what God is, it can be used negatively to point to his ultimate nature. The process of unknowing in order to know 'hym þat is abouen al seing & al knowyng' (II.124.6) is compared to that of a sculptor hewing out a shape from a block of wood discarding all material inessential to it. Metaphorically speaking, the shape released corresponds to what the pseudo-Dionysius calls 'the nakid, vnmaad, & vnbigonne kynde' [*nakid*: absolute; *vnbigonne*: eternal] (II.125.2) which is both essential to man and at the same time transcendent: that in man which is part of the One. The *Cloud*-author calls it the 'nakyd beyng' of God (*The*

Cloud, 5.14.11) which is cause and substance of man's being: 'For he is þi being, & in him þou arte þat at þou arte, . . . he is in þee boþe þi cause & þi beyng'(*P.C.*75.31–3). The language of spatial dimension is used both negatively and paradoxically to convey a sense of this immanent and transcendent nature which is:

> euermore free – wiþinne alle creatures, not inclusid; wiþouten alle creatures, not schit oute; abouen alle creatures, not borne up; bineþe alle creatures, not put doun; behynde alle creatures, not put bak; before alle creatures, not dreuen forþe – neuerþeles ȝit, to mans vnderstondyng, þe whiles it is knittyd to þis corumpid bodi, he is neuermore cleerly schewid, bot as it were a þing þat were couerhid & ouerlappid & ouerleide wiþ vnnoumerable sensible bodies & vnderstondable substaunces, wiþ many a merueilous fantastik ymage, conielid as it were in a kumbros clog abouten hym, as þe ymage of þe ensaumple wretyn before is hid in þe þik, greet, sounde stok.
>
> (II.124.25–35)
>
> *corumpid*: corrupt; *conielid*: massed; *sounde stok*: solid block of wood.

The series of negatives 'not shut out', 'not put down', 'not driven forth', etc., all emphasise the dynamic all inclusive nature of being which gives movement rather than being subject to it.

THE *CLOUD*-AUTHOR AND LANGUAGE

Dionysius also uses paradox to gesture towards the state of unknowing in which such being is experienced, calling it a 'souereyn-schinyng derknes of wisest silence' (119.18–19). His discourse is both theological argument and poetic theology and it meets the *Cloud*-author's teaching needs in *The Cloud of Unknowing*. Indeed he uses the same strategy when he describes the darkness of the cloud of unknowing as a blinding with abundance of 'goostly liȝt', and the abrogation of all earthly knowledge which makes the disciple feel that he has nothing, as, in reality, having 'Al' (68.68.16–20). But, although he uses such language, he betrays a constant nervous anxiety that the inevitable involvement with physical experience in the use of metaphor should not be misunderstood. So he laboriously warns his disciple not to think that the darkness of the cloud of unknowing is an atmospheric cloud that flies in the air or the kind of darkness that fills the house when the candle is blown out at night:

> For when I sey derknes, I mene a lackyng of knowyng; as alle þat þing þat þou knowest not, or elles þat þou hast forȝetyn, it is derk to þee, for þou seest it not wiþ þi goostly iȝe. & for þis skile it is not clepid a cloude of þe eire, bot a cloude of vnknowyng, þat is bitwix þee & þi God.
>
> (4.13.18–22)

skile: reason.

And he points out that stirring of love in the heart does not refer to a physical heart but to the will of man (51.52.28–30). Part of his concern is that his language should not encourage a substitution of physical straining after piety for a real inner conviction and understanding of spirituality. He satirises those who foolishly and meaninglessly strike attitudes with an almost discomforting venom – describing some as staring with glazed eyes like a sick sheep who has been stunned with a blow, others carrying their heads down or on one side as if they had something unpleasant in their ears (53.54), and he uses the language of spatial dimension to emphasise its complete lack of propriety to the nature of the spiritual reality which is his subject:

> For heuen goostly is as neiȝ doun as up, & up as down, bihinde as before, before as behynde, on o syde as oþer, insomoche þat whoso had a trewe desire for to be at heuyn, þen þat same tyme he were in heuen goostly. For þe hiȝe & þe nexte wey þeder is ronne by desires, & not by pases of feet . . . & þerfore ȝif we wil go to heuen goostly, it nediþ not to streyne oure spirit neiþer up ne doune, ne on syde ne on oþer.
>
> (60.62.28–32, 36–8)

þeder: thither; *pases*: paces.

His constant concern to warn against mistaking the physical for a spiritual reality is rooted in the view of the working of human nature which he has inherited: immediately from Richard of St Victor's *Benjamin Minor*, but ultimately, like Walter Hilton, from an Augustinian tradition.[34] The *Cloud*-author understood the direction of the will to be influenced by sensual desires, and the judgement of reason to be fed by the images of the imagination about the nature of existence. He believed that if man were without sin all these faculties would be integrated in true knowledge and love of God and his creation. As it is, they are hopelessly corrupted and misled by sin. Imagination mistakes the nature of physical and spiritual reality unless it is disciplined by a reason illumined by God's grace; sensuality indulges in greed and impatience unless, through grace, it is restrained by the will. It has more than once been remarked that, paradoxically, the *Cloud*-author denigrates the imaginative faculty which largely governs his style[35] but what he is denigrating is the imagination unillumined by grace. It is not that bodily things cannot point to ghostly things, but that too often man fails properly to distinguish the one from the other. Although it is true that in the apprehension of spiritual truths he thinks that the process of understanding of necessity involved with physical images is potentially misleading,[36] there are points in the text where he states a clear belief in the divinely ordained propriety of union between body and spirit. Thus in talking about the practice of vocal prayer he says:

> God forbede þat I schuld departe þat God haþ couplid, þe body & þe spirit; for God wil be seruid wiþ body & wiþ soule, boþe togeders, as seemly is . . . .
>
> (48.50.14–16)

And in the case of physical manifestations of spiritual truths like, for instance, St Stephen's visions of Christ standing in heaven, where the act of standing signifies both readiness to support and the Ascension of Christ himself, he comments on the physical manifestations as furthering, rather than hindering the work of the spirit. It is the cup which holds the wine and should be reverenced as such, 'for men will kysse þe cuppe, for wine is þerin' (58.60.11–12). This reference to the Mass implies a sacramental view of the world, rightly understood, which explains why he says in chapter sixty that Christ's Ascension is not proof of the physical location of heaven, it is simply that in manifesting the return of Christ to the Father, upwards was most seemly and appropriate:

> Bot elles ne were þis semelines, him nedid neuer þe more to haue wente upwardes þen downwardes, I mene for nerenes of þe wey.
>
> (60.62.26–7)
>
> *elles*: otherwise.

And the only reason for upwards being appropriate lies in the metaphorical connotations of 'up'. For the *Cloud*-author there is an iconographic quality in the nature of things which enables them to point beyond themselves. Man must be the prime example:

> & for þis seemlines it is þat a man, þe whiche is þe seemliest creature in body þat euer God maad, is not maad crokid to þe erþewardes, as ben alle oþer beestes, bot upriȝte to heuenwardes; for whi þat it schulde figure in licnes bodely þe werke of þe soule goostly, þe whiche falleþ to be upriȝt goostly & not crokid goostly. Take kepe þat I sey upriȝt goostly, & not bodely. For how schulde a soule, þe whiche in his kynde haþ no maner þing of bodelines, be streinid upriȝt bodely? Nay, it may not be.
>
> (61.63.20–7)

But the connotations of the physical understanding of spatial dimension are nevertheless crucial to the understanding of a reading which rejects them. This relationship between physical and spiritual is at the heart of language itself – the *Cloud*-author makes no great bother about it:[37]

> For þof al þat a þing be neuer so goostly in itself, neuerþeles ȝit ȝif it schal be spoken of, siþen it so is þat speche is a bodely werk wrouȝt wiþ þe tonge, þe whiche is an instrument of the body, it behoueþ alweis be spoken in bodely wordes. Bot what þerof? Schal it þerfore be taken & conceyuid bodely? Nay, it bot goostly.
>
> (61.63.30–5)

What he deplores is not the fact that the imagination feeds the reason with visible images for its cognition of spiritual realities[38] but that in fallen man reason and imagination can muddle the two. The fact that the *Cloud*-author, as a fallen man, uses language imaginatively to point to a reality which transcends the imagination is no more paradoxical than his suggesting that fallen will, the faculty 'þorou þe whiche we chese good, after þat it be determinid wiþ reson; & þorow whiche we loue God' (64.65.9–10) is the faculty through which, with grace, man can reach God. His whole teaching depends on the belief that man can achieve discretion in judging the operation of rational knowledge and its limitations, and a settled directional impulse for the will, which empty the mind of everything but a desire for God beyond all that can be known:

> loke þat noþing leue in þi worching mynde bot a nakid entent streching into God.
>
> (*P.C.*75.19)
>
> *leue:* remain

His emphasis in the text on the difficulties presented by the imaginative means on which human knowledge depends is dictated by the particular nature and level of contemplative discipline with which he is concerned. It may indicate more about the level of education and particular disposition of the disciple and intended audience in relation to their capacity for contemplative experience than about the *Cloud*-author's distrust of imaginative metaphor. His sometimes almost naive insistence that the reader does not take in a bodily sense what is meant spiritually acts as a perpetual corrective and check in the experience of the inner 'werk' of emptying the mind in contemplative prayer. In view of his inheritance of an explicitly sanctioned anagogical use of language in which sensible things are used to designate things which are invisible and divine[39] and of the general understanding of figurative reading in art and literature in the Middle Ages, the *Cloud*-author's preoccupation with the relationship between tenor and vehicle in metaphor must surely arise from particular circumstances. Certainly in his *Epistle on Prayer* where he describes the development of prayer from fearing the loss of salvation, through hope of gaining it to a disinterested love of God for himself (the 'nakid entent' of *The Book of Privy Counselling*), in terms of a fruit which is only fully ripe when plucked from the tree on which it grows, he does so without any wagging of his finger, reminding the reader that he is speaking about a ghostly and not a physical matter:

> of þe whiche tre drede is þat party is wiþinne in þe erþe, þat is þe rote, and hope is þat partye þat is aboue þe erþe, þat is þe body with the bowes. In þat hope is certein & stable, it is þe body; in þat (þat) it steriþ men to werkes of loue, it is þe bowes. Bot þis reuerent affeccioun is euermore þe frute. And þan euermore as longe as þe frute is fastned to þe tre, it haþ in party a grene smel of þe tre. Bot whan it haþ a certein tyme ben departed fro þe tre and is ful ripe, þan it haþ lost al þe taste of þe tre and is kinges mete, þat was bifore bot knaues mete.
>
> (103–4.34–3)

THE PATTERN OF THE INCARNATION

The *Cloud*-author's presentation of the iconographical nature of experience is incarnational; and although reference to Christ does not operate in the imagistic way adopted by Hilton in *The Scale*, it is, nevertheless, present and unifies his account of contemplative experience as part of a continuum of spiritual experience.[40] Because of the nature of the spiritual experience on which the *Cloud*-

author's attention is focused, when the conscious activity of the mind is transcended in a loving knowledge of God who cannot be fully comprehended by the human intellect, the disciple is now recommended to cease practising meditation because it can distract the work of fostering the 'nakid entent' to God that is being discussed. The *Cloud*-author calls this distraction 'scattering', pulling man away from a 'simple' awareness of God which integrates his whole being in what the *Cloud*-author calls 'onyng wisdom' (*P.C.* pp.81–2).[41]

Far from fostering the cultivation of an unspecifically Christian experience, however,[42] the *Cloud*-author takes for granted a consciousness already prepared by the discipline of penance and meditation on the Passion of Christ:

> what man or womman þat weniþ to come to contemplacion wiþoutyn many soche swete meditacions of þeire owne wrechidnes, þe Passion, þe kyndenes & þe grete goodnes & þe worþines of God comyng before, sekirly he schal erre & faile of his purpos.
>
> (7.15.16–20)

weniþ: expects; *sekirly*: certainly.

And to the disciple, whom he dramatises as (very reasonably in the circumstances) asking why, if meditation on the Passion and works of God increases devotion, he should cease pursuing it (8.16.10f.), he explains that the process of meditation is an activity which is pursued by both those in active and contemplative life, but which is transcended in the kind of contemplative prayer with which he is concerned. This engages with the nature of reality, beyond the confines of the dimensions of time though it is accessed through them, where there 'schal be no nede to use þe werkes of mercy, ne to wepe for oure wrechidnes, ne for þe Passion of Criste' (21.30.13–15). The whole process of this growth in contemplative life is typified for the *Cloud*-author by his understanding of the example of the career of Mary Magdalene whom medieval readers identified with Mary of Bethany, the sister of the busy Martha who was 'busy about much serving' and indignant at her sister's lack of help as she sat at Jesus' feet and 'heard his word' (Luke 10:38–42).This figure, conflating the two Marys, progressed from bitter penance for her sin to a love for Christ as God beyond the 'vnderstondyng in hir reson' (chapters 16.25.38) and it was she who sought and found the risen Lord (16–23 *passim*). It is for this reason that the *Cloud*-author says to the disciple:

> Wepe þou neuer so moche for sorow of þi sinnes or of þe Passion of Criste, or haue þou neuer so moche mynde of þe ioies of heuen, what may it do to þee? Sekirly moche good, moche helpe, moche profite, & moche grace wol it gete þee; bot in comparison of þis blinde steryng of loue, it is bot a litil þat it doþ, or may do, withouten þis. Þis by itself is þe best partye of Mary, wiþouten þees oþer.
>
> (12.21.26–32)

Not only does the *Cloud*–author liken this progress in contemplative prayer to the Incarnational pattern of death, resurrection and ascension in time:[43]

> Ensaumple of þis schewid Criste in þis liif. For whi, ȝif it so had ben þat þer had ben none hier perfeccion in þis liif bot in beholdyng & in louyng of his manheed, I trowe þat he wolde not þan haue assendid vnto heuen, whiles þis woreld had lastid, ne wiþdrawen his bodely presence from his specyal louers in erþe
>
> (*P.C.*98.8–12)

he also sees the specific work of the contemplative, stripping away from himself all conscious aspects of his being except a desire for God, as an offering of 'þi nakid beyng' (*P.C.*79.30). At its own level this is a crucifixion of self before the contemplative can feel himself one with God:

> Lo! here mayst þou see þat þee behouiþ soroufuly desire to forgo þe felyng of þiself, & peynfuly bere þe birþin of þiself as a cros, er þou maist be onyd to God in goostly felyng of himself, þe whiche is parfite charite.
>
> (*P.C.*90.4–7)

Such an offering extends the work of redemption manifest in the Incarnation because the contemplative's experience of God which Adam lost is, as it were, doing a restoration job on the damaged body of Christ as this is expressed by all believers. It involves not just his own realisation of salvation, but an offering of love which is made for, and furthers the salvation of all, since all are part of one organic body of Christ.[44] It is a view which allows for a spiritual commonwealth of a diversity of gifts:

> For as alle men weren lost in Adam, & alle men, þat wiþ werke wil witnes þeire wille of saluacion, ben sauid, & scholen be, by vertewe of þe Passion of only Criste – not in þe same maner, bot as it were in þe same maner – a soule þat is parfitly affecte in þis werk, & onyd þus to

> God in spirit, as þe preof of þis werk witnessiþ, doþ þat in it is to maak alle men as parfite in þis werk as itself is. . . .
>
> For Crist is oure hede, & we ben þe lymes, if we be in charite; & whoso wile be a parfite dissiple of oure Lordes, him behouiþ streyne up his spirite in þis werk goostly for þe saluacion of alle his breþren & sistren in kynde, as oure Lorde did his body on þe cros.
>
> (*The Cloud*, 25.33.26–31, 34–8)
>
> *affecte*: disposed; *preof*: proof.

Thus the *Cloud*-author sees the pattern of Incarnation operating at every level of the contemplative's experience: as an object of meditation to induce self-awareness in the early active stages, and internally experienced in the work of contemplation. Small wonder that he exclaims in *The Book of Privy Counselling*:

> Neuerþeles ȝit ben þees faire meditacions þe trewest wey þat a synner may haue in his begynnyng to þe goostly felyng of himself & of God. & me wolde þenk þat it were inpossible to mans vnderstondyng – þof al God may do what he wil – þat a synner schuld com to be restful in þe goostly felyng of himself & of God, bot ȝif he first sawe & felt by ymaginacion & meditacion þe bodely doynges of hymself & of God, & þerto sorowed for þat þat were to sorowen, & maad joie for þat þat were to joien. & whoso comeþ not in bi þis weye, he comeþ not trewly.
>
> (*P.C.*90.27–35)
>
> *þof al*: although

Christ, the manifestation of God, is the key to the significance of contemplative life as the *Cloud*-author understands it. In his gloss on Christ's words in John 10:9: 'I am the door. By me, if any man enter in, he shall be saved: and he shall go in, and go out, and shall find pastures',[45] he embodies his perception of the redemptive purposes of God – the dynamic of grace – in terms of the relationship between the creative power of the Godhead and the humanity of Christ:

> þat is to þin vnderstondyng as ȝif he seide þus acordyng to oure mater: 'I þat am almiȝty by my Godheed & may leuefuly as porter late in whom I wol, & bi what wey þat I wol, ȝit, for I wol þat þer be a comoun pleyne wey & an open entre to alle þat wolen come, so þat none be excusid by vnknowyng of þe wey, I haue cloþid me in þe comoun kynde of man, & maad me so opyn þat I am þe dore by my manheed, & whoso entreþ by me, he schal be saaf.[46]
>
> (*P.C.*91.5–12)
>
> *mater:* matter; *leuefuly*: lawfully; *porter*: door-keeper.

At the very beginning of *The Cloud* the author also distinguishes related functions of the Godhead and manhood of Christ:

> he by his Godheed is maker & ȝeuer of tyme. He bi his Manheed is þe verrey keper of tyme. & he, bi his Godheed & his Manheed togeders, is þe trewist domesman & þe asker of acompte of dispending of tyme.
>
> (4.12.4–6)

domesman: judge; *acompte*: account.

The Cloud of Unknowing and *The Book of Privy Counselling*, because of their accessible witness to the transmission of the medieval tradition of Dionysian theology, have been the focus of scholarly attention and intellectual commentary of a kind that their original recipients would probably not have been able to follow. In fact the mode of discourse adopted in these two texts is designed to clarify in its own terms the way to an experience of oneness with God the dynamic of which integrates and releases human energies to realise the presence of a transcendent creative wisdom. This wisdom is of a quite different order to that of scholarly erudition:

> He is a blisful man þat may fynde þis onyng wisdom & þat may abounde in his goostly worching wiþ þis louely sleiȝt & prudence of spirit, in offring up of his owne blynde feling of his owne beyng, alle corious kunnyng of clergie & of kynde fer put bak.
>
> (*P.C.*81–2.40–4)

onyng: unitive; *sleiȝt*: intelligence; *fer*: fair.

In a passage which affirms the creative capacity of the imagination illuminated by grace to point beyond itself the *Cloud*-author evaluates intellectual knowledge and learning 'be it neuer so sotyl ne so holy'; in comparison with this inner creative wisdom it is:

> as fer fro þe verrey soþfastnes whan þe goostly sonne schiniþ as is þe derknes of þe moneschine in a mist at midwinters niȝt fro þe briȝtnesse of þe sonnebeme in þe clerest tyme of a missomer day.
>
> (*P.C.*82.16–19)

verrey soþfastnes: veritable truth; *missomer*: midsummer.

This imagery is particularly apt in view of the identification of wisdom with the second person of the Trinity, Christ.

The internal structures of *The Cloud of Unknowing* and *The Book of Privy Counselling* are so organised as to help the reader grasp the way to this wisdom which is his union with God.

THE CLOUD OF UNKNOWING

Chapters 1–26: the work of the soul

The first twenty-six chapters of *The Cloud of Unknowing* stress and define the dynamic nature of the contemplative calling which will involve the disciple in what the *Cloud*-author calls the 'werk of the soul'. It is essentially a desire for God which dominates his whole existence. The reality of this desire is that it is a sign of the acceptance of the immanence of God for 'þis desire behoueþ algates be wrouȝt in þi wille bi þe honde of Almiȝti God & þi consent' [*algates*: always] (2.9.1–3). This is the impulse to redemption that Hilton described as the longing for health in all men, and the *Cloud*-author uses the resources of rhetoric to ram home the enormity of its implications to his disciple. The monosyllabic alliterative statement which opens his address in chapter two followed by the modulation into the increasingly lyrical cadence of the following rhetorical questions are designed to stimulate a shock of recognition of the nature of the human situation:

> Look up now, weike wreche, & see what þou arte. What arte þou, & what hast þou deserued, þus to be clepid of oure Lorde? What weri wrechid herte & sleping in sleuþe is þat, þe whiche is not waknid wiþ þe drawȝt of þis loue & þe voise of þis cleping.
>
> (2.8.19–22)
>
> *clepid*: called; *sleuþe*: sloth; *drawȝt*: drawing.

The *Cloud*-author creates a sense of urgency about the need for inner response:

> Do on þan, I preie þee, fast. Look now forwardes, & lat be bacwardes. & see what þee faileþ, & not what þou haste
>
> (2.8.34–5)

before he comes to the business of definition of how this is to be made. After the tension of the statements, orders and questions of chapter two, chapter three has a quieter certainty as it defines the response as unremitting work towards a selfless love of God, what he calls 'a nakid entent vnto God' (3.9.31). And since this is to be divested of all love for the benefits of creation and directed at a source of being beyond the knowledge of intellect and, at this stage, certainty of love, the *Cloud*-author can only describe it as involving an experience of the unknown – a darkness, but not a completely empty darkness, because of the presence of the desire for God which he has already defined as a divine gift:

> For at þe first tyme when þou dost it, þou fyndest bot a derknes, & as it were a cloude of vnknowyng, þou wost neuer what, sauyng þat þou felist in þi wille a nakid entent vnto God. Þis derknes & þis cloude is, howsoeuer þou dost, bitwix þee & þi God, & letteþ þee þat þou maist not see him cleerly by liȝt of vnderstonding in þi reson, ne fele him in swetnes of loue in þin affeccion.
>
> (3.9.28–34)

This desire is the means to the end of which it is evidence,the instrument by which the loss inevitably inherent in the time-sequence which governs human existence, is redeemed.

Before examining the 'work' involved in releasing this 'nakid entent vnto God' in human nature, the *Cloud*-author puts it in the context of the Incarnation. For him the whole work of the contemplative is a striving to regain a state of being undamaged by sin, when all the inner drives and faculties were perfectly integrated in the love of God, and man was as the *Cloud*-author puts it 'lorde of . . . þoo sterynges' [*sterynges*: stirrings] (4.10.18–19). The undiverted desire for God which is how man works when he is functioning properly[47] would have continued, for 'þis is þe eendles merueilous miracle of loue, þe whiche schal neuer take eende' (4.11.1) but for sin. The contemplative's work is to acquire the mechanical skills to repair the human psyche and get it working properly again by releasing in the self a love for God which is fundamental to its being. Julian would think of this as discovering God as the substance of one's being,[48] the *Cloud*-author talks of ways by which the infinite and finite naturally fit together in love:

> For he is euen mete to oure soule by mesuring of his Godheed; & oure soule euen mete unto him bi worþines of oure creacion to his ymage & to his licnes. & he by himself wiþouten moo, & none bot he, is sufficient at þe fulle, & mochel more, to fulfille þe wille & þe desire of oure soule. & oure soule, bi vertewe of þis reformyng grace, is mad sufficient at þe fulle to comprehende al him by loue, þe whiche is

> incomprehensible to alle create knowable miȝt, as is aungel & mans soule.
>
> (4.10.22–9)
>
> *euen mete*: exactly proportional; *mesuring*: tempering; *knowable miȝt*: itellectual ability.

Time, the dimension in which this relationship has suffered multiple fractures, is also that in which it is mended: 'only through time time is conquered'.[49] The *Cloud*-author warns the disciple how vital it is not to waste the fleeting moment 'for noþing is more precious þan tyme' (4.11.19). The act of will involved in the disciple's consent to the God-given desire for Him is, says the *Cloud*-author, the fastest and therefore shortest work imaginable; it takes the briefest irreducible instant (what he calls an 'atom') of time conceivable. Conversely the will is oriented in some direction or other as many times in an hour as there are atoms and the aim is to account for every action of will. Small wonder that the disciple is imagined coming near to throwing in the towel as he acknowledges twenty-four years of time unaccounted for before even starting to live at such a stretch of awareness in the future. 'Help me now, for þe loue of Iesu' (4.11.39–40) he cries, a masterly rhetorical conflation of colloquial frustration and theological propriety by which the *Cloud*-author gives himself just the well-signalled entrée he needed for a discussion of the theology of time.

Later, in *The Book of Privy Counselling* the relationship between the Godhead and manhood of Christ is explored in terms of Christ's words reported in John 10:9: I am the door. By me, if any man enter in, he shall be saved: and he shall go in, and go out, and shall find pastures. The function of Christ's Godhead is clarified as keeping charge of the door to everlasting life, and that of his manhood as being in itself the door through which man enters.[50] Here the *Cloud*-author anticipates this understanding by seeing the Godhead as the maker and giver of time, the manhood as the 'verrey keper of tyme' (4.12.5) a combination which involves God as the true judge of how time is spent.

The *Cloud*-author says that he does not think that anyone can truly follow Christ 'bot ȝif it be soche one þat doþ þat in hym is, wiþ helping of grace, in kepyng of tyme' (4.12.17–18). The Middle English expression 'kepyng of tyme' can be understood as employing one's time and employing it in a proper manner, but the verb 'kepe' also has senses of being on guard and preserving from loss.[51] Both senses are operative in the *Cloud*-author's use of the word. He says that the disciple's love for God unites him with Mary 'þat ful was of alle grace in kepyng of tyme', with angels 'þat neuer may lese tyme' and with the saints in heaven and earth that through grace 'keepen tyme ful iustly in vertewe of loue' (*ibid*, 10–13). The angels may never lose time because they belong to an eternal dimension, which according to Augustine is to participate in the changeless light of God.[52] Man, in his work of releasing in himself the desire of God which brings its own wisdom, can be partner with Mary who through grace enabled Christ to be born. Christ so spent time, used it, that he redeemed it from loss. As love incarnate he is 'þe verrey keper of tyme'. This activity of willed consent to a desire for God – itself a gift of grace – is at the heart of the *Cloud*-author's understanding of the contemplative's work. This is how he participates in redemption, keeps time and is 'seen to be a profiter on his partye, so litil as is, vnto þe comunite' of Christ, Mary the angels and saints' (*ibid*, 15–20). It involves a constant longing existentially to realise love for God in the present moment – a living in the present – because the time to be accounted for: 'is neiþer lenger ne schorter, bot euen acording to one only steryng þat is wiþinne þe principal worching miȝt of þi soule, þe whiche is þi wille' (4.10.12–14);[53] and this is the way in which time is 'kept' in all its senses.

In chapters five to twenty-six the *Cloud*-author develops his understanding of what is involved in the process of the patient cultivation of the contemplative's ever-present consent to the God-given desire for Himself. He defines the tension involved between 'natural' inclination to mixed feelings and discursive thought (what the *Cloud*-author calls 'scateryng'[54]) and a desire for a reality which these modes of partial and fragmented ways of knowing cannot fulfil because it transcends all such particularity. But the desire is the means by which God and man are united – what the *Cloud*-author calls 'onyng wisdom' (*P.C.*81–2.40–1)[55] which can re-order human consciousness. If it is to be facilitated and realised the disciple has to learn techniques to subdue the clamour of conscious thought rooted in physical experience. This includes not just worldly interests that inevitably stir up emotions associated with them like anger, greed or lust, but also disciplined meditation[56] – even thoughts of the angels and saints can refract a simple concentrated intention to God (the 'nakid entent') in much the same way as meditation can be distracted by simultaneous thoughts arising from the preoccupations of active life.[57] The work of the contemplative, which in fact takes for granted the prior conditioning of the consciousness by meditative disciplines[58] involves, then, a progressive stilling of all the diverse physical and mental activities by which man defines himself, in order that he may be open to the transcendent being of God.

The *Cloud*-author describes the position of the contemplative as, metaphorically, between two clouds: a cloud of forgetting beneath which the contemplative must struggle to blot out all normal active consciousness of the created world, and a cloud of unknowing which 'is betwix þee & þi God' (5.13.29) and which can be pierced by that love implanted in man's will by God. The language and syntax emphasise the meshing of man's activity with God's in this kind of prayer. The *Cloud*-author describes the attempt of love to pierce the cloud as an effort of human will ordering the disciple to 'smyte apon þat þicke cloude of vnknowyng wiþ a scharp darte of longing loue, & go not þens for þing þat befalleþ' (6.14.29–30) and to push discursive thought beneath the cloud of forgetting 'ȝif euer schal he peerse þe cloude of vnknowyng bitwix him & his God' (7.15.22–3).[59] But these activities are only enabled by a 'plesyng stering of love' (6.14.28) which is the 'werk of only God' (26.34.18–19) and so he qualifies himself:

> Bot ȝif I schal sey þe soþe, lat God drawe þi loue up to þat cloude; & proue þou þorou help of his grace to foreȝte alle oþer þing.
>
> (9.19.10–12)

The *Cloud*-author advises his disciple to use a mantra to further this kind of prayer 'a litil worde of o silable' like 'God' or 'Love' will help to take him into the silence of unknowing that he desires. And again emphasising the shift between effort and grace-filled moments he comments:

> þis worde schal be þi scheeld & þi spere, wheþer þou ridest on pees or on werre.
>
> (7.15.31–2, 37–8)
>
> *scheeld*: shield.

The *Cloud*-author constantly emphasises the desire in man for God as not just the means of union but its substance. It is the ground of the growth of true goodness in man. Without it no amount of masochistic self-mortification will succeed in rooting out sin; and although penance and meditation on the Passion are means of grace, they are less powerful than this stirring of love which includes all virtues because they are the natural consequence of such a love and most fully expressed in it. Thus meekness which is the natural concomitant of self-knowledge may come from a conviction of sin and weakness, but it may also arise from the creature's sense of the reality of the creator.[60] This is a perfect meekness proper to man's knowledge of himself and of God which lasts beyond time. The *Cloud*-author sees it as exemplified in Mary the sister of Martha in her growth from penance for sin to contemplative love.[61] Charity too is born out of this love for God. The 'nakid entent vnto God' (3.9.31) enables an equilibrium in all human attachments and emotional needs since it brings a freedom to love others for themselves, and see them, whether friends or enemies, as opportunities for such love. In this way the negative emotions are redeemed and time is kept.

This introductory definition of contemplative work ends with the *Cloud*-author reformulating his sense of the interaction between human energy and a greater power of God. He bids his disciple 'do on þi werk, & sekirly I behote þee it schal not fayle on hym' (26.34.19–20). It is the way to gifts of insight for:

> þan wil he sumtyme parauenture seend oute a beme of goostly liȝt, peersyng þis cloude of vnknowing þat is betwix þee & hym, & schewe þee sum of his priuete, þe whiche man may not, ne kan not, speke.
>
> (26.34.31–4)

Although the *Cloud*-author will not speak further with his 'blabryng fleschely tonge' of the 'werke þat falliþ to only God' (26.34.36–8) he does have more to say about the techniques to be employed by contemplatives in the part that falls to them.

Chapters 27–50: 'gamenly be it seyde'

Despite the apparent austerity of the *Cloud*-author's approach to God, there is also a fundamental lightness of heart which corresponds to his understanding of the essential nature of the contemplative experience of the realities of his faith. Despite the difficulties of the discipline caused by the recalcitrant disorder of human nature, he nevertheless perceives it as a game of faith which enacts in human terms the creative play of divine wisdom.[62] In *The Book of Privy Counselling* when he is advising its recipient on how he may recognise whether or not he has a vocation for the contemplative life, he says that besides the nature of his response to his daily devotional pattern which will indicate the direction of his instincts, he will also be obsessed by all that he hears about the nature of contemplative activity, and overwhelmed by joy in a natural perception of the significance of the calm fulfilment of the integration it seeks; it will totally absorb him like a child at play:

> A schorte worde of þi mouþ conteneþ a woreld ful of wisdam, ȝit semeþ it bot foly to hem þat wonen in here wittis. Þi silence is softe, þi speche ful speedful, þi preier is preue, þi pride ful pure, þi maners ben meek, þi mirþe ful mylde, þi list is lykyng to pleye wiþ a childe.[63]
>
> (*P.C.*95.29–33)

wonen in here wittis: live by their intellectual faculties; *speedful*: profitable; *preue*: inward; *þi list* etc.: see note.

Chapters twenty-eight to fifty of *The Cloud* explore the techniques (the skills of the game) which will help his disciple in his particular work of contemplative prayer. Since the *Cloud*-author has taken for granted the acquisition of the most basic skill (that involved in acquiring the self-knowledge which comes from the practice of penance[64] and induces clear recognition of both the limitations of man and the greatness of God) he can also take it for granted that the disciple will immediately perceive why there must be a cloud of unknowing between man and God and a cloud of forgetting beneath which time-bound preoccupations have to be blotted out. In a sentence whose pattern of alliteratively accentuated emphases stresses the sense of longing for a state of wholeness which is conceived as possible, if not immediately realised, he indicates that the barrier of sin between man and God is not insuperable:

> & þerfore, whoso coueitiþ to come to clennes þat he lost for synne, & to wynne to þat welþe þer alle wo wantiþ, him bihouiþ bidingly to trauayle in þis werke, & suffre þe pyne þerof.
>
> (29.35.33–35)

wantiþ: is lacking; *bidingly*: patiently; *pyne:* pain.

The *Cloud*-author focuses on the intensely personal nature of 'þis werke' and points to the impropriety of any kind of competitive spirit and impulse to judgement in his comment that it is well to remember that it is not always the conventionally pious who come fastest to the realisation of God;[65] his disciple's job is to manage his own 'game' '& lat oþer men allone' (30.36.21). Since, like Hilton, the *Cloud*-author believes that only the individual concerned can learn to manage himself the guidance he gives is of a very general nature but it always has a down-to-earth practicality governed by briskly positive thinking. One piece of advice is that, once past sins have been recognised and absolved through the Church's sacrament of penance (c.31), these should not continue to be dwelt on, so as to form a conscious barrier between man and God. Rather, the way forward for the contemplative at this point is a leap of faith in relaxed confidence (much like that which anyone learning to swim has to make when he takes his feet off the bottom). No amount of prescribing or describing of what has to be done can substitute for the mysterious inner action between the individual and God, what the *Cloud*-author would call 'consent', which allows the learner freedom of movement in a new element and which 'ben betir lernyd of God by þe profe þen of any man in þis liif (31.36.34–5). Nevertheless the *Cloud*-author does try to hint at gambits which may help the disciple to cope with the concerns of the stridently demanding self that deflect him from his goal. One is to ignore them and, as it were, to focus over the top of them as one might visually dodge obstructions to a view (like looking over the tops of people's heads at a theatre), or it may be that the art of dealing with them lies not in the effort which this involves, but in knowing when to give in gracefully and ask God for help with the difficulty, an act embodying the recognition of the disciple's ultimate dependence on grace. This is by no means a soft option but the difficult cultivation of a nicely judged instinct for the capacities of one's own nature. It is, perhaps, rather like realising when to stop working if work is to be fruitful:

> for, me þink in þe profe of þis sleyȝt þou schuldest melt al to watre. & sekirly, me þink, & þis sleiȝt be sotely conceyuid, it is not elles bot a trewe knowyng & a felyng of þiself as þou arte, a wrecche & a filþe, fer wers þen nouȝt: þe whiche knowyng & felyng is meeknes. & þis meeknes deserueþ to haue God himself miȝtely descendyng to venge þee of þine enemyes. . . .
>
> (32.37.14–19)

profe: experience; *sleyȝt*: strategy; *sotely conceyuid*: astutely thought out.

Such self-discipline can best be learnt from experience and the *Cloud*-author has such faith in the innate gifts of this particular disciple that he comments 'for & þou haue grace to fele þe profe of þeese, I trow þat þou schalt cun betir lerne me þen I þee [*cun*: be able; *lerne*: teach] (33.37. 24–5). This wisdom is, of course *discretion*[66] and it is known not academically, but existentially:

> For oute of þis oryginal synne wil alday sprynge newe & fresche sterynges of synne; þe whiche þee behouiþ alday to smyte doun, & be besy to schere awey wiþ a scharpe double-eggid dreedful swerde of discrecion. & herby mayst þou see & leerne þat þer is no soþfast sekyrnes, ne ʒit no trewe rest in þis liif.
>
> (33.37.37–41)
>
> *schere*: cut; *sekyrnes*: security.

Yet, paradoxically, the work which this *discretion* is the means of furthering is experienced not so much as effort to achieve, as allowing the achievement to be realised. Always at the heart of the *Cloud*-author's understanding of contemplative experience is the reciprocal movement between stirring of love and consent in the game of redemption. The contemplative has to learn so to discipline his nature that the instinctive drive which can impel the will to engage with the dynamic of love ('drawʒt of þis loue' 2.8.22) has a free run. The *Cloud*-author stresses that if the calling to contemplative life is real, it carries embryonically in itself the ability to pursue it;

> þe abilnes to þis werk is onyd to þe selue werk, wiþoutyn departyng; so þat whoso feliþ þis werk is abil þerto, & elles none.
>
> (34.38.32–3)
>
> *abilnes*: capacity; *departyng*: distinction; *elles none*: otherwise not.

The disciple is ordered to be still, like a house giving shelter to the activities of the owner within: 'be þou bot þe hous, & lat it be þe hosbonde wonyng þerin' [*wonyng:* dwelling] (34.39.5).

But despite the intensely personal nature of this sense of *discretion* there are skills which, like the practice of penance, are basic to the game. Such are to be found in the practice of the traditional disciplines of reading, meditation and prayer.[67] Here the *Cloud*-author gives further evidence that his particular disciple is not highly educated in a formal sense inasmuch as he translates the technical terms 'Lesson, Meditacion, & Oryson' as 'Redyng, þinkyng

& Preiing' (35.39.24–6) and explains that Reading can also be hearing books read aloud:

> alle is one in maner, redyng & heryng; clerkes redyn on bookes, & lewid men redyn on clerkes, whan þei here hem preche þe worde of God.
>
> (35.39.32–4)

Such practices build up a bank of reserves of knowledge which can then be processed by the experienced contemplative in a different way:

> þeire meditacions ben as þei were sodein conseites & blynde felynges of þeire owne wrechidnes, or of þe goodnes of God, wiþoutyn any menes of redyng or heryng comyng before.
>
> (36.40.16–18)
>
> *conseites*: conceptions; *menes*: intermediaries.

This instinctive revulsion from all that within the self which separates it from God – 'mene synne a lump, þou wost neuer wot, non oþer þing bot þiself' [*mene:* focus on] (*ibid*, 30) – enables the prayer which focuses the 'entent' of the disciple 'nakidly directe vnto God' (34.39.9–10). Like the mantra advised in chapter seven this is prayer which the shortest syllable serves to spearhead. Much as when a man calls out 'fire' the word concentrates a whole wealth of meaning, basic information, warning cry and urgent need for active help, and communicates more effectively than long explanations, 'so doþ a lytyl worde of o sylable' (37.41.23):

> preyer in itself propirly is not elles bot a deuoute entent directe vnto God, for getyng of goodes & remowyng of yuelles.
>
> (59.42.32–3)
>
> *goodes*: good things; *yuelles*: evils.

The *Cloud*-author explains to his disciple that if he can pray in a way that expresses his whole being's constant urgent rejection of all that separates him from God, then the more minute details of how he should govern his existence will look after themselves (c.41, 42). It is this kind of insight that the disciple addressed in *The Epistle of Discretion of Stirrings* so needs. To use a modern analogy, just as the difference between the theory of driving a car and the actual ability to do it consists in knowing instinctively when to change gear, or accelerate according to the conditions the driver finds him/herself in, so the contemplative will get to know by instinct as he goes along how to conduct himself:

> But parauenture þou askest me how þou schalt gouerne þee discreetly in mete, & in slepe, & in alle þees oþer. & herto I þink to answere þee riȝt schortli: 'Gete þat þou gete mayst'.
>
> (42.44–5.42–2)

gete þat þou gete mayst: take what comes.

Thus the discursively acquired knowledge in penance, reading, meditation and formal prayer becomes the means by which the game of contemplative prayer is played, and the purpose of the game – the experience which the acquired skills (*discretion*) are designed to enable – is the sense of wholeness, oneness with God, which is the fulfilment of man's being.

But this wholeness involves a painful stage where the contemplative, stripped of all conscious thought and desire other than the 'nakid entent' to God, has a stark sense of his own separate existence:

> For, & þou wilt besily set þee to þe preof, þou schalt fynde, when þou hast foreȝten alle oþer creatures & alle þeire werkes, ȝe, & þerto alle þin owne werkes, þat þer schal leue ȝit after, bitwix þee & þi God, a nakid weting & a felyng of þin owne beyng: þe whiche wetyng & felyng behouiþ alweis be distroied, er þe tyme be þat þou fele soþfastly þe perfeccyon of þis werk.
>
> (43.46.2–8)

preof: experience; *leue:* remain; *wetyng*: knowledge.

This 'nakid weting' must finally be overcome in the realisation of the essential union between the being of man and being of God; it involves the pain and frustration inherent in any sense of longing. The *Cloud*-author hastens to add, however, that this does not mean that the disciple wishes that he did not exist, for 'þat were deuelles woodnes & despite vnto God' [*woodnes*: madness] (44.47.3). In *The Book of Privy Counselling* the *Cloud*-author picks up and explores further this contemplative awareness of his own individual being in relation to that of God – the essence of the game. For the moment, as if tripped up by the possibility that his disciple (or perhaps another reader) might take his discussion of a sense of sorrow at his separate existence in the wrong way, he stops to explore the whole problem of the manner in which spiritual matters are conceived in terms of physical existence. Although the *Cloud*-author has explained the techniques of the game and the whole experience it is designed to incarnate, he believes that he has not sufficiently dealt with the nature of the substances energised in the game. If you play polo you not only have to know about the potential properties of balls in conjunction with sticks, but how to ride a horse in such a way as to maximise this potential. So for the *Cloud*-author playing a contemplative game involves being very clear about the relationship between body and soul and able not only to distinguish the energies of the spirit from those of the body but to know how to harness the latter in order to release the former. The eager lifting of the heart to God must not be conceived in terms of physical or nervous straining (c.45) in a greedy attempt to snatch satisfaction which cannot be attained in this way:

> & lache not ouer-hastely, as it were a gredy grehounde, hungre þee neuer so sore.
>
> (46.48.28–9)
>
> *lache*: grab.

The game of the spirit is played differently, even if it has to be gestured towards in physical terms, and the author urges ('gamenly be it seyde' [*gamenly*: in play] (*ibid*, 30)) that the disciple should actually steer past this danger of translating spiritual fervour into terms of physical, emotional and nervous striving by acting (playing a role) as if he does not want God to see how much he desires Him. It is an astutely simple ploy which, if anything can, shows the *Cloud*-author's understanding of the proper relationship between body and soul and the imaginative apprehension thereof:

> & God forbede þat I schuld departe þat God haþ couplid, þe body & þe spirit; for God wil be seruid wiþ body & wiþ soule, boþe togeders, as seemly is, & rewarde man his mede in blis boþe in body & soule.
>
> (48.50.14–17)

And it is a strategy which from experience the *Cloud*-author says leads directly to participation in the game of integrating man's consent to the drawing of God's love in a unified energy:

> þis is childly & pleyingly spoken, þee þink, parauenture. Bot I trowe whoso had grace to do & fele as I sey, he schuld fele [God] gamesumli pley wiþ hym, as þe fadir doþ wiþ þe childe, kyssyng & clippyng, þat weel were him so.
>
> (46.48.34–7)
>
> *gamesumli:* playfully; *clippyng*: embracing.

The contemplative has to learn, with help, how to manage his whole being to give it the freedom of a spiritual dimension of love – the element where ultimately both body and soul find their true fulfilment.

> & þerfore I preie þee, lene listely to þis meek steryng of loue in þin herte, & folow þerafter; for it wil be þi gyde in þis liif, & bring þee to blisse in þe toþer. It is the substaunce of alle good leuyng, . . . Soche a good wille is þe substaunce of alle perfeccion.[68]
>
> (49.51.17–19,23)

lene listely: incline readily; *substaunce*: essential nature.

Spiritual comfort and ease may be intermittent in time but they are of the essence in the life to come when the body and soul also will be one in love:

> for þere schul þei be onyd wiþ þe substaunce wiþouten departyng, as schal þe body in þe whiche þei worche wiþ þe soule.'
>
> (49.51.28–9)

This whole nature of the relationship between body and soul in the fallen world, though, prompts the *Cloud*-author into his long discussion of the proper psychological approach to the understanding of the nature of language which is fundamental to the appreciation of his highly imaginative book.[69] It occupies chapters fifty-one to sixty-seven of *The Cloud*. Then in chapter sixty-eight he returns to summarise his exposition of the work of the contemplative, humorously capitalising on the discussion he has just conducted with a fireworks display of paradoxical imagery which illuminates something about the nature of the reality of the spiritual game which is his subject. Referring back to his discussion of the possibility of misunderstanding the way in which language rooted in sense-experience can refer to spiritual experience, he laughingly says that he is not going to advise the disciple on spiritual activity in bodily terms at all:

> Bot þus wil I bid þee. Loke on no wyse þat þou be wiþinne þiself. & schortly wiþoutyn þiself wil I not þat þou be, ne ȝit abouen, ne behynde, ne on o side, ne on oþer.
>
> (68.67.34–6)

This is the cue for an incredulous exclamation by his disciple 'wher þan, schal I be? Noȝwhere, bi þi tale!' [by your account] which, as the *Cloud*-author triumphantly points out, hits the nail on the head 'for whi noȝwhere bodely is everywhere goostly' (68.67.38–9). And although the work advised is apparently nothing that the senses or reason can grasp, the author comments that he would rather play with nothing nowhere than be a great lord enjoying everything everywhere:

> For I telle þee trewly þat I had leuer be so nowhere bodely, wrastlyng wiþ þat blynde nouȝt, þan to be so grete a lorde þat I miȝt when I wolde be euerywhere bodely, merily pleiing wiþ al þis ouȝt as a lorde wiþ his owne.
>
> (68.68.7–10)

wrastlyng: wrestling [in prayer]; *ouȝt*: something.

Indeed in this apparent 'nothing' the *Cloud*-author recognises the source of all that is: and the real truth about the darkness of the cloud of unknowing is that it stems from a light so great that it simply blinds those with earthly vision 'so the darkness shall be the light, and the stillness the dancing'.[70]

This contemplative game is played out between the polarities of man's existence defined as sin and God; it can involve pain and grief because of the existence of sin but also a peace so great that the contemplative thinks it is God. Both are states indigenous to the cloud of unknowing into which man's consent to the stirring of love for God brings him (69.69.11–12). This, says the *Cloud*-author is the darkness of unknowing talked of by Dionysius, too often the occasion for speculative intellectual theology and exhibitionist erudition, instead of understanding as the literary means, like the author's own text, to an existential truth for those able to hear properly:

> For whoso haþ eren, lat hem here, & whoso is sterid for to trowe, lat hem trowe; for elles scholen þei not.
>
> (70.70.14–15)

He does admit, though, that some will find it more difficult to follow than others, since although the game is simple, some are more naturally suited to learn it than others: all is subject to:

> þe ordynaunce & þe disposicion of God, after þeire abilnes in soule þat þis grace of contemplacion & of goostly worching is ȝouen to.
>
> (71.70.21–22)
>
> *disposicion*: dispensation; *ȝouen*: given.

He embodies his perception of the differing nature of contemplative gifts in his adaption of the account of Moses on mount Sinai receiving instructions on the building of the ark of the covenant (Exodus 25f.). This was used by Richard of St Victor in his mystical theology.[71] The process of constructing the ark is the contemplative's work with his 'nakid entent vnto God' which is the source of all virtue. Moses, who could learn about it only by the grace of God after the labour of climbing the mountain, figures those contemplatives who find the work difficult but who do come to experience the joy of the game sometimes as an act of grace. Beȝeleel who made the ark, and with whom the *Cloud*-author identifies himself, is like those with some aptitude for the game, who can play it themselves through God's grace and can show it to others. In Aaron, who had charge of the ark in the temple and could see it at will thanks to the efforts of Beȝeleel, the *Cloud*-author recognises the great natural gifts of his disciple to so play the game that he may come to the sense of being in which all the distortions of the relationship between body and soul by sin are transfigured so that the natural man becomes the icon of the spiritual man.[72] It is these gifts which he hopes to help in fostering by writing his treatise:

> Lo! goostly freende, in þis werk, þof it be childly & lewdely spoken, I bere, þof I be a wreche vnworþi to teche any creature, þe ofice of Beȝeleel, makyng & declaryng in maner to þin handes þe maner of þis goostly arke. Bot fer betir & more worþely þen I do, þou maist worche ȝif þou wilt be Aaron; . . . & siþen we ben boþe clepid of God to worche in þis werk, I beseche þee for Goddes loue fulfille in þi partye þat lackiþ of myne.
>
> (73.72.16–24)
>
> *siþen*: since; *clepid*: called.

The *Cloud*-author is insistent on the fact that his little book is an organic whole and must be read as such. (74.73.2–8). He is also aware that others besides his particular disciple may read the book and be attracted by its substance. He advises them to test this attraction to see if it is a true vocation by submitting to the discipline of penance under a spiritual director to see if they remain irresistibly drawn by a desire for that God who can only be known in the cloud of unknowing (75.73.19–35). And he warns that the dynamic impetus of this desire, especially in the initial stages of the contemplative life, may sometimes be withdrawn. This is part of the nature of the game of faith which is inevitably played by means of failure and limitations in time.[73] But part of the test of the player's aptitude to play the game is the ability to hold on in patience and to greet the impetus when it returns with greater joy and passion than before;

> & þis is one of þe rediest & souereynist tokin þat a soule may haue to wit by, wheþer he be clepid or not to worche in þis werk: ȝif he fele after soche a delaying & a longe lackyng of þis werk, þat when it comeþ sodenly as it doþ, vnpurchasid wiþ mene, þat he haþ þan a gretter feruour of desire & gretter loue-longing to worche in þis werk, þan euer he had any before, insomochel þat oftymes I trowe he haþ more ioie of þe fyndyng þerof, þen euer he had sorow of þe lesing. & ȝif it be þus, sekirly it is a tokin verrey wiþoutyn errour þat he is clepid of God to worche in þis werk, whatsoeuer þat he be or haþ ben.[74]
>
> (75.74.9–18)
>
> *wit*: know; *lesing*: losing.

For the identity of the contemplative is determined not just by what he has been or is, but by what he desires to be. For the *Cloud*-author (as for Augustine) it is indeed the case that the 'nakid entent' to God is in fact fundamental to all Christian life: 'al þe liif of a good Cristen man is not elles bot holy desire' (75.74.26–7)[75] and the contemplative has a special gift to experience intuitively the source from which this desire springs – God in whom the self has its being. This is the subject which the *Cloud*-author takes further in *The Book of Privy Counselling*.

THE BOOK OF PRIVY COUNSELLING

Audience

The *Book of Privy Counselling* is a short treatise also written ostensibly for a particular disciple. The author makes it clear that although he would be pleased if others interested in contemplative life profited by reading it, he is really only addressing himself to the needs generated by the disposition of an individual disciple:

> þerfore I write none oþer þing bot soche as me þink þat is moste speedful & acording to þin disposicion only.
>
> (75.5–7)

There is no certainty that *The Book of Privy Counselling* was addressed to the same disciple as that in *The Cloud* despite the fact that he invited that young man to submit any further questions he might have (74.73.9–11); and despite the fact that in *Privy Counselling* he develops further the nature of the relationship between the contemplative and God from the sense of his own existence separate from the source of all being (*The Cloud*, 43) to the point where he feels dissolved in 'onyng to loue in þe souereyn poynte of þi spirite'(*P.C.*97.16).[76] It is true that he certainly seems to take the terminology and concepts developed in *The Cloud* for granted, as, for example, when he says the disciple can leave formal meditation in pursuit of contemplation because:

> in comparison of þis blynde felyng & offring up þi beyng, þei ben ful diuerse & scateryng from þe perfeccion of onheed, þe whiche falliþ for to be bitwix God & þi soule.
>
> (78.17–19)
>
> *onheed*: unity; *falliþ*: is appropriate.

But in his direct allusion to *The Cloud* and other writings in his attempt to elucidate the value of the 'nakid entent' to God (87–8.40–3) there is not that sense of confidence in the natural gifts of this disciple that the author evinces in *The Cloud*. In *The Cloud* the disciple's questions are managed with a rhetorical skill by the author to further a recognition of the nature of spiritual development that both can share. At the end of this treatise the disciple recognises what the *Cloud*-author had been trying to say about the 'werk' of contemplation giving birth to wholeness and confidence at the heart of being which permeates, puts into perspective, and relieves the stresses of existence in time:

> for 'þou schalt gracyously rest' in þis louely onheed of God & þi soule; '& þi sleep schal be ful softe', for it schal be goostly fode & inly strengþe, as wel to þi body as to þi soule.
>
> (83.28–30)

But the book ends on a down-beat as he complains that far from finding rest in this work he finds nothing but suffering and stress ('pyne & batayle', 98.42) in his divided self torn between his desire to pursue a 'nakid entent' to God and the demands of the conscious self '& þis þenk me a queynte rest þat þou spekist of' (99.3–4). To this the author replies that it is because he is only in the early stages of his development; but at least he has the fundamental security of his calling:

> Bot in þat I clepe it a rest, for þe soule is not in dwere what it schal do, and also for a soule is maad sekir (I mene in þe tyme of þis doynge) þat it schal not moche erre.
>
> (99.9–12)
>
> *dwere*: doubt; *sekir*: secure.

Consistent with the expression of this difficulty, the disciple is represented as raising intellectual objections to the nature of contemplative life because its nature is not accessible to intellect and reason. The author points out that the objections signal a lack of humility and trust in the advice he is being given; although his very care in meeting the objection signals the author's trust in the disciple's vocation:

> Lo! here maist þou see þat I coueite souereinte of þee & trewly so I do, & I wol haue it
>
> (87.6–8)
>
> *coueite souereinte of þee*: want to direct you.

while recognising that ultimately only God's grace, that is the experience of the game itself, will put things right for the disciple 'God amende þat is amys, for he wote fully, & I bot in party' (87.10). This argument is not amenable to intellectual proof, but the author nevertheless tries to meet some of the disciple's conscious unease on its own terms:

> Bot now, siþen we mowe not speke it, lat us speke of it, in confusion of proude wittys, & namely of þine, þe whiche is only, occasionly at þe leest, þe cause of þis writyng at þis tyme.
>
> (87.21–4)
>
> *in confusion of proude wittys*: to the confusion of intellectual pride; *occasionly*: on this particular occasion.

It is perhaps significant that it is in *Privy Counselling* that the author develops teaching on the way in which the disciple can test and be sure of his vocation,[77] and that in this context he dwells on how the contemplative can survive periods of barrenness and spiritual desolation through patience. They are the means by which the reality of the dynamic of love is proved. As in Rolle's *Meditations on the Passion*, a sense of God's absence, far from implying that he does not exist, is the very condition for knowing his coming:

> For sodenly, er euer þou wite, alle is awey, & þou leuyst bareyn in þe bote, blowyn wiþ blundryng, now heder now þeder, þou wost neuir where ne wheder. ȝit be not abascht, for he schal come, I behote þee, ful sone, whan hym likiþ [to leþe þee] & douȝtely delyuer þee of all þi dole, fer more worþely þen he euer did before. ȝe! & ȝif he eft go, eft wol he come aȝeyn; & iche tyme, ȝif þou wel bere þee by meek suffryng, wil he come more worþelyer & merilier þen oþer. & alle þis he doþ for he wil haue þee maad as pleying to his wille goostly as a roon gloue to þin honde bodely.[78]
>
> (96.11–20)
>
> *leuyst . . . bote*: are left abandoned in the boat; *behote*: promise; *leþe*: relieve; *pleying*: pliant; *roon*: [implies soft skin; see note].

Indeed, *The Book of Privy Counselling* repeats in its own terms the understanding of how the contemplative life extends the pattern of the Incarnation in time:

> Bot it suffisiþ now vnto þee to do hole worschip vnto God wiþ þi substaunce & for to offre up þi nakid beyng, þe whiche is þe first of þi frutes, in contynowel sacrifiȝe of preising of God, boþe for þiself & for alle oþer as charite askiþ . . . þis is soþ by witnes of Scripture, bi ensaumple of Crist . . . offring himself up in verreiest sacrifiȝe, al þat he was . . . for alle: riȝt so a verey & a parfite sacrifier of himself þus by a comon entent vnto alle doþ þat in him is to knit alle men to God as effectuely as himself is.[79]
>
> (79.29–32,40; 80.3–7)
>
> *substaunce*: essential nature; *by a comon entent*: with a general intention.

Although it could be argued that *The Book of Privy Counselling* might be addressed to the disciple of *The Cloud of Unknowing* at a later stage in the development of his vocation, the more cerebral nature of the disciple, the stress on the difficulties of his vocation, and the elements of repetition in the teaching in the two texts militate against this.

The tone of the book is different. It is more on the defensive. Despite the author's disclaiming any intention to speak in general terms about his subject (75.4) he does, on occasions, address a reader beyond the immediate recipient. With some asperity he anticipates objections that the surrender at the heart of the contemplative's life of all his particular needs to the pursuit of his need for God, is in fact tempting God's providence:

> Lateþ be ȝoure manly obieccions, ȝe half-mekyd soulys, & seiþ not in ȝoure resonable trasing þat soche a meek & an vtter forsaking of þe kepyng of a mans self, whan he feliþ hym þus touchid bi grace, is any temtyng of God, for ȝe fele in ȝoure reson þat ȝe dor not do so ȝowreself.
>
> (84.33–7)
>
> *trasing*: analysis.

As in *The Cloud* he used the story of Martha and Mary to distinguish the way of perfect meekness and lack of self-concern from the very proper concerns with the needs of the active life, so here the author defends contemplative life as hazarding all the material and emotional securities that others dare not venture simply to realise, and thus witness to others, the reality of sustaining love at the heart of being as distinct from the care for self that is the expression of love in this active life (pp.84–6). Indeed, on the next occasion that the author addresses the general reader ('whatsoeuer þou be þat þis writyng schalt ouþer rede or here', 92.21–2) he develops this. In his exposition of the contemplative calling going beyond the practice of penance, prayer and meditations on the manhood of Christ to enactment of, and participation in, the redeeming love it manifests (90.11f.) (thereby anchoring his mysticism firmly in incarnational theology), he breaks off to warn readers that they must recognise and accept their own vocation, whether it be for active or contemplative life, with a good grace for both are enabled by God:

> Haue pees wiþ þi parte. Wheþer þat þou haue, þee nedeþ not to pleyne þee; for þei ben boþe precious.
>
> (92.34–5)
>
> *wheþer*: whichever.

And thus, as in *The Cloud*, he warns against any competitive or judgemental impulse:

> loke neiþer þat þou deme ne discusse in þe dedes of God ne of man, ferþer þen only þiself.
>
> (92.24–5)

Both active and contemplative lives are rooted in a conscious desire to serve God. But whereas with actives this is achieved by acts of will expressed in deed and thought which manifest obedience to the love of God, in contemplatives this sense of striving gives way to an experience in which the whole being of man is invaded by the being of God:

> In dedes þat ben actyue & leueful, he is wiþ us boþe by suffring & consent, to oure reproef ȝif we go bak & oure grete mede ȝif we do forþ. In dedes þat ben contemplatyue he is wiþ us, principaly steryng & worching, & we only bot suffring & consenting, to oure grete perfeccion & goostly onyng of oure soule vnto hym in parfite charite.
>
> (93.34–9)

leueful: legitimate; *onyng*: uniting.

The tone of *The Book of Privy Counselling* is more intellectually argumentative than *The Cloud of Unknowing*, even given the fact that such discourse is used to persuade of the reality of a mode of being that transcends it. But these arguments designed to clarify the nature of the contemplative calling are prefaced by, and integrated with, passages in which the author embodies an understanding of the way the being of man engages with the being of God in the game of contemplation beyond that expressed in the more dramatically staged exploration of *The Cloud of Unknowing*.

'Þis Felyng of God'

Privy Counselling initially picks up the author's definition of the contemplative game in chapters forty-three and forty-four of *The Cloud of Unknowing*. There he talked of it as a sense of one's own being which is both the means of knowing God and yet also a final barrier between the self and God which must be overcome (46.5–8). Now, at the start of *Privy Counselling* he says that this sense of one's own being, simply that one *is*, quite apart from any individually identifying traits, must be absorbed into the 'nakid entent' for God and offered to him:

> as ȝif þou seidist þus vnto God wiþinne in þi menyng 'þat at I am, Lorde, I offre vnto þee, wiþoutyn any lokyng to eny qualite of þi beyng, bot only þat þou arte as þou arte, wiþouten any more.
>
> (75.26–8)

þat at: that which; *lokyng*: regard.

This offering of love is the means of breaking down the barrier perceived to exist between the creature and the creator:

> For he is þi being, & in him þou arte þat at þou arte, not only bi cause & bi beyng, bot also he is in þee boþe þi cause & þi beyng . . . euermore sauyng þis difference bitwix þee & him, þat he is þi being & þou not his.
>
> (75.31–3, 36–7)

As in *The Cloud*, the author insists that the game which activates this recognition is easy. You do not need a Ph.D. to realise that you have being:

> Bot for to þenk þat þou arte, mayst þou haue of þi lewydnes & þi boistouste wiþoutyn any grete kunning of clergie or of kynde.
>
> (77.15–16)

But if what was called in *The Cloud* the 'lump of synne' (that is, none oþer þing þan þiself, 43.29–30) is felt as an impediment, then the disciple is advised to make an act of faith in God's power to heal sin:

> take good gracyous God as he is, plat & pleyn as a plastre, & legge it to þi seek self as þou arte.
>
> (77.27–8)
>
> *pleyne as a plastre*: exactly like a plaster; *seek*: sick.

The treatise is anchored in a confident assertion of the experience of oneness with God which transcends all particularities and gives momentary sense of a completeness normally denied to the component part by virtue of its particularity, but which when seen makes sense of its whole being and is its security.

Just as in *The Cloud* the little prayer of one syllable is to focus the 'nakid entent' and energise the dynamic of the game, so here, the word 'is' focuses the being of God who is otherwise limited by any definitions of his attributes. The consent to the stirring of love adumbrated in *The Cloud* leads to the inner realisation that this love in man is God and is the certainty of his being (80–1.30–24). It is in essence a profoundly simple realisation and the author sees it as the means of integrating man's existence. In *The Cloud* he taught that growth in contemplative prayer fostered a natural *discretion* in the disciple. Here he says:

> holde þee hole & vnscaterid as forþ as þou maist bi grace & bi sleiȝt of goostly contynowaunce. For in þis blinde beholdyng of þi nakid beyng, þus onyd to God as I telle þee, schalt þou do al þat þou schalt do: ete & drink, sleep & wake, go & sit, speke & be stille, ligge & rise, stonde & knele, renne & ride, trauaile & rest. þis schalt þou iche day offre up vnto God as for þe moste precious offring þat þou canst make. & it schal be þe cheef of alle þi doynges wheþer þei be actyue or contemplatyue.
>
> (83.15–23)
>
> *vnscaterid*: undistracted; *sleiȝt*: strategy; *contynowaunce*: perseverance; *ligge*: lie down.

The game is easy in a theological sense because, although it may be difficult for the emotions and intellect of fallen man to abandon themselves to its simplicity, it gradually generates the lightness of confident spontaneity in love it covets – it is the profound realisation of the easy yoke of Christ (Matthew 11:29–30):

> For, as Salamon seiþ in þis processe, 'ȝif þou slepe' in þis blynde beholdyng from al þe noise & þe steryng of þe fel fende, þe fals woreld & þe freel flessche, 'þou schalt not drede any peril' ne any deceyte of þe feende.
>
> (83.23–6)
>
> *fel fende*: cruel devil; *freel:* frail.

The author places his statement born out of illuminated understanding about the oneness between man's being and the being of God at the beginning of the book (75.31–3) to make it clear to the disciple from the start that his simple concentration on his own being and the being of God is a way to the experience of their essential union:

> For wite þou wele for certeyn þat, þof al I bid þee forgete alle þinges bot þe blynde felyng of þi nakid beyng, ȝit neuerþeles my wille is, & þat was myn entent in þe biginning, þat þou schuldest forȝete þe felyng of þe beyng of þiself as for þe felyng of þe beyng of God. & for þis skyle I prouid þee in þe bigynnyng þat God is þi beyng.
>
> (88–9.39–1)
>
> *skyle*: reason.

The separation felt by the creature is transcended by love, the work of which is impeded by the sense of alienation which is the residual legacy of sin and the cross which the contemplative must bear (89–90). But through the Incarnation, it is also the means for experiencing the ultimate ascendancy of love. There are times when the contemplative enters fully into the game with a foretaste of his oneness with God, despite his temporary separation:

> þis siȝt & þis felyng of God, þus in hymself as he is, may no more be departyd fro God in hymself (to þin vnderstondyng þat þus felist or þus seest) þen may be departyd God himself fro his owne beyng, þe whiche ben bot one boþe in substaunce & also in kynde.
>
> (97.23–26)

Both the intellectual formulations of *The Book of Privy Counselling* and the imaginative exploration of *The Cloud of Unknowing* are offered as means to further a working knowledge for which they cannot substitute. When the author speaks of the work of all Christians both active and contemplative being contingent on the being of God, he quotes the words of Christ (John 15:5) 'without me you can do nothing' which, in Scripture, are prefaced by the words 'he that abideth in me, and I in him, the same beareth much fruit'; and he glosses it:

> 'Wiþouten me first steryng & principaly mouyng, & ȝe only bot consentyng & suffryng, ȝe mowen nowȝt do þing þat is parfiteli plesyng to me', as schuld be in maner þe werk of þis writyng.
>
> (92.40–43)

One commentator has translated this:

> 'Unless I first stir and prompt you, so that you have only to agree and accept it, there is nothing you can do that is perfectly pleasing to me'. And this is as it ought to be in the kind of work that this book is about.[80]

This interpretation of 'as schuld be in maner þe werk of þis writyng' blurs an important ambiguity in the original which allows the sense that any efficacy in the book itself is due to the spirit of God which is the gift of understanding in both author and reader. This sense is emphasised by his strictures in the following paragraph on those who might think the efficacy of their scholarship is to be credited to themselves, whereas:

> verrely þe contrary is soþ in þinges contemplatyue. For only in hem ben alle corious skyles of clergie or of kyndely kunnynge fer put bak, þat God be þe principal. Neuerþeles, in þinges leueful & actyue, man's clergye & his kyndely kunnyng shal worche wiþ God by & by, only by

> his consent in spirit prouid by þees þre witnes: Scripture, counseil & comoun custum of kynde & degre, eelde & conpleccyon.
>
> (93.3–8)
>
> *prouid*: tested; *counseil*: advice; *comoun custum of kynde*: ordinary practice of nature; *degre*: status; *conpleccyon*: temperament.

The *Cloud*-author knows precisely the creaturely value of intellectual knowledge and sense experience – they are instrumental in providing delightful knowledge of creation:

> it is wel seide, a man kyndely desireþ for to kunne
>
> (98.33–34)

but they are not the entrance qualifications for understanding of the love of God; indeed they can hinder this by a false sense of status: *sciencia inflat, karitas edificat*, 'knowledge puffeth up; but charity edifieth' (I Corinthians 8:1). The wisdom which is derived from a sense of value, itself born of the realisation of the union of man's being with God's, is the goal of man's existence and the author glosses his quotation from Corinthians 'in knowyng is trauaile, in feling is rest' (98.39).

In both *The Cloud of Unknowing* and *The Book of Privy Counselling* the author uses the resources of language to point to the truth that informs his theology: that the Incarnation creates a pattern of suffering in time as a means to the knowledge and love of God, and the contemplative expresses this through his discipline which can be seen as a game, learnt with pain, but the means of accessing the joy and love at the heart of his being. 'Labour', which is transformed to 'blossoming or dancing', brings an experience of man's love for God as God in him, where, for a while, he cannot distinguish the 'dancer from the dance' and this is the perfection of 'kepyng of tyme'.[81]

NOTES

1. See above p.159.
2. See further *The Cloud of Unknowing and Related Treatises*, ed. Hodgson (1982 xii–xix), hereafter cited as Hodgson (1982). I am grateful to James Hogg for permission to quote from this edition published in his Analecta Cartusiana.
3. See Hodgson (1982, xiv–xv).
4. See *The Book of Privy Counselling*, ed. Hodgson (1982, pp.87–8, 42–3). All

references to this text (*P.C.*) are given by page and line number. References to *The Cloud of Unknowing* (*The Cloud*) are given in the order chapter, page and line number.

5. See further Watson (1987).
6. See analysis in Hodgson (1982, xiv–xvi), but see also Ellis (1992).
7. The attribution was made as early as the fifteenth century. (See Hodgson (1982, xi). Modern academic argument has been conducted over a long period. See for example: McCann (1924); Gardner (1933); Hodgson (1955); Gatto (1975); Riehle (1977); Minnis (1983).
8. Hodgson (1982.ix).
9. For further references see Clark (1980, pp.108–9).
10. Hodgson (1982, p.170, note 50/41).
11. See Tugwell (1984, p.170).
12. See Lees (1983); but for a modification of her view see Minnis (1982, pp.71–2).
13. See Doyle (1953, pp.203–5, 276–80; Lees (1983, 399–424).
14. See Hodgson (1982, xvii).
15. See Lees (1983,411–12); Deanesley (1920).
16. Lees (1983) speculates that it was possibly written at Beauvale Charterhouse which was quite close to Thurgarton and moreover the foundation which Hilton's friend, Horsley entered. This, she conjectures, may account for the early connections made between Hilton and the *Cloud*-author.
17. Lees (1983, p.428); Nieva (1971, p.2).
18. See *The Cloud*, 3.11.32f.
19. See John (1964, p.110).
20. See above 1.7–8.39–10; see also 6.14.14f; 68.67.34f. For a full exploration of this aspect of the *Cloud*-author's approach to his subject see Watson (1987).
21. See above pp.77.
22. Lees (1983, p.455) who suggests that the disciple was a Carthusian novice with inadequate latin.
23. See Doyle (1953, pp.277, 299f.) and White (1949, p.101). The general concern of the *Cloud*-author for teaching theology to the uneducated is demonstrated by Dr Lees herself in her analysis of the *Cloud*-author's use of language in his translation, *Deonise Hid Diuinite* (*H.D.*). For example, she shows his concern in translation to make Latinate terms which might not be in general use comprehensible by means of gloss. Thus she cites (p.207) his use of the word

'temporal' (4.127.22) glossed 'bi proces of tymes' and his preference for a vernacular vocabulary where Latinate terms were available to him (pp.200f.).

24. See chapters 6, 8, 12, 35.

25. E.g. Prologue; chapters 7, 15, 16, 29, 45, 51–67, 69.

26. *Confessions*, trans. Sheed (1944. XI.7.p.213).

27. See above p.12–13.

28. See Hodgson (1944, lxii); *Benjamin Major* IV.22. & V.2. PL 196, 165 and 171.

29. For a specifically phenomenological approach to the *Cloud*-author, see Forman (1987).

30. *Cloud*, Prologue 2.5; 74.73.19–24.

31. 'Whoso had þis werk, it schuld gouerne him ful semely, as wele in body as in soule, & make hym ful fauorable vnto iche man or womman þat lokyd apon hym; insomuche þat þe worst fauored man or womman þat leueþ in þis liif, & þei miȝte come to by grace to worche in þis werk, þeire fauour schuld sodenly & gracyously be chaunged, þat iche good man þat hem sawe schulde be fayne & ioiful to haue hem in companye, & ful mochil þei schulde þink þat þei were plesid in spirit & holpen by grace vnto God in þeire presence' [*leueþ:* lives] (*The Cloud*, 54.55.25–32).

32. 'þis writyng þat next foloweþ is þe Inglische of a book þat Seynte Denys wrote vnto Thimothe, þe whiche is clepid in Latyn tonge *Mistica Theologia.* Of þe whiche book, forþi þat it is mad minde in þe 70 chapter of a book wretin before (þe whiche is clepid þe *Cloude of Vnknowing*) how þat Denis sentence wol cleerli afferme al þat is wretyn in þat same book: þerfore, in translacioun of it, I haue not onliche folowed þe nakid lettre of þe text, bot for to declare þe hardnes of it, I haue moche folowed þe sentence of þe Abbot of Seinte Victore, a noble & a worþi expositour of þis same book' (*H.D.* 119.2–10. See further Minnis (1982, 1983).

33. T.S. Eliot, *Four Quartets*: 'Little Gidding'.

34. See above p.138.

35. See, for example, Burrow (1977); Tugwell (1984, p.171; Minnis (1983, p.346).

36. '& al þe whiles þat þe soule woniþ in þis deedly body, euermore is þe scharpnes of oure vnderstonding in beholding of alle goostly þinges, bot most specialy of God, medelid wiþ sum maner of fantasie; for þe whiche oure werk schuld be vnclene, & bot if more wonder were, it schuld lede us into moche errour' [*bot if . . . were*: unless it were most exceptional] (8.18.18–23).

37. Burrow (1977) makes the point that the *Cloud*-author's teaching on the habit of fallen imagination to make 'a bodely conseyte of a goostly þing, or elles a

goostly conseyte of a bodely þing' (65.65.29–30) points to a proper respect for the integrity of both the physical and spiritual worlds (p.289). But his later point that the *Cloud*-author does not want the reader to carry something of the physical reality over into the realms of the spirit (p.296) perhaps does insufficient justice to the fact that while events can carry spiritual significance without losing their integrity as physical events, their spiritual significance for the understanding comes precisely from the nature of their physicality. If Stephen's vision of Christ standing in heaven is to be seen as his standing ready to help (c.58) that is only possible because we understand that in certain circumstances man on his feet is better prepared for rendering active help and support than man recumbent. Similarly, because we know about the property of clouds to obscure the sun or even, hillwalking, to cut off the line of vision of the physical landscape altogether, we can glimpse the possibility of the concept of the cloud of unknowing. This perception of physical events as icons throws light on the spirituality of Margery Kempe.

38. Cf. 'Reason never rises up to cognition of the invisible unless her handmaid, imagination, represents to her the form of visible things. For through the appearance of visible things she rises to the knowledge of invisible things, as often as she draws a kind of similitude from one to the other' (Richard of St Victor, *Benjamin Minor*, ed. Zinn, 1979, c.5.p.57) cf. Hodgson (1982, p.134.6–24)

39. See Minnis (1983, p.333).

40. For an opposite view see Tugwell (1984, pp.171–2).

41. See further Englert (1983).

42. See Johnston (1975); Cf. Moore (1987).

43. A traditional Augustinian argument, see *Sermo* cxliii.iii. *PL* 38.786. Cf. Hilton, see above pp.150–3, 158–9.

44. Cf.'for as alle men weren lost in Adam, for he fel fro þis onyng affeccion, & as alle, þat wiþ werk acordyng to here clepyng wol witnes here wille of saluacion, ben sauid & schul be by þe vertewe of þe Passion of only Crist, offring himself up in verreiest sacrifiȝe, al þat he was in general & not in specyal, wiþoutyn special beholdyng to any o man in þis liif, bot generaly & in comon for alle; riȝt so a verey & a parfite sacrifier of himself þus by a comon entent vnto alle doþ þat in him is to knit alle men to God as effectuely as himself is' (*P.C.* 79–80.41–7).

45. Cf. Hilton, *Scale 2*, c.27. See above p.150.

46. In view of this interpretation of every stage of contemplative experience as integral to the significance of the Incarnation which itself rescues through grace the imaginative faculty, it is hard to accept the view that the *Cloud*-author finds it difficult to ascribe to Christ anything more than a rather temporary significance – i.e. as a subject of humanly misleading meditations

(Tugwell, 1984, p.172). In a more fundamental sense than is implied, of course, Christ's rather temporary significance is of profound importance.

47. For þis is þe werk, as þou schalt here after, in þe whiche man schuld haue contynowed ȝif he neuer had synned, & to þe whiche worching man was maad . . . (4.11.9–12).

48. See below pp.252–3.

49. T.S. Eliot. *Four Quartets*: 'Burnt Norton'.

50. p.90. 27f. *Ego sum ostium. Per me si quis introierit, saluabitur; et siue egredietur siue ingredietur, pascua inveniet.* cf. above p.183.

51. See *MED sub* 'kepen' esp. 4a; 11a; 12a; 15b; 19a; 22b.

52. *City of God*. XI.9. Bettenson (1972, p.440).

53. See further Johnston's discussion of vertical as opposed to horizontal thinking in Christian mystical experience as part of a more general cultural phenomenon (1975, Appendix pp.264–74) Cf. also below pp.189-90.

54. See above p.181.

55. Cf. '. . . a soule þat is parfitely affecte in þis werk, & onyd þus to God in spirit, as þe preof of þis werk witnessiþ . . .' (*Cloud*, 25 33 29–30).

56. See chapters 7–9.

57. See 8.18.1–14.

58. See above pp.181, 183.

59. Cf. 12.21.14–16.

60. See chapters 12–14.

61. See above p.181.

62. See above p.8. For a tangential study of the *Cloud*-author in these terms see Tixier (1990).

63. 'þi list is lykyng to pleye wiþ a childe': this phrase, while making perfectly good sense literally [your enthusiasm is delighting to play with a child] has proved difficult in context – see further Hodgson (1982) p.181, Note 95. Tixier (1990, p.249) reads it literally but, interestingly, suggests the possibility of an allegorical understanding – i.e. reading the child in terms of the Victorine allegory (see above p.18) as Benjamin, that is contemplation, the child of Rachel. Such a sudden adoption of an unexplained allegory is not typical of the *Cloud*-author in these texts and is unlikely.The literal interpretation is awkward in the context of this passage concerned with contemplation and the silence of understanding. It is more likely to refer to the lightness of spirit and total creative absorption of a child at play. Thus it might be glossed 'your desire

for, and delight in, contemplation is like that which a child has in playing'. This is in keeping with *Cloud*, 46.48.36, where again the contemplative is likened to a child playing games with God his father. For a psychological analysis of this state in the work of the *Cloud*-author see Englert (1983, p.82f.).

64. See above p.181.

65. See chapter 29.

66. See above p.18.

67. On the relationship between the *Cloud*-author's teaching on this subject and that of Guigo II in his *Scala Claustralium* see Tugwell (1984, chapters 9, 10, 11 and 15). Certainly the *Cloud*-author does not follow the order in Rolle and Hilton of Reading Prayer Meditation. See above pp.85–9; 135.

68. The *Cloud*-author's use of the word 'meek' here draws on all the connotations he has built into it, see above p.190.

69. See above pp.176–80.

70. T.S. Eliot, *Four Quartets*: 'East Coker'.

71. See *Benjamin Major*, V. i. PL 196.169.

72. Chapter 61. See also above pp.178–9.

73. Cf. Julian of Norwich. E.g. see below pp.234, 240–1.

74. Cf. *P.C.* p.96.4f.

75. See *In Epistolam. Joannis Ad Parthos. Tractatus IV.6.Tota vita christiani boni, sanctum desiderium est.* [The whole life of a good Christian consists in holy desire.] *PL* 35.2008 Cf. *Tractatus* vii 8. Dilige, et quod vis fac. 2033 [love and do what you will].

76. See further Minnis (1982).

77. *P.C.* pp.94–7; see above p.191.

78. See Tixier (1990, p.238 and note).

79. Cf. p.88.6–17; pp.91–2.3–2; p.98.8–24.

80. Wolters (1961, p.189).

81. W.B. Yeats, 'Among Schoolchildren'.

Chapter 5

Julian of Norwich: 'Endles Knowyng in God'

Certain fourteenth- and fifteenth-century wills mention a recluse known as Julian of Norwich[1] but we know nothing about her personal life except what she herself tells us in her account of her visionary experience. That has not, however, prevented speculation based on both her writing and the historical circumstances of her time. It varies from suggestions that she was a professional religious who entered a convent in her teens,[2] to conjectures that she was a widow who had lost her husband, and possibly also a child during the plague, but who received her visions while still living in her own household which included her mother and servants.[3] All such accounts are essentially conjectural and not very fruitful. Julian tells us all she thinks needs to be known about her circumstances in order to clarify the implications of her visionary experience. Her 'story' is one of the most remarkable texts of the Middle Ages.

It exists in two forms, one a great deal longer than the other. In the shorter version, of which there remains a single copy made in the fifteenth century, the scribe tells us that a vision was shown 'to a deuoute woman and hir name is Iulyan that is recluse atte Norwyche and ȝitt ys on lyfe anno domini millesimo ccccxiii' (1.39.1–3).[4] Both versions tell us that when she was thirty and a half years old (the long text dates this in May 1373) she became seriously ill. In her younger days she had actually desired such a sickness believing, medieval-fashion, in the illuminative possibilities of suffering for those whose lives are dedicated to the desire to know the reality of God. Julian says that she wanted such an experience in order to empty her of all but spiritual comfort. And there were other desires. She also wanted to be granted a visual experience of Christ's Passion in order to sharpen her devotional understanding. In this she manifests the kind of devotional mode catered for by texts like the immensely popular Franciscan *Meditationes Vitae*

Christi.[5] These two specific desires, she tells us, did not last; but she was always filled with a third intense longing to experience the kind of pain involved in the knowledge of, and sorrow for, sin, the suffering involved in love, and a will totally subsumed in a desire for God – what she calls three wounds: 'the wound of very contrition, the wound of kinde compassion and the wound of willful longing to God' (2.3).[6]

Her illness in 1373, in fact, was the occasion for the fulfilling of all three of her desires. In her visionary experience which is centred on Christ's cross, and which is the special illumination given to Julian of the pattern of Incarnation that informs in various ways the experiences of all the five writers with whom this book is concerned, she comes to understand the psychological reality of the 'three wounds' as an inner process which restores man to a creative integrity and frees him from his own manifest inadequacy. Although it may well be felt as wounding it is, in fact, a healing surgery and death is simply part of a process. At about four o'clock in the morning at the critical point of her illness, when she felt herself to be dying, a priest was called who set a crucifix before her face. She found it a source of light in surroundings which were dark to her. Then, suddenly, her experience of pain was miraculously transformed to one of well-being and she had a series of sixteen visions on the nature of redemption: they started with Christ crucified and ended with his ruling as king within the soul which appeared to her as having immense space – that of a whole kingdom. The first fifteen occurred in an unbroken sequence until 'none of the day overpassid' (c.65, p.81). If this is None and not noon – and since she also refers to Prime (c.69, p.84) it is arguable that she refers to canonical rather than horological time – then the first series of her revelations ended after three in the afternoon, the hour which commemorated Christ's death[7] and with a vision of man suddenly and permanently delivered from pain and suffering in the form of a white child who springs out of a shapeless stinking corrupt body. After this Julian experienced another return to, and remission of, her sickness before the last vision on the following night.

We know from the longer account of her visions, which she calls both 'sheweings [showings] or revelations' (1.1) interchangeably, that fifteen years or so after they first occurred she was given a particular spiritual insight into the meaning of the whole experience

– 'wete it wele: love was his mening' [*wete*: know] (86.102) – and that for just short of twenty years she continued to be given further inward teaching about its implications (51.56). It is generally supposed that the shorter version represents an account first written down soon after the original experience and that the longer version came later and incorporates her growth in understanding over the subsequent twenty years. The fact that the heading to chapter eighty-six states that 'the good lord shewid this booke shuld be otherwise performid than at the first writing' is perhaps evidence of this.[8] It could, however, simply refer to the first sentence of that chapter: 'This booke is begunne be Gods gift and his grace, but it is not yet performid, as to my syte', which either suggests that the writing of the book is simply part of a process of growth in understanding which is continued in lived experience, or that Julian is not yet satisfied with her account. In fact, the assumption that the short text was written shortly after 1373 and the longer one sometime shortly after 1393 is currently being challenged. It is argued that internal evidence in the short text points to a date of composition after 1388 and that the long text may not have been written until after 1413 since, if the scribe of the original of the short text knew that Julian was still alive, then he is unlikely to have copied an out-of-date text which the short version would by then have become if the long text is dated in the 1390s.[9] The question of chronology is complicated. Even if the evidence that the shorter version was written in the late 1380s proves finally convincing, this does not rule out a date sometime in the early 1390s for the long text. The twenty years during which Julian received inward illumination and the fifteen years after which she was told that 'love was our lords mening' must have run concurrently. A date after 1413 would make Julian over seventy years of age, and while it is not impossible that she wrote up the longer version of her experience then, it seems inherently less likely. It would also seem odd, given her expressed concern to share her experience with her fellow Christians (long text c.9), that she should delay so long before embarking on this expanded account. There is no absolute evidence that the shorter version is not in fact part extrapolation, part summary of the longer one: this might be suggested by the fact that it appears in a manuscript which contains excerpts from other longer devotional works including Rolle's *Form of Living* and *Ego Dormio*.[10] But the nature of the passages unique to the longer version render it extremely unlikely that it predated the shorter account. On some occasions (e.g. chapter ten) a passage relates how it is the result of understanding granted subsequent to the original showing. On another occasion, in the showing for prayer, a passage in the short version (xix.69–70.28–7) on man's fear of the wrath of God is replaced by a lengthy addition in which Julian wrestles with her conviction that in fact there is no wrath in God. Other differences between the two texts also point to a development between the short and long versions. In the shorter text she twice directs her account specifically to contemplatives (4.45.8–12; 12.59.18–21) but these references are cut from the long text[11] which stresses only Julian's references to a general audience.[12] The tone of the long text is also more confident. The defensive protestations in chapter six of the short text (48.8–14) on her right to speak of what she has been shown despite the fact that she is a woman do not appear in the longer.[13]

In spite of the greater assurance of its tone, however, the long text does explicitly state that Julian lays no claim to formal education: 'these revelations were shewed to a simple creature that cowde no letter' (2.2). There are varieties of opinion as to the extent to which this statement can be taken at its face value. Some consider it beyond doubt that she was widely read in Latin and vernacular spiritual classics.[14] But the fact that those trained in the history of theology may engage with her text in a particular way, recognise in it theological stances intellectually formulated in other writings, and pick up echoes of the Scriptures and Church Fathers, does not prove that Julian was herself formally educated to a high degree.[15] There is no direct evidence of formal learning in the shape of either learned reference or Latin quotation in her text. And that such a practice would not be ruled out by the nature of her audience can be demonstrated both from Langland's *The Vision of Piers Plowman* and the vernacular sermon tradition. A woman of Julian's obviously luminous intelligence might well absorb theological concepts and terminology from conversation with, or teaching by, priests or learned men, or from hearing readings. Examples of such width of reference and wisdom at the command of a formally uneducated religious can certainly be found in the present day. Moreover, to take Julian's own direct denial of formal learning as a merely rhetorical modest 'disclaimer' would be jarringly at odds with a work of such painstaking intellectual honesty.[16] Either way, the pursuit of echoes and parallels to their possible outside source deflects attention from the peculiar nature of Julian's own text, its internal structures and its literary qualities.

Whatever the truth about the relationship of the short text to the long, it is clear that the longer represents the fuller version of Julian's understanding of her own experience. This chapter will introduce the way that the passages, which we may call additions, peculiar to this text relate to the account which is common to both, and highlight the distinctive quality of the long text – a fusion of feeling and understanding in a state of visionary awareness which Julian calls 'knowing'. The hall-mark of her witness lies in the interpenetration of theology and experience; she will not allow one to falsify the other. Her physical sickness and relief are both the initial condition in which she experiences redemption and emblematic of it. Through her physical circumstances she is involved in a process of transfiguration which she comes to understand sacramentally as part of a cosmological process of redemption. She formulates her understanding in medieval theological terms, but in such a way as to reveal that psychological dynamic which is the starting point of theology.

THE MANUSCRIPTS

It is necessary to distinguish between three copies of the long text that have come down to us. All post-date Julian herself by a considerable margin. One, in the Bibliothèque Nationale in Paris, is late sixteenth- or early seventeenth-century in date (P); British Library, Sloane Manuscript 2499 (S1) belongs to the early seventeenth century. A further Sloane Manuscript (3075) is an eighteenth-century modernised copy of the former and can be disregarded for the purposes of this discussion. But between P and S1 there are many differences. There are passages which occur in one but not the other; some, but not all, of these can be accounted for as mistaken omissions by one or other scribe. There are numerous differences in single words; sometimes it is clear by comparison with the short text that these differences arise from misreading, but this is not always the case. S1 is closer to the vocabulary and syntax of late Middle English than P which modernises words and extends syntax. The Paris text is without doubt rhetorically superior to S1 but this does not therefore mean that that is how Julian conceived it;[17] such polish may be the work of a subsequent scribe. Some of the differences in detail, such as the use of prepositions, can radically affect the theological implications of a sentence or the literary impact of a theological insight. Analysis of these differences shows that S1 frequently conveys a more immediate sense of a theological dynamic. P is a beautifully executed piece of deliberately archaised calligraphy. S1 bears all the marks of a scribe copying, rather than 'working' on his text. It is messy, the hand varies in its clarity and words are crossed out and corrected as the text progresses. As both manuscripts are much later than Julian's own time and there is no external evidence to suggest which might be closer to her own original formulation, any attempt to produce an eclectic text would involve an unwarranted degree of editorial interpretation. It has to be accepted that we probably cannot know exactly what Julian actually wrote or dictated. However, despite some notable omissions, the work of the scribe of S1 does not suffer from the kind of editorial interpretation evident in P. Here we probably come closer to Julian's own language. Its sometimes difficult grammatical structures and syntactical ambiguities have a vibrant theological resonance and complexity often clumsily ironed out by the more orthodox clarity of P.[18] For all these reasons it is to the text in S1 that all references will be made.[19]

THE WHOLE REVELATION

In perhaps the most compelling addition to the long text, the example of the lord and the servant, a lengthy narrative icon in which the figures of a lord and a servant enact her understanding of the Incarnation,[20] Julian makes it clear that although she received distinguishably separate showings they all constitute one 'hole revelation from the begynning to the end' (51.56). There is a clear shape to the basic sequence of visions common to both texts which as it unfolds, communicates a vivid simultaneous awareness of time and eternity. There are what Julian would call 'ii manner of beholdyng' (46.49): one of suffering and growth in time as a means of realising an inner security and joy which 'passyth al that herte may willen and soule may desire' (26.28); the second a realisation that this joy has always been, and always will be there, but because human faculties are imperfect, impaired by involvement with evil in a state of 'blindness' ('blindhede'),[21] the only means by which man can grow towards a realisation of this joy is faith. Like the *Cloud*-author, Julian conveys a sense of the life of faith as a game. Her visionary experience brings her by her own special route to a felt understanding of how man shares in the creative play of divine wisdom[22] and practises the skills and disciplines needed for such activity. Her showings illuminate for her the moves in the game of redemption played by both God and man, and her attempt to convey their implications and their essential shape is informed by her constant openness to a creative lightness of spirit.

The first twelve showings are concerned with Christ's Incarnation and Passion; they operate like icons triggering communication of how man and God share in the means of transfiguring the disfiguring effects of sin in time. Alienation, suffering and dying co-exist with security, joy and life, not as meaningless contradictions but as complementary states. Suffering is the only means available in time of proving the reality of the transfiguring power of love. This exposition comes to a climax in the eleventh and twelfth showings. Here Julian understands that her vision of the Virgin at the Annunciation (4.5) enabling Christ to be born and thus participating in his *kenosis*, and at the Crucifixion sharing his suffering, is completed by her knowledge of Mary exalted in glory; and all these perceptions are a means to her spiritual understanding that Mary projects the pattern of transfiguration possible for all men to 'worshippe and ioye' in Christ whose glory is ineffably the completion of all partiality. (c.25, p.28. and c.26).

There follows the thirteenth showing which transposes the double awareness of alienation and security into another mode. Here Julian receives a visionary experience of man cut off from fulfilment in Christ by a barrier. The theological name for this is sin; it has no substantive identity but is recognised by the pain and suffering which it causes. But simultaneously with the experience of deprivation, Julian is assured that 'al shal be wel' (27.28) though she finds it hard to reconcile these two states of awareness. The fourteenth showing reveals prayer to be the means by which man in time can engage in a process which liberates him from the frustrations of this barrier; and the fifteenth showing sees him finally and completely released. The sixteenth and final showing combines an awareness of both God's immanence and transcendence: Christ is discovered reigning in the soul – a vast kingdom where he has (in fact) always been. As so often, the end of man's interior journey is to know the place for the first time.

The basic shape of Julian's showings relates to the way the Office in the Primer celebrates the meaning of life in time.[23] The first fifteen relating to the Passion and redemption appear to start early in the morning, 4 a.m. (65.81), so round about Lauds, and continue until just before Evensong.[24] But whereas the office at that time remembers Christ's death, the visionary nature of Julian's showings is emphasised by the breaking of the pattern of the Hours of the Cross with an experience of the salvation that the context of these Hours celebrates. The death of Christ and thoughts on the deposition and entombment proper to Evensong and Compline are by-passed. At the point when Julian expected to witness the death of Christ he is transfigured manifesting the realities of love, joy and endless life and she is granted showings which relate to the nature of salvation. Between the fifteenth showing and the last, which occurs during the following night, Julian suffers a period of sickness and doubt[25] from which she is delivered by faith, an experience which represents in its own way both the desolation of the loss of Christ and his power to harrow hell not inappropriate to the Canonical time of day. In her final vision she sees just that 'liyf and glorie wiþ-outen ende' and Christ who 'lyuest and regnest god' which are prayed for repeatedly in the prayer which follows the memorial of the Passion in the Hours of the Virgin.[26] Her references to Mary also echo the way the office in the Primer counterpoints Mary as an instrument of salvation to the account of the Passion in the Hours of the Cross.[27]

The whole sequence of showings clearly relates to an experience of ultimate reality, understood in Christian terms, which is at the heart of Julian's experience of being in time. Her understanding of the Incarnation is not expressed in the intellectual albeit imaginative terms of Hilton, but experienced as a catalyst which transfigures everyday experience. Julian uses the language and assumptions of medieval theology but her text is shaped by literary means to convey creatively her psychological understanding of the realities such theology seeks to discover. Ultimately, of course, literary means, and the reader's response to them, cannot recreate Julian's mystical experience, but they can embody signs by which her faith and the grounds for it may be recognised. The structure and detailed formulation of this sequence of showings cohere in a visionary perspective on the dynamic of being in time. This becomes particularly apparent from a study of the way the additional material in the long text welds with the common core of visionary showings.

THE FIRST REVELATION: 'ALL THINGS FOR LOVE' (CHAPTERS 4–9)

At the end of Julian's account of this first showing, and again towards the end of the whole series, she comments that her visionary experience presented itself in three ways by 'sight', 'word' and 'gostly sight' (9.11; 73.88). In this Julian has been said to employ the Augustinian visionary terminology which distinguishes between corporeal, imaginative and intellective vision.[28] However, it is clear from Julian's account of her experience that she does not analyse it in terms of a consistent division between these three categories; they overlap in the process of illumined understanding which developed for nearly twenty years after the original experience.[29] From her text it would seem that 'gostly sight' refers to the spiritual understanding which coincides with, and develops from, insights received both in visual and linguistic terms, what she calls 'bodily sight' and 'word formyd in my understonding' (9.11). The visual showings concerned with the Passion are presented with a strangely intense yet dispassionate concentration on precise and horrifying details involved in Christ's physical suffering. They hang as if vividly lit in a silent darkness for contemplation, and function sacramentally in that they crystallise forms which allow a depth of insight into the inner realities of human existence as perceived in Christian terms.

The first chapter of the long text represents a contents list of the showings to follow. It is an addition to the short version and almost certainly by Julian herself.[30] There it is stated that the first showing is fundamental to all that follow; in it they are 'grounded and onyd' (1.1). In both versions, at the very moment Julian feels at the point of death, although relieved from pain, the crucifix on which her eyes are fixed becomes suddenly palpably alive:

> In this sodenly I saw the rede blode trekelyn downe fro under the garlande, hote and freisly and ryth plenteously, as it were in the time of his passion.
>
> (4.4)

freisly: freely.

But this visual sight is accompanied by another kind of seeing – a joyful understanding that the Passion is part of a larger pattern of salvation for all creatures and essential to the defeat of the powers of evil (4.4–5). It is easy to intuit how such visionary immediacy of 'sight' (understanding) might be fed by meditations on the Passion like those designed by Rolle, or by the pattern of daily prayer established in the Primer.[31]

The description of the flowing blood here is the start of further showings in which Christ's blood streams as love poured out regardless of suffering – which is the condition of salvation. In the first showing it is followed by a vision of Mary, apparently as she was depicted at the Annunciation in the iconography of medieval art and literature.

> I saw hir ghostly in bodily likeness, a simple mayde and a meke, young of age and little waxen above a child.
>
> (4.5)

But it is important not to let the familiar visual image divert attention from what Julian is really saying. She stresses that in this showing God brought 'our blissid lady to my understonding' ('I saw hir ghostly'). The visual image almost immediately dissolves in the point of Julian's realisation that Mary's attitude, 'the wisedam and trueth of hir soule' which participated in the divine *kenosis*, raised her to become 'mare than all that God made beneath hir in worthyness and grace'.

It is at this stage in the first showing that Julian perceived the universe as 'a littil thing' in the palm of her hand; it was no greater than a hazel nut and apparently as precarious for it seemed poised on the brink of destruction. What Julian understands from this, however, is that, paradoxically, it is assured in the very contingency of its being since it is made and kept by the being of God. Again, far from being a visual image of the world as a hazel-nut held safely in the palm of her hand, this is a 'gostly sight' in which Julian uses the image as a simile to express both existential angst and a knowledge of ultimate security:

> I loked thereupon with eye of my understondyng and . . . I mervellid how it might lesten, for methowte it might suddenly have fallen to nowte for littil. And I was answered in my understondyng: 'it lestith

> and ever shall, for God loveth it; and so allthing hath the being be the love of God.[32]
>
> (5.5)

This ambivalent sense of being at once ludicrously insignificant and vulnerable but also totally safe in God's love, is fundamental to all Julian's showings and it delineates the parameters of her understanding of the dynamic of salvation which is engaged with the growing discovery of the conditions of safety; it can only be lived, not explained. At this stage in her original experience, however, Julian is aware of a gap between these two perceptions:

> In this littil thing I saw iii properties: the first is that God made it, the second is that God loveth it, the iiid, that God kepith it. But what is to me sothly the maker, the keper, and the lover I canot telle; for, till I am substantially onyd to him, I may never have full rest ne very blisse; that is to sey, that I be so festinid to him that there is right nowte that is made betwix my God and me.
>
> (5.5)
>
> *onyd*: united.

It is in this gap that the game of salvation integrating man and God is played.

The mode of the game is encapsulated in the physical circumstances which accompany Julian's vision. They are both appropriate and integral one to another. Her experience of sickness and death and miraculous release from pain is a microcosm of the whole process of healing through suffering shared by God and man by way of Incarnation. Julian's recovery from sickness is a powerful physical emblem of the truth revealed in the subsequent showings, that joy and health are the ultimate realities. They are validated by faith which works as a catalyst to transform the experience of suffering inherent in human existence from one of negative frustration to that of being the sole means of discovering the ultimate viability of love and sure hope. Faith is a channel for joy; both may not always be experienced simultaneously in time, but in Julian's visionary awareness they are inextricably linked. The additions to the long text highlight this.

As soon as Julian has described her understanding that the showing of the blood trickling from beneath the crown of thorns has been given her by God she adds that this was suddenly accompanied by inner joy which she feels to be given by the Trinity:

> For the Trinite is God, God is the Trinite; the Trinite is our maker and keeper, the Trinite is our everlasting lover, everlasting ioy and blisse, be our lord Iesus Christ. And this was shewed in the first and in all; for where Iesus appereith the blissid Trinite is understond, as to my sight.
>
> (4.4)

For her, the Passion focuses the active care of God who 'made all things for love' (8.9) and so it is the cause for joy. The subsequent showings concerned with the Passion deepen her understanding of this simultaneity of pain and joy. Other additions to the first showing introduce the idea of a continuum of joy running between God and man and man and God: God's joy is in man's seeking of Him as his fulfilment; man's joy is in the awareness of the possibility of fulfilment. This lies behind the prayer added to the long text:

> God, of thy goodnesse, give me thyselfe; for thou art enow to me and I may nothing aske that is less that may be full worshippe to thee. And if I aske anything that is lesse, ever me wantith, but only in thee I have all
>
> (5.6)

and Julian's subsequent comment that God 'hath made us only to himselfe'. This is followed by a long passage which describes her understanding of prayer as a growth in awareness on man's part of the joy of being that is the fulfilment of his longing and the foundation of his existence:

> for our kindly will is to have God and the gode will of God is to have us. And we may never blyn of willing ne of longing till we have him in fullhede of ioy, and than may we no more willen.
>
> (6.7)
>
> *blyn*: cease.

The description of the first showing in the list of contents reads:

> the first is of his pretious coroning with thornys; and therewith was comprehended and specifyed the Trinite with the incarnation and unite betwix God and man soule, with many faire sheweings of endless wisedome and teacheing of love, in which all the sheweings that follow be grounded and onyd.
>
> (1.1)

The phrase 'his pretious coroning with thornys' conflates connotations of great value, glory and elevation with the traditional iconography of the suffering and scorn associated with this episode of the Passion. It is a verbal icon whose imploded significance explodes in the mind. Julian says that it 'comprehended and specifyed the Trinite' (i.e. it is a sign which includes all the significance of the Trinity). For the reader it points forward to Julian's own visionary perception in all her revelations of how that continuum of being which joins eternity and time, joy and suffering, God and man, is all one lasting reality; and it would also trigger a remembrance of this retrospectively. In the extended account of the first showing Julian adds a passage on the relationship of the showings to faith. They stand to faith as does the Scriptural revelation of the Incarnation: both focus in particular time and in lived experience the substance of faith which works dynamically throughout time in the inner lives of those who engage with it.

> And whan the shewyng, which is goven in a tyme, is passyd and hid, than the feith kepyth be grace of the Holy Ghost into our life end. And thus by the shewyng it is not other than the faith, ne less ne more, as it may be seene be our lords meneing in the same matter be than it came to the end.
>
> (7.9)

It is with the exposition of this dynamic of faith that the passages in the long text, absent from the short one, are often concerned. Julian finds a language to embody the implications of her showings for the life of faith 'whan the shewyng which is goven in a tyme is passyd and hid'.

THE SECOND REVELATION: 'A PARTE OF HIS PASSION' (CHAPTER 10)

The second showing has a surreal quality: Julian's field of vision is dominated by the face of the crucified Christ suffering a sequence of the effects of physical violence and a spreading discoloration of dried blood. At the time she was in doubt about the status of this bodily sight but later she recognises both the iconographical source of the image in depictions of the vernicle (a handkerchief which was believed to have been lent to Jesus on the way to Calvary by

Saint Veronica and which subsequently bore the impression of his face) and its visionary import. The account of Julian's understanding of this showing in the long version demonstrates very clearly the integration of bodily and spiritual sight at the heart of the showings. The disfiguring effects of the violence are the shame of evil actions which hide Christ.

Julian tells us that it was from this glimpse of the beauty of Christ hidden by foul abuse which she only partially understood, that she became aware of the therapeutic value of a constant direction of the will towards finding God, however overwhelming the evidence to the contrary seems:

> And thus was I lernyd to myn vnderstondyng that sekyng is as good as beholdyng for the tyme that he will suffer the soul to be in travel.
>
> (10.12)
>
> *travel*: travail.

All these senses are inherent in the strangely powerful evocation of the interior consciousness of fallen man drowned fathoms deep from direct sight of God. It is slowly brought into intellectual focus through the delicate evocation of a drowned landscape:

> One tyme mine understondyng was led downe into the see-ground, and there I saw hill and dalis grene, semand as it were mosse begrowne, with wrekke and gravel.
>
> (10.11)
>
> *see-ground*: sea-bed; *wrekke*: sea-weed.

But just as in the image of the Passion, the apparently overwhelming potential for destruction is no match for God's creative presence with a man continually, even 'under the broade watyr', if he can only see it. This kind of seeing involves a continual activity of faith which both engages with, and is enabled by, the reality – God – it seeks:

> for he wille that we levyn that we se him continually, thowe that us thinkeith that it be but litil, . . . for he wil be sene and he wil be sowte.
>
> (10.11)
>
> *levyn*: believe; *sowte*: sought.

This sense of engaging with a divine energy that can be felt as an impulse to wholeness at the heart of psychological disintegration is picked up again later in her description of prayer as a growth in consciousness of the potential for love and joy in which men are united to God. Before she can develop this, however, she has much more to assimilate on the nature of the illuminative activity of faith and the nature of that 'sin' that blocks her sight of God.

Julian's showings unfold a progressive understanding of the full significance of human inadequacy and how this negative charge can be made positive. Such understanding as she received in this showing was to be extended later in the eighth, as she points out, but the intervening five showings build up a process of enlightenment which the eighth completes and develops in a new way.

THE THIRD REVELATION: 'OUR LORD GOD DOTH ALLE' (CHAPTER 11)

In the expanded version of the third showing Julian adds to her visionary awareness of God as the being which informs that of all men – ('God in a poynte . . . for he is the mydde poynt of allthyng and all he doith' (11.13) – and the concomitant realisation that sin has no being, in fact, since it has no part in God – an illumined double awareness of what God does, 'for ther is no doer but he' (11.14). She distinguishes between the work of God, which she calls 'mercy and grace', to counteract the inadequacy of men (about which she says more will be revealed later in the showing about sin), and the nature of his being 'rightfulhede' (11.13) that is a just working in all things that never fails. The expression of her thought in this chapter is constantly pointing beyond the normal categories of logical argument and perception into a new kind of consciousness in which wisdom is born in accepting through faith the reality of transcendent love working in the world instead of trying to understand the metaphysical scheme of things with limited faculties. Just as Julian had used paradox to point to the truth that the beauty of the wisdom of God was both obscured by sin, yet revealed through it in the Passion[33] so she now expresses her understanding of the 'rightfulhede' of God in the manner of a Zen *koan*. This is a kind of riddle used in the discipline of Zen Buddhism designed to tease the disciple out of striving for solutions in terms which cannot provide them and to experience and accept themselves in a new way.[34] The tension expressed in her first showing between existential insecurity and awareness of the truth of salvation is a live issue at the heart of Julian's visionary experiences. It is finally resolved not through intellectual explanation but her transformed consciousness. In this showing she challengingly points to the limits of human judgement:

> a man beholdith some dedes wele done and some dedes evil, but our lord beholdyth hem not so; for as al that hath being in kinde is of Godds makyng, so is althing that is done in propertie of God's doing. (p.14)

Realisation of this fundamental reality, however superficially puzzling, leads Julian to recognition of the truth suggested to her as a rhetorical question from God 'How should anything be amysse?' Her state of reverent assent is described in S1 as 'enioyand in God'; P dilutes the dynamic impact of this fusion of understanding and joy between Julian and God to 'than saw I verely that my behovyth nedys to assent with great reverence and ioy in God'.

'Werkyng' is a word which Julian uses subtly to convey a range of meaning: effortful labour; creative potential (in the sense of 'how does this work?); the aesthetic implications of something 'working'; and the activity of a transforming agent much as yeast 'works' in dough. And in this third showing the 'rightfulhede' of God's working is revealed to her in the last two senses. The showing expresses to her the nature of God's being and the fact that the 'rightfulhede' of God's working will somehow bring all deeds in time – both those called evil and those called good – to a 'fulhede of godenes'(11.14). Julian still does not understand *how* such 'rightfulhede' 'works', only that it does. In this elaboration of her original showing in the long text it is at least possible – even probable – that the understanding about sin that she received in the thirteenth showing has retrospectively coloured her understanding.[35]

THE FOURTH REVELATION: 'HIS BLISSID BLODE' (CHAPTER 12)

The fourth showing starts to close the perceivable gap between the recognition of God's 'rightfulhede' and man's limited judgement which can only see the obvious evidence that something is immediately, if not ultimately, 'amysse'.

The blood which Julian saw trickle from under the crown of thorns in the first showing now pours profusely from Christ's violently abused body – a sight which at this stage of the showings subsumes the association between physical injury and the shame of evil deeds. Julian adds to the shorter account of the showing the observation that skin and wound were not distinguishable in the pouring blood which seemed as if it would soak her bed. In the original showing she associated the pouring blood with life-giving earthly water, a sacramental perception which is expanded as she 'sees' the blood descend to hell and ascend to heaven – literally streaming in the universe to efface the disfigurement of sin – and she ends with the image which crystallises her awareness that the work of the Passion was not confined by the historical moment which revealed the Incarnation but coexists with time:

> and there is in him bleding and praying for us to the Father – and is and shall be as long as it nedith. And evermore it flowith in all hevyns enioying the salvation of al mankynde that arn there and shal ben, fulfilling the noumber that failith.
>
> (12.15)

This awareness of the activity expressed in the Passion coexisting with the risen Christ is fundamental to Julian's later showings about the work of salvation. Her additions in the longer text clarify this.

REVELATIONS FIVE TO EIGHT: 'GAME' AND 'ARNESTE' (CHAPTERS 13–21)

The fifth showing also relates to the juxtaposed but unreconciled opposites in the third showing, God's 'rightfulhede' and man's inadequacy, in that she understands that through this ongoing passion the fiend is overcome. Two kinds of working co-exist: evil, which she calls the malice of the fiend; and the patient suffering of love which mysteriously processes the effect of this malice from wretchedness to joy. In the long text Julian adds riders which will later become important. One is that this is the work of salvation and there is nothing in it which shows God as wrathful towards sin; and the second that when God declares to her that the fiend is scorned, this is simply a way of saying that ultimately the work of redemptive suffering will leave him no place – he will go to hell.

Julian uses the conventional word 'hell', but the formulation of the showing reveals it as a state of annihilation, in that what the fiend has done has been transfigured through suffering, and he has no reality but his own pain.

In this showing Julian openly uses the language of the game of faith. The passage is common to both versions:

> I see iii things: game scorne and arneste. I se game that the fend is overcome. I se scorne that God scornith him and he shal be scornyd. And I se arneste that he is overcome be the blissfull passion and deth of our lord Iesus Criste, that was done in ful arnest and with sad travelle.
>
> (13.16)
>
> *arneste*: seriousness; *sad*: grave.

The suffering which transmutes the destructive potential of evil to one for joy, which she will see that all men can share with Christ through the Incarnation, is experienced as pain, a critical condition; but the fact that this can lead creatively to the defeat of that which causes the pain is matter for laughter and joy.

The whole structured sequence of Julian's visions and her reflections on them, linked with her personal experience of sickness and health, illuminates the developing skill to balance these senses of 'game' and 'arneste' in the healing integrity of faith. Thus the sixth showing assures Julian of the nature of the joy that outweighs suffering – likened, in an addition to the short text, to that joy created by a lord who fills his house with comforts specially to gladden those whom he loves (an image which is to be picked up later in her account of the lord and the servant). Similarly, the seventh showing internalises the theological truths demonstrated in the revelations thus far in Julian's own experience. She is made to feel a joy and security that surpasses all expectations of longing, alternating with pain and desolation in such a way that in the

> same tyme of ioy I migte have seid with Seynt Paul 'Nothing shal depart me fro the charite of Criste'. And in the peyne I migte have seid with Peter: 'Lord save me I perish'.[36]
>
> (15.17)

She experiences in her own situation both the reactions she had to the showing of the created universe: awareness of the threat of destruction and the confidence of joy and security. Although in her depression she intellectually acknowledges the existence of faith, hope and charity, she does not feel their comfort in experience; but the reality she understands from the showing is that 'God wille we knowen that he kepyth us even alike sekir in wo and in wele' (15.17–18). The means by which this knowledge becomes a matter of living faith rather than formulated dogma is through experience of doubt and pain.

There follows the greatly extended account of the eighth showing which coheres round a bodily sight of Christ's physical suffering, as his flesh dries in death. The sequence of showings that follow the densely impacted elements of the first revelation[37] starts to unfold its implications. Julian has been given assurance that ultimately, in a way not clear to her, the righteousness of God will prevail in his creation; that the Passion of Christ is part of this process and that it becomes a matter of lived experience as the suffering inextricably linked with existence in time activates the self-validating and thus redemptive life of faith. She is coming to the point where she will see that Christ and man are identified in the work of salvation. The core of the eighth showing in the short version is Christ's thirst on the cross which she understands physically and spiritually. As the full implications of the spiritual thirst are not processed until the thirteenth showing (about sin), she holds these back until then in the interests of allowing the shape of her original experience to speak for itself.[38]

In this eighth showing the physical thirst concentrates Julian's awareness of a process of suffering and failure in time with which she identifies but which finally does not run its course. The description of Christ's sufferings is greatly extended in the long version in an appalling image of dehydration: he hangs in the empty desolation of a failing inward vitality cruelly accelerated by a cutting freezing wind; his flesh sags and shrivels and billows in the wind like cloth hung out to dry. In both versions Julian finds this process an agony to see, and identifies with the compassion of the disciples and Mary, but in the long version this personal suffering is extended to a cosmological level:

> the firmament, the erth faledyn for sorow in hyr kynde in the tyme of Crist's deyng; for longith it kyndely to thir properte to know hym for ther God in whome al ther vertue stondyth.
>
> (18.20–1)

faledyn: fail, die; *kynde:* nature; *vertue*: inherent power.

This experience stands in apposition to the vision of creation sustained and upheld in the first showing and is modified by it. Just so Julian distinguishes between God's 'rightfulhede' that 'nedith neither the werkyng of mercy ner grace, for it ben al rightfull, wherin feilith nougte' [*feilith*: fails] (11.13–14) and his working of mercy and grace in a world of creatures prone to failure. Just so she learns through her own experiences, not only of physical sickness and health but also of spiritual desolation and joy, that life not death is the final reality. This process of failure is historically revealed at the moment of the crucifixion as he that is 'maker of kynde suffryth' and it stands for all time:

> thus was our lord Iesus nawted for us, and we stond al in this manner nowtid with hym; and shal done til we come to his blisse.
>
> (18.21)
>
> *nawted, nowtid*: set at nought.

Julian senses that there is no way to his bliss (sustaining love, truth, health and joy) except through suffering in time, and this truth has its epiphany in her physical inability to take her eyes from the cross (c.19). In the long text she adds here a gloss which reveals how the seventh showing had permeated her consciousness. She distinguishes between feelings experienced simultaneously, a natural shrinking from all the levels of pain suffered in mortality which she calls an outward sensation, and an overriding compelling inner certainty of love. For Julian these are, respectively, the 'arneste' and 'game' involved in the game of faith. It is by means of them both that she discovers how man is grounded in a reality beyond time which draws him to it, and finally, how, through the activity of faith, all the process of failure in time will ultimately be assimilated to the final reality of joy. In her formulation of this insight her language, characteristically, betrays the pressure of the synthetic nature of her revelations. She is both aware that the truth she understands is realised through the energy of Christ and also that this was showed to her by that same power:

> that the outeward part should draw the inward to assent was not shewid me; but that the inward drawith the outeward by grace, and both shal be onyd in blisse without end by the vertue of Criste this was shewid.
>
> (19.22)

Any editorial punctuation of the last phrase disturbs the fluidity of its meaning.

Another example of the way that Julian conceives the essential unity of all the separate showings can be seen in the way she anticipates the ninth showing at the end of the eighth in the passage on the three 'beholdyngs' of the Passion. Here, all her showings concerning the pain involved in the Incarnation as focused in Christ's Passion come to a head and show this pain to be but one aspect of the truth of the Incarnation. Her first 'beholding' she says concerns Christ's pain and that of the contrition and compassion that responds:

> the first is the herd peyn that he suffrid, with contrition and compassion; and that shewid our lord in this tyme . . .
>
> (21.23)

The other two, concerned more directly with the love and joy that prompts such suffering, are yet to come as a separate showing though they are anticipated at this point as Julian sees the ebbing vitality in Christ and all created being suddenly reversed:

> And I loked after the departing with al my myght and [wende] have seen the body al ded, but I saw hym not so. And ryth in the same tyme that methowte, be semyng, the life myght ne lenger lesten and the shewyng of the end behovyd nedis to be, sodenly, I beholdyng in the same crosse, he chongyd his blissfull chere. The chongyng of his blisful chere changyd myne, and I was as glad and mery as it was possible.
>
> (21.23)
>
> *chere*: expression, manner.

She shares in the joy and bliss which is the ever present reality, despite the suffering in time that obscures it and she understands that there is for man no way to this union with God – 'endles knowyng in God' – but through 'time of passion'.[39]

REVELATIONS NINE TO TWELVE: 'A IOY, A BLIS AN ENDLES LYKYNG' (CHAPTERS 22–6)

The ninth to the twelfth revelations escalate a sense of joyful identity between God and man and rehearse Julian's understanding of the implications of her experience of 'onyng' with God. The ninth showing describes the last two of the three ways of 'beholding' the Passion about which she spoke at the end of the eighth showing. They are: first an awareness of the love which is only manifested through suffering as that which transfigures the 'arneste' of the life of faith into a game the playing of which leads to joy; second, a sense of this joy itself.

The awareness of the suffering of Christ, of his love thus shown, and of the joy of the Trinity in his love are identified by theologians as the 'classical *ascensio mentis in deum* [ascent of the mind into God] of the Western tradition'.[40] For Julian her three 'beholdings' reveal a psychological dynamic of suffering transfigured by love to joy, whereby the transcendent God becomes known, immanent in the game of faith. The showing is by the word formed in the understanding that opens chapter twenty-two:

> Than seide our good lord Iesus Christe, askyng: 'Art thou wele payd that I suffrid for thee?' I sayd: 'Ya good lord, gramercy. Ya good lord, blissid mot thou be!' Than seyd Iesus, our kinde lord: 'If thou art payde, I am payde. It is a joy, a blis, an endles lekyng to me that ever suffrid I passion for the; and I myht suffre more, I wold suffre more'.
>
> (22.24)
>
> *payd*: satisfied.

This expresses with a startling simplicity the perception of salvation as a mutual working between God and man – 'if thou art payde, I am payde'. It is a condition which participates in the Trinity, itself described as 'iii hevyns', the joy of the Creator Father, the bliss of the Son and the 'endles lykyng' of the Holy Ghost (23.25) – all of which are revealed together, 'evyn lyke in blis', in the 'manhode of Criste'. Julian is aware that man is crucial to this unity. The joy of the Father is expressed as reward to the Son for his work in the Incarnation. This, says Julian, looking back to the first showing where she saw that 'allthing hath the being by the love of God' (5.5), means that:

> we be not only his be his beying, but also by the curtes geft of his Fader we be his [Christ's] blis, we be his mede, we be his worshippe, we be his corone.
>
> (22.24)
>
> *corone*: crown.

Since the image of the crown at this point in the Revelations resonates with the associations of the crown of thorns which is the cause of pain and bloodshed so vividly present in the first showing, it concentrates in itself the whole theology of salvation and the transfiguration of ways of being which is at its heart. In this ninth showing of the joy generated by the work of salvation, Julian learns that we are able to embrace this work – this game of faith – with a joy 'like to the joy that Criste hath of our salvation as it may be while we arn here' (23.25).

She seeks to convey the astonishing perception of how the limiting and temporal nature of the Incarnation focuses the eternal nature of God in time with a passage on the word 'ever' that ends this showing. At its start, in chapter twenty-two she hears Christ say that it is a source of endless joy to him that '*ever* suffrid I passion for the'. In chapter twenty-three this perception is enlarged when she comments that only in time does Christ suffer but the joy of what he accomplished never ceases:

> And al that he hath done for us, and doth, and *ever* shal, was never coste ne charge to hym, ne myte be; but only that he dede in our manhood.
>
> (23.25, italics mine)

She concludes with a meditation on how this word *ever* concentrates these revealed truths about time and eternity. As a piece of writing, the meditation reveals how Julian received amplification of the 'gostly sight' of her showings, and it is pertinent to juxtapose the relevant passages in the short and long texts. The short version has it:

> Thynke also wyselye of the gretnesse of this worde: That euer I suffred passion for the, for in that worde was a hye knawynge of luffe and of lykynge that he hadde in oure saluacion.
>
> (xii.58.19–22)
>
> *luffe:* love.

Here 'worde' refers to the whole phrase. In her expansion of the long text Julian unpacks with painstaking precision the implications of the ninth showing.

> Thynke also wisely of the gretnes of this word 'ever', for in it was shewid an high knowing of love that he hath in our salvation, with manyfold ioyes that folow of the passion of Criste; one is that he ioyeth that he hath done it in dede, and he shal no more suffre; another, that

> he browte us up into hevyn and made us for to be his corone and endles blisse; another is that he hath therwith bawte us from endless peynys of helle.
>
> (23.26)
>
> *bawte*: bought.

In both passages the language betrays pressure of an illuminated understanding to which it is inadequate. In the long version, however, the ambiguity of the word 'ever' is isolated as a means of spear-heading, with finer theological precision, a reflection on the reality of joy in the work of salvation which crowns Christ's work in time.

Indeed Julian's account of the tenth showing reveals a similar pressure on traditional exegesis, as her awareness is dominated by what promises to be a bodily sight but is instantly transposed to convey ghostly understanding. The familiar iconography of Christ's wounded side in both art and literature was understood sacramentally as an icon of the means by which man is returned to the love of God.[41] Julian's tenth showing in the long version is simply an elaboration of this traditional image; as a verbal icon it has a surreal quality which represents the meditational response the visual image is designed to enable:

> Than with a glad chere our lord loked into his syde and beheld enioyand; and with his swete lokyng he led forth the understondyng of his creture be the same wound into hys syde withinne. And than he shewid a faire delactabil place, and large enow for al mankynd that shal be save to resten in pece and in love.
>
> (24.26)

The traditional associations of the image are still present:

> And therewith he browte to mende his dereworthy blode and pretious water which he lete poure al oute for love. And with the swete beholdyng he shewid his blisful herte even cloven on two.
>
> (24.26)

But the perception lies in the way that the work of the Passion embraces all time – that, as in the fourth revelation, in Christ there is still 'bleding and praying for us' although this can now be accomplished in certain joy.

In the eleventh showing Julian is reminded of her sight of Mary suffering at the foot of the Cross in the eighth showing, and receives a 'gostly sigte' of her exalted above all creatures and the paradigm for all those who share in the Incarnation of Christ. She emphasises that she had longed for a bodily sight of Mary but learns from the understanding given to her in 'gostly sigte' that the most important thing is to desire Mary's truth, wisdom and charity as these were exemplified in the first showing, for they are the grounds for her exaltation and joy, and an epiphany of the life of faith of every Christian:

> And also to more vnderstondyng this swete word our lord God spekyth to al mankynde that shal be save as it were al to one person, as if he seyd: 'Wilt thou seen in hir how thou art lovid?'
>
> (25.27)

Mary's glory is followed in the twelfth showing by a revelation of Christ's glory. This 'passyth al that herte may willen and soule may desire', and may not be contained by language which constantly, in this chapter, gestures towards a totality of meaning beyond the partiality of its semantics and syntax, though these at least provide some partial means of recognition of the ineffable. The insistent repetition of 'I it am' with its implication of a being which transcends all others, variously qualified by verbs of longing ('I it am that thou longyst; I it am that thou desyrist; I it am that thou menyst') followed by the completion of 'I it am that is al', points towards Julian's experience of wholeness in her oneness with God. And it brings her close to the *Cloud*-author.

These twelve showings thus convey an awareness of the significance of the Incarnation and Passion of Christ; and unfold a process of suffering in time as a means to a joy and bliss beyond it which is continually reborn in the inner experience of man. It is the dynamic of this inner experience that the remaining showings reveal.

THE THIRTEENTH REVELATION: 'SYNNE IS BEHOVABIL' (CHAPTERS 27–40)

In the thirteenth showing Julian receives deeper understanding of 'time of passion' as being the only way to 'endles knowyng in God' through teaching about sin which she sees is all that stands between her and Christ's joy. The showing capitalises her experience of 'wele and wo' of the seventh showing. She wonders why sin is permitted since it alone stands between man and God; but receives a visionary assurance that it is actually appropriate, 'behovabil' and that 'al manner of thyng shal be wele' (27.28). The core of the showing common to both versions, concerns her realisation that all she has seen of the significance of Christ's Passion is also relevant to the pain of all those 'that shal be savid', and that the compassion that man has to his fellow-christians is 'Criste in him' (28.29–30). As she understands it, the love for which sin is the opportunity is vastly the more powerful of the two forces; this is the grounds for joy both in God and man which man can 'see' is his salvation even though he does not know exactly how all that is patently amiss will ultimately be righted. It is simply further grounds for playing the game of faith and so entering into a continuum of joy between the self and God which she expresses:

> in this will our lord we be occupyed, ioyeng in him for he onioyeth in us; and the more plentivously that we take of this with reverens and mekenes, the more thanke we deserven of hym and the more spede to ourselfe; and thus may we sey, enioyeng our part is our lord.
>
> (30.31)
>
> *onioyeth*: joys; *spede*: profit.

The syntax of the final clause makes it impossible to distinguish man's joy in the work of salvation from Christ's – an identification also present in the way her understanding of the thirst of Christ is implemented beyond that in the eighth showing (16–17). There she had seen it as a sign of failing creativity blasted by sin; now, in her expanded text, she sees this at the heart of a thirst which is also Christ's love-longing to make good such loss and have 'have us al togeder hole in him to his blis' (31.32). This longing will never be quenched until all men are one with God and it, in turn, quickens the human response – brings life from death:

> And of the vertue of this longyng in Criste we have to longen ageyn to him, withoute which no soule comyth to hevyn.
>
> (31.32)

Julian is coming to understand the 'time of passion' that leads to 'endles knowyng in God' as a period when the dynamic of love charged between God and man can act as a catalyst to transfigure the impediments of sin. Her vision gives her a double understanding of human cognition. It can both conceive a knowledge of this endless life out of time – Christ glorified – which naturally draws the will; and it can also recognise the disfigurement that follows from sin and obscures the glory of the body of Christ, still in time in so far as Christ's identity is inextricably involved with man's:

> For arnernst that Criste is our hede, he is glorifyed and onpassible, and anernst his body in which al his members be knitt, he is not yet ful gloryfyed ne al onpassible; for the same desire and threst that he had upon the cross . . . was in him fro withoute begynnyng, the same hath he yet, and shal into the tyme that the last soule that shalbe savid is cum up to his bliss; for as verily as there is a properte in God of ruth and pity, as veryly there is a property in God of threst and longyng. (31.32)
>
> *arnernst*: concerning; *onpassible*: beyond suffering; *threst*: thirst.

The basic substance of the showing for sin thus starts to subsume the visionary understanding achieved through the showings of Christ's Passion into an understanding of how man 'works' as a spiritual creature. It is with this 'working' that a great deal of the rest of the book is involved, and also the additions to this thirteenth showing in the long text. These additions are of two kinds. In the first she greatly elaborates her own difficulty in reconciling the assurance that 'al shal be wele' with what she understands of the Church's teaching on salvation about judgement for sin on those who do not die in the faith. Although she accepts that 'al that is besiden our salvation'(30.31) is hidden from her and she can only play the game of faith, she still worries that the Church's teaching on damnation is at odds with her assurance of ultimate 'wele'; and this is a matter which will recur. In the second kind of expansion of the thirteenth showing she makes the eighth showing, already echoed in the reference to the thirst of Christ in the short version, more central by widening the pains of Christ's flesh hung out like a cloth to dry to include the sufferings of all Christians. Moreover, the double view of pain and joy as Christ changed his 'chere' (c.21) in the earlier showing now includes the whole process of salvation in time. And now she starts to understand how this suffering of pain and death, the 'werks' of Christ's manhood, are involved with the process by which all things are made 'wele'.

Her earlier experiences begin to take on an exciting interior significance for her as she reinterprets God's care for creation revealed in the first showing, and the 'rightfulhede' of his works in the third, as 'al that is good our lord doith'. She completes this phrase by 'and that is evil our lord suffrrith' (35.36). This 'suffering' has an active quality by means of what she calls the 'werkyng of mercy and grace'. It is operative in the Passion and coterminous with sin. Julian says that through our experience of it in time we have a foretaste of the joy of salvation. But just how she understands that this mercy and grace 'work' within man is discussed later in the development of the fourteenth showing for prayer. The great bulk of the passages peculiar to the long text occur from now on; they have to do with the insight given her in subsequent meditations of the way in which the transfiguration of pain and evil by joy and love shown in the Passion of Christ is realised as an inward process activated by prayer.

THE FOURTEENTH REVELATION: 'PRAYOR ONYTH THE SOULE TO GOD' (CHAPTERS 41–50)

Julian develops the showing as reported in the short text, where she sees prayer as a willed longing for God; this must be sustained even in times when the only indication of God's presence is his absence, and it cannot be ultimately refused since this longing comes from God himself: 'I am ground of thy besekyng' (41.42). It is the means by which man becomes complete – one with God. In the long text Julian's understanding is developed by her use of the rhythmic and semantic potential of language which informs her account with a clarity of perception and a sense of joy. As with the *Cloud*-author prayer is born out of a God-given longing for God who himself longs to have us 'al togeder hole in him to his blis' (31.32) and through it man's prayer engages with the divine love which informs all creation. It is a process which can grow from a dry and barren seeking, to one which is experienced as joy: and then further to a prayer where the longing and trust necessarily implicated in a state of absence from full knowledge of God, is superseded by visionary understanding where 'we knowen the frute and the end of our prayors' (42.44) ('seking' becomes 'beholdyng', 10.12). Julian understands prayer to be not so much petition as a way of life. It involves a growth in consciousness of the realities of the game of faith – a kind of balancing between faith and understanding which creates the stability it desires.

> Than menyth he thus: that we sen that he doth it and we prayen therfor; for that on is not enow; for if we prayen and sen not that he doth it, it makyth us hevy and doutful, and that is not his worshippe. And if we sen that he doth, and we pray not, we do not our dette; and so may it not ben, that is to seyen, so is it not in his beholdyng; but to sen that he doth it and to pray forthwith, so is he worshippid and we sped.
>
> (42.44–5)

do not our dette: do not behave properly; *sped*: helped.

The rhythms of the prose here, as it moves through statement and explanatory conditional clauses to the confident unravelling of 'but to sen that he doth it and to pray forthwith, so is he worshippid and we sped', mirrors the progress towards the lucidity which it describes – a state of balance where self and God are reconciled. Julian sees prayer in relation to her understanding of the significance of Christ's thirst as a longing with which man engages:

> fayling of our bliss that we ben kyndly ordeynid to makyth us for to longen; trew vnderstondyng and love, with swete mynd in our savior, graciously makyth us for to trosten. And in these ii werkyngs our lord beholdith us continuly.[42]
>
> (42.45)

This sense of incompleteness which impels man to find wholeness, she calls 'ablyng of ourselfe to Iesus' (43.46), her understanding of prayer, however, is that even in this life it can allow man to experience oneness with God, which she expresses by recalling the terms of the tenth showing where the wounded Christ shows himself the way into God for man and by using language of the senses only to transcend them:

> And than shal we all come into our lord, ourselfe clerely knowand and God fulsomely havyng; and we endlesly ben al had in God, hym verily seand and fulsumly feland, hym gostly heryng, and hym delectably smellyng and hym swetely swelowyng; and than shal we sen God face to face.
>
> (43.46)

fulsomely: abundantly; *swelowyng*: swallowing.

In the short version the showing for prayer ends with a passage in which Julian asserts both God's constant love for man and also the feeling in man that God is wrathful with him because of his sins, a fear that prompts in him contrition and confession which are the means of renewing access to God. (There then immediately follows the fifteenth showing.) The longer version is greatly extended. Chapter forty-three is the last chapter to incorporate material from the short version but the fifteenth revelation is not reported until chapter sixty-four. In the sequence of intervening chapters, Julian conveys a remarkable growth in insight into God's unvarying love which seems at odds with her belief in the Church's teaching on judgement for sin. The double view of the Passion depending on both eternal and temporal perspectives, where compassion for suffering co-exists with joy in redemption, increasingly dominates Julian's understanding. Now she comes to see God's single and endless unchangeable 'rightfulhede' coexisting for the duration of time with man's doubleness: his capacity for union with God and his changeable propensity for sin which blocks him off from, and blinds him to, this ultimate reality. She builds on her understanding of the first showing of the Annunciation and Passion as signs relating to men's inner lives, valid for all time in delineating how the soul 'works'. God is endlessly truth and wisdom and love, and these elements are created in man's soul and naturally drawn back to their source: 'Treuth seith God, and wisedam beholdyth God, and of these ii comyth the thred: that is an holy marvelous delyte in God, which is love' (44.47). Her understanding of the significance of the showings of Mary at the Annunciation are subsumed in this recognition of a creative reciprocity between God and man. In her previous references to Mary in the first and eleventh showings (chapters four and twenty-five) she had stressed the virtues of her soul, 'wisedam' and 'trueth', as the efficacious powers which enabled the Incarnation of love then and for all time.

However, this understanding is held in tension with Julian's own experience that this continuum is often choked and man cut off from God, blind to the true sources of his creativity.[43] It is this block which is the sphere for the operation of mercy and grace demonstrated at a historical point in time in the Passion but active continually in man as the means by which he 'werkyth' God's will 'evermore' (44.47). Whereas God sees in his unerring 'rightfulhede', man sees and judges from the basis of his fallible nature which often clouds his perception. Then 'our good lord Iesus reformyth it be mercy and grace throw the vertue of his blissid passion, and so bringith into the rythfulhede' (45.47). But before Julian feels free to develop her delighted understanding of how this process 'works', she is impeded by her inability to grasp how the Church's teaching that sinners merit blame and anger fits in with this constant salving activity, because she can see no wrath in God at all. She says that the only answer she ever gets to this problem is the example of a lord and a servant which is described in chapter fifty-one.[44] In the expanded version of the showing for prayer Julian's account of her growth in perception on how man works at his channels of communication with God prepares the ground for the significance of this example which stands as a natural flowering of her transformed consciousness. She remains true to her double perception of the work of salvation, on the one hand assurance of security, on the other fear of judgement as taught by the Church, and relates them to her own inner drives ('manner of werkyngs', 47.50), elation and depression ('enioying' and 'morning', p.50), desire, dread and sure hope. All these relate intimately to her experience of longing for God and fear of loss and failure; but she comes to realise that the activity she called mercy which she had presumed related to God's forgiveness of our sins after his wrath (47.50), in reality relates to a process in time which constantly turns failure and falling to become the means of knowing the strength of love. It is the dynamic of grace that flows from God and transfigures man's experience. Her account is luminously informed by the way she has understood the showings of Christ's Passion:

> I cowth not aperceyven of the partye of mercy otherwise but as it were alone in love, that is to sey, as to my syte. Mercy is a swete gracious werkyng in love medilyd with plentevous pitte; for mercy werkith, us kepand, and mercy werkyth turnyng to us althyng to good. Mercy be love suffrith us to faylen be mesur; and in as mech as we faylen, in so mekyl we fallen, and in as mekyl as we fallen, so mekyl we dyen, for us behovyth nedes to deyen in as mech as we failen syght and felyng of God that is our lif. Our faylyng is dredful, ovr falling is shamefull and our deyng is sorowfull; but in al this the swete eye of pite and love cummyth never of us, ne the werkyng of mercy cessyth not. For I beheld the properte of mercy and I beheld the properte of grace, which have ii manner werkyng in one love; mercy is a pitifull propirte which

> longyth to the moderid in tendyr love, and grace is a worshipful propirte which longith to the ryal lordshipp in the same love; mercy werkyth: kepyng, suffring, quecknyng and helyng, and al is of tendernes of love; and grace werkyth: reysing, rewardyng and endlessly overpassyng that our lovyng and our travel deservyth, spredyng abrode and shewyng the hey, plentivous largess of Godds ryal lordship in his mervelous curtesye.
>
> (48.51)
>
> *moderid*: motherhood.

So mercy is concerned not with turning away the wrath of God but with making good the deficiencies in man. Yet she still considers that this insight into God's intervention in the perverse nature of man sits uneasily with her faith in the teachings of the Church. It is at this point that she relates the account of a lord and a servant. It stands like a poetic image concentrating meanings hitherto unfolded in her account and anticipating those to come.

'A MERVELOUS EXAMPLE OF A LORD AND A SERVANT' (CHAPTERS 51–63)

This example is different in kind from any of the sixteen named showings. They are either concerned directly with Christ's Passion and the work of transfiguration, or an apprehension of this as immanent, and are shown by heard speech, and visionary image, both of which are understood spiritually. The 'example' is also substantially longer than the account of any single showing in its extended development of the image of the lord and the servant. It combines the static representational qualities of an icon, and the fluidity of allegorical narrative, to focus an intuitive understanding of the redemptive work of love at the heart of the Incarnation, through which Christ and man are one in the game of faith.

Furthermore, Julian never uses the word 'showing' in an unambiguous or unqualified way about the example. It is not mentioned at all in the short version, and in the long, Julian speaks of it as given as an answer to her difficulties in accommodating the Church's teaching on God's wrath that she talks of only in that version.[45] All this might suggest the possibility that the example occurred in her meditations subsequent to the original showings which are incorporated into the long text. On the other hand, Julian tells us that the example is relevant to three aspects of her visionary experience between which she cannot distinguish: what she understood at the time, what she has understood since, and the significance of the whole book (pp.55–6):

> I have techyng wherby I owe to leyvyn and trostyn in our lord God, that of the same godenes that he shewed it, and for the same end, ryth so of the same goodnes and for the same end he shal declaryn it to us whan it is his wille. For xx yeres after the tyme of the shewing, save iii monethis, I had techyng inwardly, as I shal seyen: 'It longyth to the to taken hede to all the propertes and condition that weryn shewid in the example thow thou thynke that they ben mysty and indifferent to thy syte'.
>
> (51.56)

leyvyn: believe.

It therefore seems that she connects the example with the original experience but sees it not so much as a separate showing contributing a distinct element to a sequential cumulation of meaning, as pertinent to the meaning of the whole which still continues to unfold.[46]

The significance of the example grows in stages which Julian describes in her account of it. She first sees the figure of a lord who sits peacefully, and his servant standing before him ready to do his will; when sent, the latter runs eagerly to perform his service, but falls into a bog and is unable to rise unaided or to see his lord. This evokes not blame but pity from the lord who determines to reward him more generously than if the mishap had not occurred. At this point in the account Julian says the example vanished. And it is at this point that she explains that at the time when she received her 'example', she remained puzzled:

> . . . the mervelyng of the example cam never from me; for methowth it was goven me for an answere to my desir, and yet cowth I not taken therin ful vnderstondyng to myn ese at that tyme; for in the servant that was shewid for Adam, as I shal seyn, I saw many dyvers properties that myten be no manner wey ben aret to single Adam. And thus in that tyme I stode mekyl in onknowyng.
>
> (51.55)

aret: attributed.

But she adds that that her understanding increased during twenty years of meditation and she felt herself directed to pay close attention to details which she is about to elaborate. First, she sees further into the state of the fallen servant who is indeed Adam, and thus every man, whose sorrow arises from the fact that he cannot see his loving lord, nor how his lord sees him. These two aspects of his distress relate directly to Julian's own problem over God's attitude to sin, and she says that 'when these ii are wysely and treuly seyn, we shall gettyn rest and peas her in parte, and the fulhede of the bliss of hevyn . . .' (51.56). She understands that it is only the servant's blindness that makes his painful experience seem punishing; the lord longs to comfort and restore him. She then proceeds to elaborate: the lord is dressed in blue robes and sits in a brown wilderness, thus representing the steadfast presence of God in the heart of man. The servant is dressed in a short, sweaty kirtle suitable for the labour he has to perform, to be a gardener – a physical activity she describes in prose as vital in its discrimination as that she uses to delineate the stirrings of emotion and understanding at a spiritual level. The gardener has to:

> delvyn and dykyn, swinkin and swetyn, and turne the earth upsodowne, and sekyn the depnes, and wattir the plants in tyme. And in this he shuld continu his travel and make swete flods to rennen, and noble and plenteous fruits to springen . . .
>
> (51.58)

dykyn: dig; *swinkin and swetyn*: work and sweat.

He also has to recover a treasure which is simultaneously buried in the earth and grounded in the lord. A further dimension to the image is now clarified as Julian understands that the servant is not only Adam but Christ. Thus by the Incarnation, the work of gardening and recovering treasure becomes the work of both Christ and man in redemption: 'for Iesus is al that shal be savid and al that shal be savid is Iesus' (51.59).

By the end of her account the example seems to have developed in visual terms altogether beyond those vouchsafed at its first showing. Initially Julian saw the lord regarding the fallen servant with pity, and she understood inwardly that the falling and the woe of the servant shall be turned to bliss; then the example vanished (p.55). At the end, however, not only has she recognised the servant as Christ, but she 'sees' him transfigured in robes the brightness of which eclipse those of the lord who, himself, no longer sits in the wilderness but in his most noble seat which he made in heaven, and the servant is set by him in an equality of joy.

All this imagery (ghostly in bodily likeness) is integrated into the web of visionary experience by means of a mesh of conceptual and verbal echoes. The depiction of the servant's distress ensuing from the fact that he cannot 'see' that the lord regards him with love continues Julian's double view of pain and joy, secure 'rythfulhede' (45.47) and insecure 'blyndhede' (50.53). In the example, however, as she sees the servant identified with Christ, the implications of her personal showing of gladness and grief (c.15) are deepened as she sees how all these apparent opposites are not irreconcilable, but means to quicken faith to life. With memorable simplicity she retracts the whole pattern of sacred history,[47] of necessity revealed in a process, to a single point of understanding: that the reality manifested in the Incarnation is coexistent with time:

> Whan Adam fell, God Son fell; for the rythfull onyng which was made in hevyn, God Son myte not fro Adam, for by Adam I understond all man. Adam fell fro lif to deth into the slade of this wretchid world and after that into hell. Gods Son fell with Adam into the slade of the mayden wombe, which was the fairest dauter of Adam, and therfor to excuse Adam from blame in hevyn and erth; and mytyly he fetchid him out of hell.
>
> (pp.58–9)
>
> *slade*: valley, boggy place.

Julian perceives that man's predicament is inextricably involved in the meaning of God:

> for in al this our good lord shewid his owne Son and Adam but one man.
>
> (51.59)

St Paul's words in the Epistle to the Ephesians seem peculiarly relevant to her insight:

> Blessed be the God and Father of our Lord Jesus Christ, who hath blessed us with all spiritual blessings in heavenly places in Christ: As he chose us in him before the foundation of the world, that we should be holy and unspotted in his sight in charity.
>
> (1:3–4)

In the example she starts to 'see' how this works. She understands that the lord regards the fallen servant with love; and further, as the servant is identified with Christ, she perceives him released from the two fixed positions of the original example, either to the left of the lord or stuck in the bog, to change to his final state at God's right hand. The precise moment in the account of the example when this *stasis* breaks into fluidity, is when Christ has reached the lowest point of his fall into humanity, his physical death: then he first began 'to shewen his myte', he goes into hell and raises up the 'grit rote out of the depe depenes which rythfully was knit to hym in hey hevyn' (51.60). The showing crystallises the grounds for the saying in the thirteenth showing that 'sin is behovabil', so that in the chapters that follow the example she accepts falling and rising as part of one process of redemption and affirms that finally when all the mysteries in the process of salvation hidden in time are revealed:

> Than shall non of us be stirid to sey in ony wise 'Lord, if it had ben thus, than it had bene full wele,' but we shall seyn al without voice: 'Lord, blissid mote thou ben! For it is thus, it is wele'.[48]
>
> (85.101)
>
> *mote*: may.

It is perhaps not surprising that this shared activity between Christ and man should be conceived in terms of gardening. The figure of the gardener links with economy a trio of medieval iconographical motifs: the activities of fallen Adam/everyman as a labourer, Christ the true gardener cultivating the virtue of the Church[49] and God as the gardener planting Christ, the tree of love, in the heart of man.[50] The image of labour releasing a generous fecundity also concentrates elements of the whole revelation. In the fourth showing, Julian saw the excessive bleeding which threatened to soak the bed as the generous outpouring of love descending to hell (like Christ in chapter fifty-one) to 'braste her bands' (12.15). In that showing the blood reminded Julian of 'waters plentivous in erthe to our service and our bodily ease' (12.15). In the example they are identified. The labour to make 'swete flods to rennen, and noble and plenteous fruits to springen' is the work of mercy and grace, restoring and fulfilling, accomplished through passion, Christ's and man's, but not without joy because of the fruit of the labour, bringing to completion the work of redemption, which later Julian expresses in terms of Christ's 'us al werkeng into hym; in which werkyng he will we ben his helpers' (57.70).

The connection of the servant's digging to produce fruit with that digging for buried treasure looks back to Julian's account of how she reconciles her understanding in faith that 'althyng shal be wele' with the inability of her reason to see how this can be in the face of palpable evil. While recognising that such full knowledge is beyond human limitations, she has faith in a:

> dede the which the blisful Trinite shal don in the last day. . . . This is the grete dede ordeynyd of our lord God from without begynnyng, treasured and hid in his blissid breast, only knowen to hymself, be which dede he shal make al thyngs wele.
>
> (32.33)

It also anticipates future references to the final salvation of mankind: 'we shal be withoute end, . . . tresurid in God, and hidde' (53.64) 'for our soule is . . . groundid in God, and so endlesly tresorid (56.67) and at the last day we shall receive goods from God which are 'treasurid and hidde in hymselfe' (75.91). At the end of the example, when the Son is crowned before the Father, she picks up an image from the ninth revelation (c.22) that man is Christ's crown and joy, and the hidden treasure of redemption now becomes metaphorically 'a corone upon his hede of pretious richess' (51.60). And the description of the servant in the 'heyest noblyth of the Fadirs ioyes' (51.61) subsumes the image in the first revelation of the lord who honours his servant by his intimacy (c.7) and a reference in the sixth revelation where the honour shown to sinful creatures who come to heaven was compared to that shown to servants whom a great king publicly thanks. In that revelation too, she understood heaven to be like a feast prepared by a lord who reigns in his own house and extends its lavish hospitality to all his servants and friends. This is echoed and transformed in the last showing where the house is the kingdom of man's soul and the 'place that Iesus takith in our soule, he shal never removen it without end as to my syte' (67.82). The internalisation of the image starts to happen in chapter 51 where, by the end, the suffering servant who is both Christ and man sits 'in his cety in rest and peace' (p.61). The use of the word 'city'in deliberate contrast to the 'wildernes' of the world (pp.56, 58) enables the reader to move from the material form of the image with its implications of a carefully wrought community established on a foundation of religious authority to its abstract spiritual dimension as the City of God. Here man redeemed is one with the Trinity:

> Now sittith the Son, very God and man, in his cety in rest and peace, which his Fader hath adyte to him of his endles purpose; and the Fadir in the Son, and tho Holy Ghost in the Fadir and in the Son.
>
> (51.61)
>
> *adyte*: ordained.

Julian is expressing in her own way a perception, again formulated by St Paul in the Epistle to the Ephesians that in Christ we are 'predestinated according to the purpose of him who worketh all things according to the counsel of his will' (1:11). She will describe the process of how this transformation occurs in the soul of man in the following chapters.

The whole example thus enacts a process of transfiguration which is at the heart of Julian's showings. And her account of it seems to trigger a release of more abstract understanding of how this is enacted in the inner workings of the human psyche. It gives her anagogical terms to anchor her dual perspective on man, temporal and eternal:

> We have in us our lord Iesus uprysen, we have in us the wretchidnes of the mischefe of Adams fallyng, deyand;
>
> (52.61)

and she now develops this in relation to an analysis of human nature as two-fold in its composition. She sees an essential continuum between the nature of God and the nature of man's soul which she calls his substance. With characteristic use of ambiguity she achieves a startlingly simple statement about creaturely dependence on, and union with, the creator, 'and thus is man soule made of God' (53.64). It is in our substance that we have our 'lord Iesus uprysen' and sense this as an eternal reality.

> For he will we wetyn that our soule is a lif, which lif, of his goodnes and his grace, shall lestin in hevyn without end, him loveand, him thankand, him prayand.
>
> (53.64)
>
> *wetyn*: know; *lestin*: last.

Christ's soul is the fullest substance because it is one with and includes 'al the soules that shal be savid'.[51] But man is not just substance – an essential spiritual core, he also has sensuality derived from the 'slyppe of erth' [*slyppe*: wet clay] (53.64) from which his body is made, and it is in his sensuality that he both feels the 'wretchidnes' of Adam's falling and also shares in the Incarnation of Christ:

> for our substance is hole in ilke person of the Trinite, which is on God. And our sensualite is only in the second person, Crist Iesus, in whom is the Fader and the Holy Gost; and in him and be him we arn mytyly taken out of helle and out of the wretchidnes in erth, and worshipfully browte up into hevyn and blisfully onyd to our substance . . . .
>
> (58.71)

This is the work of redemption entered into by faith which is a creative power latent in the constitution of human nature. But it remains entropic unless activated when it closes the fissures of alienation in human experience. It emanates from man's substance (which is God) to illuminate the truth about his double nature:

> for it is not ell but a rythe vnderstondyng with trew beleve and sekir troste of our beyng that we arn in God, and God in us, which we se not.
>
> (54.65)
>
> *ell*: else; *rythe*: right.

It is the means by which God is seen, in a 'glass darkly' – to use a Pauline phrase, through lived experience of falling and rising. It is Julian's experience of faith as an active principle which 'werkith in us grete things' (54.65) that informs her understanding. For her, its dynamic reality is known in playing the game of redemption which itself acts out what God is. In chapter fifty-six Julian describes it as involving the energies of what she calls 'substantial kindhede' (God, the life of the soul), mercy and grace, which 'werkyng altogeder' (56.68) enable man's integrity. In chapter fifty-eight she expresses this in conventional Trinitarian terms, but they are illuminated by inner understanding of the reality which gives them relevance. Our substance, essential being, is in the Father towards whom we grow in the time of our sensuality through the principle of mercy in the Son by the dynamic of grace – the Holy Spirit which brings us to fulfilment. All is a unifying activity of God in Christ who is endlessly in our soul 'us al werkeng into hym' (57.70).

Julian certainly uses the language of dogma and philosophy but to gesture towards understanding of an achievement of human wholeness, which can only be known as it is lived. Her epistemology, consciously or unconsciously, is Augustinian in its confidence that God's word has been revealed in Christ; and this enables man to use language as signs pointing to a reality fully known only through experience – incarnation. Salvation is not a matter of intellectually formulated theology which can only point to a reality known through the dynamic of faith:

> for only be our reson we may not profitteyn, but if we have verily therwith mynd and love; ne only in our kindly ground that we have in God we may not be savid, but if we have connyng of the same ground, mercy and grace.
>
> (56.68)

She ascribes the achievement of this balance between reason and experience in the knowledge of God to the work of Christ described as a mother who expresses the creative care of God in a labour of mercy during the Incarnation which gives us birth to endless life (c.58–63). But the growth to spiritual maturity comes only by means of falling, and Julian now sees again that the insight given in her seventh showing for 'wele and wo' is central to the means by which the strength of love is realised and the principle by which 'synne is behovabil' in the plan of salvation:

> for it nedith us to fallen, and it nedith us to sen it; for if we felle nowte we should not knowen how febil and how wretchid we arn of ourselfe; ne also we shuld not fulsomely so knowen the mervelous love of our maker; . . . And by the assay of this failyng we shall have an hey, mervelous knoweing of love in God without end; for herd and mervelous is that love which may nowte, ne will not, be brokin for trespas.
>
> (61.75)

fulsomely: abundantly.

This is the love which 'suffrith us never to lose tyme' and which is the 'kindhede' [compassionate nature] of God (62.76). It expresses itself in the work of redeeming failure by transforming it to an opportunity to know its power until 'all his derworthy children be born and forth browte' (63.77).

> for wickednes hath ben suffrid to rysen contrarye to the goodnes, and the goodnes of mercy and grace contraried ageyn the wickidnes, and turnyd al to goodness and to worship to al these that shal be savid.
>
> (59.72)

contraried: opposed.

Julian sees all men like children in their frailty being brought to blissful wholeness by the very means of their alienation from God's will; through it they know in themselves the transcendent creative working of 'kindhede', 'mercy' and 'grace' for 'our fader wyllyth, our moder werkyth, our good lord the Holy Gost confirmith' (59.72).

THE FIFTEENTH REVELATION: 'CLENE DELIVERANCE' (CHAPTERS 64–5)

Julian's account of her growth in understanding of the psychological realities embodied in the 'example' (c.52–63) is preparing the ground for the full significance of the fifteenth revelation, which has to do with the delivery of the fully formed spiritual child. In the short version she is simply given to understand that man will finally be suddenly delivered 'oute of payne into blysse' (xx.71.1–2), but in the long version she records a visual showing which concentrates the thinking she has just developed on the motherhood of God active in maturing her children. She discerns a stinking, shapeless, decomposing, lump of a body lying on the ground out of which springs a little child 'full shapen and formid' (c.64. p.79) who glides up into heaven. This is not an expression of antagonism between the flesh and spirit, for Julian is at pains in her text to see man's sensuality as well as substance redeemed by the Incarnation; the decomposing body is the 'gret wretchidnes of our dedly flesh' (64.79). Julian understands by this showing that man is 'taken fro peyne' (64.79), the symptom of death-bringing sin – mortality; the child is the cleanness of purity in the soul (the substance of the self) now fully formed and refined through its experience of wretchedness and born into 'endless life' (63.77).

A passage right at the end of the short version (xxiii.75–6.27–24) which was dropped from the long version illuminates the import of this visual showing. Here Julian is concerned with man's involvement with, and deliverance from, sin, which she calls 'wretchedness'. She observes that 'wrecchydnesse is alle thynge that is nought goode' (23.76.2–3) and that:

> ȝif alle ware departed fra vs that is nouȝt goode, we schulde be goode. When wrechidnesse is departed fra vs, god and the saule is alle ane, and god and man alle ane.
>
> 23.76.8–10

ane: one.

Her familiar double perspective on earthly existence is informed by how 'synne is behouelye' (13.60.11):

> Whate is alle in erthe that twynnes vs? I answere and saye: In þat that it serues vs it is goode, and in that that it schalle perisch it [is] wricchednes, and in that that a man settys his herte þeropon othere wyse than thus it is synne. . . . And when he loves nouȝt synne, botte hates it and luffez god, alle is wele.
>
> 23.76.11–17

twynnes: separates.

In the long version this is worked out at length in the added passages on the interaction between 'kindhede' [compassionate nature], 'mercy' and 'grace' which enable man to be 'served' by earthly experience. In the short text she concludes that if a man really hates sin and loves God:

> þowȝ he syn sum tyme by frelty or vnkunnynge in his wille, he falles nought, for he wille myghtely ryse agayne & behalde god wham he loves in alle his wille.
>
> (23.76.18–21)

vnkunnynge: ignorance.

And the understanding conveyed in this coda is integrated in a more coherently structured theological exposition in the long version which is completed by the addition to the fifteenth showing.

Julian understands two opposite currents in time. One carries man from birth to death through experiences of falling, failure and compromise:

> For sikerly, when I was bore, anon
> Deeth drough the tappe of lyf and leet it gon.[52]

The other rips back through this tide of death, raising man from falling and continually reversing the fleeting order of time; it provides the element within which man matures towards his birth into endless life and pushes him back to be united with the source of his being.

This tide is Christ, its dynamic is exemplified in his incarnation, death and resurrection in which all men share. Small wonder that Julian adds in the long text's development of the fifteenth showing a passage of affirmation which has a lyrically triumphant tone celebrating her visionary gift of assurance of the reality of God which validates the game of faith:

> for it is his will that we wetyn that al the myte of our enemy is token into our frends hand; and therfore the soule that wott sekirly this, he shall not dredyn but him that he lovith.
>
> (65.80)

She is well aware of the difficulties for fallen natures in maintaining this essential lightness of spirit; but she sees it as an underlying condition men must constantly work to release.

> All our dreds he setteth among passions and bodely sekenes and imaginations, and therfore thow we be in so mech peyne, wo and disese that us thinkith we can thynke ryte nowte but that we arn in, or that we felyn, as sone as we may, pass we lytely over and sett it at nowte.
>
> (65.80)

lytely: lightly.

For as she remarks in the previous chapter – a passage also in the short version (xx.71.9–11) – 'the lyter we taken hem and the less price we setten at hem for love, the lesse peyne shall we have in the feling of hem . . .' (64.79).

THE SIXTEENTH REVELATION: AN 'ENDLES WORLD' AND A 'BLISSFULL KYNGDOM' (CHAPTERS 66–8)

This perception of the insecurity of fallen man obsessed with his own 'disese' in chapter sixty-five of the long version puts in a fuller context her account of her experience after the fifteenth revelation (common to both texts) when her sequence of showings is interrupted by a return of her sickness, during which she supposes her visionary experience mere hallucination, and is afterwards filled with grief at what she feels to be her treachery. She has a nightmare experience of the devil – the description of the lurid close up of his black-speckled fiery face with its grinning white teeth, and his paws shooting out to strangle her, an addition to the shorter account, smacking of a recall of a dramatic representation of the devil.[53] Its dream-like quality underlines her previous understanding that our fears spring from passions, sickness and imagination. It is the only experience in her account which she describes as taking place during sleep. But even so she tells us in the long version that while it was happening she trusted to be saved, and, in a phrase which 'fixes' the whole import of her showings, and movingly anticipates her growth in understanding, yet to be told, in the last showing, she says: 'and our curtes lord gave me grace to waken' (66.82). She does so aware of a time of suffering inextricably linked with the evil of the fiend, both of which are cleared away as she consciously exercises her faith (66.82).

She now receives her sixteenth showing. Just as her eyes were wakened from the nightmare fever of sickness to assurance and health, so now she says her 'gostly eye' is opened and she experiences her human reality, her 'substance', as a place of infinite space, 'an endles world' emanating from its still centre where Christ sits in rest and peace. In the long version she adds to this passage, with its self-evident links with the imagery of the 'example', the more conventional gloss that just as people expect the most noble building in a great kingdom will be the king's palace, so is this the dwelling-place of Christ to which man's soul is naturally drawn because it cannot rest in things beneath itself. There follows a passage in which the whole apparatus of language, limited as it is to the created world of sense-impression and natural reason, is pressured into signalling a reality in which the dimensions of time do not apply. The physical sense of rising above, yet entering into, the centre of the self suggests an expanded consciousness of an ineffable reality, as does the conflation of the physical apprehension of light with the more abstract experience of love:

> and thus I vnderstode sothly that our soule may never have rest in things that is beneathin itselfe. And whan it cometh aboven all creatures into the selfe, yet may it not abyden in the beholdyng of the selfe, but all the beholding is blisfully sett in God that is the makar wonand therinn; for in manys soule is his very wonyng; and the heyest lyte and the brightest shynyng of the cite is the glorious love of our lord.
>
> (67.83)
>
> *wonand*: dwelling.

Julian's last words relating to the immediate visionary experience concern its validity as grounds for a faith, in which she is assured 'thou shalt not ben overcome' (68.84). And she adds, with a sharp sense of the reality of her experience of our 'changeabil sensualyte'

(45.47) which renders her experience of faith not only charismatic but soberly convincing:

> He seid not 'Thou shalt not be tempestid, thou shalt not be travelled, thou shalt not be disesid', but he seid: 'thou shalt not be overcome'. (68.84)

Then the visions cease, and she concludes with quiet monosyllabic finality: 'and sone after al was close and I sow no more' (68.84).

THE REVELATIONS AND THE GAME OF FAITH (CHAPTERS 69–86)

However, there are eighteen chapters still to go in her long text. In both versions Julian recounts the return and final banishment of her sense of the devil – a kind of literal enactment of her final insight. The short version then ends with an account of the manner in which Julian's visions manifested themselves to her, and an analysis of the psychological forces which run counter to the dynamic of love – impatience and despair, which render man unable to play the game of faith and realise its wisdom in joy. The last chapter of the short version ends with the way that these negative energies can be accommodated in the game so as to avoid what in the long text she calls 'unskilfull hevyness' (73.89). In this term 'unskilfull' Julian's contemplative contemporaries would have recognised the lack of balance which is the opposite of *discretion*, sometimes glossed as 'skil' in Middle English.[54] It is for this reason that in the long text she glosses 'onpatience' as 'slaith' [sloth] (73.88), the failure to make the effort to bear difficulties with a good grace. Julian sees the game of faith as the arena where these tendencies towards impatience and despair can be harnessed to good effect. She sees them both as fuelled by three kinds of fears. The two anxieties which produce impatience are born of insecurity and failure to endure pain, both of which she points out are the means of enlightening the creature about the efficacy of God's love, for 'he is not abil for the time to perceivyn the soft comfort of the Holy Gost till he have vnderstonding of this drede of peyne, of bodily deth and of gostly enemyes' (74.89; ST.25.78.15–19). Moreover their stabs of panic stir and wake man from the 'sleepe of synne' (*ibid*). The third fear that leads to despair is born of radical doubt and negative thinking that undermines the skilful balance constantly practised in the game of faith. This can be re-routed by grace to a transcending certainty which enables further playing of the game, as she puts it in the long version: 'God will have it turnyd in us into love be the knowing of love' (74.89). She distinguishes a fourth fear unrelated to the others, the proper awe of the creature before God which is part of love, for 'I am sekir he that lovith, he dredith, thow that he fele it but a littil' (74.90; ST.25.78.31–2). Julian ends the short version with a statement which has the full force of the showings behind it, that man is enabled by revelation and self-knowledge to direct his potentially conflicting energies to the game of faith in which they will be reconciled and transcended as they are released into the mainstream of the dynamic of God's love. The trick is to know the remedy for the divisions in human nature. This is the ability to recognise its potentialities and 'refuse þe fals' (25.79.6–7). In the long version before chapters seventy-three and seventy-four, which incorporate this material from the short version, there is an expansion of the implications of the last showing and of Julian's final experience of release from the devil (c.70–2). In it she relates how the reality of the state of heightened visionary awareness may become the stuff of faith after the condition itself is gone. God tells her that the

> syte shuld passyn; which blissid shewing the feith kepith, with his owne good will and his grace; for he left with me neyther signe not token wherby I myte knowen it, but he left with me his owne blissid worde in true vnderstondyng . . . .
>
> (70.85)

The final additions in the expanded text have to do with translating perceptions born out of the visionary showings into the language of understanding. The impact of all the showings is now channelled into an explanation of the game of faith as the sole means of renewing in the time-sequence of experience the realities shown by means of vision:

> for aboven the feith is no goodnes kept in this life, as to my sight; and beneath the feith is no helpe of soule; but in the feith: there will the lord that we kepe us. For we have be his goodnes and his owne werkeing to kepe us in the feith and, be his suffrance, be gostly enmyte we are assayed in the feith and made myty; for of our feith had none enmyte it should deserve no mede, as to the vnderstondyng that I have in all our lords menyng.
>
> (70.85–6)

For Julian, to play the game of faith is to engage with the divine creative play of the Trinity. To describe the joy and wisdom generated by the playing, and the harder discipline entailed, she draws together elements in her separate showings – the double view she had of the Passion as cause for sorrow and also joy; the two contraries in human nature: outward 'grutching' of 'our dedely fleshede' (19.22) which she later calls sensuality, and the inward part 'which is an high, blissfull life which is al in pece and in love' (*ibid*); the 'ii manner of beholdyng' (46.49), assurance of ultimate security ('blisful salvation') and conviction of sin that deserves 'peyne and wreth' (*ibid*); the awareness of a duality in human nature she calls substance and sensuality. She develops the identification she has made between Christ and man – 'Iesus is al that shal be savid and all that shal be savid is Iesus' (51.59) – and therefore between man and the Trinity since 'where Iesus appereith the blissid Trinite is understond' (4.4).

All these inform her perception of three ways of being manifested in the three different 'cheres' [dispositions] she saw in Christ: 'passion' (suffering), 'pite'and bliss 'as it shal be without end' (71.86). Passion and pity belong peculiarly to the Incarnation, the game in time, but they are inextricably mingled with endless bliss – since this is what activates the game. In our suffering, Christ shows us his; in sinning we know his pity in the merciful action by which sin can become 'behovabil': but these are aspects of, and channels to, his endless bliss and we 'arn ordeynid therto in kinde, and gettyn therto be grace' (72.87). And this grace is what is experienced in the game of faith: 'the blisfull chere of our lord God werkith it in us be grace' (71.86). The reality manifest in the historical Incarnation and Passion continues in man's earthly life, for Julian Christ's story 'pennes and sets us down':[55] 'I it am that is heyest; I it am that is lowist, I it am that is all' (72.87–8). From it human knowledge derives its ultimate meaning which both informs and transcends partiality; and man enters into it through incarnation by faith:

> It longith to us to have iii manner of knowyngs: the first that we knowen our lord God; the ii that we knowen ourselfe, what we arn be him in kinde and grace; the iii that we knowen mekely what ourselfe is anempts our synne and febilness. And for these iii was all the shewing made, as to my vnderstondyng.
>
> (72.88)

anempts: as regards.

In the long text this is the context for the examination of the drives in man which work to block entrance into this meaning, and the means by which they are removed common to both texts. By the end of her account of the lord and the servant, Julian has abandoned as unprofitable her puzzlement about why things are as they are.[56] What she has grasped with visionary understanding is how the present system 'works', and her final chapters celebrate a joyful theological pragmatism. We must know our 'writchidnes' (that of 'Adam's fallyng', 52.61) as ground for further pain but as a means by which we are punished skilfully, for it is then purged by trust in God's love:

> this place is prison and this lif is penance, and in the remedy he will we enioyen. The remedy is that our lord is with us, kepand and ledand into the fulhede of ioye.
>
> (77.93–4)

The assurance of this acceptance of the two-edged sword of faith erupts into prose whose cumulative rhetorical structures embody the joy to which they refer:

> Fle we to our lord and we shall be comfortid; touch we him and we shall be made clene; cleve to him and we shall be sekir and safe fro al maner of peril: for our curtes lord will that we ben as homley with him as herte may thinke or soule may desiren. But beware that we taken not so reklesly this homleyhede that we levyn curtesy; for our lord himselfe is sovereyn homleyhede, and as homley as he is, as curtes he is; for he is very curtes. And the blissid creatures that shall ben in hevyn with him without end, he will have hem like to himselfe in all things. And to be like our lord perfectly, it is our very salvation and our full bliss.
>
> (77.94)

reklesly: carelessly; *homleyhede*: intimacy, familiarity.

Julian recapitulates our blindness and wretchedness, the recognition of which makes us long for God; so that in this desire we may be 'werked' into an ever present longing in God to draw us which lasts as long as time 'and thow some of us fele it seldam, it passeth never fro Criste till what tyme he hath browte us out of all our wo' (80.97). He stands security for the reality of this experience of desire for God.

Julian calls her visionary experience 'sheweings or revelation' but the sight received is that of understanding where 'bodily syte', 'word formyd in myn vnderstondyng' and 'gostly syte' cohere to enlighten and comfort what she calls our 'blindhede here' (85.101). It is an understanding which is the substance of faith. In the lyrical climax to her work she uses language with the concentrated creativity of poetry, and all her understanding about the self-generating wisdom of the game of faith is subsumed in the image of light, the agent of visibility and the beginning and end of the nature of our being, for 'in lyte is endless kyndhede' (83.100). In the game, the dynamic of God's being becomes known, so:

> our feith is a light, kindly command of our endles day, that is our fader, God; in which light our moder, Criste, and our good lord the Holy Gost ledith us in this passand life.
>
> (83.100)

This reference to the Trinity has behind it the weight of the analysis of the spiritual energies of 'kindhede', mercy and grace, which 'work' to comfort and raise man in his fallen blindness. The end of the showings of the Passion was Christ's sudden change of 'chere'. The thirteenth and fourteenth showings concerned ways in which man's painful sense of the absence of God is the very stuff by which his being may be known. The fifteenth revelation showed man's ultimate delivery from the wretchedness inherent in the 'tyme of his living'. The sixteenth revelation fixed all the previous showings as a revelation of how eternal being is incarnate in the depths of individual experience where the soul is an 'endles world' and a 'blisful kingdom', at the centre of which is Christ in glory known only by means of passion:

> He seid not 'Thou shalt not be tempestid, thou shalt not be travelled, thou shalt not be disesid', but he seid: 'thou shalt not be overcome'.
>
> (68.84)

Julian sees the whole process in terms of the energy of the Trinity, the great attractor which begins and ends in love. And she provides a further formulation of her understanding of the game played through incarnation as a gracious 'geft of werkyng' in which 'charite kepith us in feith and in hope, and hope ledith us in charite. And at the end al shall be charite' (84.101). It is love, God's and Julian's, which prompted the showings and they are all concerned with love: 'thus was I lerid that love was our lords mening' (86.102). In endless love men took their beginning: it is the underlying buoyancy which keeps them from falling out of being into the black hole of sin, and which penetrates their consciousness in time with glimpses of an endless joy. Finally she says, again with the verbal ambiguity by which she so characteristically links the beings of God and man, this love 'shall be seen in God without end' (86.102).

Despite the fact that Julian's text is anchored in the techniques of meditation on the Passion and the shape of the liturgy, it is misleading to separate her too widely from the *Cloud*-author. Both articulate a response to what they believe to be ultimate reality, known dynamically. The *Cloud*-author expresses this as a waking to the voice of God's calling and the gravitational pull 'drawing' of his love (*The Cloud*, 2.8.20–2), Julian as a God of love who will be 'sene' and 'sowte' despite all evidence to the contrary (10.11). Both find means to express what they understand as foretaste of man's 'heritage, þe kingdome of heuen' (*The Cloud*, 2.8.32–3). For the *Cloud*-author the way to this is through a prayerful attention which eschews images; for Julian it is miraculously given in a visionary experience in which familiar images are literally transfigured to point away from themselves to the 'Charite onmade' (84.101).[57] Her book works like an extended commentary on John 17:3

> Now this is eternal life: That they may know thee, the only true God, and Jesus Christ, whom thou hast sent.

For her Christ's Passion is at the heart of 'kepyng of time'; it is, mysteriously to the limited reason, but increasingly clearly to experience by faith, the only way to 'endles knowyng in God'.

NOTES

1. See Norwich Consistory Court, 194, Harsyk; Norwich Consistory Court, 86, Surflete; Thomas Edmund, Reg. Arundel, I.f.540d (Lambeth Palace Library).
2. See Colledge and Walsh (1978), p.43.
3. See Benedicta (1988) pp.11–31.
4. All references to the short version of Julian's text are to the edition by Beer (1978) and the numbers refer to chapter, page and line.

5. See above p.35.

6. All references to the long text (see further below pp.217–19) are to the edition by Glasscoe (1976). The numbers refer to chapter and page.

7. See above p.30.

8. See Reynolds (1956, xviii).

9. See Watson (1993).

10. For an account of the manuscript see Beer (1978, 10–12).

11. Cf. chapters 5 and 26 of the long version.

12. See chapter 8. p.9 (cf. short text chapter 7.49.1–2) and the beginning of chapter 9. p.10.

13. See Windeatt (1977); for; further analysis of the relationship between the formulation of the short and long texts in relation to their dating see Watson (1993).

14. See Colledge and Walsh (1978, p.44f.).

15. Cf. Pelphrey (1982, p.56);for an enlightening analysis of the whole question of Julian's possible indebtedness to specific sources see his chapter 2.

16. For an opposite view see Colledge and Walsh (1978, p.47).

17. See Colledge and Walsh (1978, p.26 and Appendix pp.734–48).

18. See further Glasscoe (1989); Gillespie and Ross (1992).

19. See above note 6.

20. See further below pp.246f.

21. See chapter 11, p.13. Julian explores the implications of this 'blindhede' more fully in chapter 51.Cf. also chapter 73.

22. See above p.8.

23. See above pp.30–1.

24. See above p.216.

25. Chapter 66, p.81.

26. See above p.31.

27. See above pp.31, 92–3. For a fuller analysis of the relationship between Julian's revelations and the *Prymer* see Glasscoe (1990).

28. See Augustine, *De Genesi ad Litteram*, Book XII, PL 34, 458f.

29. For discussions of Julian's use of this terminology which vary from maintaining

that she applies it with consistency to a recognition of the indivisible complexity of the way in which Julian receives understanding see Molinari (1958); Colledge and Walsh (1978, pp.71f. and notes to text); Ellis (1980); Glasscoe (1983, 156–7); Gillespie (1987, pp.132f.); Gillespie and Ross (1992); Watson (1992, pp.85–6).

30. See annotations to chapter one of the long text in Colledge and Walsh (1978, pp.281–4).

31. See above note 27.

32. Cf. Leech (1988); Gillespie (1992, p.67); Watson (1992, pp.88–9).

33. See the second revelation.

34. See Merton (1969, pp.241f.).

35. See chapters 27–40; see below pp.239–42.

36. Cf. Romans 8:35, Matthew 14:30 (cf. also 8:25).

37. I.e. the sight of the suffering Christ crowned with thorns giving rise to the rush of joy, awareness of the greatness of Mary implicit in her simplicity at the Annunciation and of the existential miracle of divine creation. See above pp.224–7.

38. '. . . for I saw in Criste a doble threst: one bodely, another gostly the which I shall speke of in the xxxi chapter' (17.19. cf. short text:10.54.4).

39. Cf. the second revelation c.10. It should perhaps be noted that P. and S1 differ in the way that they divide up the text between chapters 20 and 21. P starts chapter 21 'sodenly I beholdyng in the same crosse . . .'. There is also a minor confusion as to where the ninth revelation starts. P announces it twice, once erroneously at chapter 17 and once at chapter 22 where S1 also places it. This is obviously where it is meant to be since it agrees with the way that the scribe indicates the major divisions in the text of the short version (see B.L. Additional manuscript 37790 104v). Colledge and Walsh (1978) introduce a new complexity by intervening editorially in the text: they change the start of chapter 21 as it exists in P to the point which in S1 reads 'And I loked after the departing with al my myght . . .' and they insist that this is where the ninth revelation begins. For further discussion of this matter see Glasscoe 'On the Eighth Revelation of Julian of Norwich' (forthcoming).

40. See Colledge and Walsh (1978, p.389, note 6).

41. See for example the little Franciscan lyric (Gray, 1992, 26a) quoted above p.33; see also Gray, (1992, 26b). In depictions of the last judgement Christ is seen displaying his wounds to indicate the means by which man is reconciled to God. See also Woolf (1968, 183f. and plate 1).

42. For further comment on this passage see Glasscoe (1989, p.112).

43. Cf. Rolle's *Meditations on the Passion*; Horstman (1895, I, p.87); see above p.100.

44. Cf. above p.218.

45. 'I cryed inwardly with al my myte, sekyng into God for helpe . . . and than our curtes lord answerd in shewing full mystily a wonderful example of a lord that hath a servant . . .'(c.50; c.51. p.54).

46. Julian thus seems to support both the view that this example is an original showing suppressed in the shorter version (Colledge and Walsh, 1978,pp.24–5) and the view that it witnesses to an interplay between creative imagination and growth in understanding through meditation on the meaning of the Incarnation (Schmidt, 1980, pp.31–3).

47. See above p.9.

48. Cf. Watson (1992, p.99).

49. See Odo of Cluny *Sermo II In Veneratione Sanctae Mariae Magdalanae, PL*133,720; Gueririci, *Sermo Cantici Canticorum VIII*, 13, PL 185,212.

50. See *The Book of Vices and Virtues*, ed. Nelson Francis (1942, p.96).

51. Cf. 'And be the endles assent of the full accord of al the Trinite, the mid person would be ground and hede of this fair kinde out of whom we be al cum, in whom we be all inclosid, into whome we shall all wyndyn' [*kinde*: mankind; *wyndyn*: go] (53.64).

52. Chaucer, ed. Robinson (1957, 'The Reeve's Tale', 3892–3).

53. The devil might have appeared thus in the mystery cycles.

54. See *Vices and Virtues*, ed. Holthausen (1888, p.149, 8 and 22).

55. George Herbert, 'The Bunch of Grapes'.

56. Cf. also Watson (1992, p.99).

57. For related studies see Gillespie (1987) and Gillespie and Ross (1992).

Chapter 6

Margery Kempe: The Form of her Living

The nature of Margery Kempe's religious experience gave rise to controversy during her lifetime and continues to provoke modern readers. The source of the difficulty appears to be in the style of the woman herself, in the way she perceived, reacted to and to some extent created the events of her life and presented these in the two books of narrative known as *The Book of Margery Kempe*. Although she sees herself as receiving gifts of contemplation[1] her experience of this interrelates with what, in the understanding of the writers so far considered, would be called active life. She certainly shares with them a mystical sense of the reality of the redeeming love of God at work in human experience but her writings are in a different category to these others.[2] Their work tells us little or nothing of the external circumstances of their lives, but a great deal about a pattern of meaning which they perceive as fundamental to existence. Even Rolle presents details of his life only in so far as he judges them to have facilitated or hindered his realisation of that meaning in inner life. Although there is a sense in which Margery could be said to do the same her *Book* provides a very different literary experience.

Her understanding of inward spiritual realities is inextricably bound up with the distinctive forms of the active life which she chose to pursue. She does not slot easily into any of the recognised ways of living evolved to satisfy an inner need to live out a religious faith during the medieval period. Her position as a married woman who won the consent of her husband that they should live a life of mutual chastity opened up the possibility of an anchoritic life of prayer,[3] but she obviously, temperamentally, needed more active life to substantiate her inner experiences of God. The ethos of lay piety in England of which the Lollard movement was symptomatic, and the context of the *mulieres sanctae* in Europe from the twelfth to the fifteenth centuries, do illuminate Margery's *Book*, but they also highlight its unique quality. In it we confront her perception of her experiences as patterns of truth. Physical and meditative realities, biographical and Scriptural narrative, coexist together and overlap to illuminate her sense of the world charged with the immanence of the Word.

It is no accident that until relatively recently Margery's writing was known only through short extracts selected and printed by Wynkyn de Worde in 1501 with the *incipit*:

> Here begynneth a shorte treatyse of contemplacyon taught by our lorde Jhesu cryste/or taken out of the boke of Margerie kempe of lynn.

The extracts, abstracted from material less tractable to convenient religious *mores*, are cleverly arranged to highlight the meditative passages in Margery's account and suggest a book more akin to the spiritual writings of continental pious women like Catherine of Siena.[4] Hence Henry Pepwell described Margery as an *ancresse* when he reissued the selection in 1521 in a quarto volume of mystical writings. While de Worde's editing removed those aspects of her experience which have caused critical disagreement both in her own time and since the recovery of her complete account, the fact that it was carried out at all signifies a contemporary validation of the spirituality of the book in a period when devout works in English were highly valued.[5] Margery's full text came to light in 1934 in the possession of a north-country Catholic family, the Butler-Bowdens, but long before it passed into their hands it was evidently in the possession of the Carthusians of Mount Grace Priory.[6] That Margery's complete book seems to have occupied the attention of such austere religious may be a fact to be stressed when considering the variety of critical responses it has elicited since its reappearance in the 1930s, many of which are unfavourable and patronising.[7]

The book begins not with her childhood but with her marriage *circa* 1393 when she was about twenty. This is because it was her married life which precipitated the experience that resulted in an inner compulsion to lead a life totally dedicated to religion and incompatible with her role as a wife.[8] Margery was clearly a woman of strong will and high spirits who had a tender conscience and was highly impressionable to religious teaching. She started her first child shortly after her marriage and had a difficult pregnancy. In the pain and trauma of childbirth she thought she was going to die and her distress was compounded by her obsession with the fact that she had been involved in a sin which she had never been able to bring herself to confess. She makes it clear that she had faced up to it herself and done penance (1.7.5–8) but she had a neurotic fear that she would be damned because she had not formally confessed and been shriven.[9] In the crisis of childbirth she sent for her confessor, but there was a failure of communication between them. He does not appear to have been a good listener and, because he cut in with reproof before she had really made a clean breast of what she wanted to say, she failed even then to confess to her satisfaction and had a complete breakdown. For eight weeks she felt herself to be tormented by devils, suffered from suicidal depression and loss of faith, mutilated herself and was forcibly restrained and tied up in her room. A visionary experience delivered her from this wretchedness. From the black impotence of feeling herself cut off from creative healing – 'sche knew no vertu ne goodnesse' (1.7.35-6) – she recognised the beauty of Christ and the security at the heart of the Incarnation, recovered her stability and balance, and was restored to the control of her household. The experience is described in very literal terms but it carries a feeling of calm, radiance and healing. Christ healed her with a look and was absorbed into light as she watched. He appeared to her

> in lyknesse of a man, most semly, most bewtyuows, & most amyable þat euyr mygth be seen wyth mannys eye, clad in a mantyl of purpyl sylke, syttyng up-on hir beddys syde, lokyng vp-on hir wyth so blyssyd a chere þat sche was strengthyd in alle hir spyritys, seyd to hir þes wordys: 'Dowtyr, why hast þow forsakyn me, and I forsoke neuyr þe?' And a-noon, as he had seyd þes wordys, sche saw veryly how þe eyr openyd as brygth as ony levyn, & he stey up in-to þe eyr, not rygth hastyli & qwykly, but fayr & esly þat sche mygth wel beholdyn hym in þe eyr tyl it was closyd a-geyn.
>
> (1.8.15–25).
>
> *chere:* expression; *levyn:* lightning; *stey*: ascended.

From this time she dates her feeling of being specially obliged to serve God (2.9.8–9) although she disarmingly confesses that at first she found it difficult to relinquish her sense of social status as the daughter of John Brunham, a man of consequence in King's Lynn who was not only Mayor but also a Member of Parliament.[10] Indeed, she threw her sense of superiority in her husband's face: she projected it in her style of dress – her clothes worn slashed to reveal layers of colour so that she would attract attention and 'þe mor ben worshepd' (2.9.15–18) – and flaunted her financial independence in her ventures into the brewing and milling trade. These all failed: the ale went flat and the horses refused to work the treadmill, so that those who were exasperated by her self-importance put it about that she was cursed and no man or beast would work for her. These biographical details, however beguiling in themselves, are recounted for a larger purpose, for she tells us that only then did she see the hand of God, not cursing her, but impelling her to recognise her own vanity and pride.

At this time an ineffable auditory experience filled her with an unshakeable certainty of spiritual joy in heaven and of her own religious calling. Unlike Rolle's mystical perception of the reality of God which he describes as transposing speech to song, Margery's account of her experience has an unambiguously literal quality which is characteristic. While she was in bed with her husband, she heard a melody so ravishing that she thought she must be in Paradise and, leaping out of bed, cried 'Alas, þat euyr I dede synne, it is ful mery in Hevyn' (3.11.15–16). The experience affected her reactions to earthly merry-making and music – whether because of the gap between this and her spiritual experience, or because she perceived it as only a faint echo of this heavenly joy is not clear. Perhaps both of these realisations were operative as catalysts for her tears of longing for heavenly joy about which she could not stop herself from talking so volubly that, to those who knew her only as the indefatigable social climber, she lacked all credibility. They remarked with some acerbity 'why speke ȝe so of þe myrth þat is in Heuyn; ȝe know it not & ȝe haue not be þer ne mor þan we' (3.11.30–2). The experience was a turning point. From then on she found the idea of sex with her husband revolting because she was so consumed with a desire for God (3.11–12.34–6). It was at this time that the characteristics of Margery's piety which were to persist and develop were firmly established: her tears, irrepressible talk of God and desire for chastity. Some years later she and her husband agreed to discontinue sexual relations and Margery started a life of pilgrimage and also of persecution which arose partly from her own manner. She so wearied others that they refused to eat with her unless she promised not to speak of the Gospel (21.65.32–7); her crying became so convulsive that she was thought to be possessed (33.83.18), epileptic (44.105.18–21), or possibly a mere charlatan (c.78.185.28–9), and so disturbing that some preachers would not tolerate her in church (c.61).

There is always a physicality about her expression of religious experience. Her understanding of the spiritual dimension of the Incarnation which came in her experience of marriage to God the Father was followed by a physical penumbra of comforting sensations and sounds and a curious sight of 'many whyte thyngys flying al a-bowte hir on euery syde as thykke in a maner as motys in the sunne' (35.88.6–9). Her perception of the closeness between Christ and herself is expressed in rather naive sexual terms:

> Dowtyr, thow desyrest gretly to se me, & þu mayst boldly, whan þu art in þi bed, take me to þe as for þi weddyd husbond.
>
> (36.90.18–20)

When she talks of the Trinity she thinks of the members each seated on distinct coloured cushions: God the Father on gold, the Son on red velvet, the Holy Ghost on white silk (86.210–11.32–10). Nevertheless the literal terms can signal a spiritual experience. Her understanding of the tenderness of physical love was a medium through which she could express her sense of fulfilment in the love of Christ. The colours of the cushions on which the Trinity sat are symbolic: the gold of God's sovereign power, the red of Christ's blood shed in love, the white for purity and holiness. Moreover this literal level of the symbol is yoked, comically if the text is read superficially, to the spiritual context in which it has meaning: the Trinity is seated in Margery's soul and it is to the soul of man as theatre for the enactment of an inner realisation of essential unity with God that all the mystics testify. In words she attributes to Christ Margery spells out her theological and experiential understanding of the unchangeable unity of the divine nature whose operations of creative love are extended in time in incarnation:

> And also þu thynkyst sumtyme, dowtyr, þat þe Fadyr is al myghty
> & al witty & al grace & goodnes, & þu thynkyst þe same of þe
> Sone þat he is al myghty & al witty and al grace & goodnes. And
> þu thynkyst þat þe Holy Gost hath þe same propirteys euyn wyth
> þe Fadyr & þe Sone, procedyng of hem bothyn. Also þu thynkyst þat

> eche of þe iij personys in Trinite hath þat oþer hath in her Godhed, & so hath þu beleuyst verily, dowtyr in thy sowle þat þer be iij dyuers personys & oo God in substawnce, & þat eche knowyth þat oþer knowyth, & ech may þat oþer may, & eche wil þat oþer wil.
>
> (86.211.14–24)

She lacks the subtle abstract vocabulary which expresses both an inner approach to the mystery of God and cognition of the nature of this experience which the *Cloud*-author, Hilton and Julian all convey in different ways; but it is an indiscreet and biased judgement to suggest that Margery lacks spiritual discernment and muddles spiritual and physical realities.[11]

It is easy to point to aspects of her style that give rise to such judgement. Although Margery refers to herself as 'þis creatur' and talks of herself in the third person, the narrative has an air of self-absorption and self-justification, exacerbated by the fact that so many of the situations she describes involve persecution or disbelief by others, and her subsequent vindication. So she reports that in spite of the annoyance her ostentatious piety afforded to her travelling companions on pilgrimage:

> not-wythstondyng al her malyce, sche was had in mor worshep þan þei wher-þat euyr þei comyn.[12]
>
> (26.62.21–2)

Her conviction of God's loving purposes for her is also sometimes expressed rather oddly. She was told that she could choose whom she wished to have in heaven with her (8.20.20–1). She conceives salvation in economic terms telling God that she wished him to credit the goodness he had released in her to the salvation of other souls and being assured that she will have a double reward in heaven for her charity (8.20–1.31–7). Even while acknowledging that all her visionary understanding is a gift of God, she believed that it was to count as if it were her own merit to earn her reward in heaven (86.209–10.35–4).[13]

Careful reading, however, will often show how easy it is to receive false impressions of superficiality from the verbal register with which she is equipped to express her spiritual intuition. In chapter eighty-six she follows up the statement with a rephrasing which indicates that she understood that what was at stake was the crucial interaction between the dynamic of God's love and the assent of her own will. Like Mary she had allowed God to work in her and to reveal Christ, she hears words from 'owre Lord':

> But hyly I thanke þe, dowtyr, þat þu hast suffyrd me to werkyn my wil in þe & þat þu woldist latyn me be so homly wyth þe.
>
> (86.210.2–5)

Another time she comments that her gifts are to point to the goodness of God not 'commendacyon of þe creatur' (23.54.31). She also acknowledges her own difficulty in discriminating between spiritual and physical concepts – a commonplace of visionary literature but expressed by Margery with a pointed and disarming directness together with her recognition of a potential for self-deception in her own inner feelings:

> For sumtyme þat sche vndirstod bodily it was to ben vndirstondyn gostly, & þe drede þat sche had of hir felyngys was þe grettest scorge þat sche had in erde & specialy whan sche had hir fyrst felyngys, & þat drede made hir ful meke for sche had no joye in þe felyng tyle sche knew be experiens wheþyr it was trewe er not. But euyr blissyd mote God ben, for he mad hir al-wey mor myty & mor strong in hys loue & in hys drede & ȝaf hir encres of vertu wyth perseuerawns.
>
> (89.220.9–18)

scorge: scourge.

In view of the fact that she has always been the subject of uneasy approval or downright disparagement by those who find her piety qualified by a hysterical self-absorption, we do well to remember not only her own self-criticism but also the fact that highly intelligent religious of her own day, like Julian of Norwich and Thomas Arundel, Archbishop of Canterbury, apparently perceived the truth of her witness.[14]

Perhaps the most helpful perspective from which to view Margery's spirituality is that provided by modern medicine. Her trouble at the birth of her first child has now been recognised as postpartum depressive psychosis with features of agitation brought on by guilt; her convulsive weeping as an epileptiform component; her flying white specks which she understood as tokens of angels, as the *scomata* that accompany migraine; her indifference to the effects of her eccentric behaviour as hysteria.[15] However, whereas hysterical behaviour often results from repression of consciousness of guilt, with Margery such behaviour was therapeutic, relieving and healing the black depression and self-destructive behaviour that resulted from a sense of failure and sin. Margery's temperament made her sensitive to both the ugliness and shame of sin and the beauty of the love of God[16] and provided the theatre within which this tension was resolved and healed. Far from being an embarrassing adjunct to an otherwise acceptably orthodox manifestation of religious devotion, her so-called hysteria is the very centre of the healing processes of the Incarnation in time. Her account (albeit unconsciously) challenges the tendency to distrust and patronise eccentric behaviour and sensibilities which disturb comforting norms, rather than to seek to understand and share the significant humanity that they manifest.

The fact that she was a lay woman and a wife in a well-defined social context who was so consumed with a desire for God that she pursued alternative life-styles which she thought would bring her closer to God, and was also finally persuaded to dictate her meditations and experiences in order to manifest God's goodness to a wider audience, has attracted the attention of critics interested in assessing her in the terms of particular analyses of cultural history. Thus she has been seen as witness to the 'special oppression of women in early capitalist society':[17] or as one who internalised the values of bourgeois society, investing in her own salvation and thus asserting her power to transcend her marginal household role and social roles and integrate them into a new power-base in which the mould of female subjection and victimisation is vindicated by the Passion of Christ.[18]

Such views, interesting in their own terms, have designs on Margery's account. Using it to illuminate a particular approach to, and view of, cultural development, they explain, and thus to some extent patronise, Margery in terms, however valid, that she would not have recognised. In so doing they miss the centre of joy in her book and fail to illuminate its avowed purpose. To paraphrase Eliot, Margery had the experience and she did not think she had missed the meaning. She states that she wrote down 'hyr felyngys & reuelacyons & þe forme of her leuyng þat hys [God's] goodnesse myth be knowyn to alle þe world' (Proem, 3–4.32–1). In significant contrast to Rolle's exploration of the 'form' of living as a shaping dynamic, Margery's use of the words 'forme of her leuyng' designates the very particular visible and concrete details of her life and behaviour which for her signalled an inward reality.[19] The phrase encapsulates the essence of that embodied and idiosyncratic spirituality which has caused such difficulty for her readers.

OUTWARD AND VISIBLE SIGNS

Visible icons and sensibly perceived signs were important to Margery. Participation in church rituals activated her vibrant sense of the redemptive reality of the Incarnation. In the Palm Sunday ritual enactment of Christ's entry into Jerusalem, she joined the procession which met the priests carrying the sacrament across the churchyard in a shrine which they then raised in the church porch for all to enter beneath and reverence. Her inward awareness of the significance of the event was so sharp that she was overcome by tears. Then, as the priest knocked on the door with the cross before entering, she felt caught up in the whole process of redemption signified in the iconography of the Harrowing of Hell where Christ effortlessly enters its gates to redeem lost souls.[20] When finally the whole procession knelt before the large cross in front of the sanctuary which had been veiled during Lent, but was now revealed again to the people by the priest, the ritual released in her an urgent sense of longing to transcend earthly knowledge and see God face to face.[21] This resolved itself into tears during the celebration of the sacrament, the bridge over the gap between earth and heaven.

Similarly her part in the Candlemas ceremony of presenting candles to the priest celebrating Mass modulated for her into the offering of Christ by Mary in the temple. She felt so moved at participating in the continuing process of dedicating love to God made possible by the Incarnation that she could scarcely walk steadily as she approached the priest.[22] Her reaction is unsurprising in the context of the Candlemas sermon in which John Mirk reminds his audience that the lighted wax candle is an incarnational image uniting man and God. It betokens the love of God lit in human form in Christ, his mother and 'also yche good man and woman þat doþe good dedes wyth good entent, and yn full loue and charite to God and his euen-cristen' [fellow-christian]. The strongly literal account of holiness so characteristic of Margery's own piety also appears in Mirk's exemplar in the same sermon.

One tells of a woman whose only good deed – to light a candle for the Virgin – saved her from death and hell; another concerns a woman who, having given her clothes away for charity felt unable to attend a public Candlemas ceremony. Her piety was rewarded with a visionary dream of the service in which the Virgin herself gave her a candle half of which remained in her hand when she awoke.[23]

Weddings also fired Margery's sense of the reality of the sacramental theology they embodied. She 'had in meditacyon':

> þe gostly joynyng of mannys sowle to Ihesu Crist, preying to owr Lord þat hir lofe & hir affeccyon myth ben joynyd to hym only wyth-owtyn ende.
>
> (82.199.1–4)

This is perhaps not surprising in view of her sense of intimacy with Christ in bed expressed in terms of a marriage relationship (36.90.10f.) and it is clear that in these moments she felt herself illuminated by the reality of God's truth:

> for sche had hem not of hir owyn stody ne of hir owyn witte, but of hys ȝyfte whos wisdom is incomprehensibyl to alle creaturys saf only to hem þat he chesith & illuminyth mor er lesse as he wil hys owyn selfe, for hys wil may not be constreyned, it is in hys owyn fre disposicyon.
>
> (82.199.11–15)

Her tears were another tangible sign of grace for her. They were the involuntary physical response to an inward sense of the reality of God manifesting an inextricable love and penitence, and representing, for her, a source of fertility in her contemplative life:

> But hir thowt it was no sauowr ne swetnesse but whan sche myth wepyn, for þan sche thowt þat sche cowde preyin.
>
> (82.199. 33–5)

This echoes an insight which informs the moving medieval lyric based on a sinner's vision of the *Pieta* in which Mary weeps and addresses the sinner 'who cannot wepe, come lerne at me':

I said I cowd not wepe, I was so harde hartid.
Shee answerd me shortly with wordys that smarted:
'Lo, nature shall move the; thou must be converted;
Thyne owne Fader thys nyght is deed' – lo, thus she thwarted –
'So my soon is bobbid,
And of his lif robbid.'
Forsooth than I sobbid,
Veryfyng the wordes she seid to me:
'Who cannot wepe may lern at me'.[24]

thwarted: replied; *bobbid*: buffeted.

Margery's tears focus all the difficulties her piety presents. She describes how, when she visited Mount Calvary her involuntary tears at the remembrance of Christ's Passion developed into the especially disturbing paroxysms of grief with which she was visited for many years following, and which frequently prompted suspicious antagonism in others (28.68.20f.). But however extraordinarily violent and disruptive her tears were, they were also a long recognised sign of grace[25] though they were given different emphasis by different writers. Hilton, for instance, perhaps in a very English way, considered that for those advanced in the contemplative experience of God (reformed in feeling) outward tears give way to an inward peace and security which does not manifest itself in 'bodily feruours',[26] yet his contemporary and Margery's predecessor, Catherine of Siena, perceived involuntary weeping to belong to all stages of spiritual development; such tears spring from fear of the consequences of sin, express compassion for the sufferings of Christ and one's neighbour, and, for those perfect souls peacefully at one with God in what she calls his 'pesable see', they express and nourish their love.[27] Certainly tears as the expression of grace were the subject of the Common Memorial prayers for tears of contrition in the Sarum Missal, where the collect with lucid economy combines an allegorical understanding of Biblical history with a sense of its anagogical significance:

> Almighty and merciful God, Who to quench the thirst of Thy people, broughtest a spring of living water out of the stony rock; draw from our hard hearts tears of contrition, that we may bewail our sins, and through Thy mercy obtain pardon for them.[28]

For Margery they were a sign that the Incarnation is not simply a historical event but an ever-present reality. She explains that, for her, all human suffering became an icon of Christ's Passion and that she never knew where or when this strong sense of the enormity of such experience would overcome her. It could be

> sumtyme in þe cherch, sumtyme in þe strete, sumtym in þe chawmbre sumtyme in þe felde.
>
> (28.69.15–16)

It is this very strong embodied sense of spirituality that distinguishes Margery's *Book* from the writings of her predecessors. Whereas they find literary forms to wrestle with a mystery they know they cannot express, Margery can only signal her sense of a God she knows to be transcendent by investing familiar iconographical territory with personal significance. The contrast between her response to Christ's Ascension and that of Hilton demonstrates this very clearly. It figures for him the transcending of active meditation by contemplative knowledge in a pattern of inner spiritual growth;[29] but for Margery it was a difficult event on which to meditate. She saw Christ ascend up into heaven (73.174.30f.) but she could not bear either to contemplate loss of his presence or to wait to be united with him in heaven:

> þerfor sche desiryd to a gan wyth hym, for al her joy & al hir blysse was in hym and sche knew wel þat sche xulde neuyr han joy ne blys tyl sche come to hym.
>
> (73.175.1–4)

gan: go; *xulde*: should.

Thus she looked forward to the time of her death (74.176.6f.) But in the light of her incarnational understanding of the fallen world her strong propensity to understand spiritual truth through bodily images should not be lightly dismissed. She is not indulging in 'fantasye' in the *Cloud*-author's sense of the word[30] when she sees lepers and wounded men as icons of the bleeding Christ and wished to care for them (74.176.23f.).

For Margery the events she includes in her book are recorded because they were for her in various ways rites of passage to the realisation of truth and it is important not to lose sight of this in the astonishingly beguiling detail of the narrative. In this respect it is no accident that one of the most memorable aspects of her book is her phenomenal capacity for travel. Literal journeys by their very nature can be obvious ways of both experiencing and expressing the growth of significant inner change. In addition to journeying all over England in the course of pilgrimages and visits to particular churchmen[31] she also set out at the age of forty to go to the Holy Land, travelling across Europe to Venice and from thence by boat to Jaffa, the port for Jerusalem from whence she returned to Italy and went on via Assisi to Rome before returning to King's Lynn. After that, we hear of her going to the shrine of St James at Compostella, and, in the second part of the book there is an account of the most remarkable of her journeys, that to Danzig, undertaken on the spur of the moment with no proper luggage or clothing. All these journeys have religious significance. They are either made for specifically religious purposes – to consult spiritual advisers or as pilgrimages to holy places – or as a response to God's will.

Pilgrimage had a high cultural profile in the Middle Ages. That to the Holy Land was associated with the very foundation of the Christian message – the literal geography of the Incarnation making possible a special sense of identification with Christ; while Rome brought the pilgrims into contact with the foundations of the apostolic church; indeed it was obligatory for Catholic bishops to make a pilgrimage to Rome. During the period from the seventh to the eleventh centuries, when Islam ruled the Holy Land and access to its sacred places became increasingly difficult and was finally denied, shrines which duplicated their function appeared in Europe. That at Compostella commemorates St James's missionary activities in Spain. There St James was believed to have received a vision of the Virgin Mary who left behind a small statue of herself and commanded him to build a church at a particular place. The principal English Marian shrine in England, at Walsingham, a centre of pilgrimage second only to Canterbury, was believed to have been erected in the eleventh century as a result of a vision in which the Virgin commanded a lady of a local Norman household to build a replica of the house of the Annunciation.[32]

Pilgrimage provides a mode of experience through which the pilgrim can freely live out his faith at all kinds of levels.[33] The challenge of a journey from a known environment to a distant goal enables the pilgrim to enact a sense of purposeful existence in the scheme of God's providence, to understand himself, his limitations, and dependence on a strength greater than his own, in a new way. The pilgrimage thus takes on some of the functions of sacramental rituals, participation in which mediates the realities of the faith. The enactment of Christian pilgrimage is that of Christ's way of the cross in the Incarnation. The experience is thought of as a penitential journey in which the individual suffers in his own way for sin but moves towards a real place, associated with the source of renewal, resurrection and healing. There he can identify historically and anagogically with Christ the foundation of his faith, and with the saints and believers with whom he shares it – both those present with him on the journey, and the wider community alive and dead.

It is this aspect of pilgrimage which leads anthropologists to see it as 'liminoid',[34] a means, which, as it cuts across the structures and divisions of society, may enable the self to be restructured both in interior awareness of the faith and external relations with fellow pilgrims with whom an essential equality in the sight of God is now thrown into high relief. One of the high points in late medieval literature is the passage in the alliterative *Morte Arthure* when Arthur, at the peak of his triumph in Europe, overshadowed by a dream of his downfall but unable to make any change in his *modus vivendi*, defies his fate and, clad in the scarlet robes of the pride of life, turns towards Rome, the summit of his dreams. On the highway, he meets a penitent on a pilgrim's way thither, who figuratively points the way to a salvation which forever eluded the Round Table. It is small wonder that such an activity should have been deemed extroverted mysticism: 'the pilgrim physically travels a mystical way; the mystic sets forth on an interior pilgrimage. For the former, concreteness, historicity dominate; for the latter, a phased interior process leads to a goal beyond conceptualisation.'[35] All these aspects of pilgrimage are central to the spirituality of Margery Kempe. They provide means by which she orders her very literally experienced piety. In the circumstances of her life, and the way she recalls and orders them in her book, pilgrimage supplies both a mode by which she develops her understanding of her inner spirituality and an outward sign of this.

MARGERY'S BOOK IN ITS MEDIEVAL CONTEXT

The context of piety in England and Europe which Margery no doubt took for granted and against which she seems less unusual, highlights her distinctive qualities.[36] Certainly some of her preoccupations and modes of expression are illuminated by awareness of the whole ethos of female piety in Europe from the twelfth to the fifteenth centuries and of the way in which uneducated lay people in England received instruction about their faith in contemporary sermons, perceived it in the liturgy and demonstrated it in parish guilds – Margery almost certainly became a member of the Trinity Guild of Lynn.[37] Her anxiety over the consequences of her unconfessed sin are more understandable not only in the context of sermons which stress the importance of confession[38] but in the religious climate generated by the challenge of the reforming zeal of the Lollards. Although their literal iconoclasm goes right against the grain of Margery's piety,[39] the fact that one of the accusations they were called to answer concerned their belief that oral confession was superfluous for the truly contrite puts Margery's extreme anxiety on this subject into an understandable perspective.[40]

It is not surprising that she attracted hostile attention in the ethos of controversy generated by the fervently pious and articulate Lollards.[41] Her reputation for compulsively exhibitionist and loquacious piety provoked a mistaken reaction among the clergy and that sector of the population who supported them in their efforts to suppress Lollardy in the interests of social stability and to stamp out unlicensed preaching. It is even more understandable in view of the evidence for female participation in Lollard activities.[42] Although Margery was not a Lollard the movement provides an enlightening perspective on her particular kind of earnest and personal religious practice. As in her relation to the European *mulieres sanctae*, she was both like and very unlike.

The preaching to the laity of which Margery was so fond, statutory in England since the fourteenth century,[43] was part of a European movement given greater impetus by the mendicant orders; it both aroused, and responded to, a need expressed by lay men and, particularly, women, not just for instruction in the faith, but for a *modus vivendi* by which they might live it out.[44] Although the ways evolved to satisfy this need do not provide exact role models for Margery, they do bring her lifestyle into a proper contemporary focus and sharpen perception of her particular individuality.

Certain aspects of Beguine piety, its integration of a secular, active mode of life with religious ideals, the intensity and sometimes mystical nature of the devotions recorded in the lives of individual women (e.g. Mechtild of Magdeburg, Christine of Stumbalen, Mary of Oignies) illuminate Margery's devotions. She knew of the life of the early but prototypical Beguine, Mary of Oignies. In her *Book* she records that when she was at the height of her unpopularity in Lynn because of her weeping, the priest who was later to become her amanuensis distrusted her until he read of a parallel situation in the life of Mary of Oignies. Mary's inability to hear of Christ's passion without tears offended a priest similarly until he, while reading the Gospel, also received the gift of tears so strongly 'þatt he wett hys vestiment' (62.153.19).[45] Other aspects of Mary's life also bear on Margery's. Although she married at her parent's wish, her husband out of 'naturel goodnes'[46] eventually agreed to share a chaste life of piety with her and they selflessly looked after lepers at Willambroux, though she later went to live in a cell at the Augustinian priory at Oignies. In addition to her tears which, 'doune rennynge on þe kirke paumente shewed where she ȝeed',[47] her piety manifested itself in her life of prayer and her austere life-style: she ate no meat but was 'sustenyd with frutes of trees, erbys and potage' [*potage*: soup].[48] She wore the simplest of clothes, next to her skin a coarse sack and a white woollen garment over that,[49] which affords the biographer an opportunity to inveigh against vanity in dress in a way shared by Margery after her conversion:

> What seye ȝee to þis, ȝee superflue wymmen, ful of pompe & pryde, þat chargiþ ȝoure caryouns wiþ many-folde of clothes . . .[50]
>
> *superflue*: extravagant; *caryouns*: bodies.

Mary, like Margery later, had assurance that she would go straight to Paradise when she died;[51] they both had a visionary experience at Mass:

> Also often, whan þe preste lifte vp þe sacramente, she sawe bytwix þe prestys handes þe lyknes of a feyre childe and an oost of heuenly spirites doune commynge wiþ mykel lighte.[52]
>
> *mykel*: great.

But there were also marked differences in temperament and lifestyle. Mary worked to support herself and lived out her life of piety quietly in one place:

> þerfore in reste and silens, after þe apostil, she wirkynge wiþ hir handes ete hir brede – for hir strengthe was in silens & hope. In so mykel, sooþly, she fledde noyse & company of men & loued stillnesse and reste, þat on a tyme fro holy-rood daye to paske she kepte silens vnneþes spekynge any worde.[53]
>
> *holy-rood daye*: feast of the exaltation of the Cross (September 14th); *paske*: Easter; *vnneþes*: scarcely.

Other more active women (who were later canonised) enacted roles by which Margery may well have been influenced. Like her they travelled, but they were unlike her in enjoying considerable prestige not only for visionary piety but for their influential and active part in religious affairs. Dorothy of Montau, Catherine of Siena and Bridget of Sweden must all have been known to Margery though she refers directly only to Bridget.[54]

She had the revelations of Bridget of Sweden whom she venerated read to her (17.39.24; 58.143.27), sought out people and places connected with her in Rome (39.95.10f.) and visited Syon Abbey in 1434 (*Book* 2, 10.245.31). Bridget, who learned Latin in her middle age, spent time at the Swedish court and was concerned at the highest levels of power with the reform of the church, is a far cry from Margery. Yet elements of their experience are shared.[55] Bridget was married at thirteen and had eight children, but she developed an increasingly ascetic lifestyle and eventually secured her husband's consent to a life of mutual chastity. After his death in *c.*1343 she devoted herself to a version of religious life lived out in a socio-political context, at first in Sweden, and then in Rome where she stayed until her death.[56] She felt herself ordered by Christ to visit the Holy Land. In much the same way Margery felt that Christ commanded her to go to Jerusalem, Rome and Compostella and, later, to Danzig (15.32.5–8; *Book* 2, 2.226.30f.).[57] It may be that Margery's sense of a divine calling to go to Danzig was fuelled by St Bridget's experience; but the place itself must almost certainly also have been attractive as the home of the Blessed Dorothy of Montau when she was married. It is odd that Margery never mentions Dorothy; although Dorothy had died nearly forty years before, it is hard to believe that Margery had not heard of her through her pious son and daughter-in-law who came from there.[58]

Dorothy was another woman who, devout from early childhood, found that the demands of her piety and her duties as a married woman were incompatible. She also eventually won her husband's consent to a mutual vow of chastity, but not until she had borne him nine children and exasperated him by putting her pious practices before the practicalities of housekeeping and motherhood.[59] Like Bridget, and later Margery, she went on pilgrimages. Once a widow, she became a recluse and was allowed to receive Communion three times daily, an act which was the occasion of great emotion in her: she displayed the gift of tears and wept not only for herself but for all sinners.

There are obvious parallels to be drawn between various aspects of the experience of these continental women and that of Margery; their concern to forge a lifestyle which embodied the authority of their religious calling despite their status as lay women; their dependence on confessors; their visionary and ascetically inclined piety linked with strong devotion to the manhood of Christ which expressed itself in tears of compassion and penitence; Mary's love of preachers; Bridget's and Dorothy's practice of pilgrimage. But Margery stands out with a distinctly more naive individuality, forging her own pattern of living out of the reality of the faith.

THE WRITING OF HER BOOK

Despite the fact that Margery did not actually write out her own book, there seems little reason to doubt that she was responsible for the final organisation of material. In the short proem to Book One she tells us that despite the fact that she was urged by others to record her experience fairly early on – the Carmelite friar, Alan of Lynn who worked on the revelations of St Bridget, had even offered to be her amanuensis – she felt the time was not yet right. It was not until much later, twenty years after she had first dedicated herself to God, that she felt herself bidden to 'wryten hyr felyngys & reuelacyons' (Proem, 3.32) and then the job was done in a very botched up fashion by a man who could speak both English and German but who could not write clearly in either tongue.

Eventually she managed to persuade a friend who was a priest to transcribe the original text. He started to do this in 1436 and says that when he had finished:

> he added a leef þerto, and þan wrot he þis proym to expressyn mor openly þan doth þe next folwyng whech was wretyn er þan þis.
>
> (p.5.30–2)

leef: leaf (of a book); *proym*: introduction; *er þan*: before.

He explains that the first scribe was an Englishman by birth who had married in Germany and had a child, but because he knew what Margery wanted he came to England to stay with her and wrote down all that she could tell him before he died, though he comments that the book was 'euel wretyn . . . neiþyr good Englysch ne Dewch, ne þe lettyr was not schapyn ne formyd as oþer letters ben' (Proem, 4.14–17). It has been conjectured that this scribe was Margery's son of whom she tells us in Book Two.[60] Certainly the son did marry abroad and certainly he came to England with his wife to see Margery and died there. It does, however, seem extraordinary that Margery, who was not slow to tell quite a lot about his life, did not identify him as her scribe if that was the case, and also extraordinary that he apparently wrote only in broken English. Margery finally persuaded her second amanuensis to overcome his understandable reluctance to wrestle with a text so corrupt that it foxed even a friend of the original writer familiar with his handwriting (Proem, 4.29–40). She countered his expostulations of difficulty in actually focusing on the writing, even with the aid of spectacles, by assuring him that his affliction was a devilish plot to thwart the work and that he must persevere with God's help. This proved effective as 'whan he cam a-geyn to hys booke, he myth se as wel, hym thowt, as euyr he dede be-for þe day-lyth & þe candel-lygth boþe' (Proem, 5.27–9).

He tells us that he read the original manuscript to Margery and she helped over difficulties in understanding before he copied it. On occasions the narrative has a textured feeling as the speaking voice shades from that of Margery to that of the scribe: for instance, in the stories he tells against himself in his early relationship with Margery (c.24) and in the comments in defence of her weeping in the Holy Land (28.70.23). But there seems to be no reason to doubt that the material is presented in accordance with Margery's wishes. He signs off:

> Her endith þis tretys, for God toke hym to hys mercy þat wrot þe copy of þis boke, &, þow þat he wrot not clerly ne opynly to owr maner of spekyng, he in hys maner of wrytyng & spellyng mad trewe sentens þe whech, thorw þe help of God & of hir-selfe þat had al þis tretys in felyng & werkyng, is trewly drawyn owt of þe copy in-to þis lityl boke.[61]
>
> (89.220.18–24)

sentens: meaning.

Margery's book shows progress towards an increasingly spiritual understanding of her experience. It has been seen both as didactic odyssey, which culminates in her dialogue with Christ and shows her becoming wise in God's ways rather than man's,[62] and also as a process in which physical problems are transcended in a creative spirituality which she expresses through sequences of thematic clusters related to sex, words, tears and food.[63] Certainly there is a purposeful thrust in the way Margery remembered events. Despite the fact that she could not remember exact chronology 'þe tyme & þe ordyr whan thyngys befellyn', she conveys a sense of a spiritual order in her life, discernible in the way 'þe mater cam to þe creatur in mend' [mind] (Proem, 5.16, 14). The conclusion of this chapter points to an order in her recollection, selection and arrangement of events which reveals her understanding of the pattern of the Incarnation at the heart of the Church's teaching and her perception of its presence as a dynamic development in her own experience.

THE SHAPE OF HER BOOK

Chapters 1–11: spiritual awakening

The ethos of pilgrimage made possible an existential validation of Margery's faith, it provided her with a figurative mode of understanding her whole life and it governs the shape of her book. This consists of those sequences of events which she remembered as significant markers on the 'wey whech wold leden hir to þe place þat sche most desyred' (3.13.13–14). She starts with those which she thought set her feet on this inward 'wey of euyr-lestyng lyfe' (2.11.10) and continues with those which illuminated her development of a life-style through which she understood something of the nature of that 'kendly cuntre' to which she looked forward when she had 'passyd þis wretchyd wordelys exile' [*kendly*: natural; *wordelys*: worlds] (42.100.28–9).

After the initial account of the traumatic experiences of childbirth which precipitated Margery's visionary awareness of the redemptive love of Christ the book continues with a description of her meditative participation in the births of the Virgin, St John the Baptist and Christ, and then a midsummer picnic at which she and her husband John agreed to a vow of mutual chastity. As she bore fourteen children (48.115.32), this sequence of events must cover at least fourteen years and during this time her centre of gravity moved from an assertion of independent power on the domestic front to a sense of freedom under the authority of God.

For two years after her initial vision she indulged in a rather self-righteous devotional zeal which she saw retrospectively as pride (4.14.2f.). It was smartly cut down by a humiliating experience of sexual attraction to a local man who led her on only to reject her in no uncertain terms as Margery's penitential vividness conveys: 'he seyd he ne wold for al þe good in þis world; he had leuar ben hewyn as smal as flesch to þe pott' (4.15.26–8). Margery was devastated and in despair at her own behaviour; but, significantly, in view of her attitude to Church ritual, her dejection was lifted in the Advent season, a time for contemplation not only of sin and judgement, but also of the light which is coming in the darkness. On the Friday before Christmas, she received a visionary certainty of Christ's love which lifted her above the despairing harshness of her penitential discipline and infused her with an inward assurance of forgiveness and the sense of a possibility of a life which, sacramentally, would channel God's grace. As she was told to leave off her hair-shirt to experience a new inner sense of God and herself, it is as if, at her own level, she moves from purgation to illumination. Indeed, Christ bade her to cease from set prayers and commune directly with him 'I schal ȝefe to þe hey medytacyon and very contemplacyon' (5.17.30–1). Margery may not mean the same by this as the *Cloud*-author, but she certainly both exemplified, and talked about, a transfiguring certainty of the truth of the Incarnation and her relation to it. That she rang true on both counts was testified by a Dominican recluse to whom Christ sent her for authentication of her vision (5.17–18.31–3).

It is in this context that she remembers her absorption in meditative experiences centred on the birth of the Virgin, the Annunciation, Visitation, Nativity and Epiphany – all familiar icons which together celebrate the meaning of the Incarnation. The chronology of the experiences is uncertain; what is important is that these meditations have a propriety at this point in her account. It would seem that they are based on the popular Franciscan *Meditationes Vitae Christi*. Certainly, like Margery, Nicholas Love in his version uses the term 'contemplacioun' to describe what the other writers with whom this book is concerned call 'meditation', the mental activity of dwelling on the significance of the

Incarnation by meditating on physical details of its stories.[64] And certainly Margery's apocryphal detail of how the Virgin was present at the birth of John the Baptist and in token of his holiness herself presented him to his mother Elizabeth is also present in Love.[65]

That Margery's account of her meditations has the same factual quality as the surrounding narrative of circumstances in her own life may not just point to the literal quality of her imagination, but reflect on the way she expected her own story to be read. 'Contemplacyon' and action interact with each other as signs of her perception of grace. Margery's recall of her meditative experiences of the birth of the Virgin, John the Baptist and Christ at this juncture in her narrative reflects back on her own experience of salvation at the birth of her first child and also signals a new interior awareness of Christ – 'I am in þe, and þow in me' (10.23.3) – and birth into a life of prayerful action in which she would contribute in her own way to the redemptive work of love. This characteristic interplay between 'contemplacyon' and action reveals itself in the two episodes in her life which stood out for her as definitive of her changed status at this time. The first is her vision of Mary in which she is given assurance of her entry to heaven and an opportunity to name another to join her. (Her naming of her confessor in preference to her husband and children signifies her sense of priorities, though her family was also subsequently included in the 'deal', c.8.). The second is her apparently miraculous preservation when nine pounds of masonry and timber from the vaulting of the church fell on her while she was praying (c.9). Small wonder in all these circumstances that, as Margery developed a clearly spectacular certainty of her inner calling, and gained public recognition, John Kempe bowed to the inevitable and agreed to a vow of chastity. But on touchingly practical terms. Margery was not only to live and eat with him, Fridays included, but to pay his financial debts before she went off on pilgrimage to the Holy Land. Margery's emergence into the life-style she so passionately desired is celebrated at a midsummer picnic. She gives her account of the event a sacramental quality, telling how she and John knelt to pray at a wayside cross and then ate and drank together 'in gret gladnes of spyryt' (11.25.17–18).

Chapters 12–25: 'dredyth ȝe not of ȝowr maner of leuyng'

The following fourteen chapters are not in strict chronology. They include accounts of events that occurred before and after the summer picnic, but they belong together thematically in establishing Margery as a figure of religious authority in an enlarged theatre. So far she has concentrated on her private sense of passage to an inner healing; now she shows how she experienced the saving power of faith in various public situations. The events described range from public persecution and ridicule to increased inner certainty and endorsement by authoritative figures such as the Bishop of Lincoln, the Archbishop of Canterbury and a group of religious at Norwich which included Julian and, finally, Christ himself.

Her account conveys a lively sense of both her own personality and the religious tensions of her time. Thus she describes how she so embarrassed her husband by her devotional tears on a visit to Canterbury that he went off and pretended to disown her. This left her open to the taunts of irritated monks who clearly did not trust women who not only wept loudly but were articulate about religion. One of them wished her walled up in a stone cell out of ear-shot (the anchoritic option) while another, obviously impressed by her loquacity, said she was certainly inspired, but whether by the Holy Ghost or the devil, he was not sure (13.27.32f.). She left the cathedral pursued by ugly cries that threatened death at the stake for heresy: 'þow xalt be brent, fals lollare. Her is a cartful of thornys redy for þe & a tonne to bren þe wyth' [*tonne:* barrel *bren:* burn] (13.28.29–31). In a moment of desolation and panic, longing for the support of her husband (13.28.34f.), she prayed for help and was instantly befriended by two young men who took her back to her lodgings.

As before, the contemplative experiences she recalls at this point directly relate to the events of which she speaks. She saw her own ability to suffer persecution as part of her compassion for Christ's suffering – an extension of it. For he told her 'I am an hyd God in þe . . .' (14.30.26–7) – and that he was the source of the tears which expressed her joy and understanding of the Passion (31.4–6).[66]

Similarly this visit was one of many to various authorities which might authenticate her calling and compensate for the public scorn and betrayal by fair-weather friends (5.32.29f). She went to see Philip Repyngdon, Bishop of Lincoln, at a time when she felt an inner calling to wear a white habit and ring as palpable sign of her chastity. As a former Wycliffite subject to persecution (he had abjured in 1382) the Bishop would have been keenly sensitive to the need for discretion in religious practices. Although he ratified Margery's vow of chastity, he clearly had reservations about her adopting any clothing which would single her out for attack and stalled in making a decision until she returned from her planned visit to Jerusalem. Despite her craving for the approval of authority Margery was not easily dissuaded from her inner convictions. To her, Repyngdon's reply did not seem to display discretion, but a fear of public opinion which he placed above love for God (15.35.20). When he tried both to accommodate her and to pass the buck by suggesting that she should appeal to a higher authority, the Archbishop of Canterbury, she replied that she did have certain matters to discuss with him but that was not one. 'God wyl not I aske hym þeraftyr' (15.35.37).

What these matters were we can readily infer from her visit to Thomas Arundel, Archbishop of Canterbury, to secure his permission for weekly communion and freedom to choose her confessor: probably a deliberate bid to establish her orthodoxy publicly, since he was known for his severity in bringing known Lollards to trial. He might well have been sympathetic to Margery's piety as she revealed it to him since he had himself licensed for popular devotional reading the Franciscan *Meditationes Vitae Christi* translated by Nicholas Love.[67] The visit must have been memorable and says much for both of them. He submitted 'ful benyngly & mekely' to Margery's remonstration about the foul-mouthed members of his staff she had encountered – she expostulated that God had not put him where he was in order to subsidise a group of swearers. However, they must have found common concerns since they chatted until 'sterrys apperyd in þe fyrmament' (16.37.11,13–14).

The account prompts her memory of an earlier journey to Norwich where among other religious figures she met the visionary friar, William Southfield, who confirmed her life-style as the work of God's grace – 'dredyth ȝe not of ȝowr maner of leuyng, for it is þe Holy Gost werkyng plentyuowsly hys grace in ȝowr sowle' [*leuyng*: living] (18.41.13–14) – and with Julian. Margery's earlier account of a contemplative experience when she hears Christ say:

> I swer to þi mend, & it wer possybyl me to suffyr peyn a-geyn as I haue do be-forn, me wer leuar to suffyr as mech peyn as euyr I dede for þi sowle alon raþar þan þow schuldyst partyn fro me wyth-owtyn ende
>
> (14.30.17–21)

strongly recalls the ninth revelation of Julian. Perhaps they had talked of it on this visit.[68] Echoes of Julian's Revelations certainly now resonate in Margery's report of their conversation. Julian assured her that her tears of contrition and compassion were from God.[69] Her parting advice to Margery points to a shrewd assessment of her temperament, circumstances and the mode in which she was most likely to experience the reality of the Incarnation:

> I prey God grawnt ȝow perseuerawns. Settyth al ȝowr trust in God & feryth not þe langage of þe world, for þe mor despyte, schame, & repref þat ȝe haue in þe world þe mor is ȝowr meryte in þe sygth of God. Pacyens is necessary vn-to ȝow, for in þat schal ȝe kepyn ȝowr sowle.
>
> (18.43.12–18)
>
> *pacyens*: patience.

This part of her book, establishing Margery's credentials, comes to a climax in her recall of visionary experiences in which she felt herself officially confirmed as a pious woman by Christ himself. She has a vision of the dove above the Host at Mass and is given an insight into the ills of mortality as an opportunity to prove the love of God in patience; at the same time she understood that God put her on a footing with St Bridget (c.20). In view of Bridget's renowned prophetic gifts it is not surprising that at this point Margery's sense of being in a special relationship with Christ – 'þu art to me a synguler lofe, dowtyr' (21.50.32) – seems linked in her mind with a series of incidents which foreground her prophetic insight (c.22–25). Typically their distinctly parochial dimensions point up the difference between Margery and her role model[70] but at the same time they obviously served to authenticate her calling and status in England. She now extends this by her account of her pilgrimage experience abroad.

Chapters 26–43: to be a pilgrim

It may be that her home town of King's Lynn provided the ethos which was the catalyst for Margery's perception of pilgrimage. Not only was it a thriving trading town,[71] it was an important and lively religious centre by virtue of its position as a port to which pilgrims from Scandinavia and Northern Europe came to England.[72] Swedish Bridgettines came through King's Lynn *en route* for Syon Abbey[73] and there was a way-station for pilgrims coming to Walsingham. As the daughter of an alderman and several-times mayor of Lynn, and as wife of a substantial trader, Margery must have been in close contact with such comings and goings. They would have provided a window on the world for her restless and ambitiously independent spirit, a stimulus to look beyond the confines of her own domestic horizons. From King's Lynn she embarked on a journey to God in which outward and visible signs of her life-style manifested its inner reality. Just as the reclusive contemplative seeking God exercises a discipline which moves her beyond a state of penitential awareness for sin to an inner awareness of the reality of love, so Margery, in her own manner, sought ways of living which would further illuminate her inner experience of God. Although she was assured of Christ's forgiveness for her sin (5.16.34–5; 14.30.17–24) she wanted to deepen her faith by going

> to se þo placys wher he was born & wher he sufferyd hys Passyon & wher he deyd, wyth oþer holy placys wher he was in hys lyue & also aftyr hys Resurrexyon.
>
> (15.32.2–5)

Her desire was answered by a sense that God commanded her to go to Jerusalem, Rome and the shrine of St James at Compostella.

In the Holy Land her devotions took on appropriate symbolic structures. She rode into Jerusalem (and also Bethlehem) on a donkey. In the church of the Holy Sepulchre which enclosed Mount Calvary she undertook a twenty-four hour vigil which must have been a powerfully emotive experience, familiar as she was with the Canonical Hours and their daily reminder of the Passion.[74] It is small wonder that her meditative experience of Christ's crucifixion echoes the Passion meditations of Richard Rolle[75] or that her specifically convulsive crying first occurred as she lay cruciform on the site. In the Franciscan convent of Mount Zion, believed to house the room of the Last Supper, she received communion, again in tears, and in the same building, on the believed site of Pentecost, she received more inward assurance that this pilgrimage was not to be regarded as a penance but as an occasion which answered her felt need for merit and reward:

> þu comyst not hedyr, dowtyr, for no nede but for meryte & for mede, for thy synnes wer for-ȝouyn þe er thow come her . . . .
>
> (29.72.31–3)

hedyr: hither; *for-ȝouyn*: forgiven.

Margery uses the language of social success, but as a means to express her intense desire for the attainment of spiritual grace in which she felt confirmed as she heard Christ reiterate the assurance that her pilgrimage to Rome and Compostella was not pentitential but his command.

In addition to the devotional goal of pilgrimage, the challenges of the journeys became the means whereby she constantly realised the reality of Christ's care first experienced in the trauma of her postnatal depression: 'Dowtyr, why hast þow forsakyn me, and I forsoke neuyr þe?' (1.8.20). Since her longing to travel was, at the beginning, frustrated by lack of means, when Christ himself told her to go she replied: 'Wher schal I han good to go wyth to þes holy placys?' Christ not only assured her that he would send friends to help, but promised:

> I xal go wyth þe in euery contre & ordeyn for þe; I xal ledyn þe thyder & brynge þe a-geyn in safte.
>
> (15.32.9–10, 13–14)

On her return to Venice from Jerusalem, finding herself deserted by companions who said that they would no longer travel with her, even if paid to do so, she felt wretched and panicky about continuing alone; but on receiving inward assurance of Christ's presence to help in all needs, she plucked up her courage to go on and instantly came across one, Richard, an Irishman, who was not only the answer to her present needs but the fulfilment of a prophecy made to her before she left England (see 18.44.11–15) and so especially marked as an agent of God's providence. On another occasion in Rome, perhaps influenced by contact with Franciscans not only in Palestine (they conducted her round the Holy Places) but in her subsequent journey via Assisi, she felt called to live in poverty. In a gesture of total commitment she gave away not only all her own money but also a loan from Richard as well. Grandly meeting his understandable annoyance with the assurance that God's grace would bring them safely to England, she suffered a back-lash of panic at having thus totally abandoned all financial security, only to be reminded by Christ that she was not more destitute than he was in his Passion and assured that help was on the way: 'drede þe not, dowtyr, for þer is gold to-þe-ward' (38.92.38). Whereupon she went out and straight away bumped into a total stranger who was so impressed by her piety that he gave her money to tide her over.

In addition to this aspect of the pilgrimage enactment of faith, Margery also turned the difficulties arising from the clash of personalities in a small group of pilgrims into an opportunity to transform the teaching of faith into lived reality. Obviously she cannot have been easy to live with. Her compulsive need to proclaim her faith publicly at all kinds of levels, the eccentric clothes she felt she had to wear, her dominating conversation, vegetarianism and sobbing[76] so annoyed her fellow pilgrims that instead of her sharing the joy and security of *communitas* in a shared faith, they not only deserted or ridiculed her, but cut up her clothes, refused to let her speak (26.62.15f.), took her money (27.64.15) and even stole her sheets:

> whan it was tyme to makyn her beddys . . . a preste wech was in her cumpany toke a-wey a shete fro þe forseyd creatur & seyd it was hys. (28.67.2–5)

But all her experiences were transformed for Margery by her ability to see them as occasions for sharing Christ's suffering in patience and love.

If the definition of play is that it is intrinsically rewarding, and faith is a game wherein the wisdom of God is born in man, then pilgrimage for Margery gave her a mode of play. Such a perspective throws light on her understanding of the merit and reward which were her goal.[77] Always liable to express physically what was to be understood spiritually (89.220.9f.), she lays herself open to denigrating interpretation; but there is the possibility that this may reflect more on the interpreter than on her.

Her particular kind of incarnational understanding was intensified by her contact with the Franciscans. The affective nature of their piety, deeply involved with images of the humanity of Christ, able to imbue domestic realities with significant spirituality and inspire followers to rejoice in poverty and simplicity as an expression of love for Christ, appealed to Margery.[78] She wept with joy as she saw Italian women respond to the image of the Infant Christ, because she had shared similar experiences in her meditations (30.78.1–6).[79] Her encounter with a poor woman in Rome encapsulates her sacramental understanding:

> An-oþer tyme, ryth as sche cam be a powr womanys hows, þe powr woman clepyd hir in-to hir hows & dede hir sytten be hir lytyl fyer, ȝeuyng hir wyn to drynke in a cuppe of ston. & sche had a lytyl manchylde sowkyng on hir brest, þe whech sowkyd o while on þe moderys brest; an-oþer while it ran to þis creatur, þe modyr syttyng ful of sorwe & sadnes.
>
> (39.94.8–14)

ston: stone; *manchylde:* male child.

For Margery the experience triggered a vivid realisation of the suffering humanity of Christ which released her tears and she received a visionary understanding of God's presence there:

> þan owr Lord Ihesu Crist seyd . . . 'Thys place is holy'.
>
> (39.94.20–1)

She is not alone in this understanding. A German priest who befriended her in Rome clearly understood that Margery's devotion needed some kind of literal enactment to express itself when he ordered her to look after a destitute old woman and share her poverty, which she did scrupulously, fetching sticks for her fire and begging bread for them both.

It is in conjunction with the memory of this obedient self-denial in the service of active love that Margery places her account of the culminating point of the pilgrimage experience – her marriage to the Godhead. The terms of the marriage service are used to express her sense of union:

> And þan þe Fadyr toke hir be þe hand in hir sowle be-for þe Sone & þe Holy Gost & þe Modyr of Ihesu and alle þe xij apostelys & Seynt Kateryn & Seynt Margarete & many oþer seyntys & holy virgynes wyth gret multitude of awngelys, seying to hir sowle, 'I take þe, Margery, for my weddyd wyfe, for fayrar, for fowelar, for richar, for powerar, so þat þu be buxom & bonyr to do what I byd þe do'.
>
> (35.87.13–20)

buxom & bonyr: gentle and obedient.

Although Margery self-confessedly had a literal turn of mind, here she seems to be trying to express the awakening of her sense of the creative source of her faith which she knew she imperfectly understood. When she heard God call her to him as his wife she:

> kept sylens in hir sowle & answeryd not þerto, for sche was ful sor aferd of þe Godhed & sche cowde no skylle of þe dalyawns of þe Godhede, for al hir lofe & al hir affeccyon was set in þe manhode of Crist.
>
> (35.86.19–22)

cowde: knew; *dalyawns:* conversation.

Her very hesitation and lack of confidence are, however, a potential response which she sees embodied in the words of the Christ with whom she identifies:

> Fadyr, haue hir excused, for sche is ȝet but ȝong & not fully lernyd how sche xulde answeryn.
>
> (35.87.13–14)

And it is at this point that she sees herself as the spouse of God. It is not so very remarkable that Margery used the language of the marriage service; such language expressed the love between man and wife as a sacramental reflection of the love of Christ for the Church and provided her with a paradigm for her feeling of oneness with God in the redemptive work of patience and love. It had also been used by other medieval saints and pious women.[80] Margery focuses the experience in all its intensity accompanied by physical sensations of sweet smells and sounds and an inner warmth and comfort which she identified as the fire of love (35.88.33). She was filled with a certainty of ultimate spiritual security 'for þi sowle xal partyn fro thy body but God xal neuyr partyn fro þi sowle, for þei ben onyd to-gedyr wyth-owtyn ende' and of confirmation of her life-style 'for þis is an holy lyfe & þe tyme is ryth wel spent' (35.89.13–19). Her sense of spiritual intimacy was mediated through an extremely literal image of love-making:

> & þerfor þu mayst boldly take me in þe armys of þi sowle & kyssen my mowth, myn hed, & my fete as swetly as thow wylt.
>
> (36.90.24–6)

But in the context of Hilton's use of the body of Christ as an image[81] it is easy to see how it would have a propriety in Margery's particular circumstances. As usual the shape of her narrative is a key to its significance. It is appropriate that she placed the account where she did, just after her memories of service to an old woman – behaviour which in the terms of the Gospel was an act of love towards Christ, and of embracing a life of poverty so complete that she not only gave away her own goods but those on loan to her.[82]

Perhaps her account at this point of her visits to the Bridgettine sites in Rome witness to her sense of security as a woman whose life-style expressed her divine mission. Her public reputation for holiness is also now stressed as she remembers the priest who had heard in England of her reputation in Rome and came to look for her and bring her the wherewithal for her return journey (40.96). Unsurprisingly her account of this journey in which she was miraculously preserved from dramatic storms (43.101) and safely brought across the North Sea in a boat so small that her companion got cold feet about embarking in it (43,102.9–10), has a distinctly emblematic quality.[83]

Back home, when her friend Richard Caister, Vicar of St Stephens in Norwich[84] welcomed her, marvelling that after such hazards she had such merriment, she replied that it was born of her experience of the reality of God's care (43.102.34–6). She displayed the same equanimity in the face of the hostile reception afforded her by a Benedictine anchorite she visited. He had clearly given ear to gossip arising from Margery's independent life-style and sourly enquired as to the whereabouts of the child he had heard that she had conceived and borne while away. Unconvinced by Margery's disavowal of the matter, he waxed sarcastic about her white clothes. Her reply acts as a succinct summary of her whole position: 'Ser, I mak no fors so þat God be plesyd þerwyth' [*fors:* care] (43.103.20). Her words appropriately usher in the events of the next period she remembered – her travels in England when she was both imprisoned and tried as a Lollard, but finally vindicated by the highest ecclesiastical power in the country.

Chapters 44–55: persecution for the faith

It is significant that although this next period in her story includes her trip to Compostella in July 1417, she tells us more about the difficulties of the embarkation from Bristol due to lack of shipping and the hostility of her fellow pilgrims (c.44–5) than of her experience there. This is probably because it seems to have offered no memorable trials to bear: the tone of this section is set, in fact, by her remark, made in the context of her appearance in new white clothes on Trinity Sunday 1415 in Norwich:

> & sithen hath sche sufferyd meche despyte & meche schame in many dyuers cuntreys, cyteys, & townys, thankyd be God of alle.
>
> (44.104.24–6)

Her account follows the chronology of her travels to Leicester *en route* from Bristol to York where she went on pilgrimage to the shrine of St William Fitzherbert – a site of reputed miracles[85] – and then home via Beverley and Hull. At this time anti-Lollard feeling was very strong. After the Oldcastle rising in 1414 the authorities, both ecclesiastical and secular, were especially vigilant in investigating any unusual lay religious activity in the dioceses. That John Oldcastle was still at large increased the social tension, and the hunt for his whereabouts was particularly active in the summer of 1417 in the Midlands and Welsh borders. Margery's eccentric behaviour, white clothes, irrepressible loquacity and sense of vocation which she flaunted in the face of all opposition, together with her appearances at Bristol and Leicester, both centres where Lollards had long been active, obviously marked her down as suspect.[86]

In Bristol while she was still waiting for a ship to Santiago and causing a lot of disturbance among her fellow pilgrims, she was summoned to the Bishop of Worcester, Thomas Peverell, who was staying at his Manor at Henbury about three miles outside the port. He had pronounced as heretic one of the few Lollards to be actually burnt – John Badby, a tailor from Evesham.[87] Although nothing is said on this occasion about Lollardy it is clear that he must have wished to take Margery's measure for himself. He obviously responded to the integrity of her witness and sought her prayers in the face of his impending death (45.110.2–7). As in Lambeth, Margery found the episcopal retinue lacked seemliness. She was confronted by a group of very natty dressers ('al-to-raggyd & al-to-daggyd in her clothys' [slashed and scalloped] 45.109.11–12) and it says as much for them as for her that they took in good part her comment that they looked less like the Bishop's servants than the devil's.

On her return from Compostella, while travelling through England she was arrested and tried on suspicion of Lollard activity at Leicester, York and Beverley. In her life of patience under these persecutions she identifies her particular imitation of Christ, sometimes quite explicitly, and her accounts of her experiences now begin increasingly to echo the Gospel narratives. Thus just before she begins these journeys, in King's Lynn where her convulsive weeping and famous white clothes roused suspicion of demonic possession (44.105.13) and people spat at, and cursed her, she took it all

> pacyently for owr Lordys lofe, for sche wist wel þat þe Iewys seyd meche wers of hys owyn persone þan men dede of hir.
>
> (44.105.15–17)

And when she was abused and slandered at Bristol she prayed to the Christ who forgave his killers to forgive those who scorned her (44.107.17–24). In York her white clothes so affronted one priest that he took her by the scruff of the neck in the Minster and said 'þu wulf, what is þis cloth þat þu hast on?' Like Christ before his accusers, she was silent and would not 'answeryn in hir owyn cause',[88] though a group of passing children did not share her discretion and called out cheekily 'Ser it is wulle' [wool] (50.120.19–22). On trial in Beverley similarly Margery seems to have interpreted the incidents as an extension of the Passion in her own life. In the house where she was imprisoned she talked to the crowd through an open window and asked for a drink 'for sche was euyl for thryste' (53.131.3) – which she is offered from a ladder.[89] And as she appeared before the Archbishop of York, he announced like a more famous predecessor that he had examined her and 'fond no defawte in hir' (54.131.33).[90] Margery herself departed on a high note to Lincoln; there her ability to defend herself against attack so amazed people that they asked her how she knew what to say and she replied with an echo of Christ's words: 'Stody not what ʒe schal sey, for it schal not be ʒowr spiryt þat schal spekyn in ʒow, but it schal be þe spiryt of þe Holy Gost' (55.135.32–5).[91]

These incidents, however, also reveal Margery's ability to defend herself with some cogency, an ability she believed to be a divine gift (52.124.3–7; 55.135.30–1). In Leicester the Mayor clearly felt threatened, both as a man and as an official, by her independence and ability to answer with informed lucidity the questions on Articles of the Faith posed by the presiding judge, the Abbott of the House of Augustinian Canons and the Dean of the College of St Mary. Her statement on the intrinsic validity of the sacrament (48.115.10–18) would have been one of the chief factors in determining her orthodoxy.[92] In York, however, when she appeared before the Archbishop at his palace at Cawood, although she indulged in the, by now almost statutory, reproof of unmannerly officials, (52.124.4–6) she evidently found the experience traumatic. She describes herself as trembling so violently 'þat sche was fayn to puttyn hir handys vndyr hir cloþis þat it schulde not ben aspyed' (52.124.25–6). But neither her courage nor her wit failed her and she was able to answer questions on the Articles of the Faith 'wel & trewly' (52.125.9). The Archbishop clearly found her an embarrassment and offered to let her go if she left the diocese immediately. She not only refused to do so before returning to see her friends in York, but also declined to take any oath that she would not teach people while she was there quoting the Gospel to back up her claim that 'God al-mythy forbedith not, ser, þat we xal speke of hym' (52.126.1–13).[93] And to the thrusting clerk who in return showed her chapter and verse for St Paul's prohibition against women preaching in church[94] she replied coolly that she was not claiming to be a licensed preacher using a pulpit.

This section of the *Book* is brought to a close with Margery's visit to London to obtain a letter vouching for her orthodoxy from the Archbishop of Canterbury, now Henry Chicheley, who was committed to eradicating Lollard practices. She came home to King's Lynn with the healthy respect of those to be reckoned with in the ecclesiastical hierarchy only to find a fresh set of problems in store for her.

Chapters 56–76: 'a welle of teerys'

In the last series of events Margery recalls she is back home in Lynn where she started. These events do not have the sequence of a journey to order them and tend to be disordered chronologically, but they refer to a period between 1417 and the late 1420s when she was brought to a low point in her fortunes and they bring us hard up against some of the most difficult aspects of Margery's account of herself.

It is as if the absence of the stimulus of pilgrimage laid her open to a period of depression and suffering. She was afflicted by periods of doubt and isolation when she had misgivings about the revelatory insights she felt were given her by Christ. She thought that she was being punished for this lack of faith by tormentingly degrading sexual fantasies before she was comforted and reassured by Christ. Beneath the claustrophobically limiting way in which she conceptualises this process,[95] there is a basic experience of doubt and delusion remarkably similar to Julian's where she is tempted to doubt her revelations but feels herself delivered by faith in Christ.[96] Looked at carefully, it is clear that Margery is struggling to express what she understands to be a hell of disbelief:

> I wold not, Lord, for al þis world suffryn swech an-oþer peyne as I haue suffryd þes xij days, for me thowt I was in Helle, blyssed mote þu be þat it is passyd.
>
> (59.146.29–31)
>
> *mote*: may

The problems attendant on her weeping also came to a head during these years. On Good Fridays she wept uncontrollably for all sinners, including herself, for five or six hours on end, to the point of exhaustion. One of the difficulties with the chronology of this period arises from a statement that she now makes about the nature of her crying and its duration:

> þan wex sche al blew as it had ben leed & swet ful sor. And þis maner of crying enduryd þe terme of x ȝer, as it is wretyn be-forn.
>
> (57.140.23–5)
>
> *wex:* grew; *blew:* blue; *leed:* lead.

In the period between her return from Rome and her departure to Bristol (1415–17) she describes her violent weeping in a manner which recalls her description at this point saying that in her convulsions she 'wex al blew & al blo as it had ben colowr of leed' [*blo*: leaden-coloured] (44.105.20–1). If the 'as it is wretyn be-forn' of chapter fifty-seven is a clumsy way of qualifying 'þis maner of crying' rather than the 'terme of x ȝer' then it would be possible to date the cessation of her convulsive form of weeping to about 1427. This would not be at odds with the events she describes in this section concerning a friar who came to Lynn to preach (c.61f.) but who, despite representations as to her sincerity from priests, mayor and people, refused to allow her in church disrupting his sermons with her fervent responses unless she admitted that her noisy weeping was an illness of some kind (61.151.8f.). She recalls his arrival in Lynn in conjunction with her memories of prayers for the recovery of a priest who used to read to her:

> many a good boke of hy contemplacyon & oþer bokys, as þe Bybyl wyth doctowrys þer-up-on, Seynt Brydys boke, Hyltons boke, Boneventur, Stimulus Amoris, Incendium Amoris, & swech oþer.
>
> (58.143.25–9)

His sickness and return to health can be dated to 1420 because she says that at that time she went to Norwich to give special thanks at St Stephen's church where Richard Caister (*ob.*1420) had just died. If the friar who so opposed Margery's weeping came to Lynn shortly after this, her remark in chapter sixty-one (151.33–5) that it was years before she was allowed to hear him preach, fits with a date *c.*1427 for the remission of the convulsive weeping which allowed her to resume her place in his congregation. The friar clearly commanded influence in the community since he turned so many people against her (including the priest who later became her amanuensis)[97] that her confessor, Robert Spryngolde, remarked: 'an-nethe is þer any man þat heldith wyth ȝow but I a-lone' (63.155.13–14). Margery neither despaired nor lost her faith in herself or Christ, but, interestingly, she did eventually experience as a gift from God the cessation of her particularly convulsive form of sobbing – though not a retraction of the gift of tears. Margery brings the too obvious interpretation into the open as she recounts that this led many in Lynn to conjecture that she had simply calmed down for her own convenience and that her weeping was far from uncontrollable. She found herself in a no-win situation, wryly remarking that 'as summe spoke euyl of hir aforn for sche cryed, so sum spoke now euyl of hir for sche cryid not' (63.156.5–6).[98]

Not surprisingly, she associates this period with contemplative experiences of strong reassurance about the efficacy of her tears. They are revealed as drink for angels (65.161.1) and signs of how her goodness in time engages with eternal love. In the next world:

> þer þu schalt se wyth-owtyn ende euery good day þat euyr I ȝaf þe in erth of contemplacyon, of deuocyon, & of al þe gret charite þat I haue ȝouyn to þe profyte of thyn euyn-cristen. For þis schal be thy mete whan þu comyst hom in-to Heuyn.
>
> (64.157–8.36–3)
>
> *mete:* food.

There is a feeling of completing both a literal and a spiritual journey in this section of the book as Margery, back on home ground, confronted formerly threatening situations with a faith that transformed them. She was the instrument of healing, through her presence and prayers, for a woman severely afflicted with the postnatal depressive psychosis that she herself had suffered. The poor creature was confined, howling, in chains to restrict her violence but was perfectly calm and rational with Margery, whose prayers were answered and the woman restored to health – an occurrence regarded by many as miraculous, not least by the priest who was Margery's scribe (75.178.36f.). And she now found the domestic restriction from which she had broken free to be the very means of expressing her vocation. Her husband John, an old man of seventy and living alone since their chaste cohabitation and companionship had rendered them vulnerable to ridicule and slander, fell downstairs incurring horrific head injuries which left him helpless and eventually senile. Although regretfully aware of the constriction it would impose on her contemplative life-style, Margery took him home, looking after him for the love of Christ as she felt compelled to do. The account of her duties is touching. John was incontinent

> and þerfor was hir labowr meche þe mor in waschyng & wryngyng & hir costage in fyryng & lettyd hir ful meche fro hir contemplacyon . . .
>
> (76.181.7–9)
>
> *lettyd:* hindered.

Although the comment that she regarded looking after his worn out body as a penance for her former pleasure in it seems a clumsily sad product of certain medieval attitudes to sex, her feeling of helping him as she would have done Christ himself corrects the seeming inhumanity of the remark. It is not surprising that this reunion of husband and wife with its reminders of the initial period of her autobiography concludes the chronicle of events in her life which she felt to be markers of her spiritual growth. It was an appropriate point from which in the remaining chapters of Book One she could look back over the whole of her meditative and contemplative experience.

Chapters 77–89: 'gostly dalyawns'

This review as we may call these chapters brings into focus the core of her 'mysticism' – the particular ways in which she experienced God. In her unbidden tears she felt the force of a power operative in the whole universe:

> I xal make þe buxom to my wil þat þu xalt criyn whan I wil, & wher I wil, bothyn lowde & stille, for I teld þe, dowtyr, þu art myn & I am thyn, & so xalt þu be wyth-owtyn ende. Dowtyr, þu seist how þe planetys ar buxom to my wil, þat sum-tyme þer cum gret thundir-krakkys & makyn þe pepil sore a-feerd. . . . Also sumtyme þu seest þat I sende gret wyndys þat blowyn down stepelys, howsys, & trees owt of þe erde & doth mech harm in many placys, and ȝet may not þe wynd be seyn but it may wel be felt. & ryth so, dowtyr, I fare wyth þe myth of my Godheed; it may not be seyn wyth mannys eye, & ȝyt it may wel be felt in a sympil sowle wher me likyth to werkyn grace, as I do in þi sowle.[99]
>
> (77.182.8–22)

stepelys: steeples.

Church rituals and processions of Palm Sunday and Candlemas orchestrated a sense of the numinous and enabled for her some understanding of both the means and the meaning of redemption.

Her meditative experiences when she found herself participating in events connected with the story of Christ's life and Passion suggest how she united contemplative and active life. She felt bidden by Christ to comfort his mother at the Passion and in her meditation she brought 'owr Lady a good cawdel to comfortyn hir' [*cawdel:* broth] (81.195.8). Such meditative compassion and her care for the old woman in Rome[100] when she comforted the old lady with good new wine finishing up the old sour dregs herself (34.86.5–7), are components of one action. The patience of the Incarnation and the social dimension of the body of Christ illuminated for her her whole existence; she cared for her helpless husband as if she were caring for Christ; weddings were icons of the union of God with the soul (82.198.34f.), small boys of the childhood of Jesus (83.200.20f.).

And she received divine confirmation of her kind of understanding of the body of Christ:

> þu makyst euery Cristen man & woman þi childe in þi sowle for þe tyme & woldist han as meche grace for hem as for þin owyn childeryn.
>
> (86.212.7–9)

Margery's 'very contemplacyon' (5.17.30–1) may have been rather concrete but the very literalness of her active mysticism was the means by which she accessed the kingdom[101] and she knew that she could not really convey completely the way her understanding was illuminated. She had:

> so many holy thowtys, holy spechys, and dalyawns in hir sowle techyng hir how sche xulde louyn God, how sche xulde worschepyn hym & seruyn hym, þat sche cowde neuyr rehersyn but fewe of hem; it wer so holy & so hy þat sche was abaschyd to tellyn hem to any creatur, & also it weryn so hy abouyn hir bodily wittys þat sche myth neuyr expressyn hem wyth hir bodily tunge liche as sche felt hem. Sche vndirstod hem bettyr in hir sowle can sche cowde vttyr hem.
>
> (83.201.30–9)

But she did convey in her own way her sense of the creative Word at the heart of her being:

> And I telle þe trewly, dowtyr, euery good thowt & euery good desyr þat þu hast in þi sowle is þe speche of God, al yf it be so þat þu her me not spekyn to þe sumtyme as I do sumtyme to þi cler vndirstonding. And þerfor, dowtyr, I am as an hyd God in þi sowle, and I wyth-drawe sum-tyme þi teerys & þi deuocyon þat þu xuldist thynkyn in thy-self þat þu hast no goodnes of þi-self but al goodnes comyth of me, and also þu xuldist verily wetyn what peyn it is for to forbere me, & how swet it is for to fele me . . .
>
> (84.204–5.37–9)
>
> *wetyn*: know; *forbere*: forego.

She also expressed an awareness that her contemplative experience developed beyond the vivid sense of the manhood of Christ to a greater spiritual understanding of the creative purposes of God. This came, she says, after she had been to Jerusalem and Rome and been scorned for her gift of tears:

> owr Lord of hys hy mercy drow hir affeccyon in-to hys Godhed, & þat was mor feruent in lofe & desyr & mor sotyl in vndirstondyng þan was þe Manhod
>
> (85.209.5–7)

and she linked it with an increased experience of the inward fire of love (*Ibid*, 8). It seems that she here refers to her marriage to the Godhead in Rome and to the sixteen years that followed during which she grew in this relationship between her soul and God (see 35.88.26–33).[102] Certainly it is at this point in her recall of her contemplative experiences that she talks of her understanding of the dynamic potentiality and love in the Trinity, so transcendent, yet so deliciously and decorously at home on their ceremonial cushions in her soul (86.210–11),[103] and of how her domestic situation was translated and transfigured in her marriage to the Godhead as she hears Christ say:

> þu wost wel þat I far lyke an husbond þat schulde weddyn a wyfe. What tyme þat he had weddyd hir, hym thynkyth þat he is sekyr a-now of hir & þat no man xal partyn hem a-sundyr, for þan, dowtyr, may þei gon to bedde to-gedyr wyth-owtyn any schame er dred of þe pepil & slepyn in rest & pees ȝyf þei wil. And thus, dowtyr, it farith betwix þe & me . . .
>
> (86.213.20–6)

So Margery concluded her account of her contemplative 'visitacyons' which were 'mech mor sotyl & mor hy wythowtyn comparison þan be wretyn' and that had continued 'mor than xxv ȝer' (1390s to 1430s) (87.214.26–8,30). Although very different from the *Cloud*-author and Julian, and although hesitant about her own ability to understand her experience (see 89.219.32) Margery knew, like them, that devotional experience of God in her soul was the means by which experience in time was redeemed from loss: 'and dowtyr, þu xalt neuyr lesyn tyme whil þu art ocupijd þerin, for ho-so thynkyth wel he may not synnyn for þe tyme' (84.206.1–3). Although at first sight Margery's *Book* appears to lack an organising principle, it has a shape which disregards autobiographical chronology, in favour of tracing events, both mental and physical, which are tied into a growth in inner certainty for which they are both the catalyst and the authentication.

BOOK TWO: 'ȜYF GOD BE WYTH US, HO SCHAL BE A-GEYNS US?'

There is a sense of completeness about Book One that makes Book Two something of a postscript. The scribe, who started to work on her original version of Book One in 1436, tells us that in April 1438 he began to write down some of the things that happened to Margery subsequently. Clearly, Margery's account of her experience was, and is, irresistible, and we may be thankful to the scribe for compiling the second book. Although it does not add anything new to our understanding of her 'mystical' spirituality, it sets the seal on all that has gone before and trenchantly illustrates her strong sense of God's power active in the circumstances of her life.

The opening story provides a fascinating glimpse of Margery as a mother, a role conspicuously absent from Book One and here present as her particular version of the story of the prodigal son.[104] It is easy to be amused by the account of her puritanical attitude to the youth who 'fled her cumpany' (1.221.21–5) as she did 'as meche as in hir was' (and that must have been considerable) to get him to give up the world and follow Christ, or, at the very least, to live chastely until he married a nice girl (1.222.4–5). She even threatened divine punishment for non-compliance with this course of action which enabled the young man, when his escapades had rendered him jobless and sick with venereal disease, to put it about that his mother had cursed him – a view which those who disliked Margery were happy to endorse. It is clear, however, that the bond between mother and son was strong enough for him to be able to return to her and find support in achieving a reformed life-style. For Margery it was a case of the parental role becoming a channel for God's grace as the boy recovered, eventually married a Prussian girl and settled to a life of conspicuous piety (1.222–3.25–11).

His premature death while visiting Margery with his wife in 1431, followed by that of John Kempe, precipitated the events which are the main substance of Book Two: Margery's amazing journey with her daughter-in-law to Danzig and even more astounding return with no arranged escort at a time when there were hostilities between England and the cities of the Hanseatic League. The account of how she felt called to embark from the port of Ipswich to which her confessor had given her leave to travel with her daughter-in-law and a hermit escort, emphasises how events conspired both to reinforce Margery's sense of a divine calling and to offer her an opportunity to demonstrate her complete faith and obedience.

En route she began to receive a strong conviction that, despite her terror of sea travel and lack of preparation for a voyage, God was telling her to go all the way to Danzig. In answer to her own fears she heard Christ say 'Yf I be wyth þe, ho schal be a-geyns þe? (2.227.14) and subsequently, at Walsingham, she heard a sermon on the same text (Romans 8:31). This naturally worked strongly on her resolve to go – a resolve strengthened by a Franciscan friar at Norwich who encouraged her to follow the will of God and travel on – much against the wishes of her daughter-in-law, who did not relish her as a travelling companion. The outward journey during the Holy Week of 1433 through a storm so violent that the boat could do nothing but run before it, has an emblematic quality concentrating the way Margery's experience authenticated her faith. It is as if she is offering her own typically embodied version of the figurative teaching in 'Hyltons Boke'[105] about how the anchoress should seek Christ in the inner experience of fallen man as the disciples woke the sleeping Jesus to help them in the storm on Lake Galilee.[106] In an extremity of fear she prayed:

> schewe þu art sothfast God & non euyl spiryt þat hast browte me hedyr in-to þe peryllys of þe see, whoys cownsel I haue trustyd & folwyd many ȝerys & xal don thorw þi mercy yf þu delyuyr us owt of þis greuows perellys. Help us & socowr us, Lord, er þan we perischyn er dispeyryn, for we may not long enduryn þis sorw þat we ben in wyth-owtyn þi mercy & þi socowr.
>
> *greuows*: grievous; *perellys*: perils; *dispeyryn*: despair.

Christ replied 'Why wilt þu mistrostyn me? . . . Suffyr paciently a while and haue trost in my mercy' (230.2–9, 11–15). With significant timing, the ship was driven on to the Norwegian coast in time for Easter. When Margery saw the cross raised up in a local church it concentrated, for her, all her experience of, and faith in, a divine care from which she, like Julian, felt that she could never be parted 'ne in þe see, ne in no place þat sche cam to' (3.231.9).[107]

The details of her return journey from Danzig where she stayed for six weeks despite the antagonism of her daughter-in-law are mesmerising. The tension of travelling through hostile territory with a panicky companion who was exasperated by Margery's pious reassurances as to their safety is beautifully caught in her memory of an occasion when an aggressive-looking figure emerged from a wood ahead of them. Her companion rounded on her in fear: 'Lo, what seyst þu now?' to which she replied 'Trust in owr Lord God & drede no man'. It is easy to imagine the escalation and then sudden evaporation of fear as 'þe man cam by hem & seyd non euyl worde to hem' (5.234.11–12). Margery so irritated her various fellow travellers that they deliberately went too fast for her though she 'ran & lept as fast as she myth' (7.239.11; cf. 5.234.13–17), gave her the slip – like the London woman she encountered (7.238.11–12) – or abandoned her to the miseries of finding lodgings by herself and of sexual harassment by two priests (6.236.28–32). Despite these hazards and the rather mixed blessing of the God-sent beggars who gave Margery company but abashed her by their habit of stripping off in the countryside to pick and scratch themselves, she reached Calais. It is significant that the route took her via the famous relics at Wilsnak and Aachen, a pilgrimage centre which had been visited by both Dorothy of Montau and St Bridget of Sweden.[108]

As the journey began with a voyage that demonstrated Christ's saving power, it ended with one which demonstrated Margery's imitative behaviour. Spared by God from sea sickness during a rough channel crossing, she tended the needs of passengers who had done their best to avoid her company altogether but were now 'voydyng & castyng ful boistowsly & vnclenly' [*voydyng & castyng*: vomiting and being sick] (8.242.22) – especially the London lady who was among the group. It is hard for a modern reader not to attribute a triumphant irony to the apparently ingenuous remark that Margery comforted her especially, 'for owr Lordys loue & be charite – oþer cawse had sche non' (8.242.27–8). But a straight reading is quite consistent with the projection of Margery as a saintly exemplar of God's grace elsewhere in the *Book*.[109] Indeed her genuine and compelling witness to her faith is reaffirmed by the necessarily considered response of a male Bridgettine postulant to her tears when she visited Syon Abbey on her return home via London.[110] Just as Book One had ended with a review of the contemplative experiences which signal the spiritual nature of her whole narrative, so Book Two, very appropriately, finishes with prayers used by Margery which combine penitent recognition of her own limitations with a paean of thanksgiving for all the circumstances of her life which had enabled her to engage with the love and patience which transcend time and participate in heaven.

Her 'mystical' piety may not appeal to those who naturally gravitate towards discipline and restraint and who respond more easily to the implications of subtle and abstract expressions of the inner experiences of the contemplative life. There is an innocent lack of discretion and also naivety in the account that she gives of herself[111] but if mysticism has to do with an inward experiential sharing in the wisdom of God generated in playing the game of faith, then Margery's witness in her time cannot be ignored. The medieval piety which shaped her understanding and expectations and gave her a language illuminates 'the felyngys & reuelacyons & þe forme of her leuyng' which she felt called to write about, but she stands out with a sharp individuality. She seems to have been something of a 'natural', akin, but again, very much in her own way, to those, like St Francis, who found a vocation in being fools for God because only in roles which outraged worldly priorities could they realise, and become signs of, God's wisdom.[112]

Efforts to 'account' for her in terms of historical or sociological theory fail to contain that fundamental vitality and buoyancy of spirit characteristic of the 'holy fool' and also of this woman who made light of the scorn of men. She scandalised those who thought piety was a solemn affair – 'holy folke xulde not lawghe' – by the attitude she articulated in her reply to the officer of the Archbishop of York; but it embodies her sense of oneness with Christ:

> Ser, I haue gret cawse for to lawghe, for þe more schame I suffyr & despite, þe meryar may I ben in owr Lord Ihesu Crist.
>
> (54.135.1–4)

Maddening she may have been, egocentric she may sound, but she knew she had access to that ultimate transforming dynamic about which others may write more cogently and which Herbert, two centuries later, called the elixir:

> All may of thee partake:
> Nothing can be so mean,
> Which with his tincture (for thy sake)
> Will not grow bright and clean.

A servant with this clause
 Makes drudgerie divine:
Who sweeps a room, as for thy laws,
 Makes that and th'action fine.

 This is the famous stone
 That turneth all to gold:
For that which God doth touch and own
 Cannot for lesse be told.[113]

NOTES

1. See *The Book of Margery Kempe*, ed. Meech and Allen (1940). c.5. p.17.29–31; c.7. p.19.27. Hereafter this text will be cited as *Book* and the number references will refer to chapter, page and line in that order.

2. Cf. Hirsh (1984, p.113).

3. See Warren (1985, pp.27–9).

4. See below pp.282f. See also above pp.38–40, and for a Middle English translation of Catherine's *Dialogue*, see *The Orcherd of Syon*, eds Hodgson and Liegey (1966).

5. See further Holbrook (1987, p.41).

6. On the verso of the binding leaf there is a fifteenth-century inscription: *Liber Montis Gracie*; see Hogg (1980); for the role of the Carthusians in the transmission of Medieval spiritual writings see Sargent (1976). When the manuscript first came to light it was identified by Hope Emily Allen at the request of Colonel Butler Bowden who rapidly made it available to a wider reading public in his modernised version in 1936.

7. For a different view on the Carthusian provenance of Margery's *Book* see Aers (1988, p.114f.) For examples of twentieth-century views on Margery see for example: Thurston (1936); O'Connell (1937); Burns (1938) Undset (1939); cf. Watkin (1953); Delaney (1975); Bosse (1979); Beckwith (1986).

8. The dating of events in Margery's life is approximate and arrived at by reference she makes in her *Book* to historical events. Her age is thus deduced from mention she makes in *Book* of hostilities between Poland and Danzig in 1433 when she says that she was sixty years old (*Book* 2 c.4). For a clearly set out chronology of her life see *The Book of Margery Kempe*, trans. Windeatt (1985, pp.29–30). Hereafter cited as Windeatt (1985).

9. On the stress laid on the importance of confession in popular religious teaching see above pp.26–7.

10. See further *Book*, Appendix, II, pp.359f.

11. For an alternative view see Tugwell (1984, pp.109–10, 162–5); Stargardt (1985, pp.300f.).

12. Cf. chapters 24, 27, 70, 89.

13. See further Aers (1988, pp.71f.) and Delany (1975).

14. See for example Thurston (1936); O'Connell (1937); Colledge (1962), and see further below pp.291–2.

15. See Ober (1985); Ober conjectures that the guilt was for a sexual offence because of Margery's preoccupation with sexual temptation – see for example c.59.

16. Cf. the thirteenth revelation of Julian of Norwich.

17. Delaney (1975, p.109).

18. Delaney (1975); Ellis (1985); Beckwith (1986).

19. *MED sub* 'forme', esp. 1a &b; 5a; 11a.

20. 'And þan on þe same Sonday, whan þe preyste toke þe crosse-staf & smet on þe chirche-dor & þe dor openyd a-geyn hym, & þan þe preyst entryd wyth þe Sacrament & al þe pepil folowyng in-to chirche, þan þowt sche þat owr Lord spak to þe Deuyl & openyd Helle-ȝatys confowndyng hym & alle hys oste . . .'. (78.186–7.34–4). Cf. *Piers Plowman* (1978, Passus XVIII, p.228.260–4).

21. 'þan was hir mende al holy takyn owt of al erdly thyngys & set al in gostly thyngys, preying & desyryng þat sche myth at þe last han þe ful syght of hym in Heuyn whech is boþin God and man in oo persone' (78.187.15–19).

22. 'On þe Purifcacyon Day er ellys Candilmesse Day whan þe sayd creatur be-held þe pepil wyth her candelys in cherch, hir mende was raueschyd in-to beholdyng of owr Lady offeryng hyr blisful Sone owr Sauyowr to þe preyst Simeon in þe Tempyl, as verily to hir gostly vndirstondyng as ȝyf sche had be þer in hir bodily presens for to an offeryd wyth owr Ladys owyn persone' (82.198.1–6).

23. See *Mirk's Festial*, ed. Erbe (1905, no.14, pp.56–62).

24. See Gray (1975, p.21).

25. See further McEntire (1987).

26. Hilton, *Scale* 2, c.29. (101r. –251).

27. Christ speaks to Catherine of the soul resting in him: 'þanne sche resteþ in me, þat am þe verry pesable see; her herte is oonyd in me by affeccioun of loue. And so by þe feelyng of myn eendelees godheed, þe iȝe bigynneþ to wepe teeris of swetnesse, þe whiche teeris ben as a maner of mylk þat norischeþ þe soule with verry pacience. Alle siche teeris ben as a maner of swete oynement, þe which casteþ out riȝt a greet smelle of swetnesse.' *The Orcherd of Syon*, eds Gabriel and Liegey (1966, pp.195–6, 35–2).

28. *The Sarum Missal in English* p.565. Cf. the continuation of this section: *Secret.* Mercifully look down, O Lord, on this offering which we present unto Thy Majesty for our sins, and draw from our eyes plenteous floods of tears, whereby we may be able to quench the fiery flames which we deserve. *P.Comm.* We, being satisfied with Thy Body and Blood, beseech Thee, O Lord, ever freely to bestow upon us repentance and sorrow of heart for our sins, and abundant tears; to the end that we may hereafter find heavenly comfort.

29. *Scale 2,* c.30. See above p.152.

30. *The Cloud of Unknowing*, c.65. p.65.28–31; Cf. Tugwell (1984, p.109).

31. She describes visits to Lincoln, Norwich, Canterbury, London, Bristol, Hailes, Leicester, York, Bridlington, Walsingham and Syon Abbey.

32. See further Turner (1978, chapters 4 and 5); Stephenson (1970).

33. See Turner (1978, chapter 1). I owe a great deal of my response to Margery Kempe to the purposes of pilgrimage documented in this book.

34. Turner (1978, chapter 1, pp.34–5).

35. Turner (1978, pp.33–4).

36. As long ago as 1938 the scholarly and anonymous Benedictine of Stanbrook pointed out the importance of the liturgical context within which Margery's faith had meaning. Allen (Meech and Allen 1940) was aware of the context of female piety on the Continent particularly that of Dorothy of Montau and Bridget of Sweden who were nearly contemporary with Margery. Recently scholars have started to explore these connections further. See, for example, Dickman (1980 and 1984); Atkinson (1983); Wallace (1984); Stargardt (1985).

37. See *Book* (1940), Appendix III.I. See also above pp.24–43.

38. See above pp.26–7.

39. Cf. the view of Goodman (1978, p.350) who argues that Margery 'lacked the intellectual robustness to strike out into unorthodoxy'.

40. See McFarlane (1952). The theology of the subject was a matter of contemporary concern; see Hilton, *Scale* 2, chapter 10, and Clark (1978c, pp.76–80).

41. See below p.299.

42. See McFarlane (1952, chapter 4); Cross (1978); Aston (1980, pp.49–70).

43. See above p.26f.

44. See above p.37f.

45. For an account of the versions of the books known to Margery and her scribe

and the suggestion that both had a tendency to substitute the letter for the spirit of the text see R. Ellis (1990).

46. *Prosalegenden,* ed Horstman (1885, p.136.25).

47. *Ibid*, p.137.31–2.

48. *Ibid*, p.140.19–20.

49. *Ibid*, p.147.17–18.

50. *Ibid*, p.147.30–2.

51. *Ibid*, p.148.17–18.

52. *Ibid*, p.165.1–3.

53. *Ibid*, p.148.11–15.

54. It is curious that she does not mention either Dorothy (see below) or Catherine who was not only a visionary who experienced a mystical wedding to Christ and had the gift of tears but had considerable political influence for reform within the Church. The piety which she stimulated was characterised by the Franciscan meditational devotion to the manhood of Christ. She died in 1380 and the testimony to her sanctity was being collected in Venice when Margery was there in the winter of 1413–14.

55. See further Cleve (1992).

56. See Roger Ellis ('The Swedish Woman, the Widow, the Pilgrim, and the Prophetess: Images of St Bridget in the Canonization Sermon of Pope Boniface IX' (forthcoming)).

57. See further below pp.293, 308–10.

58. See below p.308.

59. See Atkinson (1983) See also Stargardt (1981, pp.62f.).

60. See Hirsh (1975, p.146).

61. For an alternative view see Hirsh (1975). He sees this passage together with the information that the scribe read the original over to Margery before writing (Proem, 5.12) as evidence that he reworked the material. However, the scribe needed to read over the account with Margery before writing to establish the text before transcribing it. Significantly, when Hirsh quotes the scribe reporting that the text was 'drawyn out of þe copy' he omits the word 'trewly' in the original. Of course it is true that even with this left in the matter could still be open to interpretation; though Hirsh's further argument that when the scribe introduced himself into the text 'he did so without any hint that he is departing from his usual practice or doing anything at all different' (p.148) and we may therefore assume that he in fact 'did more than transcribe the earlier text, . . . he rewrote it, from start to finish' (p.147) seems rather extreme.

The scribe certainly does introduce himself into the text (24.55.6; 25.59.31; 62.153, 28) as the 'prest whech wrot þis boke' but these may be just later additions to material about him already present in the first draft – certainly in chapter 25 he speaks of himself as the 'preste whech aftyrward wrot þis boke' (59.31). Since he is scrupulous in making it clear that the first Proem is his own addition, it seems likely that he would have announced any similarly reformulated additions in the text itself and that, therefore, when he tells us (p.5.12) 'thys boke is not wretyn in ordyr, euery thyng aftyr oþer as it wer don, but lych as þe mater cam to þe creatur in mend whan it schuld be wretyn, for it was so long er it was wretyn þat sche had for-getyn þe tyme & þe ordyr whan thyngys befellyn. And þerfor sche dede no þing wryten but þat sche knew rygth wel for very trewth', we may assume that the order in which things appear is Margery's own, and that what is there is her own experience. There seem no grounds, for example, for going along with Hirsh's suggestion that in chapter 28 Margery is responsible for the details of the pilgrimage journey to the Holy Land but that the priest is 'clearly responsible for the description of the contemplation of Mount Calvary' (p.149) which he inserted from his own devotional reading having ascertained that some such revelation had taken place. It is of course true that it is impossible to be certain about the precise nature of any cooperation between Margery and her amanuensis over the drafting of the book, but the scribe does seem to be clear that the whole has been authenticated by Margery herself.

62. Hirsh (1975, pp.148–9).
63. Holbrook (1985).
64. See Nicholas Love, ed. Powell (1908, p.33).
65. *Ibid*, p.39.
66. Cf. the teaching of Catherine of Siena on tears: *The Orcherd of Syon*, eds Hodgson and Liegey (1966), p.195.
67. See Salter (1974, p.1).
68. Cf. *A Revelation of Love*, c.22. p.24.
69. Cf. Margery's account of how Julian assures her that her tears come from God and 'God & þe Deuyl ben euyrmor contraryows, & þei xal neuyr dwellyn to-gedyr in on place . . .' (18.43.8–10) with Julian's Revelations chapter 72, pp.86–7: 'But now behovith me to tellen in what manner I saw synne dedly in the creatures which shall not dyen for synne, but liven in the ioy of God without end. I saw that ii contrareties should never be to God in one stede . . . in all this I saw sothfastly that we be not dede in the syte of God.'
70. Her insights range from the ability to foresee death (c.23) to the outcome of parish rows over church matters (c.25) and the ability to spot sharp practice

(c.24) – there is a particularly diverting story of an old man peddling non-existent breviaries to a gullible priest (later Margery's scribe).

71. See further Darby (1974, p.21).
72. See Carus–Wilson (1962–3).
73. See Stephenson (1970).
74. Margery tells us that she was given to going to church at two or three in the morning (in time for Lauds and Matins presumably) and staying until noon and after (3.12.26–9).
75. Cf. above note 61.
76. See chapter 26, and also 30.75.35f.; for particular references to white clothes see 31.80.5–6; 33.84.25f.; 37.92.4.
77. See above p.8.
78. See further Wallace (1984).
79. See above pp.288–9.
80. Cf. *The Life of St Catherine of Siena* trans. Lamb (1960, p.100).
81. See above p.122.
82. See above pp.294, 296 and Matthew 25:35–40; see also below pp.305–6 and note 101.
83. Cf. below pp.309–10.
84. Margery gives an amusing account of her first meeting with him when she asked if she might speak to him for an hour or two about the love of God. He refused to eat anything until he had heard her, so amazed was he at the prospect of of a woman being able to sustain any such discussion for that duration of time. He subsequently became her firm champion (c.17).
85. See Drake (1736, p.420)
86. See McFarlane (1952, c.6. pp.181–2); Thomson (1965, chapters 2 and 4); Aston (1984, p.130).
87. See McFarlane (1952, p.154).
88. Matthew 26:63; 27:12–14.
89. John 19:28–9.
90. Cf. Luke 23:14 and John 18:38.
91. Matthew 10:19–20.
92. Cf. Thomson (1965, pp.23–8).

93. See Luke 11:27–8.

94. 1 Corinthians 14:34–5.

95. Cf. Hirsh's view of Margery's experience as what he calls 'paramystical' (1989, especially chapter 6).

96. *A Revelation of Love*, chapters 66 and 69.

97. See above p.283.

98. It is interesting to note that if the chronology is right and this remission of her convulsive weeping occurred round about 1427, then Margery would have been somewhere in her fifties and it is possible that hormonal changes, perceived as a divine gift, tempered the extremity of her behaviour.

99. Margery was sensitive to weather and it entered into her experience of God's power in various ways. On her journey from Rome she foretold a great storm (c.42) and in her sea journey home on that occasion and, later, across the North Sea to Danzig and the Channel to England, she experienced God's saving power in storms at sea (chapter 43, and Book 2 chapters 3 and 8) In Leicester her travelling companions who were arrested on grounds of their association with her were delivered when a violent storm frightened the populace into believing it to be a divine punishhment for their imprisonment (47.113–14). In King's Lynn Margery's prayers for weather that would save the parish church from the great fire in 1421 resulted in a snowstorm (c.67. p.163).

100. See above p.296.

101. Cf. Matthew 25:34–45: 'Then shall the King say . . . Come, ye blessed of my Father, possess you the kingdom prepared for you from the foundation of the world. For I was hungry, and you gave me to eat; I was thirsty, and you gave me to drink,' etc.

102. See above pp.296–8

103. See above p.272–3

104. See Luke 15:11–32.

105. See above p.303.

106. See above pp.139–40.

107. Cf. *A Revelation of Love* (c.10, p.11).

108. At Wilsnak there were three Hosts miraculously preserved in a church that had burnt down. At Aachen there were relics believed to be the swaddling clothes of Jesus and a garment worn by Mary at Christ's birth.

109. E.g. 63.156.19–27. When Christ comforts Margery for the shame she has suffered at the hands of the Friar who was so implacable about her weeping: 'As hys name is now, it xal ben throwyn down & þin schal ben reysed up. & I

xal makyn as many men to lofe þe for my lofe as han despisyd þe for my lofe. Dowtyr, þu xalt be in cherch whan he xal be wyth-owtyn. In þis chirche þu hast suffyrd meche schame & reprefe for þe ȝyftys þat I haue ȝouyn þe & for þe grace & goodnes þat I haue wrowt in þe, and þerfore in þis cherche & in þis place I xal be worschepyd in þe.' This passage seems to hint at her future sainthood. Cf. Windeatt (1985, 323.63. note 3); Collis (1964).

110. The Bridgettine Rule fixed the minimum age on entry to twenty-five for men (chapter 22). See Ellis (1984, p.36).

111. See for instance when she tells her confessor that the sick and lepers reminded her of Christ in his Passion and she felt moved to kiss them, and then continues '& he warnyd hir þat sche xulde kyssyn no men, but, ȝyf sche wolde al-gatys kyssyn, sche xuld kyssyn women' [*al-gatys*: anyway] (74.177.5–7).

112. Cf. 1 Corinthians 1:22–31. See also Maisonneuve (1982) and references cited.

113. George Herbert, The Elixir.

Epilogue: Patterns of Incarnation

In the terms of their own culture and belief these five 'writers' participate in the witness of all mystics to ways of being which challenge the comfortable, protective norms which society adopts to cater for its immediate survival and ease. Alarmingly, and with a joyful confidence that disarms scepticism and reductive explanations in terms of compensatory behaviour, they by-pass the routes to self-confidence which go via self-promotion and self-projection in favour of a desire for a wholeness which transcends the individual. In this completeness the fissures in human experience between active and contemplative life, feeling and intellectual understanding, security and insecurity, disease and health, pain and joy may be bridged in an experience of a reality in which all opposites are subsumed as opportunities for engaging with it. These medieval mystics understand the ability to both recognise and pursue this desire as a gift – that of God in the self – to which they assent and thus, like Mary at the Annunciation, allow the work of Incarnation.[1] Julian perceives God as 'ground' of her 'besekyng' (c.41. p.42) and the *Cloud*-author talks of a calling from God – of waking to 'þe drawȝt of þis loue & þe voise of þis cleping' (*The Cloud*, 2.8.22). All realise that this gift, which is God, has a dynamic potential enabling a growth to fulfilment which ultimately exceeds their powers of expression.

Mystics in all religious traditions witness to an experience of oneness with ultimate reality, but it is characteristic of Christian mysticism that this is enabled not by freeing the self from desire as in Buddhist enlightenment[2] but by channelling all longing into desire for God which transforms the limitations of consciousness. So Julian prays:

> God, of thy goodnesse, give me thyselfe; for thow art enow to me and

I may nothing aske that is less that may be full worshippe to thee. And if I aske anything that is lesse, ever me wantith, but only in thee I have all.

(5.6)

Richard Rolle states that when the soul loves Christ 'all þinge þat he will haue he trowes he has' (*Emendatio Vitae*, xi.124.23); Hilton advises his disciple to 'coueite noȝt bot on, & þat is Iesu' (*Scale* 2, 21.85r. –228); the *Cloud*-author directs his love to a transcendent God: 'I wole leue al þat þing þat I can þink, & chese to my loue þat þing þat I cannot þink' (*The Cloud*, 6.14.20–2); and Margery, typically, sees herself following the way that will lead her to 'þe place þat sche most desyred' (3.13.14). All these mystics find a structured way of realising the potential of such God-given desire through the patterns of meaning they engage with in the story of the Incarnation. They may engage with it at different levels and in different ways, but for all of them it provides a paradigm for an all-absorbing way of being. As it is played out it proves a creative, self-validating process in which temporal fragmentation, destruction and pain are not just transcended but redeemed as the very medium through which the creative power of God is realised. For all of them this experience may be seen as an immensely challenging inward game which requires specific skills and disciplines for effective play. The acquisition of such skills may involve a painful and difficult process of self-knowledge but it brings the player hard up against an awareness of a being of grace and wholeness felt to be beyond man's unaided grasp but, mysteriously, available as a gift – that of God's love. And the desire for this not only witnesses to something of God in the self, but it provides a bridge between the limited self and transcendent being, a way in which the gift of growth in grace may be received and the wisdom of Christ extended.

Different though the ways may be in which these writers engage with the paradigm of the Incarnation, all witness to a fundamental pattern of mortality subsumed in glory. Rolle is a gifted writer in the vernacular who finds ways of giving a sense of the reality of this inner life. In his shorter prose meditation on the Passion he projects a suffocating sense of all that kills a relish for true life, but he also finds structures to embody his experience of a transfigured consciousness in which the work of time is orchestrated to the music of God:

When mai I negh þe nere, þi melody to here,
Oft to here sang,
þat es lastand so lang?
þou be my lufyng
þat I lufe may syng.

(*Ego Dormio*, 69.252–56)

Hilton maps out the development of the inner life through an anagogical understanding of the significance of Christ's death, resurrection and ascension. The *Cloud*-author, whose chief preoccupation is to address himself to those with a special gift for contemplation, is mainly engaged with those skills which further an awareness of a transcendent God. But although he is concerned to liberate consciousness from the limitations of finitude, he also acknowledges that only through the processes of redemption in the self demonstrated in the Incarnation can such a gift be received. In the context of comment on John 10:9–10 he exclaims:

> It is a merueilous housholde, goostlines, for whi þe Lorde is not only portour hymself, bot also he is þe dore; þe porter he is bi his Godheed, & þe dore he is by his manheed. . . .
>
> (*Privy Counselling*, 90–1.41–1)

Although Margery Kempe finds it hard to conceptualise the movements of the inner life in which the spirit discerns God, she nevertheless witnesses in her own way to an inner experience of the truth which was revealed to Julian in her visionary experience rooted in Christ's Passion. Both women in their own way know how the joyful reality of the ineffable being of God works as a catalyst whereby the seeds of failure grow a harvest of love.

For all of them the transformation of consciousness, present to whatever degree, prompts an immediate and urgent awareness of time as a dimension through which a way of being which transcends it may be realised. Since they understand this way of being, known through faith, as the wisdom which is Christ, it is not surprising that Rolle believes that man without Christ loses not only all he is but all he might get (*The Form*, 1.85.19–21) and that 'ilke tyme þat we thynke not on God, we may cownt it als þe þyng þat we have tynt [lost]' (*The Form*, 4.95.38–9), or that Margery Kempe is told that she will 'neuyr lesyn tyme' that is filled with the gift of love for God (84.206.1–3). Such thinking on time in relation to eternity is behind Hilton's understanding of the opportunity for reforming in feeling which repairs the wholeness of perception fractured in temporal distinctions so that the 'soule sumwhat feliþ in vndirstandynge of þat þinge þat it had bifore in nakid trowynge' (33.110r. –378). Julian comes to experience the 'work' of Christ incarnate as a creative energy of love which 'suffrith us never to lose tyme' (62.76) and which will make possible an eschatological recognition that in God finally all will be well 'than shall non of us be stirid to sey in ony wise "Lord, if it had ben thus, then had it bene full wele"; but we shall seyn al without voice: "Lord, blissid mot thou ben! For it is thus, it is wele"' (85.101). Such perception is behind the terms of the *Cloud*-author's awareness of the relationship between time and God. As divine creator Christ is the 'maker & ȝeuer of tyme', incarnate he is the true 'keper' of time and as both together he is the truest judge of how time is spent (*The Cloud*, 4.12.4–6).

All these five mystics witness to an interaction between their will to 'have' God and an answering grace which Julian describes as God's will to 'have' them (6.7). It is through the inward game of faith which furthers this longing that Christ is known. For all of them, in terms of their own culture, it lives out, to paraphrase Eliot, the 'prayer of the one Annunciation'[3] – the redemption known by the 'message of an Angel' is the means to the glory of Christ's 'Resurrection' which each in his or her own way anticipates in mystical experience.[4] All witness to the possibility of a lightness of heart and grace of being[5] freed to an effective existence fully alive to the present moment, unhampered by any disjunction of thought and feeling and the consequent diversions of energy to evaluating acts and their consequences. But all are enabled to express their experience because they are rooted in theological traditions which give them a language. The *Cloud*-author reinforces his teaching that the essential life of man lies in his desire for God, by reference to the idea that God sees not what we are or have been but 'þat þat þou woldest be' (75.74.19–20), an idea also expressed by Margery as she hears Christ tell her that 'I receyue euery good wyl as for dede' (86.212.21–2); neither of them alludes to a direct source for this teaching although such sources existed.[6] The *Cloud*-author does knowingly quote Gregory the Great as he continues 'alle holy desires growen bi delaies; . . .' (75.74.21) and this is an insight which whether or not Julian had come across it academically she certainly knew from experience.[7] The *Cloud*-author clinches his proposition by direct reference to Augustine:

> Of þis holy desire spekiþ Seint Austyne & seiþ þat 'al þe liif of a good Cristen man is not elles bot holy desire.[8]
>
> (75.74.26–7)

TESTIMONY OF THE LIGHT

It is possible to discriminate not only between these mystics in terms of different formative influences but within the thinking of any one of them. But language is a tricky and imprecise medium, and academics are often tempted to over-value its usefulness as an accurate means of communication. Enriching though some such exercises in delineating the transmission of ideas may be, there is a constant danger of substituting limiting and provisional linguistic structures for an openness to the challenging nature of a more inclusive reality which itself informs these structures and to which they point.

Mystics do not use words to invite an endlessly regressive process of academic commentary and explanation; they use them to point to a dynamic process of transformation of consciousness free from the illusions bred by the logic of verbal distinctions – a way of being which once known does not need the sign which points to it. All of these five use language to point *away* from language – and all of them use the image of light in ways which signal both their own very particular experience and a reality which transcends it and unites them all: the scripture in which their theological tradition is grounded describes this reality as a life which is 'the light of men' (John 1:4). Margery Kempe, spellbound by the holy significance of creation, not only sees Christ absorbed in light – 'sche saw veryly how þe eyr openyd as brygth as ony levyn, & he stey up in-to þe eyr . . .' [*levyn:* lightening; *stey:* ascended] (1.8.23), but she also finds the brilliant perturbation of lightning an image by which she can convey her own understanding of the movements of her inner life. She hears Christ say:

> &, as sodeynly as þe leuyn comith fro Heuyn, so sodeynly come I in-to thy sowle, & illumyn it wyth þe lyght of grace & of vndir-standyng, &

> sett it al on fyr wyth lofe, & make þe fyr of lofe to brenn þerin & purgyn it ful clene fro alle erdly filth.[9]
>
> (1.8.23–27)
>
> *brenn*: burn.

Hilton on the other hand contrasts the light of physical existence with that of an inner enlightenment in which knowledge and love are one.[10] Typically, he embodies this in the image of a journey through shadow to illumination which, initially discerned as 'smale sodeyn liȝtynges' from a distant source (*Scale* 2,25.92v. –238), grows to fill the soul 'with schynynges' as Christ enlightens it with 'clere knowynge & . . . sikernes of luf'. (27.98r. –247). Rolle conceives mystical experience as being absorbed into an uncreated love known as a 'fire that consumes everything that is dark' (*The Fire of Love*. Prologue, p.47) and as a 'syght' by means of which contemplatives 'se intil heven with þar gastly egh' (*The Form*, 12.119.69–70). Julian too finds that her painstaking growth in visionary understanding of how the being of God 'works' in the vicissitudes of time resolves itself into images of light:

> at the end of wo, sodenly our eye shal ben openyd, and in clerte of light our sight shall be full; which light is God our maker and Holy Gost in Christ Ihesus our savior. Thus I saw and vnderstode that our feith is our light in our night; which light is God our endlesse day . . . The light is charite . . . I had iii manner of vnderstonding in this light, charite: the first is charite onmade; the second is charite made; the iii is charite goven. Charite onmade is God; charite made is our soule in God; charite goven is vertue; and that is a gracious geft of werkyng in which we loven God for himselfe and ourselves in God . . .[11]
>
> (83,84.100,101)

For the *Cloud*-author, concerned to point to an ineffable God totally out of reach of intellect though not of love, his delighted play with his reader's susceptibility to paradox serves as a sign illumined by grace: 'noȝwhere bodely is euerywhere goostly' (*The Cloud*.86.67.38–9) and the very darkness of the cloud of unknowing between man and God is one consequence of being blinded by excess of light.

The chronological order that governs the structure of this book cuts across other possible patterns of perception. It might have been tempting to suggest a scale of experience by considering Margery first, next to the introductory account of late medieval religious teaching which is clearly very formative of her thinking and embodied spirituality, and ending with the extremely disembodied spirituality of the *Cloud*-author. But any such imposition of patterned interpretation, though it may pander to our craving for order and classification by which we think we can explain things to ourselves, would certainly cut across the larger historical witness to a creative randomness within an overall self-validating pattern of incarnational meaning which informs the Christian mystical tradition. Within this larger pattern the differences of emphasis and approach of all five writers hold together.

The testimony of the mystics has a particular resonance in the new scientific understanding of reality at the present time. Quantum physics points to a fundamental web of being which language cannot adequately define and in which consciousness and matter are part of one continuum. Scientists and mathematicians describe a universe which allows both order and unpredictability – in which pattern is 'born amid formlessness' as 'life sucks order from a sea of disorder' – and they suggest the possibility of conceiving infinity within a finite space.[12] Rooted though these five medieval mystics are in the theology, iconography and rituals of their own time, they point to a transcendent teleology through which man is enabled to choose to renew the redemptive patterns of the ultimately creative play of love. There is an undeniable interaction between a complex background of formal theological doctrines and the texts of these mystics but all finally point away from discourse to an annunciation of sacramental ways of being that provide absolution from the 'complexities of the Word'.[13]

NOTES

1. Cf. Julian of Norwich, *A Revelation of Love*, 4.5. and 44.47.
2. See further Collins (1991, chapter 1).
3. T.S. Eliot, *'Four Quartets:* 'Dry Salvages'.
4. 'Pour forth we beseech Thee, O Lord, Thy grace into our hearts, that as we have known the Incarnation of Thy Son Christ by the message of an Angel, so by His Cross and Passion we may be brought unto the glory of His Resurrection'. Post Communion Collect of St Mary used from Advent to Christmas and on the Feast of the Annunciation, *Sarum Missal in English* (1868, pp.285, 358).

5. See especially the *Cloud of Unknowing*, 54.55.25–32.

6. See *The Book of Margery Kempe* (1940, p.339, note 212/21); for possible sources see especially Anselm *Epistola* cxxxiii, PL 159.167; Hugo of St Victor, *Opera Dogmatica: De Sacramentis*, VI & VII, PL 176. 561–4.

7. See especially revelation 7, chapter 15.

8. See above p.214 note 75.

9. See further above p.305.

10. See further above pp.149–56.

11. For a discussion of the variant reading in the Paris manuscript see Glasscoe (1989, p.111).

12. See further Talbot (1981, p.122); Gleick (1988, pp.299 and 98).

13. Cf. R.S. Thomas, 'the simplicity of the Sacrament absolved him from the complexities of the Word', *The Echoes Return Slow*.

Glossary of Terms

Advent: The liturgical season which looks forward both to the joy of Christmas when Christ first came into the world and to the 'last judgement' at his second coming. Advent now begins on the Sunday nearest to St. Andrew's day – 30 November.

Annunciation (the): The name given to the event described in Luke 1:26–38 when the angel Gabriel announced to Mary that she would conceive Jesus, the Son of God. The feast day remembering this is 25 March (Lady Day).

Articles of Faith: Fundamental expressions of Christian belief.

Ascension (the): The term refers to the event recounted in Acts 1:4–11 of the last post-resurrection appearance of Jesus when he was lifted from the sight of men. The feast which commemorates this is celebrated on the fifth Thursday after Easter (cf. Mark 16:19; Luke 24:51).

Candlemas: The feast which remembers the purification of the Virgin Mary and the presentation of Jesus in the temple (see Luke 2:22–38). It is combined with blessing, distributing and processing with candles which stand as symbols of Christ the light of the world and it may be based on a pre-Christian Roman procession with lights and is celebrated today on 2 February.

Consecration: Generally speaking, the setting apart for a divine purpose. In the context of the Mass the 'consecration' refers to that part of the Liturgy in which the bread and wine become the body and blood of Christ.

Corpus Christi: The feast in honour of the Eucharist celebrating the presence of Christ in the sacrament of Communion. It is observed on the Thursday after Trinity Sunday and was officially instituted for the whole Church in 1264.

Crucifixion (the): The putting to death of Jesus by nailing to a cross (see Matthew 27:35f.; Mark 15:24f.; Luke 23:33f.; John 19:18f.).

Epiphany (the): The feast which, in the West, remembers the manifestation of Christ to the Gentiles at the adoration of the Magi (see Matthew 2:1–12). It is celebrated today on 6 January.

Fall (the): The Fall refers to the account in Genesis chapters 2 and 3 of how Adam and Eve ate the fruit of the tree of knowledge of good and evil contrary to the command of God. The story embodies a religious perception of the evils of the human condition interpreting them as a consequence of estrangement from God.

Fathers of the Church: The term now refers not only to those writers in the early Church whose holiness of living and teaching on spiritual realities were approved by the Church as orthodox and sound witnesses to the Christian faith, but to a wider range of early Christian writings which contributed to the development of Church doctrine. A collection of their writings may be found in J.P. Migne, *Patrologia Graeca* and *Patrologia Latina*.

Harrowing of Hell (the): This refers to events connected with the belief that during the period when Christ's body was dead in the tomb his soul passed into the abode of the souls of the dead known in Greek as Hades which was thought to be situated in the depths of the earth. The belief which concerns the reality of Christ's experience of death was incorporated into the Creed (formally authorised statement of basic Christian doctrine) of the Christian Church in the fifth century. Also in the fifth century the apocryphal Gospel of Nicodemus describes Christ's descent into this region and his liberation of Old Testament saints and it is this event which is known as the Harrowing of Hell.

Holy Spirit (the): See **Trinity** below. The Holy Spirit is thought of as the dynamic in the being of God whose effects in man are understood as a divine gift (see Galatians 5:22; Romans 8: 9–11, 26).

Incarnation (the): The term relates to the complex theology based on Scriptural teaching that Jesus of Nazareth was the eternal Word, God, who became flesh – he revealed God in human form and thus mediates between fallen man and God.

Kenosis: The term refers to thinking about the ways in which the Godhead was limited in the Incarnation. It is concerned with the nature of Christ based on Philippians 2:7–8 where Christ is described as humbling himself to become a servant and subject to death.

Last Judgement (the): The term engages with a complex Christian theology of judgement which understands individual human life as either furthering or hindering God's purposes. The 'last judgement' refers to a belief in a final act of God in which his loving designs for the universe as an interrelated whole to which all individual beings belong are completed.

Liturgy: The forms evolved to express the public worship of the Church.

Mass (the): The term used in the Roman Catholic Church for the enactment of the liturgy of the Eucharist which celebrates, re-enacts and thus commemorates Christ's redemptive actions through the ritual of breaking bread and pouring wine in a shared meal in which Christ is recognised as the true sustainer of life. The ritual is related to biblical accounts of the events known as the 'last supper' (see Matthew 26; Mark 14; Luke 22; John 13–17).

Maundy: From Old French *mande*, Latin *mandatum*, commandment. It is applied to the Thursday before Easter when Christians remember how Christ washed the disciples' feet at their last supper together before the crucifixion and 'commanded' them to love one another as he loved them (see John 13).

Nativity (the): The term used without qualification in the context of Christian theology refers to the birth of Jesus (see Luke 2:1–20).

Office: The full term 'divine office' refers to the daily services of psalms prayers and readings set down in the Breviary (a book containing the texts of such services) which ordained ministers in the Church recite at the various appointed hours of the day (Canonical Hours).

Original Sin: The corruption which is inextricably part of the human condition and in Christian theology understood in terms of the consequences of the Fall (see above).

Passion (the): All the physical and psychological suffering of Jesus from the night before the Crucifixion in the Garden of Gethsemane to his death (see Matthew 26–7; Mark 14–15; Luke 22–3; John 18–19.

Pentecost: A festival of the Christian Church observed on the seventh Sunday after Easter commemorating the coming of the Holy Spirit to the disciples after Christ's ascension (see Acts 2).

Pietà: Iconography depicting Mary the mother of Christ grieving over the body of her dead son lying across her lap and used to stimulate affective piety.

Redemption: The term used in a religious sense refers to a release from evil and death, and in Christian thinking involves intercourse with God.

Resurrection (the): The belief that Christ was raised to new life after his death by crucifixion based on Biblical accounts (see Matthew 28; Mark 16; Luke 24; John 20–1; Acts 1).

Sacrament: A religious rite which has the funtion of an outward and temporal sign of a spiritual reality and grace.

Second Coming (the): The term refers to the belief in the return of Christ in manifest glory at the end of time when both the living and the dead are finally judged (see above, Last Judgement).

Stigmata: Bodily wounds (on hands, feet, sides and back) which are felt to be visible signs of participation in Christ's Passion.

Transfiguration (the): This term is derived from the account of Jesus' appearance in glory witnessed by Peter, James and John before whom he was 'transfigured'. (See Matthew 17:1–13; Mark 9:2–13; cf. Luke 9:28–36). On this occasion they saw Moses and Elias with Jesus and heard words from God 'this is my beloved Son' (cf. 2. Peter 1:16–18). The feast day remembering this event is 6 August.

Trinity (the): The term refers to the belief that there are three ways of being in one God, that of the creator Father, that of the wisdom of the Son and that of the love of the Holy Spirit.

Visitation (the): This term refers to Mary's visit after the Annunciation (see above) to her cousin Elisabeth who was pregnant with John the Baptist. He was later to preach in preparation for Jesus and to baptise him. At the 'Visitation', although still a baby in the womb, John leapt for joy at Mary's coming. This was the occasion of Mary's song known in the Liturgy as the Magnificat from its opening lines 'my soul doth magnify the Lord'. (see Luke 1:39–56). The feast remembering this event is now celebrated on 31 May (formerly 2 July).

For fuller references see *The New Catholic Encyclopaedia*.

Bibliography

The following abbreviations are used:

AS	*Acta Sanctorum*, eds Johannes Bollandus, Godefridus Henschenius, etc., reprinted Paris and Rome, 1865–.
CCSL	Corpus Christianorum Series Latina.
EETS	Early English Text Society.
MED	*Middle English Dictionary*, eds Hans Kurath and Sherman M. Kuhn, (Michigan, 1952–).
MMTE	*The Medieval Mystical Tradition in England*, Exeter Symposia I–V, ed. Marion Glasscoe (Exeter, 1980 and 1982; Cambridge, 1984, 1987 and 1992).
PL	*Patrologia Latina*, ed. J.P. Migne.
RS	Rolls Series.
YW	*Yorkshire Writers: Richard Rolle of Hampole and his Followers*, ed. C. Horstman, 2 vols (London, 1895–6).

NOTE

References to Biblical texts are taken from the Latin Vulgate (the Bible used in the Medieval period) and the translation in the Douay Rheims version.

EDITIONS AND PRIMARY SOURCES

Aelred of Rievaulx:

Ayto and Barratt (1984) *Aelred of Rievaulx's De Institutione Inclusarum*, eds John Ayto and Alexandra Barratt, EETS o.s., 287 (Oxford).

Alexander of Hales:

Alexander of Hales (1951–7) *Glossa in Quattuor Libros Sententiorum Petri Lombardi*, 4 vols, Bibliotheca Franciscana Scholastica Medii Aevi, 12–15 (Quarrachi).

(1960) *Quaestiones Disputatae*, 3 vols, Bibliotheca Franciscana Scholastica Medii Aevi, 19–21 (Quarrachi).

Ancrene Riwle:

Salu (1955) *Ancrene Riwle*, trans. M.B. Salu (London, reprinted Exeter, 1989).

Ancrene Wisse:

Tolkien (1962) *Ancrene Wisse*, ed. J.R.R. Tolkien, EETS o.s., 249 (London).

Angela of Foligno:

Steegman (1909) *The Book of Divine Consolation of the Blessed Angela of Foligno*, trans. M. Steegman (New York).

Aquinas, Thomas:

Mandonnet (1927) *Expositio Super Boethium, De Hebdomadibus*, in *Opuscula Omnia* . . . vol. I, ed. P. Mandonnet (Paris).

Gilby (1951) *St. Thomas Aquinas: Philosophical Texts*, selected and trans. Thomas Gilby (London).

Augustine, Saint Augustine of Hippo:

Sheed (1944) *The Confessions of St Augustine*, trans. F. Sheed (London).

Bettenson (1972) *City of God*, trans. Henry Bettenson (Harmondsworth).

Blake, William:

Keynes (1966) *Complete Writings*, ed. Geoffrey Keynes (London).

Bonaventure, Saint, Cardinal:

Okey (1910) *The Little Flowers of St Francis, The Mirror of Perfection. The Life of St. Francis*, trans. Thomas Okey (London).

Healy (1955) *De Reductione Artium ad Theologiam*, trans. Sister Emma Therese Healy, Franciscan Institute (New York).

(1883–1902) Bonaventure, *Sermones De Tempore, De Sanctis, De B. Virgine Maria et De Diversis*, 1901, vol. 9, in *Opera Omnia*, edita studio et cura PP Collegii a S Bonavanturae, 10 vols (Quarrachi).

Book of Vices and Virtues:

Nelson Francis (1942) *The Book of Vices and Virtues*, ed. W. Nelson Francis, EETS o.s., 217 (London).

Breviavum ad Usum Insignis Ecclesiae Sarum:

Procter and Wordsworth (1879, 1882, 1886) *Breviavum ad Usum Insignis Ecclesiae Sarum*, eds F. Procter and C. Wordsworth (Cambridge).

Catherine of Siena:

Lamb (1960) Raymond of Capua, *The Life of Catherine of Siena*, trans. G. Lamb (London).

Chatwin, Bruce:

Bruce Chatwin (1987) *The Songlines*, (London: Jonathan Cape).

Chaucer, Geoffrey:

Robinson (1957) *The Works of Geoffrey Chaucer*, ed. F.N. Robinson (London).

The Cloud of Unknowing:

Hodgson (1944) *The Cloud of Unknowing and the Book of Privy Counselling*, ed. Phyllis Hodgson, EETS O.S., 218 (London).

Hodgson (1982) *The Cloud of Unknowing and Related Treatises*, ed. Phyllis Hodgson (Salzburg).

Wolters (1961) *The Cloud of Unknowing and Other Works*, trans. C. Wolters (Harmondsworth).

Early English Carols:

Greene (1977) *The Early English Carols*, ed. R.L. Greene (Oxford).

Edmund of Abingdon, St:

Horstman (1895) *The Mirror of St Edmund*, ed. C. Horstman, in *YW* 1, pp.219–61.

Eliot, T.S.:

T.S. Eliot (1963) *Collected poems* (London).

Gregory the Great:

Adriaen (1979) *S. Gregorii Magni Moralia in Job*, ed. M. Adriaen, CCSL 143, 143A (Turnholt).

Schaff and Wace (1964) *The Book of Pastoral Rule*, eds P. Schaff and H. Wace, A Select Library of Nicene and Post Nicene Fathers (New York, reprinted).

Gregory of Nyssa:

Ferguson and Malherbe (1979) *The Life of Moses*, trans. E. Ferguson and A.J. Malherbe, Classics of Western Spirituality (London).

Guigo II:

Colledge and Walsh (1978) *The Ladder of Monks, A Letter on the Contemplative Life and Twelve Meditations by Guigo II,* trans. Edmund Colledge and James Walsh (London and Oxford).

Harvey, Andrew:

Andrew Harvey (1991) *Hidden Journey* (London).

Herbert, George:

Patrides (1974) *The English Poems of George Herbert*, ed. C.A. Patrides (London).

Hilton, Walter:

Clark and Dorward (1991) *Walter Hilton : The Scale of Perfection*, trans. and with an Introduction by John P.H. Clark and Rosemary Dorward (New York).

Ogilvie-Thomson (1986) *Mixed Life*, ed. from MS Lambeth Palace 472 by S.J. Ogilvie-Thomson (Salzburg).

Underhill (1923) *The Scale of Perfection*, ed. Evelyn Underhill (London).

The Honor and Forest of Pickering:

Turton (1895) R.B. Turton, *The Honor and Forest of Pickering*, ed. R.B. Turton (North Riding Record Society).

Instructions for a Devout and Literate Layman:

Pantin (1976) *Instructions for a Devout and Literate Layman*, ed. W.A Pantin, in *Essays Presented to Richard William Hunt*, eds J.J.G. Alexander and M.T. Gibson (Oxford).

Julian of Norwich:

Beer (1978) *Julian of Norwich's Revelations of Divine Love*, ed. Frances Beer (Heidelberg).

Colledge and Walsh (1978) *A Book of Showings to the Anchoress Julian of Norwich*, eds Edmund Colledge and James Walsh, 2 vols (Toronto).

Glasscoe (1976) *A Revelation of Love*, ed. Marion Glasscoe (Exeter).

Reynolds (1956) A.M. Reynolds, 'Julian of Norwich: Revelations' (Leeds University Ph.D. Thesis).

Kempe, Margery:

Meech and Allen (1940) *The Book of Margery Kempe*, ed. Sanford Brown Meech with Prefatory Note by Hope Emily Allen. EETS o.s., 212 (London).

Windeatt (1985) *The Book of Margery Kempe*, trans. B. A. Windeatt (Harmondsworth).

Lancaster, Henry Duke of:

Arnould (1940) *Livre de Sayntz Medecines*, ed. E.F.J. Arnould, Anglo Norman Texts (Oxford).

Langland, William:
Schmidt (1978) *William Langland: The Vision of Piers Plowman*, ed. A.V.C. Schmidt (London).

Lay Folks' Catechism:
Simmons and Nolloth (1901) *The Lay Folk's Catechism*, eds T.F. Simmons and H.E. Nolloth, EETS o.s., 118 (London).

Lay Folks Mass Book:
Simmons (1879) *The Lay Folks Mass Book*, ed. T.F. Simmons, EETS o.s., 71 (London).

Love, Nicholas:
Powell (1908) *The Mirrour of the Blessed Lyf of Jesu Christ* ed. C.F. Powell (Oxford).

Matthiessen, Peter:
Peter Matthiessen (1980) *The Snow Leopard* (London).

Meditations on the Supper of Our Lord:
Meadows Cooper (1875) *Meditations on the Supper of Our Lord*, ed. J. Meadows Cooper, EETS o.s., 60 (London).

Merton, Thomas:
Thomas Merton (1949) *Elected Silence* (London).
Thomas Merton (1962) *New Seeds of Contemplation* (London).
Thomas Merton (1969) *Mystics and Zen Masters* (New York).

Middle English Sermons:
Ross (1940) *Middle English Sermons*, ed. from B.L. MS Royal 18 B xxiii by W.O. Ross, EETS o.s., 209, (London).

Mirk, John:
Erbe (1905) *Mirk's Festial: A Collection of Homilies by Johannes Mirkus*, ed. T. Erbe, EETS e.s., 96 (London).

Orcherd of Syon:
Hodgson and Liegey (1966) *The Orcherd of Syon*, eds P. Hodgson and Gabriel M. Liegey, EETS o.s., 258 (London).

Pecock, Reginald:
Babington (1860) *Repressor of Overmuch Blaming of the Clergy*, ed. C. Babington, RS 114 (London).

Pope, Alexander:

Butt (1963) The Poems of Alexander Pope, ed. John Butt (London).

Prosalegenden:

Horstman (1885) *Prosalegenden*, ed. C. Horstman, *Anglia*, 8, 102–96.

Prymer:

Littlehales (1895–7) *The Prymer or Lay Folks Prayer Book*, ed. H. Littlehales, 2 vols, EETS o.s., 105 and 109 (London).

Religious Lyrics of the Fourteenth Century:

Brown (1952) *Religious Lyrics of the Fourteenth Century*, ed. Carleton Brown (Oxford).

Rewyll of Seynt Sauioure:

Hogg (1978) *The Rewyll of Seynt Sauioure and other Middle English Brigittine Legislative Texts*, vol. 2 (Salzburg).

Hogg (1980) *The Rewyll of Seynt Sauioure*, vol. 4, *The Syon Additions for the Sisters* (Salzburg).

Richard of St Victor:

Zinn (1979) *Richard of St Victor: The Twelve Patriarchs, The Mystical Ark, Book Three of the Trinity*, trans. Grover A. Zinn, Classics of Western Spirituality (Toronto and London).

Rolle, Richard:

Allen (1963) *English Writings of Richard Rolle, Hermit of Hampole*, ed. Hope Emily Allen (London, reprinted).

Deanesly (1915) *The Incendium Amoris of Richard Rolle*, ed. M. Deanesly, (Manchester).

Harvey (1896) *The Fire of Love and The Mending of Life or The Rule of Living. The First English in 1435 from the De Incendio Amoris, The Second in 1434, from the De Emendacione Vitae of Richard Rolle*, ed. Ralph Harvey, EETS o.s., 106 (London).

Ogilvie-Thomson (1988) *Richard Rolle: Prose and Verse,* ed. from MS Longleat 29 and related manuscripts by S.J. Ogilvie-Thomson, EETS 293 (Oxford).

Wolters (1972) *The Fire of Love*, trans. Clifton Wolters (Harmondsworth).

Ryman, James:

Zipitza (1892) 'Die Dedichte des Franziskaners Jakob Regum', ed. Julian Zipitza, *Archiv Für das Studium der neueren Spracken und Litteraturen*, 89, 167–338.

Sarum Missal:

Wickham Legge (1916) *The Sarum Missal*, ed. J. Wickham Legge (Oxford).

Selection of Religious Lyrics:

Gray (1975) *A Selection of Religious Lyrics*, ed. Douglas Gray, (Oxford, reprinted as *English Medieval Religious Lyrics*, Exeter, 1992).

Speculum Christiani:

Hohnstedt (1937) *Speculum Christiani*, ed. Gustaf Hohnstedt, EETS o.s., 182 (London).

Thomas, R.S.:

R.S. Thomas (1988) *The Echoes Return Slow* (London).

Thornton Manuscript:

Perry (1914) *Religious Pieces in Prose and Verse Edited from the Thornton Manuscript*, ed. G. Perry, EETS o.s., 26 (London).

Traherne, Thomas:

Margoliouth (1958) *Centuries, Poems and Thanksgivings*. ed. H.M. Margoliouth (Oxford).

Vices and Virtues:

Holthausen (1921) *Vices and Virtues*: *Stow MS 240*, ed. F. Holthausen, EETS o.s., 159 (London).

Vitry, Jacques de:

Vita Mary Oigniancis A.S. June V, *Dies* xx–xxiv.

Walsingham, Thomas:

Riley (1866) *Historia Anglicana*, ed. H.T. Riley, RS 28 (ii) (London).

William of St Thierry:

Hart (1970) *Exposition on the Song of Songs*, trans. Mother Columba Hart, Cistercian Fathers Series 6 (Shannon).

Shewring (1930) *The Golden Epistle of Abbot William of St Thierry to the Carthusians of Mont Dieu,* trans. by Walter Shewring (London).

York Breviary:

(1879 and 1882) *The York Missal,* Surtees Society 71 and 75 (Durham).

York Missal:

(1872) *The York Missal*, Surtees Society 59 (Durham)

SECONDARY SOURCES

Aers (1988) David Aers, *Community, Gender and Individual Identity* (London and York).

Allen (1966) Hope Emily Allen, *Writings Ascribed to Richard Rolle, Hermit of Hampole, and Materials for his Biography* (New York: Kraus Reprint).

Allen (1984) R. Allen, 'Singuler Lufe: Richard Rolle and the Grammar of Spiritual Ascent', in *MMTE III*, pp.28–54.

Aston (1984) Margaret Aston, *Lollards and Reformers: Images and Literacy in Late Medieval Religion* (London).

Atkinson (1983) Clarissa Atkinson, *Mystic and Pilgrim: The Book and the World of Margery Kempe* (London).

Baker (1978) *Medieval Women*, ed. D. Baker (Oxford).

Barratt (1984) Alexandra Barratt, 'Works of Religious Instruction', in *Middle English Prose: A Critical Guide to Major Authors*, ed. A.G.S. Edwards (New Jersey), pp.413–32.

(1992) *Women's Writing in Middle English*, ed. Alexandra Barratt (London).

Barron (1984) Caroline M. Barron, 'The Parish Fraternities of Medieval London', in *The Church in Medieval Society*, eds C.M. Barron and C. Harper-Bill (Woodbridge).

Beale (1975) W.H. Beale, 'Walter Hilton and the Concept of Medled Lyf', *American Benedictine Review*, **26**, 381–94.

Beckwith (1986) S. Beckwith, 'A Very Material Mysticism' in *Medieval Literature*, ed. D. Aers (Brighton), pp.34–57.

Benedicta (1988) Sr Benedicta, 'Julian the Solitary', in *Julian Reconsidered,* Kenneth Leech and Sr Benedicta (Oxford) pp.11–31, 33.

Bennett, Clark, O'Barr, Vilen and Westphal-Wihl (1989) *Sisters and Workers in the Middle Ages*, ed. Judith M. Bennett, Elisabeth A. Clark, Jean F. O'Barr, B. Anne Vilen and Sarah Westphal-Whil (1989).

Berman, Connell and Rothschild (1985) *The World of Medieval Women: Creativity, Influence and Imagination*, ed. C.H. Berman, C.W. Connell and J.R. Rothschild (Virginia).

Bishop (1895–7) Edmund Bishop, 'On the Origin of the Primer', in *The Primer or Lay Folks Prayer Book*, ed. H. Littlehales, 2 vols, EETS o.s., 105 and 109 (London), vol 2.

Bolton (1978) Brenda Bolton '*Vitae Matrum*: A Further Aspect of *Frauenfrage*', in *Medieval Women* ed. D. Baker (Oxford), pp.266–70.

Bosse (1979) Roberta Bosse, 'Margery Kempe's Tarnished Reputation: A Reassessment' *Fourteenth-Century English Mystics Newsletter*, **5**, 9–19.

Bossy (1975) J.R. Bossy 'The Social History of Confession in the Age of the Reformation', *Transactions of the Royal Historical Society*. 5th series, **25**, 21–38.

(1983) 'The Mass as a Social Institution', *Past and Present*, **100**, 29–61.

(1985) *Christianity in the West* 1400–1700 (Oxford).

Bradley (1984) Ritamary Bradley 'The Speculum Image in Medieval Mystical Writers', in *MMTE II*, pp.9–27.

Burns (1938) G. Burns, 'Margery Kempe Reviewed', *Month*, **171**, 238–44.

Burrow (1977) J. Burrow, 'Fantasy and Language in the *Cloud of Unknowing', Essays in Criticism*, **27**, 283–98.

Butler (1967) Cuthbert Butler, *Western Mysticism* (London).

Bynum (1982) Caroline Walker Bynum, *Jesus as Mother: Studies in the Spirituality of the High Middle Ages* (London).

(1987) *Holy Feast and Holy Fast: the Religious Significance of Food to Medieval Women* (California).

Carus-Wilson (1962–3) E. Carus-Wilson, 'The Medieval Trade of the Ports of the Wash', *Medieval Archaeology*, **6–7**, 182–201.

Catto (1981) Jeremy Catto, 'Religion and the English Nobility in the Late Fourteenth Century', in *History and Imagination: Essays in Honour of Hugh Trevor Roper*, eds Hugh Lloyd Jones, Valerie Pearl and Blair Worden (London), pp.43–55.

Chenu (1969) M.D. Chenu, *La Théologie comme science au XIIIe Siècle*, Bibliothèque Thomiste 33 (Paris).

Clark (1977) The 'Lightsome Darkness' – Aspects of Walter Hilton's Theological Background', *Downside Review*, **95**, 95–109.

(1978a) 'Walter Hilton and Liberty of Spirit', *Downside Review*, **96**, 61–78.

(1978b) '*The Cloud of Unknowing*, Walter Hilton and St John of the Cross: A Comparison', *Downside Review*, **96**, 281–98.

(1978c) 'Intention in Walter Hilton', *Downside Review*, **97**, 69–80.

(1979a) 'Image and Likeness in Walter Hilton', *Downside Review*, **97**, 204–20.

(1979b) 'Action and Contemplation in Walter Hilton', *Downside Review*, **97**, 258–74.

(1980) 'Sources and Theology in the *Cloud of Unknowing*', *Downside Review*, **98**, 83–109.

(1982) 'Augustine, Anselm and Walter Hilton', in *MMTE II*, pp.102–26.

(1983) 'Richard Rolle: A Theological Reassessment', *Downside Review*, **101**, 108–39.

(1985) 'Walter Hilton in defence of the Religious Life and of the Veneration of Images', *Downside Review*, **103**, 1–25.

(1990) 'The Trinitarian Theology of Walter Hilton's *Scale of Perfection Book Two*, in *Langland, The Mystics and the Medieval English Religious Tradition*, ed. Helen Phillips, pp.125–40 (Cambridge).

(1991) 'Time and Eternity in Julian of Norwich', *Downside Review*, **109,** 259–76.

(1992) 'Late Fourteenth-Century Cambridge Theology and the English Contemplative Tradition', in *MMTE V*, pp.1–16.

Clay (1914) R.M. Clay, *The Hermits and Anchorites of Medieval England* (London).

Cleve (1992) Gunnel Cleve, 'Margery Kempe: A Scandinavian Influence in Medieval England', in *MMTE V*, pp.163–77.

Colledge (1962) Eric Colledge, 'Margery Kempe', *Month*, **28**, 16–29.

Collins (1991) J.E. Collins, *Mysticism and New Paradigm Psychology* (Maryland).

Collis (1964) Louise Collis, *The Apprentice Saint* (London).

Comper (1969) Frances M.M. Comper, *The Life of Richard Rolle Together with an Edition of his English Lyrics* (London, reprinted).

Copeland (1984) Rita Copeland, 'Richard Rolle and the Rhetorical Theory of the Levels of Style', in *MMTE III*, pp.55–80.

Cousins (1983) Ewart H. Cousins, 'Francis of Assisi: Christian Mysticism at the Crossroads', in *Mysticism and Religious Traditions*, ed. S. Katz (Oxford) pp.163–90.

Crone (1965) G.K. Crone, 'New Light on the Hereford Map', *Geographical Journal*, **131**, 447–62.

Cross (1978) Claire Cross, 'Great Reasoners in Scripture: The Activities of Women Lollards 1380–1530', in *Medieval Women*, ed. D. Baker (Oxford), pp.359–80.

Darby (1974) H.C. Darby, *The Medieval Fenland* (Newton Abbott).

Davies (1992) Oliver Davies, 'Transformational Processes in the Work of Julian of Norwich and Mechthild of Magdeburg', in *MMTE V*, 39–52.

Davlin (1981) Sister Mary Clemente Davlin, '*Kynde Knowynge*' as a Middle English Equivalent for Wisdom in *Piers Plowman*, B Text', *Medium Aevum*, **50**, 40–8.

Deanesley (1920) M. Deanesley, 'Vernacular Books in England in the Fourteenth and Fifteenth Centuries', *Modern Language Review*, **15**, 349–58.

Delany (1975) Sheila Delany, 'Sexual Economics, Chaucer's Wife of Bath and the *Book of Margery Kempe*', *Minnesota Review*, N.S. 5, 104–13.

(1983) *Women Writers and Women in Literature Medieval and Modern* (New York).

(1990) *Medieval Literary Politics* (Manchester).

Denley (1990) Marie Denley, 'Elementary Teaching Techniques and Middle English Religious Didactic Writing' in *Langland, the Mystics and the Medieval English Religious Tradition*, ed. Helen Phillips, 225–41.

'Teaching through print: Bridgettine Religious Didactic Writing, its Audiences and its Dissemination' (forthcoming).

Despres (1985) Denise Despres, 'Franciscan Spirituality: Margery Kempe and Visual Meditation', *Mystics Quarterly,* XI, 12–18.

Devlin (1984). Devlin, 'Feminine Piety in the High Middle Ages', in *Medieval Religious Women*, eds J.A. Nicholas, and L.T. Shuck (Michigan), pp.183–95.

Dickinson (1950) J.C. Dickinson, *The Austin Canons and their Introduction into England* (London).

Dickman (1980) Susan Dickman, 'Margery Kempe and the English Devotional Tradition', in *MMTE I*, pp.156–72.

(1984) 'Margery Kempe and the Continental Traditions of the Pious Woman', in *MMTE III*, pp.150–68.

Dillon and Hope (1897) Viscount Dillon and St John Hope, 'Inventory of the goods and chattels belonging to Thomas Duke of Gloucester, and seized in his castle at Pleshy . . .' *Archaeological Journal*, **54**, 275–308.

Dix (1945) G. Dix, *The Shape of the Liturgy* (Glasgow).

Dobson (1966) E.J. Dobson, 'The Date and Composition of *Ancrene Wisse, Proceedings of the British Academy*, **52**, 181–208.

(1976) *The Origins of Ancrene Wisse* (Oxford).

Doyle (1953) Ian Doyle, 'A Survey of the Origins and Circulation of Theological Writings in English in the Fourteenth, Fifteenth and Early-Sixteenth Centuries with Special Consideration of the Part of the Clergy Therein', Ph.D. Thesis, University of Cambridge.

Drake (1736) F. Drake, *Eboracum: or, the Histories and Antiquities of the City of York* (London).

Dugdale (1830) William Dugdale, *Monasticon Anglicanum*, a new edition by John Caley, Henry Ellis, The Rev. Bulkeley Bandinel, Vol. VI, part III (London).

Ellis (1985), D. Ellis, 'Margery Kempe and the Virgin's Hot Caudle', *Essays in Arts and Sciences*, **14**, 1–11.

Ellis (1980) Roger Ellis 'Revelation and the Life of Faith: the Vision of Julian of Norwich', *Christian*, **6**, 61–71.

(1984) *Syon Abbey: The Spirituality of the English Bridgettines* (Salzburg).

(1990) 'Margery Kempe's Scribe and the Miraculous Books' in *Langland, the Mystics and the Medieval English Religious Tradition*, ed. Helen Phillips (Cambridge) pp.161–75.

(1992) 'Author(s) Compilers, Scribes and Biblical Texts: Did the *Cloud* Author translate the *Twelve Patriarchs*?' in *MMTE V*, pp.193–221.

(Forthcoming) 'The Swedish Woman, the Widow, the Pilgrim, and the Prophetess: Images of St Bridget in the Canonisation Sermon of Pope Boniface IX', in Proceedings of the International Symposium on St Bridget of Sweden Rome 1991.

Englert (1983) R.W. Englert, *Scattering and Oneing: A Study of Conflict in the Works of the Author of the Cloud of Unknowing* (Salzburg).

Erler (1985) Mary Carpenter Erler, 'Syon Abbey's Care for Books: Its Sacristan's Account Rolls 1506/7–1535/6', *Scriptorium*, **39**, 293–307.

Evans (1986) G.R. Evans, *The Thought of Gregory the Great* (Cambridge).

Forman (1987) R. Forman 'Mystical Experience in the *Cloud*-Literature' in *MMTE V*, pp.177–94.

Forshaw (1971) A.P. Forshaw, 'New Light on the *Speculum Ecclesie* of St Edmund of Abingdon', *Archives d'histoire doctrinale et litteraire du moyen age*, **38**, 7–33.

(1972) 'St Edmund's *Speculum*: A Classic of Victorine Spirituality', *Archives d'histoire doctrinale et litteraire du moyen age*, **39**, 7–40.

Gardner (1933) Helen Gardner, 'Walter Hilton and the Authorship of the *Cloud of Unknowing*', *Review of English Studies*, **9**, 129–47.

(1936a) 'Walter Hilton and the Mystical Tradition in England', *Essays and Studies*, **22**. 103–27.

(1936b) 'The Text of the *Scale of Perfection*', *Medium Aevum*, **5**, 11–30.

(1947) 'The Cloud of Unknowing and the Book of Privy Counselling', *Medium Aevum*, **16**, 36–42.

Gatto (1975) L.C. Gatto, 'The Walter Hilton and *Cloud of Unknowing* Controversy Reconsidered', *Studies in Medieval Culture*, **5**, 181–9.

Georgianna (1981) Linda Georgianna, *The Solitary Self* (London).

Gillespie (1982) V. Gillespie, 'Mystics Foot: Rolle and Affectivity', in *MMTE II*, pp.199–230.

(1987) 'Strange Images of Death: The Passion in Later Medieval Devotional and Mystical Writing', *Zeit, Tod und Ewigkeit in der Renaissance Literatur* vol. 3 (Salzburg: Analecta Cartusiana 117), pp.111–59.

(1989) 'Vernacular Books of Religion', in *Book Production and Publishing in Britain 1385–1475*, ed. J. Griffiths and D. Pearsall (Cambridge), pp. 317–44.

(1992, with Maggie Ross) 'The Apophatic Image: The Poetics of Effacement in Julian of Norwich', in *MMTE V*, pp.53–77.

Glasscoe (1983) Marion Glasscoe, 'Means of Showing: An Approach to

Reading Julian of Norwich', *Spatmittelalterliche Geistliche Literatur in der Nationalsprache* (Salzburg: Analecta Cartusiana 106), pp.155–77.

(1987) 'Late Medieval Paintings in Ashton Church, Devon', *Journal of the British Archaeological Association*, **140**, 182–90.

(1989) 'Visions and Revisions: A Further Look at the Manuscripts of Julian of Norwich' *Studies in Bibliography*, **42**, 103–20.

(1990) 'Time of Passion: Latent Relationships between Liturgy and Meditation in two Middle English Mystics', in *Langland, the Mystics and the Medieval English Religious Tradition, Essays in Honour of S.S. Hussey*, ed. Helen Phillips (Cambridge), pp.141–60.

Gleick (1988) James Gleick, *Chaos* (London).

Goodich (1981) Michael Goodich, 'The Contours of Female Piety in Later Medieval Hagiography', *Church History*, **50**(1). 20–32.

Goodman (1978) Anthony Goodman, 'The Piety of John Brunham's Daughter, of Lynn', in *Medieval Women* ed. D. Baker (Oxford), pp.347–80.

Gray (1967) Douglas Gray, 'A Middle English Verse at Warkworth', *Notes and Queries*, **212** (n.s.14), 131–2.

Guibert (1953) Joseph de Guibert *The Theology of the Spiritual Life*, trans. P. Barrett (New York).

Hilka (1927) Alfons Hilka, 'Alt französische Mystik Und Beginentum', *Zeitschrift für Romanische Philologie*, **47**, 121–70.

Hirsh (1975) 'Author and Scribe in the *Book of Margery Kempe*', *Medium Aevum*, **44**, 145–50.

(1984) 'Margery Kempe', in *Middle English Prose: A Critical Guide to English Major Authors*, ed. A.S. Edwards (New Brunswick), pp.109–19.

(1989) J.C. Hirsh, *The Revelations of Margery Kempe: Paramystical Practices in Late Medieval England* (Leiden).

Hodgson (1955) P. Hodgson, 'Walter Hilton and the *Cloud of Unknowing:* A Problem of Authorship Re-considered', *Modern Language Review*, **50**, 395–406.

Hogg (1980) James Hogg, 'Mount Grace Charterhouse, Late Medieval English Spirituality', *Analecta Cartusiana*, **82**, 1–53.

Holbrook (1985) S.E. Holbrook, 'Order and Coherence in the *Book of Margery Kempe*', in *The Worlds of Medieval Women: Creativity, Influence and Imagination*, eds C.H. Berman, C.W. Connell and J.R. Rothschild (Virginia), pp.97–110.

(1987) S.E. Holbrook, 'Margery Kempe and Wynkyn de Worde', in *MMTE IV*, pp.27–46.

Hort (1936) Greta Hort, *Sense and Thought: A Study in Mysticism* (London).

Hudson (1971) Anne Hudson, 'A Lollard Sermon Cycle and its Implication', *Medium Aevum*, **40**, 142–56.

(1985) *Lollards and Their Books* (London).

(1988) *The Premature Reformation* (Oxford).

Hughes (1988) J. Hughes, *Pastors and Visionaries*, (Woodbridge).

Hussey (1964) S.S. Hussey, 'The Text of the Scale of Perfection Book II', *Neuphilologische Mitteilungen*, **65**, 75–92.

(1973) 'Latin and English in the *Scale of Perfection*', *Medieval Studies*, **35**, 456–76.

(1980) 'Walter Hilton: Traditionalist', in *MMTE I*, pp.1–16.

'The Audience for the Middle English Mystics' in *De Cello in Seculum: Religious and Secular Life and Devotion in Late Medieval England*, ed. Michael Sargent (Cambridge), pp.109–22.

Hutchison (1986) Ann Hutchison, 'Devotional Reading in the Monastery and in the Late Medieval Household', in *De Cella in Seculum: Religious and Secular Life and Devotion in Late Medieval England*, ed. Michael Sargent (Cambridge), pp.215–27.

James (1983) M. James, 'Ritual Drama and Social Body in the Late Medieval English Town', *Past and Present*, **98**, 1–29.

Jantzen (1987) Grace Jantzen, *Julian of Norwich* (London).

Jeffrey (1975) D.L. Jeffrey, *The Early English Lyrics and Franciscan Spirituality* (Nebraska).

Jennings (1975) Margaret Jennings, 'Richard Rolle and the Three Degrees of Love', *Downside Review*, **93**, 193–200.

John (1964) Eric John, *The Popes: A Concise Biographical History* (London).

Johnston (1974) William Johnston, *Silent Music* (London).

(1975) W. Johnston, *The Mysticism of the Cloud of Unknowing* (Indiana).

Kaske (1960) R.E. Kaske 'Eve's Leaps in the *Ancrene Riwle*, *Medium Aevum*, **29**, 22–24.

Katz (1983) *Mysticism and Religious Traditions*, ed. Steven T. Katz (Oxford).

Keiser (1987) G. Keiser, 'The Mystics and the Early English Printers: the Economics of Devotionalism', in *MMTE IV*, pp.1–26.

Kingsford (1920) C.L. Kingsford, 'Two Forfeitures in the Year of Agincourt', *Archaeologia*, **70**, 71–100.

Knowles (1927) David Knowles, *The English Mystics* (London).

(1948) *The Religious Orders in England* (Cambridge).

(1961) *The English Mystical Tradition* (London).

Leclercq (1961) Jean Leclercq, *The Love of Learning and the Desire for God: A Study of Monastic Culture*, trans. Catherine Misrahi (New York).

Leech (1988) K. Leech, 'Hazelnut Theology: Its Potential and Perils', *Julian Reconsidered*, Kenneth Leech and Sr Benedicta (Oxford), pp.1–9, 32.

Lees (1983) R.A. Lees, *The Negative Language of the Dionysian School of Mystical Theology* (Salzburg).

Leff (1958) Gordon Leff, *Medieval Thought: Augustine to Ockham* (Harmondsworth).

Little (1917) A.G. Little, *Studies in Franciscan History* (Manchester).

Louth (1976) Andrew Louth, 'Bernard and Affective Mysticism', in *The Influence of Saint Bernard*, ed. B. Ward (Oxford), pp.2–10.

(1981) *The Origins of the Christian Mystical Tradition* (Oxford).

Lubac (1959) Henri de Lubac, *Exegese Medievale* (Paris).

Macqueen (1970) John Macqueen, *Allegory* (London).

Madigan (1978) Mary Felicitas Madigan, *The Passio domini Theme in the Works of Richard Rolle: His Personal Contribution in its Religious, Cultural, and Literary Context* (Salzburg).

Main (1987) John Main, *Word into Silence* (London).

Maisonneuve (1982) R. Masionneuve, 'Margery Kempe and the Eastern and Western Tradition of the "perfect fool" ', in *MMTE II*, pp.1–17.

Mary Philomena (1964) Sister Mary Philomena, 'St Edmund of Abingdon's Meditations before the Canonical Hours', *Ephemerides Liturgicae*, **78**, 33–57.

McCall (1910) H.B. McCall, *Richmondshire Churches* (London).

McCann (1924) J.McCann, 'The Cloud of Unknowing', *Ampleforth Journal*, **29**, 192–7.

McDonnell (1969) E. McDonnell, *Beguines and Beghards in Medieval Culture* (New York).

McEntire (1987) S. McEntire, 'The Doctrine of Compunction from Bede to Margery Kempe', in *MMTE IV*, pp.77–90.

McFarlane (1952) K.B. McFarlane, *John Wycliffe and the Beginnings of Nonconformity* (London).

Milosh (1966) J.E. Milosh, *The Scale of Perfection and the English Mystical Tradition* (London).

Minnis (1982) A.J. Minnis, 'The Sources of the *Cloud of Unknowing'*,: A Reconsideration', in *MMTE II*, pp.63–76.

(1983) 'Affection and Imagination in *The Cloud of Unknowing* and Hilton's *Scale of Perfection*, *Traditio*, **39**, 323–66.

(1984) '*The Cloud of Unknowing* and Walter Hilton's *Scale of Perfection* in *Middle English Prose: A Guide to Major Authors*, ed. A.G.S. Edwards (New Jersey), pp.61–81.

(1984) *Medieval Theory of Authorship* (Aldershot).

Molinari (1958) Paul Molinari, *Julian of Norwich* (London).

Moore (1987) Peter Moore, 'Christian Mysticism and Interpretation: Some Philosophical Issues Illustrated in the Study of the Medieval English Mystics', in *MMTE IV*, pp.154–176.

Morgan (1953) M. Morgan, 'Versions of the Meditations on the Passion Ascribed to Richard Rolle', *Medium Aevum*, **22**, 93–103.

Morris (1972) Colin Morris, *The Discovery of the Individual* (London).

Neale (1969) Robert Neale, *In Praise of Play, Toward a Psychology of Religion* (New York)

Neel (1989) Carol Neel, 'The Origins of the Beguines', in *Sisters and Workers in the Middle Ages*, eds J. Bennett, E. Clark, J. O'Barr, B. Vilen, S. Westpahl-Wihl (Chicago), pp.93–109.

Nicholas and Shuck (1984) *Medieval Religious Women*, ed. J.A. Nicholas and L.T. Shuck (Michigan).

Nieva (1971) C. Nieva, *This Transcending God* (London).

Ober (1985) William Ober, 'Hysteria and Mysticism Reconciled', *Literature and Medicine*, **4**, 24–40.

O'Connell (1937) J. O'Connell, 'Mistress Margery Kempe of Lynn', *Downside Review*, **55**, 174–82.

Orme (1973) Nicholas Orme, *English Schools in the Middle Ages* (London).

Owen (1971) H.P. Owen, 'Christian Mysticism: A Study in Walter Hilton's *The Ladder of Perfection*', *Religious Studies*, **7**, 31–41.

(1983) 'Experience and Dogma in the English Mystics', in *Mysticism and Religious Traditions*, ed. Steven. T. Katz (Oxford), pp.148–62.

Park (1992) Tarjei Park, 'Reflecting Christ: the Role of the Flesh in Walter Hilton and Julian of Norwich', *MMTE V*, pp.17–37.

Parkes (1973) M.B. Parkes, 'The Literacy of the Laity', in *The Medieval World*, eds D. Daiches and A. Thorlby (London), pp.555–77.

Pelphrey (1982) Brant Pelphrey, *Love Was His Meaning: The Theology and Mysticism of Julian of Norwich* (Salzburg).

Pepler (1949) Conrad Pepler, 'The Scale', *Life of the Spirit: A Blackfriars Review*, 3 and 4, 504–11.

(1958) *The English Religious Heritage* (London).

(1959) 'English Spiritual Writers III, Richard Rolle', *The Clergy Review*, **44**, 78–89.

Pfaff (1970) Richard Pfaff, *New Liturgical Feasts in Late Medieval England* (Oxford).

Pollard (1985) W. Pollard, 'The Tone of Heaven: Bonaventuran Melody and the Easter Psalm in Richard Rolle', in *The Popular Literature of Medieval England*, ed. T. Heffernan (Tennessee), pp.252–76.

Rahner (1965) Hugo Rahner, *Man at Play*, trans. B. Battershaw and E. Quinn (London).

Rahner (1967) K. Rahner, *Theological Investigations. The Theology of the Spiritual Life,* vol.III, trans. K.H. and B. Kruger (Baltimore).

Riehle (1977) Wolfgang Riehle, 'The Problem of Walter Hilton's Possible Authorship of the *Cloud of Unknowing* and Its Related Tracts', *Neuphilologische Mitteilungen,* **78**, 31–45.

(1981) *The Middle English Mystics*, trans. Bernard Standring (London).

Robbins (1942) 'Levation Prayers in Middle English Verse', *Modern Philology*, **40**, 131–46.

Ross (1992) Maggie Ross, see above Gillespie (1992).

Rushforth (1929) G. McN. Rushforth, 'Seven Sacraments Composition in English Medieval Art', *The Antiquaries Journal,* **9**, 83–100.

Russell-Smith (1954) Joy Russell-Smith 'Walter Hilton and a Tract in Defence of the Veneration of Images', *Dominican Studies*, **7**, 180–214.

(1959) 'Walter Hilton', *The Month*, September, 133–48.

(1966) 'Letter to a Hermit', *The Way*, **6**, 230–41.

Rygiel (1978) Dennis Rygiel, 'Structure and Style in Rolle's *The Form of Living*', *Fourteenth-Century English Mystics Newsletter*, 6–15.

Salter (1974) E. Salter, *Nicholas Love's 'Myrrour of the Blessed Lyf of Jesu Christ'* (Salzburg).

Sargent (1976) Michael Sargent, 'The Transmission by the English Carthusians of some Late Medieval Spiritual Writing', *Journal of Ecclesiastical History*, **27**, 225–40.

(1988) 'Richard Rolle, Sobonnard?' *Medium Aevum*, 57, 284–9.

Schmidt (1980) A.V.C. Schmidt, 'Langland and the Mystical Tradition', in *MMTE I*, pp.17–38.

(1983) 'The Treatment of the Crucifixion in *Piers Plowman* and Rolle's *Meditations on the Passion*', *Spiritualitat Heute und Gestern*, ed. James Hogg, Analecta Cartusiana, 35 (Salzburg), 174–86.

Scholem (1955) G.G. Scholem, *Major Trends in Jewish Mysticism* (New York).

Shaw (1985) Judith Shaw, 'The Influence of Canonical and Episcopal Reform in Popular Books of Instruction', in *The Popular Literature of Medieval England,* ed. T.J. Heffernan (Tennessee), pp.44–60.

Sitwell (1949) G. Sitwell, 'Contemplation in the *Scale of Perfection*', *Downside Review*, **67**, 276–90.

(1950a) 'Contemplation in the *Scale of Perfection* II', *Downside Review*, **68**, 21–34.

(1950b) 'Contemplation in the *Scale of Perfection* III', *Downside Review*, **69**, 271–89.

(1959) 'English Spiritual Writers: VII Walter Hilton', *Clergy Review*, **44**, 321–32.

Smart (1965) Ninian Smart, 'Interpretation and Mystical Experience', *Religious Studies*, **1**, 75–87.

Southern (1970) R.W. Southern, *Western Society and the Church in the Middle Ages* (London).

Spargo (1953) Sister Emma Jane Marie Spargo, *The Category of the Aesthetic in the Philosophy of Bonaventure* (New York).

Stace (1960) W.T. Stace, *Mysticism and Philosophy* (Philadelphia).

Stanbrook (1938) A Benedictine of Stanbrook, 'Margery Kempe and the Holy Eucharist', *Downside Review*, **56**, 468–82.

Stargardt (1981) 'The Influence of Dorothy of Montau on the Mysticism of Margery Kempe', Ph.D. Thesis, University of Tennessee.

(1985) 'The Beguines of Belgium, the Dominican Nuns of Germany and Margery Kempe', in *The Popular Literature of Medieval England*, ed. E. Heffernan (Tennessee), pp.277–313.

Stephenson (1970) Colin Stephenson, *Walsingham Way* (London).

Talbot (1981) Michael Talbot, *Mysticism and the New Physics* (London).

Tart (1975) C.T. Tart, *Transpersonal Psychologies* (London).

Thomson (1965) J.A.F. Thomson, *The Later Lollards* (London).

Thurston (1936) H. Thurston, 'Margery the Astonishing: A Fifteenth-Century English Mystic', *Month*, **24**, 446–56.

Tixier (1990) R. Tixier, 'Good Gamesumli Pley': Games of Love in the *Cloud of Unknowing*', trans. Victoria Hobson, *Downside Review*, **109**, 235–53.

Tugwell (1984) Simon Tugwell, *Ways of Imperfection* (London).

Turner (1978) V. Turner and E. Turner, *Image and Pilgrimage in Christian Culture* (Oxford).

Underhill (1928) Evelyn Underhill, 'Ricardus Heremita', *Dublin Review*, **183**, 176–87.

Undset (1939) Sigrid Undset, 'Margery Kempe of Lynn', *Atlantic Monthly*, **164**, 232–40.

Wakelin (1979) M.F. Wakelin, 'Richard Rolle and the Language of Mystical Experience in the Fourteenth Century', *Downside Review*, **97**, 192–203.

(1980) 'English Mysticism and the English Homiletic Tradition', in *MMTE I*, pp.39–54.

Wallace (1984) 'Mystics and Followers in Siena and East Anglia', in *MMTE III*, pp.169–91.

Warner (1990) Marina Warner, *Alone of All Her Sex* (London).

Warren (1985) A.K. Warren, *Anchorites and their Patrons in Medieval England* (California).

Watkin (1979) E.I. Watkin, 'In Defence of Margery Kempe' in *On Julian of Norwich and in Defence of Margery Kempe* Exeter Medieval Texts and Studies (Exeter) pp.35–65. Originally in *Poets and Mystics* (London, 1953).

Watson (1987) Katherine Watson, 'Friends in God: A Study of the Relationship Between Teacher and Disciple in the *Cloud of Unknowing* and other Medieval English Letters of Spiritual Direction' Ph.D. Thesis, University of Wales College of Cardiff.

Watson (1991) Nicholas Watson, *Richard Rolle and the Invention of Authority* (Cambridge).

(1992) 'The Trinitarian Hermeneutic in Julian of Norwich's Revelation of Love', in *MMTE V* pp.79–100.

(1993) 'The Composition of Julian of Norwich's Revelation of Love', *Speculum*, 68 no. 2 (forthcoming).

Weinstein and Bell (1982) D. Weinstein and R.M. Bell, *Saints and Society* (London).

Westlake (1919) H.F. Westlake, *The Parish Guilds of Medieval England* (London).

White (1949) B. White, '*The Cloud of Unknowing and the Book of Privy Counselling*', *Modern Language Review*, **44**, 99–103.

Windeatt (1977) B. Windeatt, 'Julian of Norwich and her Audience', *Review of English Studies*, n.s., **28**, 1–17.

(1980) 'The Art of Mystical Loving', in *MMTE I*, pp.55–71.

Woolf (1968) Rosemary Woolf, *The English Religious Lyric in the Middle Ages* (Oxford).

Zacher (1976) Christian K. Zacher, *Curiousity and Pilgrimage* (London and Baltimore).

Index